The Minister's Annual Manual for Preaching and Worship Planning 1992-1993

Compiled and Edited by
Lois and Manfred Holck, Jr.

CHURCH MANAGEMENT, INC.
P.O. Box 162527, Austin, Texas 78716

Copyright© 1992
CHURCH MANAGEMENT, INC.

First Edition

Sixth Annual Volume

All rights reserved.

No part of this book may be reproduced or transmitted in any form or by any means, electronic or mechanical, including photocopying and recording, or by any information storage or retrieval system, except as may be expressly permitted by the 1976 Copyright Act or in writing from the publisher or as otherwise permitted herein. Requests for permission should be addressed in writing to Church Management, Inc., P.O. Box 162527, Austin, TX 78716.

Permission is hereby granted, however, for the convenience of parish pastors, for reprinting of brief sections of this book in a local congregation's weekly Sunday bulletin or newsletter. Where appropriate, proper acknowledgement should be given as to source.

This book has been typeset by
Wallace Engraving Company of Austin, Texas
and printed by
Capital Printing Company of Austin, Texas

Scripture quotations in this publication are from the New Revised Standard Version of the Bible, copyrighted 1989 by the Division of Christian Education of the National Council of Churches of Christ in the U.S.A. unless otherwise noted and are used by permission.

The *Hymn of the Day* for each worship experience has been prepared by Marilyn Stulken, who is a member of the music faculty of the University of Wisconsin – Parkside, in Kenosha, Wisconsin. She is also organist at St. Luke's Episcopal Church in Racine, Wisconsin and founder and conductor of the Church Organists' Enrichment Series for parish organists. She is author of the *Hymnal Companion to the Lutheran Book of Worship* and of over 40 articles and reviews in various professional journals.

The *Introductions to the Lessons* have been prepared by John R. Brokhoff, Professor Emeritus of Homiletics, Candler School of Theology, Emory University, Atlanta, Georgia.

ISBN: 0-9618891-6-0
ISSN: 0894-3966

The Minister's Annual Manual
for Preaching and
Worship Planning
1992-1993

CONTENTS

How to Use This Book 11

SERMONS

August 2, 1992	Neighbor: Threat or Opportunity? —	
	E. Dean Windhorn	18
August 9	One Thing is Needful — E. Dean Windhorn	24
August 16	Prayer Power — E. Dean Windhorn	33
August 23	How to Fail by Succeeding — E. Dean Windhorn...	41
August 30	Have No Fear — T. A. Youngquist	48
September 6	Christ the Divider — T. A. Youngquist	56
September 13	Where Are You Coming From? — T. A. Youngquist	63
September 20	On Being Humble and Hospitable — T. A. Youngquist	70
September 27	Yes or No, but not Maybe — David Z. Ring	77
October 4	Lost — and Found! — David Z. Ring	85
October 11	True to Form — David Z. Ring	93
October 18	One Powerful Parable — David Z. Ring	100
October 25	(1) Written on our Hearts —	
	Andrea La Sonde Anastos	109
October 25	(2) Only What We Ought to Do —	
	Andrea La Sonde Anastos	117
November 1	(2) Blessed Are They — Andrea La Sonde Anastos..	125
November 1	(1) Being a Samaritan —	
	Andrea La Sonde Anastos	132
November 8	Persistent-Persuasive-Powerful — Ronald H. Love...	139
November 15	The Contrite Heart — Ronald H. Love	146
Proper 26	The Seeking Soul — Ronald H. Love	152
Proper 27	Children of the Resurrection — Ronald H. Love ...	159
Proper 28	Proclaiming the Love of God, Or Whistling	
	in the Dark? — Miles Walter Jackson	165
Proper 29	God Really Does Trust Me — Miles Walter Jackson...	173
November 22	Today! In Paradise! — Miles Walter Jackson	179
November 26	Remembering to Give Thanks —	
	Miles Walter Jackson	186
November 29	Watch! — Richard Andersen	194
December 6	Repent! — Richard Andersen	202
December 13	Look and Listen! — Richard Andersen	209
December 20	Receive! — Richard Andersen	218
December 24	Do Not Be Afraid — Marie C. Jerge	227
December 25	A New Day Dawns — Marie C. Jerge	233

December 27	Joseph — Marie C. Jerge 239
January 3, 1993	Silent Night — Marie C. Jerge 246
January 6	Where Are You Going to Find God? — David deFreese 252
January 10	Touch of the Master — David deFreese 259
January 17	Following the Lead — David deFreese 267
January 24	Repent ... Wow! — David deFreese 274
January 31	These Are Blessings? — David N. Mosser 281
February 7	You Talkin' To Me? — David N. Mosser 286
February 14	What Does Exceeding Righteousness Look Like? — David N. Mosser 292
February 21	After the Mountain, Then What? — David N. Mosser 298
February 24	Return to the Lord — Beth Marie Halvorsen 304
February 28	I Am Not God. You Are Not God — Beth Marie Halvorsen 310
March 7	Let Go and Walk! — Beth Marie Halvorsen 317
March 14	Come to the Light — Beth Marie Halvorsen 324
March 21	Are You Able to Drink this Cup? — Stephen M. Larson 332
March 28	I Am the Resurrection and the Life — Stephen M. Larson 337
April 4	Truly This Was the Son of God — Stephen M. Larson 344
April 8	To Go in Peace — Stephen M. Larson 350
April 9	Behold Your Son — Stephen M. Lason 356
April 11	It Was on Fire When I Lay Down — William Wesley Elkins 363
April 18	Something Hidden. Something Pro-found — William Wesley Elkins 370
April 25	Know What You Need — William Wesley Elkins .. 377
May 2	We Know What You Said, But How Do You Mean It? — William Wesley Elkins 384
May 9	In My Father's House — Bruce A. Hedman 391
May 16	What the Spirit Does — Bruce A. Hedman 398
May 20	You are Witnesses — Bruce A. Hedman 405
May 23	Glorify Thy Son — Bruce A. Hedman 412
May 30	The Peace Christ Gives — Bruce A. Hedman 419
June 6	Faith's Eternal Story — Gary F. Anderson 426
June 13	Faith and Obedience — Gary F. Anderson 432
June 20	The Hospital of God — Gary F. Anderson 440
June 27	Following the Leader — Gary F. Anderson 447
July 4	Pennies and Sparrows — Nancy E. Topolewski.... 455
July 11	Some Basic Choices — Nancy E. Topolewski...... 462

July 18	"What is Real?" Said the Rabbit—	
	John L. Topolewski	469
July 25	Seeds, Seeds, Seeds—John L. Topolewski	476

CHILDREN'S OBJECT TALKS

August 2, 1992	Help!	17
August 9	I'm Not Ready Yet	23
August 16	Snakes and Spiders for Breakfast?	32
August 23	Want! Want! Want!	40
August 30	What To Do When You're Afraid	47
September 6	Making the Right Choices	55
September 13	Growing Up to Be Christ-Like	62
September 20	Always Being First, Or #1	69
September 27	One Way	76
October 4	Pointing Toward Jesus	84
October 11	Is Bigger Always Better?	92
October 18	Beggars All	99
October 25	(1) Formed in God's Image	107
October 25	(2) Increase Our Faith!	115
November 1	(1) The Saints of God	124
November 1	(2) Love is Greater than Fear	131
November 8	God Allows Us to Pray	138
November 15	Good at Some Things, but not All Things	145
Proper 26	Zacchaeus	151
Proper 27	The Meaning of the Resurrection	159
Proper 28	There's Safety in Following Jesus	164
Proper 29	Remember the Source of Everything	171
November 22	Celebrating the Good News!	178
November 26	God Brings Forth Fruit from the Earth	185
November 29	Don't Be Late	192
December 6	Answering the Call	201
December 13	Using Common Senses	208
December 20	Surprise!	216
December 24	Do Not Be Afraid	226
December 25	The Gift	232
December 27	Ordinary People in God's Plan	238
January 3, 1993	We Have All Received	245
January 6	Looking for God	251
January 10	God Connects Us and Uses Us	258
January 17	Jesus Says	266
January 24	God's Love Frees Us	273
January 31	Being Peacemakers	280

February 7	Light of the World	285
February 14	Telling the Truth is Enough	291
February 21	Going to the Mountain	297
February 24	Why Are We Sorry?	303
February 28	The Forty Days in Lent	309
March 7	A Pretzel!	316
March 14	The Sign of the Cross	323
March 21	The Cup of Servanthood	330
March 28	Jesus Cried Like You	336
April 4	Hosanna!	343
April 8	Try to Remember	349
April 9	The Cross of Death and Life	355
April 11	Do Not Be Afraid	362
April 18	We See What We Expect	368
April 25	We See Jesus in the Giving of the Bread	376
May 2	Whom Do You Trust?	383
May 9	Your Real Home	390
May 16	Jesus Inside Us	397
May 20	Tell People About Jesus	404
May 23	Like Father, Like Son	411
May 30	Peace with God	418
June 6	The Stories of God	425
June 13	Believe in Jesus	431
June 20	Church for our Hurts	439
June 27	The Best Leader of All	446
July 4	Whom Does God Love?	454
July 11	We are a Family	461
July 18	Drawing God's Love	468
July 25	Planting Time	475

APPENDIX

Order Form for *The Clergy Journal* 450
Order Form for *The Minister's Annual Manual for Preaching
and Worship Planning 1993-1994* 436, 451, 479
Preach Like Jesus — John R. Brokhoff 480
Resources for Preaching from the Common Lectionary
  David H. Schmidt 488
Lectionary Lessons for August 2, 1992 through July 25, 1993 494
Names and Addresses of Sermon Writers 506
Four Year Church Year Calendar 507
Calendars for 1992 and 1993 508
Additional Worship Planning Resources 509
Index of Sermon Texts 511

HOW TO USE THIS BOOK

This book is intended for use from August 1992 through July 1993.
Since many ministers prefer to plan an entire year of preaching and worship during their summer vacations, this Manual is designed to assist in summer to summer planning.

Of course, every minister develops his or her own style of preaching planning. Methods, planning, study, writing and delivery are all unique. Preaching practice comes from experiences over the years. Therefore, you will use this book in whatever ways will benefit your worship and sermon preparation most fully. Its usefulness is determined by your own style and manner of preparation.

Please read John Brokhoff's comments in this book on "Preach Jesus." This well-known preacher helps the preacher put the emphasis in preaching every sermon where it ought to be, in Jesus Christ, crucified and risen.

Initial worship planning usually consists of developing an overall thrust for the year, briefly detailing for each worship experience what you may plan to accomplish. Included in the book are helpful suggestions to guide your thinking for each Sunday as well as for several special worship events.

Many ministers then prefer to spend time several weeks in advance of a specific Sunday reviewing the texts for that day. The materials in this book will be most helpful for that task. Please read David H. Schmidt's "Resources for Preaching." A variety of resource materials, commentaries and translations are listed to help you in your exegeses.

And for each worship experience, John Brokhoff has prepared brief explanatory notes for the lessons, notes that you can use to get a feel for the texts. You can also use these notes in your Sunday bulletins to help your people grasp the central idea in the lessons for the day.

As your worship plans develop for a particular Sunday, please note the variety of prayers and calls to worship suggested by our writers to fit in with the theme for the day. You may use these in any way appropriate to your planning.

The children's object talks can be useful to your worship planning especially for those pastors who have difficulty developing ideas and presentations for this important ministry to children. The sermon materials may be used as thought starters for your own sermon preparation.

Not all preachers use the lectionary lessons on a regular basis. If you don't use these texts for your preaching, the materials in this book can still be extremely useful to you in providing sermon ideas and illustrations on specific texts appropriate for the time of year. On the other hand, if you are accustomed to using the lectionary lessons, you will find these materials especially suited to your preaching needs. All sermon material is based on the Gospel lesson for the day.

Since not all denominations use the same lectionary lesson listings during the entire year, especially during the Pentecost season, this book notes the correct dates for use of the lessons for each Sunday for all major denominations. You should have no difficulty adapting these materials easily to your own church calendar.

Materials that are included for each worship experience in this book are the following:

Lessons as assigned for liturgical preaching.
Introduction to the Lessons, brief explanation of all texts.
Theme of the day's materials.
Thought for the day to help set the tone for preaching.
Prayer of meditation prior to the worship experience.
Call to worship for the beginning of the service.
Prayer of adoration for beginning of worship.
Prayer of confession asking for forgiveness and blessing.
Prayer of dedication of gifts and self at the offering.
Hymn of the day description.
Sermon title for the day.
Announcements for next week for use in this week's bulletin.
Children's object talk for conversation with children.
The sermon including **hymns**, **scripture** and **sermon text**.

Names and addresses for all of the preachers who have prepared these materials are listed in the appendix should you like to write to any one of them.

To assist in your planning, a four-year church year calendar is included in the appendix of the book. In addition, a 1992 and 1993 calendar are provided. And a 1992-1993 calendar of all lessons for all major denominations using the Common Lectionary texts and, beginning in Advent 1992, the Revised Common Lectionary texts is included.

If you need special dedication services or litanies or readings for church events, a resource for these materials is also listed in the appendix.

And for even more worship use planning helps, you may wish to use the May/June 1992 annual planning issue from *The Clergy Journal* magazine. This resource includes another complete set of sermons, children's object talks, hymn selections, prayers, calls to worship, and dedication services. Also published by Church Management, Inc., it is available either as part of a subscription to *The Clergy Journal* or separately.

Thus, preachers who use this *Annual Manual for Preaching and Worship Planning for 1992-1993* and also have a subscription to *The Clergy Journal* will have resources of unequaled value for worship planning including:
1) three complete sets of sermons for every Sunday of the year— this book, the annual planning issue, plus "Preaching on the Lessons" in *each* issue of *The Clergy Journal*;
2) two sets of object talks for children; plus
3) almost three dozen additional sermons; as well as
4) more hymn selections to match the texts;
5) a handbook of dedication and litanies; and
6) more prayers and calls to worship.

The Minister's Annual Manual for Preaching and Worship Planning for 1992-1993 and the May/June planning issue of *The Clergy Journal* can both be helpful additional books for your library of preaching resource materials.

Lois and Manfred Holck, Jr.

Spring 1992

AUGUST 2, 1992

Lutheran: Eighth Sunday after Pentecost
Roman Catholic: Fifteenth Sunday of the Year
Episcopalian: Proper 10 (July 12)
Pres/Meth/UCC: Fifth after Pentecost (July 12)

Lessons:

Lutheran:	Deut. 30:9-14	Col. 1:1-14	Luke 10:25-37
Roman Catholic:	Deut. 30:10-14	Col. 1:15-20	Luke 10:25-37
Episcopal:	Deut. 30:9-14	Col. 1:1-14	Luke 10:25-37
Pres/Meth/UCC:	2 Kings 2:1, 6-14	Col. 1:1-14	Luke 10:25-37

Introductions to the Lessons

Lesson 1

(1) *Deut. 30:9-14* (**Lutheran/Episcopal**). The Israelites are on the threshold of entering the Promised Land after struggling for 40 years through the wilderness. Moses, in addressing them for the last time, assures the people that God will bless them so long as they obey his laws and turn to him with all their hearts. And God is not asking too much of them!

(2) *2 Kings 2:1, 6-14* (**Pres/Meth/UCC**). The time for Elijah to leave the world has come and Elisha, his spiritual son, knows it. As a parting gift, Elijah gives Elisha a double portion of his spirit symbolized in Elijah's mantel which fell when a chariot and horses of fire swooped down and took Elijah. It marked the end of Elijah's and the beginning of Elisha's ministry.

Lesson 2

Colossians 1:1-14 (**Luth/Epis/Pres/Meth/UCC**). Today we begin a series of four readings from Colossians. Paul never visited this church, but learned about it from his fellow-worker, Epaphras. Knowing about their Christian faith, love, and hope, Paul thanks God for them and prays for their spiritual understanding and for their bearing the fruit of good works.

Gospel

Luke 10:25-37 (**Luth/Epis/Pres/Meth/UCC**). In this gospel lesson Jesus answers a question with a question. The question was asked by a Biblical teacher in order to trap Jesus. The teacher's second question, "Who is my neighbor?," Jesus answered with the parable of the Good Samaritan, showing that a neighbor is anyone in need of kindness.

Theme: Don't just talk it — walk it!

Thought for the day: We love because he first loved us. If anyone says, "I love God," yet hates his brother, he is a liar. For anyone who does not love his brother, whom he has seen, cannot love God, whom he has not seen.

Prayer of meditation: Remember Jesus, who though he was rich, for our sakes became poor and lived among us. Remember Jesus, who though he had great power, did not use power to advance himself but to help others. Remember Jesus, who was Master and Lord to his disciples, yet was among them as a companion and as one who served.

Call to worship:
Pastor: O come, let us sing to the Lord;
People: Let us make a joyful noise to the rock of our salvation!
Pastor: Let us come into his presence with thanksgiving;
People: Let us make a joyful noise to him with songs of praise!
(Psalm 95:1-2)

Prayer of adoration: God of light and author of love, we gather here this morning to receive the enlightenment of your word and to experience the warmth of your love. Having received, may we share both your word and your love with all those around us. In Jesus' name we pray. Amen.

Prayer of confession:
Pastor: We confess, Lord, that sometimes we have been like the priest
    and Levite on the Jericho road.
People: We have passed by on the other side.
Pastor: We heard that our neighbor was in the hospital, but we sent no card nor did we visit.
People: We passed by on the other side.
Pastor: We knew that the widow down the street was very lonely, but we never had time to visit.
People: We passed by on the other side.
Pastor: For all the times we knew what was right to do and did not do it, Lord.
People: We ask your forgiveness. Amen.

August 2, 1992
(Epis/Pres/Meth/UCC - July 12, 1992)

Prayer of dedication of gifts and self: O Lord, enable us to use our material resources as a public blessing rather than a private possession and as a sacred trust rather than a divine right. In Jesus' name we pray. Amen.

Sermon title: Neighbor — Threat or Opportunity?

Sermon thesis: We do a lot of talking about our religion, but when do we act?

Hymn for the day: *"Lord, whose love in/through humble service"*. This hymn was one of *Seven New Social Welfare Hymns* published by the Hymn Society of America for the Second National Conference on Churches and Social Welfare, 1961. Albert F. Bayly (1901-1984), a Congregational minister, served a number of churches in England between 1928 and 1972. He wrote his first hymn in 1945 and thereafter published four volumes of hymnody. He was made an honorary fellow of Westminster Choir College in 1968 and ten years later was honored at a special service in Westminster Abbey. The hymn calls on us to worship not with voice alone, but with our hearts consecrated to his purpose.

Announcements for next week:
    Sermon title: One Thing is Needful.
    Sermon theme: Dealing with priorities and choices.
    Sermon summary: There's time for everything. The tough part is keeping it all in perspective. How does one achieve the kind of wisdom that avoids "making mountains out of mole hills and mole hills out of mountains"?

Children's object talk:

Help!

Objects: A 911 card, such as can be posted near a phone.
Lesson: Help people in need. (Luke 10:25-37)
Outline: 1. Do you like to help people?
        2. Should we help people even when they don't ask for it?
        3. We can help by calling "911" on the phone.

BOYS AND GIRLS, do you like to help people? *(Let them answer).* I like to help people too. It makes me feel good whenever I help somebody, especially when they ask for my help.

Do you think we should ever help somebody even if they aren't asking for our help? *(Talk it over.)* Suppose you are sitting in your house or in the front yard and you see somebody trying to steal a purse from the elderly woman who lives on your street? Should you try to help her? How could you do it without getting hurt? *(Let them try some answers.)*

Here is one way we can help *(hold up the 911 card).* Do you know what will happen if you call 911 on the phone? *(pause)* That's right. If you dial 911, you will be able to talk with someone who will call the police, the fire department or the ambulance.

Sometimes it is very scary to help when someone is in trouble. Be sure to listen very carefully to the sermon today where we hear about a man who, even though he was afraid, helped another man who had been beaten up by robbers.

The sermon:
Neighbor — Threat or Opportunity?

Hymns:
Beginning of worship: Praise to the Lord, the Almighty
Sermon hymn: They'll Know We Are Christians by Our Love
End of worship: Let There Be Peace on Earth

Scripture: Luke 10:25-37

Sermon Text: *"Which of these three do you think was a neighbor to the man who fell into the hands of the robbers?" The expert in the law replied, "The one who had mercy on him." Jesus told him, "Go and do likewise."* Luke 10:36-37 (N.I.V.)

SOME HOME-TOWN PHILOSOPHERS say that the way to get along with people is never talk religion or politics. I've never enjoyed talking politics but, wow! — I've sure enjoyed talking religion! How about you? Have you ever gotten involved in a late night religious "bull session"? Interesting and stimulating — that's for sure!

Can't you just picture the intellectual in our Gospel today, sitting down with Jesus over a cup of coffee at the local donut shop? "Let's talk religion, Jesus"! After a couple of opening rounds, he comes to a question that is **sure** to be good for at least an hour of stimulating discussion. The question: "Who is my neighbor?" Jesus' answer was surprising! He told a story. That story is the one we know as "The Good Samaritan."

By means of the story, Jesus answered the intellectual with great impact and clarity! In the process, he outlines several ways that humans deal with one another. The first is characterized by the robbers who beat up the man who was traveling from Jerusalem

August 2, 1992
(Epis/Pres/Meth/UCC - July 12, 1992)

to Jericho. Jesus said: "They stripped him of his clothes, beat him and went away, leaving him half dead." That's one way humans can deal with others. We can beat them up!

The abundance of news coverage today leaves most of us rather blase' when we read or hear about robberies, murders and rape. One that grabbed my attention, though, was the incident of the 28-year-old female jogger in New York's Central Park. She was raped, savagely beaten, and left for dead. The "attention grabber" is the fact that the attacker was **not** a man, but a herd of 13- and 14-year-old boys. The boys said they were out "wilding," out for a good time, looking for someone to attack, just like a pack of wild dogs!

Another one that has etched a spot in my memory is two 16-year-old girls in Gary, Indiana who professed interest in a Bible study offered by an aged woman in their neighborhood. Once inside the house, they beat her to death and had $10.00 in cash to show for their efforts.

Wife abuse. Child abuse. It doesn't take a lot of imagination to know that the option of dealing with our neighbors by "beating them up" is a popular one. Our jails and prisons are bulging with inmates. This option is as tragic in 1992 as it was in the days of Jesus!

According to the story, another option of dealing with our neighbor is simply to ignore him. Frankly, the examples used by Jesus make me rather uncomfortable. The two people who saw the injured man and "passed by on the other side" were religious professionals. Much to my shame, sometimes my schedule and the abundance of church work prevent me from doing the work of the church and helping other people in the spirit of Christ.

Here's a question for you. Which pronoun of the four I will give you, do you think is the most destructive to the work of a church or community? The pronoun choices are: I, we, it and they. Which one did you choose? I have a hunch that many of you picked the pronoun "I" as the most destructive. That's the one I picked. The answer, however, is the pronoun they. Here's how it works:

"They ought to do something about that."
"Why don't they do this?"
"Why don't they do that?"

Do you see why overuse of the pronoun they can be so destructive? What a clever way to divorce ourselves of responsibility! By contrast, I submit that the most constructive pronoun is we. When members of a congregation think in terms of "We need to do something about this," then we have learned a valuable lesson in dealing with our neighbor.

The third alternative for dealing with our neighbor is, as suggested by the Samaritan's response, to help him. A Sunday School teacher was telling this parable to her class of first graders. She vividly described the poor man who was all beaten up and bleeding by the side of the road. She obviously was seeking a response similar to that of the Samaritan when she asked: "What would you do if you saw the poor man by the side of the road?" One little girl didn't hesitate a moment and said: "I think I'd throw up!"

That's really not so far out! Sometimes when called upon by need to help our neighbor, we are frightened or intimidated. We don't know what to do or how to go about helping. The fact that Jesus used a Samaritan as the "good guy" in this story is quite remarkable. Samaritans were half-breeds and looked down upon with disgust by religious purists of the day. What a story! Here's an outcast who has more compassion for someone who is hurting than people of the church.

With whom in the parable do you most closely identify? We'd all like to think of ourselves as the Samaritan. In reflection, many of us may be closer to the intellectual who prompted the story in the first place. We like to talk about religion. We do a lot of that in the church. While careful and thoughtful discussion of religious issues is wise and prudent, there does come a time when we need "to roll up our sleeves" and live out what we profess to believe.

Is our neighbor a threat or an opportunity? Our response to that will be determined to the degree that we have the heart and will of the Samaritan.

E. Dean Windhorn
Christ Church (Lutheran)
Zionsville, Indiana

AUGUST 9, 1992

Lutheran: Ninth Sunday after Pentecost
Roman Catholic: Sixteenth Sunday of the Year
Episcopalian: Proper 11 (July 19)
Pres/Meth/UCC: Sixth after Pentecost (July 19)

Lessons:

Lutheran:	Gen. 18:1-10a (10b-14)	Col. 1:21-28	Luke 10:38-42
Roman Catholic:	Gen. 18:1-10a	Col. 1:24-28	Luke 10:38-42
Episcopal:	Gen. 18:1-10a (10b-14)	Col. 1:21-29	Luke 10:38-42
Pres/Meth/UCC:	2 Kings 4:8-17	Col. 1:21-29	Luke 10:38-42

Introductions to the Lessons

Lesson 1

(1) *Genesis 18:1-10a* (**Luth/Epis**). In the middle of a hot day, three strangers visit Abraham's tent. Abraham treats them with utmost hospitality without knowing they are angels. In return Abraham receives God's promise that though he is 100 years old and his wife, Sarah, is 90, they in due time will have their first child, Isaac.

(2) *2 Kings 4:8-17* (**Pres/Meth/UCC**). Having received Elijah's mantel, Elisha continues the ministry of Elijah. A childless couple often provides him with meals and even adds a room to their house for his sole use when he passes through. To express his gratitude, Elisha promises the wife that in a year she will have a son. And it was so!

Lesson 2

Colossians 1:21-28 (**Luth**); *Colossians 1:21-29* (**Epis/Pres/Meth/UCC**). What a change came over the church in Colossae when the people accepted Christ! They changed from enemies to friends of God made possible by the cross. Paul says he was called to reveal God's secret, the secret that the gospel is for all people, both Jews and Gentiles.

Gospel

Luke 10:38-42 (**Luth/Epis/Pres/Meth/UCC**). When Jesus and his disciples came to Bethany, a short distance from Jerusalem, Jesus was invited by two sisters, Martha and Mary, to have dinner with them in their home. While Martha was busy preparing the meal, Mary sat at Jesus' feet conversing with him. When Martha complained to Jesus, he reminded her that the one needful thing was not physical but spiritual food, which Mary had chosen.

The Minister's Annual Manual

Theme: Dealing with priorities and choices...
Thought for the day:
    I Am One
I am only one,
But I am one:
I cannot do everything,
But I can do something.
What I can do,
I ought to do;
And what I ought to do,
By the grace of God, I will.
    —Author unknown

Prayer of meditation:
The world is very busy today, Lord.
    Like Martha of old, many are hard at work
    and many are hard at play.
But we come here to be separated for a time
    from life's strain and stress.
Like Mary, we have come, kneeling at your feet,
    seeking the truth about life,
    and inquiring about things that really matter. Amen.

Call to worship: Come, let us invite the risen Christ to be our unseen guest during this hour and during all of life, for in his presence there is enlightenment and love.

Prayer of adoration:
Eternal God, our Creator,
    if we were flowers,
        we would praise you with full blossoms of color.
If we were birds,
    we would praise you with melodious sounds all day.
If we were trees,
    we would praise you by reaching high in the heavens.
But you have made us creatures who can think, meditate,
    pray, sing, speak, and love.
Therefore, we worship you today with our thoughts, with our songs, with our words, with our prayers, and with our intentions to love. Amen.

Prayer of confession: Lord, we have come into this quiet place from a busy and hectic world. During this past week, we have been very much caught up in the struggle for survival and the fight for advancement.

August 9, 1992
(Epis/Pres/Meth/UCC - July 19, 1992)

Yet we know that in the busyness of everyday life we have often lost sight of you.

So we ask you to forgive our preoccupations and our oversights. Use this hour to get our perspectives straight again. Make your presence very real to us. Surround us with the reality of your being. And, because we've been here, may we walk with you more closely this week. In Jesus' name we pray. Amen.

Prayer of dedication of gifts and self: As we sit at the feet of Christ, learning his plan for our lives; and as we follow in his steps, imitating his example; may we learn from him what it means to be truly generous and sharing. Amen.

Sermon title: One Thing Is Needful

Sermon thesis: There's time for everything. The tough part is keeping it all in perspective. How does one achieve the kind of wisdom that avoids "making mountains out of mole hills and mole hills out of mountains."

Hymn for the day: *"All depends on our possessing"* This hymn reminds us that all that is needful—our top priorities—are God's free grace and blessing. It is an anonymous hymn which first appeared in Nurnberg in 1676. It possibly dates from 1673.

Announcements for next week:

  Sermon title: Prayer Power.
  Sermon theme: Persistence in prayer.
  Sermon summary: When it comes to prayer, have faith that God surely hears every prayer, that he answers every prayer, and that he answers every prayer in the way that is spiritually best for us.

Children's object talk:

I'm Not Ready Yet!

Objects: A Bible and a TV Guide.
Lesson: Choosing the most important things in life. (Luke 10:38-42)
Outline: 1. What is the best selling book, year after year?
  2. What is the best selling magazine?
  3. Choosing between the Bible and the TV Guide is difficult.
  4. Helps for making the best choice.

  BOYS AND GIRLS, can you name a book that sells more copies every year than any other book? *(Let them answer. Looking for the answer: the Bible).* Before I tell you if you're right, let me ask you the same question about a magazine: what magazine do you think sells the most every year? *(Let them try again. Looking for the answer: TV Guide).* Now let me show you what I have in the paper sack: a Bible and a TV Guide. The Bible is usually the most popular book. The TV Guide is usually the most popular magazine. I guess that means people are really interested in the Bible and also in television.

How many of you like Bible stories? *(Let them answer).* How many of you like stories from television? *(Let them answer).* I like stories from both places too. Suppose there was going to be a time after supper every night when you would all sit down together and read a Bible story. You may be watching a television program and say "I'm not ready yet. The program isn't over."

You know what I think? We can watch television programs lots of times. But we don't always have a chance to sit down with our family and listen to Bible stories. That's very important, because the family won't always be together. Later we can go back to watching television.

The sermon:

One Thing Is Needful

Hymns:
 Beginning of worship: To God Be the Glory
 Sermon hymn: Dear Lord and Father of Mankind
 End of worship: Beautiful Savior

Scripture: Luke 10:38-42

Sermon Text: *"One thing is needful. Mary has chosen the good portion, which shall not be taken away from her."* Luke 10:42 (R.S.V.)

> This is the age
> of the half-read page;
> The quick hash
> and the mad dash.

August 9, 1992
(Epis/Pres/Meth/UCC - July 19, 1992)

> This is the age
> of the bright night
> with the nerves tight;
> And the plane hop
> with a brief stop.
>
> This is the age
> of the lamp tan
> in a short span.
> The brain strain
> and the heart pain;
> The catnaps till
> the spring snaps
> and the fun is done.

I KNOW, THAT SOUNDS KIND OF CYNICAL. But there's lots of truth in that poem. An article in the magazine, *Psychology Today*, had this to say:

"In the next 12 months, we will consume around 20,000 tons of aspirin. ...That totals 225 tablets per person, per year, or ⅔ of a tablet per person, per day. If you go by these sales figures alone, it would suggest that most everyone in the United States has a headache most of the time."

I don't know if this generation is any more "uptight" or anxious than the last one. Recently I attended a seminar where a statement was made that made quite an impression on me. If there really are such things as light bulbs going off on top of a person's head when a new idea or insight takes hold, then the light bulb above my head would have been a bright, flashing neon light.

The statement was this: *"Twenty years ago people were asking: 'How can I get to heaven?' Today people are asking: 'How can I get through this day?'"* That statement made such an impact on me because:

- That's what I've been hearing.
- That's what I've been seeing.
- That's what I've been feeling inside.

We're such busy people. Many of you are under lots of pressure at work or at school. Some of you are under stress because of a shaky marriage or problems with the children.

Obviously, we are not the first generation of people who are under lots of pressure, anxiety and stress. There were people uptight and anxious in the time of Jesus too. In fact, in our gospel text, Jesus told a good friend named Martha to slow down and "smell the flowers," so to speak.

Jesus was coming to Bethany to visit Lazarus and his two sisters, Mary and Martha. Great news! Martha didn't hesitate a minute to begin the preparations. A thorough house cleaning. And, no doubt, cooking and baking many of the foods she knew that Jesus liked.

Jesus must have arrived early. (Don't you just hate it when people arrive early? Here you are, making last minute preparations. You're still in your grubbies giving that floor a last vacuuming, when the doorbell rings. There are your guests! You had just enough time for a quick shower and change of clothes. So much for those plans. You chastise yourself and say: "I knew I should have started earlier.")

Whether Jesus arrived early or not, suffice it to say that there were more things to be done. Mary had been working feverishly too. But after Jesus arrived, all of Mary's activity stops as she visits with and listens to him.

Meanwhile, Martha's in the kitchen finishing up the meal. "When is that girl going to get in here and help me finish up?!!" The pots and pans and slamming doors get louder and louder. That doesn't work. So, finally Martha can't stand it anymore. She bursts into the living room, hands on her hips, her face flushed with anger, as she blurts out these words to Jesus:

"Lord, do you not care that my sister has left me to serve alone? Tell her then to help me!"

I picture Jesus responding with a loving smile, as he says to her: "Martha, Martha, you are anxious and troubled about many things; one thing is needful. Mary has chosen the good portion, which shall not be taken away from her."

Can't you just empathize with Martha here? Shocked. Embarrassed. What was she supposed to do, let the casserole burn in the oven? I remember vividly a Pastors' meeting held at a neighboring church. As noon time approached, we caught whiffs of delicious food being prepared in the downstairs kitchen. Noon finally came. The host pastor, with a straight face, stated that they had a very unique situation in their church in that all the women preparing the meal that day had the first name of Martha. That struck me as truly unique. It was not until later that I realized he

August 9, 1992
(Epis/Pres/Meth/UCC - July 19, 1992)

was "pulling our legs," with an obvious reference to the story we have been considering today.

If we don't know the rest of the story, we may assume that Martha had quite a shallow faith and that Mary had all the spiritual depth. Not so! Recall when Lazarus died? They had sent for Jesus several days before. When he finally comes, Martha hurries to him while Mary stays home. "If you had been here," she says to Jesus, "my brother would not have died." No recrimination. Just simple trust. "I know even now," she goes on, "that God will give you whatever you ask of him!" Notice that Martha did not say, "I hope" or "I think," but she said, "I know"! In spite of her sorrow, she exclaims: "I believe that you are the Messiah, the Son of God who was to come into the world!"

What a confession of faith! The woman who once was flustered by last minute preparations has become one of the first to recognize and proclaim who Jesus really is.

Martha's *faux pas* was not lack of spirituality. It was a matter of timing and perspective. In Ecclesiastes chapter three, we hear the rhythmic cadence of the writer who says:

"For everything there is a season, and a time for every matter under heaven...
...a time to be born, and a time to die.
...a time to break down, and a time to build up.
...a time to cry, and a time to laugh.
...a time to keep silence, and a time to speak.

There's a time for everything. The tough part is keeping it all in perspective. How does one achieve the kind of wisdom that avoids "making mountains out of mole hills and mole hills out of mountains"?

Have you have ever been in a hurry and buttoned up a long overcoat with lots of buttons and when you were done, found out that the coat was uneven? What went wrong? I'll tell you what went wrong. When you don't get the first button in the right hole, all the rest are out of sequence too, right? That's a parable about life. Jesus said it this way in the Sermon on the Mount: "Seek first God's kingdom and his righteousness, and all these things shall be yours as well." (Matthew 6:33). If the Lord is not high priority in your life, then, like the overcoat, so many other things in life will be out of whack as well.

Is it true that people today are not asking as fervently as in the past, "How can I get to heaven?" and rather, are asking: "How can

I get through this day?" Who really knows for sure. Ultimately, it really doesn't make that much difference. Even though the questions are different, they are co-dependent in a startling way! For, the closer we are to Jesus Christ, the more he will have a positive effect on our faith-walk each day. I like this prayer because it captures the themes of both questions:

"O Lord, help me to remember that nothing is going to happen today that you and I together can't handle." Amen.

E. Dean Windhorn
Christ Church (Lutheran)
Zionsville, Indiana

AUGUST 16, 1992

Lutheran: Tenth Sunday after Pentecost
Roman Catholic: Seventeenth Sunday of the Year
Episcopalian: Proper 12 (July 26)
Pres/Meth/UCC: Seventh after Pentecost (July 26)

Lessons:

Lutheran:	Gen. 18:20-32	Col. 2:6-15	Luke 11:1-13
Roman Catholic:	Gen. 18:20-32	Col. 2:12-14	Luke 11:1-13
Episcopal:	Gen. 18:20-32	Col. 2:6-15	Luke 11:1-13
Pres/Meth/UCC:	2 Kings 5:1-15ab	Col. 2:6-15	Luke 11:1-13

Introductions to the Lessons

Lesson 1

(1) *Genesis 18:20-32* (**Luth/Epis**). After Abraham royally entertained three men from God, he goes with them to a place where they can see the city of Sodom, which has a bad reputation as a sin city. Two of the men go to check out the city while the Lord and Abraham have a conversation. Abraham questions the justice of killing innocent people along with the wicked. He reasons with the Lord, who agrees not to destroy the city if ten righteous people are there.

(2) *2 Kings 5:1-15ab* (**Pres/Meth/UCC**). Elisha continues to perform miracles. This time Naaman, a four-star general and chief of staff of the Syrian army, contracts incurable leprosy. A Jewish slave girl in Naaman's mansion tells him of Elisha. He goes to Elisha who tells him to immerse himself seven times in the River Jordan. After reluctance and in protest he does so and is cured. In gratitude Naaman declares that the God of Elisha is the one and only God.

Lesson 2

Colossians 2:6-15 (**Luth/Epis/Pres/Meth/UCC**). According to Paul, the members of the Colossian church accepted Christ as Lord. Therefore, they are to live in union with Christ. They were made one in Christ by their spiritual circumcision, their death and resurrection in baptism, and by the victorious death of Christ on the cross. Because of this oneness in Christ, they are in Christ's victory procession.

Gospel

Luke 11:1-13 (**Luth/Epis/Pres/Meth/UCC**). In response to the disciples' request for a lesson in prayer, Jesus gives them a model, the Lord's Prayer. In addition, he teaches

The Minister's Annual Manual

that they need to be persistent and confident in praying because God wants them to have all good gifts.

Theme: Persistence in prayer.

Thought for the day:

True Promises

God has not promised
  Skies always blue,
Flower-strewn pathways
  All our life through;
God has not promised
  Sun without rain,
Joy without sorrow,
  Peace without pain.

But God has promised
  Strength for the day,
Rest for the labor,
  Light for the way;
Grace for the trials,
  Help from above,
Unfailing sympathy,
  Undying love.

— Author unknown

Prayer of meditation:
What a friend we have in Jesus,
  All our sins and griefs to bear!
What a privilege to carry
  Ev'rything to God in prayer.
Oh, what peace we often forfeit;
  Oh, what needless pain we bear;
All because we do not carry
  Ev'rything to God in prayer. Amen.

— Author unknown

Call to worship:
Pastor: In celebration of what God has done for us in the past;
People: In expectation of what he will do for us this hour;
Pastor: And in anticipation of what he plans for us through the ages to come;
People: Let us come before the Lord and worship him.

Prayer of adoration:
O Lord, you are greater in majesty than we can imagine.
  You are present beyond the farthest reaches of the most distant galaxies.
You are intelligent beyond the comprehension of our poor, finite minds.
How awesome to know that you have promised to hear us when we pray; and even more, how wonderful to know that you will

August 16, 1992
(Epis/Pres/Meth/UCC - July 26, 1992)

respond to our prayers as a loving, heavenly Father, in a way that is best for us. In Jesus' name we pray. Amen.

Prayer of confession:
Pastor: Forgive us, Lord, if we have faltered in using the privilege of prayer. If we have found ourselves too hurried in the morning, and too busy during the day and too tired at night to pray.
People: Forgive us, Lord, and teach us to pray.
Pastor: If we have mouthed meaningless phrases which have long since lost their significance through endless repetition,
People: Forgive us, Lord, and teach us to pray.
Pastor: If we have considered prayer to be only a way of getting things, and have seldom used it to express praise and thanksgiving,
People: Forgive us, Lord, and teach us to pray.
Pastor: If we have kept prayer in reserve, to be used only as an emergency measure,
People: Forgive us, Lord, and teach us to pray.
Pastor: If we have demanded things from you rather than saying, "Your will be done,"
People: Forgive us, Lord, and teach us to pray.
Pastor: If we have prayed without persistence or conviction,
People: Forgive us, Lord, and teach us to pray. Amen.

Prayer of dedication of gifts and self: Heavenly Father, we know that many many needy people around the world have asked but have not yet received. May we realize that very often you answer those prayers through us. May our generosity now become a means by which such prayers are answered. Amen.

Sermon title: Prayer Power.

Sermon thesis: When it comes to prayer, have faith that God surely hears every prayer, that he answers every prayer, and that he answers every prayer in the way that is spiritually best for us.

Hymn for the day: *"Lord, teach us how to pray aright"* James Montgomery (1771-1854) ranks with Isaac Watts and Charles Wesley in his contributions to English hymnody. Intended by his parents for the Moravian ministry, Montgomery instead entered a literary career in which he made a considerable Christian witness. Besides his hymns, he wrote much poetry which spoke out against slavery. As printer of a newspaper, the *Sheffield Iris*, he also raised a voice against injustice. This hymn on prayer, written in 1818, was first printed on a leaflet for the Sheffield Nonconformist Sunday School.

Announcements for next week:
  Sermon title: How to Fail by Succeeding.
  Sermon theme: True living does not consist in the abundance of our possessions.
  Sermon summary: Success is not measured by the abundance of our possessions, but rather by the priority God has in our lives.

Children's object talk:

Snakes & Spiders For Breakfast?

Objects: Plastic or rubber snake and spider.
Lesson: Trust that God will answer your prayers in the way that is best for you.
Outline: 1. Who likes snakes and spiders?
  2. Loving parents wouldn't serve you snakes and spiders for breakfast.
  3. Your loving heavenly father also will not answer prayer in a way that hurts you.

GOOD MORNING, boys and girls! Look what I have here in the sack. Some snakes and spiders. Of course, they aren't real. How many of you like snakes and spiders? *(discuss for a while)*

I have a question for you. How would you like to come to breakfast tomorrow morning and your mother asks you what you would like to eat? You say: "I would like some scrambled eggs." But then, your mother brings you a plate full of snakes and spiders instead. Yuck! You wouldn't like that, would you? I know I wouldn't! Would your mothers and fathers trick you like that? No, of course not! They love you. They would never trick you by giving you something that could harm or scare you.

Jesus told us that our Father in heaven is the same way as our mothers and fathers. God is not going to trick us with something that would be bad for us or scare us in a terrible way. If we ask for love, he will give us love—not hate. If we want help, he will give us help and not trick us with something else.

Jesus wants to teach us about prayer. When you pray to God, know that you can trust him. He will give you those things which are best for you. And you'll know for sure, they will never be things that hurt you.

August 16, 1992
(Epis/Pres/Meth/UCC - July 26, 1992)

The sermon:

Prayer Power

Hymns:
Beginning of worship: Oh, for a Thousand Tongues to Sing
Sermon hymn: What a Friend We Have in Jesus
End of worship: He Leadeth Me: Oh, Blessed Thought

Scripture: Luke 11:1-13

Sermon Text: *"One day Jesus was praying in a certain place. When he finished, one of his disciplines said to him, 'Lord teach us to pray, just as John taught his disciples,' ...If you then, though you are evil, know how to give good gifts to your children, how much more will your Father in heaven give the Holy Spirit to those who ask him!"*
Luke 11:1 and 13- (N.I.V.)

IN UNGUARDED MOMENTS, many Christians (or should I say, most Christians) will say: "I ought to pray more." I intend to. I want to. But then, something else comes up, and another prayerless day is gone.

But even though most of us feel guilty about our shallow "hit and miss" prayer life, there's an ongoing fascination with prayer. We can't seem to write it off and say, "Bah! Humbug!" and then get on with life. We keep coming back! There's a gut feeling that prayer is for real, that it's untapped spiritual power. Prayer is heaven's toll free 800 number.

A recent nationwide poll included this item: I would like for my pastor to preach more sermons on the topic of _____.
The preferred topic, by a landslide, was the topic of prayer! So, even though the Gospel for today was written centuries ago, it would seem that interest in prayer is no less intense than it was then.

The disciples had watched Jesus pray. Often. They observed first hand the strength it brought to him. Why did they wait so long to make the request: "Lord, teach us to pray, just as John taught his disciples"? Who knows? At any rate, Jesus' response was quick. Almost like he is saying, "I thought you'd never ask!" Jesus said, "When you pray, say: 'Father, hallowed be your name...'" He taught them the prayer that Protestants call "The Lord's Prayer" and Catholics call the "Our Father." But he didn't stop there. He continued on and taught them other insights about prayer.

That's the springboard this morning. Let's review basic truths about prayer as taught in God's Word.

The first Scriptural truth about prayer is this: God hears every prayer! I have attended several football games at the University of Michigan. This giant stadium is usually filled to capacity. Over 100,000 people. Imagine for a moment that Jesus Christ is there. He is standing on the 50 yard line. People realize who this is. Even the doubters recognize that Jesus Christ is for real! Wow! Then, 100,000 people try to get his attention. A cacophany of sound! Pleadingly the needs are communicated. If this were to happen, would it make any sense? Wouldn't it be like gibberish? How is Jesus going to hear all those requests? How is he going to sort it all out?

When we come to the Lord in prayer, we may feel something like the person who is sending out countless resumes looking for a job. I'm told, that even today, when a good job is offered, employers receive hundreds and hundreds of resumes. How will you get the employer's attention among so many qualified people? Some have tried all kinds of zany things to get the employer's attention. It may come in the form of a psychedelic poster, a special envelope, etc. As we reflect upon the Lord and the countless prayers offered to him, we may feel: He'll never have time to listen to me.

The person who wrote Psalm 8 was amazed that God paid attention to him, or for that matter, to any human being. Listen to a portion of this Psalm as I read it to you from the Living Bible:

"When I look up into the night skies and see the work of your fingers—the moon and the stars you have made—I cannot understand how you can bother with any puny man, to pay any attention to him! And yet you have made him only a little lower than the angels, and placed a crown of glory and honor upon his head. You have put him in charge of everything you made; everything is put under his authority..."—Psalm 8:3-6-

It does seem totally awesome and unbelieveable, doesn't it?! That God hears every prayer offered to him. But that's exactly what Scripture tells us! I don't know how he does it, just like I don't understand how a computer can come up with instantaneous answers to complex problems. But God does. He hears every prayer.

There's more. Scripture also affirms the fact that God not only hears every prayer, but he answers every prayer too! That's where today's Gospel really comes into focus. Living in the society that we do, we have come to expect instant response to our prayers. If

August 16, 1992
(Epis/Pres/Meth/UCC - July 26, 1992)

God doesn't respond immediately with his heavenly fax machine, we automatically assume that he didn't answer. Jesus told the story of the folks who had some unexpected company late at night. The cupboard was bare, and since there were no 24 hour 7-11 stores to buy some refreshments, the man went to his neighbors and woke them up from sleep to borrow some food. "Hey!" the neighbor complained, "don't you know how late it is?! We're all in bed. Come back in the morning!" But the man who was seeking some refreshments for his unexpected guests kept asking and asking. Finally, to get rid of him, the sleepy neighbor got up and provided the food.

Jesus is here emphasizing a forgotten ingredient of prayer. Don't give up so fast. Don't be so impatient! Be persistent! Keep at it! God does answer prayer. But, in his almighty wisdom, he may answer in different ways. He may say "yes" or "no" or "not yet" or "how much do you really want this gift"? Two big questions: The human being says: "God, I have prayed and prayed and prayed. Why don't you answer?" And God says: "Dear friend, I have answered and answered and answered. Why don't you listen?" Scripture does not waver on this tenet of truth. God answers every prayer!

Finally, we need to add one more ingredient to the Scriptural description of prayer. It's true, God answers every prayer, but he answers in the way which is spiritually best for us.

What do you make of Romans 8:28? This passage states:
"And we know that in all things God works for the good of those who love him, who have been called according to his purpose."
For me, the implication is that God works together for the spiritual good of those who love him.

I have a confession to make. When it comes to praying for a stronger faith, I am a spiritual wimp. You know why? Simply because I know that, at least in my life, the only times I have really sensed a deepening of faith were times of crisis. Someone has said: "Sometimes God knocks us down so that we will look up at him." Perhaps some of the tough times in life come so that God can get our attention.

Examples by the dozen come to mind of people I have known who prayed fervently to the heavenly Father and were convinced that prayers were not answered. At least, not in the way they had prayed.

When my sisters were in their teens, they had what was called a "hope chest." Many a winter evening was spent embroidering pillow cases, dish towels and other items they hoped to use when they became married. If you are familiar with embroidery, you'll know that when you look on the bottom side of the cloth, there are a bunch of knots and threads criss-crossing in a crazy quilt, meaningless pattern. However, when you look at the top side (assuming the person has done a good job), you see the beautiful pattern intended.

Life is like that. We're looking at life from our perspective, from the bottom side. The patterns of life so often don't make sense. But, if we haven't come to grips with it before, when we're with God in heaven, we'll be looking at our life from his perspective and see the pattern unfolded before him.

So, when it comes to prayer, hang in there! Have faith that God surely hears every prayer, he answers every prayer, and he answers every prayer in the way that is spiritually best for us.

E. Dean Windhorn
Christ Church (Lutheran)
Zionsville, Indiana

AUGUST 23, 1992

Lutheran: Eleventh Sunday after Pentecost
Roman Catholic: Eighteenth Sunday of the Year
Episcopalian: Proper 13 (August 2)
Pres/Meth/UCC: Eighth after Pentecost (August 2)

Lessons:

Lutheran:	Eccl. 1:2, 2:18-26	Col. 3:1-11	Luke 12:13-21
Roman Catholic:	Eccl. 1:2, 2:21-23	Col. 3:1-5, 9-11	Luke 12:13-21
Episcopal:	Eccl. 1:12-14, 2:(1-7, 11)18-23	Col. 3:(5-11) 12-17	Luke 12:13-21
Pres/Meth/UCC:	2 Kings 13:14-20a	Col. 3:1-11	Luke 12:13-21

Introductions to the Lessons

Lesson 1

(1) *Ecclesiastes 1:2; 2:18-26* (**Luth**); *Eccl. 1:12-14; 2:18-23* (**Epis**). An old man writes about the meaninglessness of life. For instance, a person works hard all his/her life, but has to leave it to one who did not have to work. This is useless. What does one have to show for all one's work? Only pain and worry. The best thing to do is to enjoy one's work. God can make this possible.

(2) *2 Kings 13:14-20a* (**Pres/Meth/UCC**). Today we bring to a close the ministry of Elijah and Elisha. While on his deathbed Elisha receives a tearful visit from Joash, king of Israel. Elisha orders the king to get bow and arrows and to shoot an arrow through a window in the direction of Syria, Israel's dreaded enemy. This is a sign that Syria will be defeated. Then Elisha dies and is buried.

Lesson 2

Colossians 3:1-11 (**Luth/Pres/Meth/UCC**). The readings from Colossians come to an end today. A Christian, according to Paul, is a new creation in Christ. In baptism a Christian dies to self and rises with Christ as a new being. Consequently, a Christian seeks what is above where Christ is and puts to death all evil desires and practices. Consequently, there are no distinctions among Christians, for we are one in Christ.

(2) *Colossians 3:12-17* (**Epis**). Since we are the people of God, we must be clothed with virtue: compassion, kindness, humility, gentleness, and patience. Best of all is love which is expressed in forgiving each other. And be thankful to the God who loves us in Christ.

The Minister's Annual Manual

Gospel

Luke 12:13-21 (**Luth/Epis/Pres/Meth/UCC**). One of the Ten Commandments is "You shall not covet." A brother asked Jesus to persuade his older brother to share his father's inheritance. Jesus refused because it was a case of coveting based on greed. To illustrate Jesus tells the story of a very wealthy man who thought he had it made for the future but died that very night.

Theme: True living does not consist in the abundance of our possessions.

Thought for the day:

A Moment With Him

We mutter and sputter
  We fume and we spurt,
We mumble and grumble,
  Our feelings get hurt.
We can't understand things,
  Our vision grows dim,
When all that we need
  Is a moment with him.

—Author unknown

Prayer of meditation:

We brought nothing into this world, and it is certain that we can carry nothing out.

Therefore, let our affection be for those things that will never be destroyed.

Let our values be the kind that will never become outdated.

Let our beauty be that which will never fade.

In Jesus' name we pray. Amen.

Call to worship:

Pastor: Fellow Christians, we have come together to praise the living God;

People: To make humble confession of our sins;

Pastor: To seek his presence anew through our prayers;

People: To join in fellowship with other Christians;

Pastor: To contemplate the message of his holy Word.

People: Let us worship the Lord in spirit and in truth!

Prayer of adoration: Heavenly Father, we have freely received so many gifts from you. For these benefits, far greater than we have any right to expect, we thank you. For the beauty of the world around us, and all the magnificent wonders of nature, we thank you. For the growth of the harvest, providing food for ourselves and others, we thank you. For the abilities given to us, whereby we can perform our daily tasks and provide for our families—heavenly

August 23, 1992
(Epis/Pres/Meth/UCC - August 2, 1992)

Father, we thank you. For the wonders of human life and the joys of our relationships with others, we thank you. For the sustaining power of your spiritual presence, to guide us in our daily living, we thank you. For the greatness of your love, revealed to us through the gift of Jesus Christ, our Savior, we offer our thanks, O God. Amen.

Prayer of confession: Lord, you know that we have tried to lose ourselves in the crowd, since we do not want to face up to who we really are. We have tried to forget our sins and mistakes by becoming busy with so many things. We do not have peace within since we have tried to live with our sin rather than repent of it. Help us to stop trying to hide from our true selves. Forgive us our sins and guide us in finding a new life through Jesus Christ. Amen.

Prayer of dedication of gifts and self: Deliver us, O Lord, from the bondage of materialism—that master which tries to control every ambition, every decision, every relationship, every ethical choice. Accept these gifts as evidence that in some respects, at least, we are already free. Amen.

Sermon title: How To Fail By Succeeding

Sermon thesis: Success is not measured by the abundance of our possessions, but rather by the priority God has in our lives.

Hymn for the day: *"God, whose giving knows no ending".* This hymn reminds us that all that we have comes from God and calls on us to "open wide our hands in sharing." The hymn was written in 1961 by Robert Lansing Edwards (b. 1915), a Congregational minister who served two churches in Connecticut. He held a Ph.D. in history from Harvard University, and a master's degree from Union Theological Seminary in New York City, and later completed a research fellowship at Yale Divinity School. He held numerous posts in the greater Hartford area, and four times was a delegate to international church councils.

Announcements for next week:
  Sermon title: Have No Fear.
  Sermon theme: Discipleship is built upon trust in the promises of God.
  Sermon summary: Fear is a natural human condition. From the birth of Christ to his resurrection, and in the course of his ministry, fear was addressed and always countered. God's promise to give us the Kingdom is our encouragement for trust and discipleship. The Kingdom means joy, happiness, and service—here and now.

Children's object talk:

Want! Want! Want!

Objects: A Christmas toy catalog.
Lesson: Wanting too much becomes greed. (Luke 12:20)
Outline: 1. The new Christmas catalog will be coming soon.
2. If you could have as many things as you wanted, what would you choose?
3. Be careful. Don't be like the greedy farmer.

LOOK WHAT I HAVE HERE TODAY. What is it? That's right, it's a Christmas toy catalog. This is last year's catalog. But I guess the new ones will be coming soon. Won't it be fun to look through the catalog and start making a list of the toys you would like to have for Christmas? Do any of you know what you would like to ask for this Christmas? *(give opportunity for sharing)*

Do the toys in the catalog cost lots of money? How do you know what each toy costs? *(have someone point out where the prices are printed in the catalog)* How long would it take to earn the money to buy the things from a Christmas catalog? That's right. A long time. Suppose someone told you that you could have whatever you wanted from this catalog — in fact, as many things as you wanted and you wouldn't have to worry about how much it costs. Wow! Wouldn't that be great!

You know what I think. I think many of us want more things than we could possibly use or need. When we get like that, we are greedy. Does anyone know what "greedy" means?

Jesus told a story about a man who got greedy. He was a farmer who had lots of crops. But instead of sharing, he kept it all for himself. The more he got, the more he wanted. Want! Want! Want! That is being greedy. Well, one night the greedy farmer died. All of this money didn't do him any good. Jesus wants us to be careful so that we don't become unhappy with what we already have and to share. Otherwise, we might get so greedy that we forget all about him.

August 23, 1992
(Epis/Pres/Meth/UCC - August 2, 1992)

The sermon:
How To Fail By Succeeding

Hymns:
Beginning of worship: Praise and Thanksgiving
Sermon Hymn: We Give Thee but Thine Own
End of worship: Now Thank We All Our God

Scripture: Luke 12:13-21

Sermon Text: *"Jesus said to them, 'Watch out! Be on your guard against all kinds of greed; a man's life does not consist in the abundance of his possessions..'"* Luke 12:15 (N.I.V.)

THIS IS A STORY about a very successful farmer-businessman. He had mastered the techniques of his business:
- He knew the proper fertilizers to use.
- He knew how to care for the soil.
- He knew the best seed to plant for greater yields.
- He obviously knew the right time to market his product so that he would get the very best price.

In fact, business was so good, he didn't have enough storage space for the bumper crops of grain. He had to tear down the old storage bins and build larger ones! Yet Jesus called him a failure. More than that, Jesus called him a fool!

Why? Was it because he was rich? No, not really. Does this mean that Jesus is suspicious and cynical about success? After all, many of you in this congregation are quite successful in your vocation. No, Jesus isn't against success. Does Jesus believe that people who have lots of money are never happy. Nope. That's not what he is saying either.

The point comes out in his words just prior to the story of the foolish "successful farmer." He said: "Watch out. Be on your guard against all kinds of greed. Life does not consist in the abundance of possessions"!

(pause) Life does not consist in the abundance of possessions! That must be stated again and again. You know why? Because that is just the opposite of the theme trumpeted by the "economic Bible." The economic Bible states that life does consist in the abundance of possessions. The person who won the million dollar lottery and said: "Now I can really start living" is not so unusual. All of us, whether

Christian or non-Christian, are bombarded and literally brainwashed with the thesis that "life — real living — consists in the abundance of possessions."

Let's pause for a moment and emphasize what Jesus is not teaching in this story. He is not saying that rich people should feel guilty about the fact that they have lots of money and property (assuming it was acquired honestly). On the other hand, Jesus is not giving out a spiritual Oscar to those who are poor, implying that somehow poverty, in and of itself, guarantees greater spirituality. The heart of Jesus' teaching is this: Rich or poor, what is the attitude we have toward our possessions?

If has been said: "When what you possess begins to possess you, then you are really possessed." *(Hold up a dollar bill)* Here's some money? Is it good or evil? I've done this in a classroom setting a number of times. There is almost always at least one person in the class who proclaims that money is evil. Actually, money is amoral. It is neutral. It is neither good nor evil, in and of itself. How you use it determines it's morality. *(Hold the dollar bill directly in front of your eyes).* Obviously, if the dominant quest in your life is to acquire more money, it can shut off your vision to other things/persons that are really more important to real living.

I heard a story about a young man who one day accidentally found a $10.00 bill in the parking lot. In the spirit of Clint Eastwood, this "really made his day!" In fact, he was so enamored about this unexpected good fortune that from then on, he spent a lot of time with his eyes to the ground while he was walking. He never again found much money, but after 40 years, here's a partial tabulation of what he found:

- *29,516 buttons*
- *54,172 pins*
- *7 pennies*
- *a bent back and a miserly disposition*

At the same time, he lost the glories of the sunlight, the smiles of friends, the songs of the birds, the beauty of flowers and trees, blue skies, the opportunities to serve his fellow human beings, etc.

As the Apostle Paul puts it so succinctly while writing to his young friend, Timothy: "The love of money is the root of all evils; it is through this craving that some have wandered away from the faith and pierced their hearts with many pangs." (1 Timothy 6:10, RSV) The rich, successful farmer-businessman was a fool, not because he

August 23, 1992
(Epis/Pres/Meth/UCC - August 2, 1992)

was rich, but because he was greedy. His possessions had begun to possess him. They were the dominant quest of his life.

The rich farmer needed to learn that life does not consist in the abundance of possessions. How true. Sometimes we're so busy making a living, we have forgotten to live.

Some examples: A young wife/mother wants others to think well of her abilities as a homemaker. She works long and hard to keep the house clean and do the right things. In the meantime, she may invest so much time to perpetuate that image that she sacrifices some quality time with the children as they grow up. And, how quickly they do.

In my own life, I carry some guilt from my younger years as a pastor. I devoted lots of quality time to the job, trying to be the best pastor there ever was! Something had to give. Unfortunately, I sacrificed quality time with my wife, but most of all, with my children during those precious growing up years.

Grandparents are often accused of spoiling the grandchildren. Now that I'm officially a grandfather, I can understand that. Picture this scenario: here's Grandpa down on the floor playing with his toddler grandchildren. The son or daughter is shocked and jealous: "Dad, I'm surprised. You never got down on the floor and played with me!" And he probably didn't. He was too busy trying to be a success.

I guess grandparents have lived long enough to learn some things. To be a success seemed so important in those younger years. The older you get, the more you appreciate the quality time spent with loved ones. When you're a grandparent, the quest for success pales in comparison to enjoying the beauty and genius of your little grandson or granddaughter. What a delightful symbol of God's artistic creation!

An artist had completed a painting of "The Last Supper" and invited his closest friends to view the work. He had worked hard on this painting for many months, pouring all his skill into the painting. No detail had been neglected. Each of the apostles had been studied diligently from the Gospels and was portrayed as the artist understood him. The table and all its appointments had been painted with great care. An elegant, beautiful cup was in the hands of our Lord.

As his friends admired the painting, several of them made special mention of the beautiful cup. "What an exquisite cup!" they were heard to exclaim.

"This is wrong," said the artist. "The cup takes the eyes of the viewer away from the face of the Master." He then took his brush and blotted out the cup upon which he had spent so much time. He replaced it by painting an ordinary, plain cup. He wanted nothing to detract from the center of his work — the face of Jesus.

Aren't there such "cups" in our own lives, that is, things which detract our attention from the face of Jesus? Whatever it might be: our possessions, our jobs, our quest for success or social acceptance — it is no longer amoral, but rather becomes immoral when it shuts out Jesus. Dear friends in Christ, hear his words today: Success is not measured by the abundance of our possessions, but rather by the priority he has in our lives.

E. Dean Windhorn
Christ Church (Lutheran)
Zionsville, Indiana

AUGUST 30, 1992

Lutheran: Twelfth Sunday after Pentecost
Roman Catholic: Nineteenth Sunday of the Year
Episcopalian: Proper 14 (August 9)
Pres/Meth/UCC: Ninth after Pentecost (August 9)

Lessons:

Lutheran:	Gen. 15:1-6	Heb. 11:1-3, 8-16	Luke 12:32-40
Roman Catholic:	Wisd. 18:6-9	Heb. 11:1-2, 8-19	Luke 12:32-48
Episcopal:	Gen. 15:1-6	Heb. 11:1-3, (4-7) 8-16	Luke 12:32-40
Pres/Meth/UCC:	Jer. 18:1-11	Heb. 11:1-3, 8-19	Luke 12:32-40

Introductions to the Lessons

Lesson 1

(1) *Genesis 15:1-6* (**Luth/Epis**). The period of preparation prior to the Persian Gulf war was called by the Allies the "Desert Shield." In today's Lesson Abraham could claim that God was his "Divine Shield." God promised Abraham to shield him from danger and through a son to provide descendants as numerous as the stars. Because Abraham trusted these promises, he found favor with God.

(2) *Jeremiah 18:1-11* (**Pres/Meth/UCC**). Today's Lesson is the first in a series of three taken from the book of Jeremiah. He was a prophet at the time the Babylonians took Judah into captivity. Because he deeply loved his countrymen, it pained him to have to tell his people they would experience death and destruction, which took place in 586 B.C. In today's passage Jeremiah forecasts God's judgment upon Judah for refusing to repent.

Lesson 2

Hebrews 11:1-3, 8-16 (**Luth/Epis**); *Hebrews 11:1-3, 8-19* (**Pres/Meth/UCC**). For the next four Sundays we will be hearing God's Word from the last three chapters of Hebrews. Today we begin with chapter 11, the faith chapter. Faith is defined for us and then is illustrated especially by Abraham. His faith was shown by his obedience to God's commands and by his trust in God's promises.

Gospel

Luke 12:32-40 (**Luth/Epis/Pres/Meth/UCC**). In last Sunday's Gospel, Jesus taught us that life does not consist of material possessions. Therefore we should not worry

The Minister's Annual Manual

about physical needs, for God will provide them. Rather we are to seek spiritual resources in terms of God's Kingdom which he wants us to have. Since the time of the Kingdom's coming is uncertain, we need to be ready and waiting for it.

Theme: Discipleship is built upon trust in the promises of God.

Thought for the day: In the midst of the changes and chances of life, the Christian seeks courage to live out the family relationship as a child of God. This courage comes from renewed faith in studying God's word and remembering his promises.

Prayer of meditation: We are here, O God, waiting and wondering. We sense your greatness. Some of us are worried; some of us are afraid of the future; some of us are grumpy. But we are here, together with the others in this place. O Lord, make us aware of our need and the greatness of your love. Grant us your Holy Spirit, and thus allow us to become what we were meant to be in your creation—children of yours through Christ our Lord. Amen.

Call to worship: O come, let us sing to the Lord; let us make a joyful noise to the rock of our salvation! Let us come into his presence with thanksgiving; and make a joyful noise to him with songs! For the Lord is a great God, and a great King above all gods. (Ps. 95:1-3)

Prayer of adoration: O Lord, our God; you humbled yourself that we might be exalted. You became poor that we might be enriched. You came to us that we might come to you. You became human like us that we might share in eternal life. We are gathered in the presence of this mystery to praise you and to receive your word. Through your Holy Spirit show us, and prepare for us, the way that leads to you; through Christ our lord. Amen.

Prayer of confession: Let us make a confession of our sins to God, and offer repentance: for being inattentive to your word and the voice of your servants; for not thinking deeply, and for being too intense about ourselves; for thinking we have the whole truth; for lack of trust; for lack of feeling and intercession for the needs of our families, the oppressed, the hungry, those in temptation, and those without hope; for an uncritical attitude toward our own part in a society ruled by the world's values; for ignoring other people, and for taking ourselves too seriously; for presumptuous sins and sins of inhibition; for a failure to think and pray and act deeply for the mission and unity of our Church; and for trying to imprison you in words and institutions. O Lord we do repent, and seek your mercy. Forgive what we have been, and help us become what you desire, through Jesus Christ, our Lord. Amen.

Prayer of dedication of gifts and self: O God, you have no need to be enriched with any gifts that we may bring, and yet you have told us of your love for the cheerful giver; we present these our offerings in a joyful spirit of gratitude. We do acknowledge that you provide for our every need—the food that nourishes us, the people who support us, and your word which enlivens us. With these gifts we present ourselves, our whole bodies, our being, as a living sacrifice. We pray it will be holy and acceptable to you, through Jesus Christ, our Lord. Amen.

Sermon title: Have No Fear

Sermon thesis: Fear is a natural human condition. From the birth of Christ to his resurrection, and in the course of his ministry, fear was addressed and always countered. God's promise to give us the Kingdom is our encouragement for trust and discipleship. The Kingdom means joy, happiness, and service—here and now.

Hymn for the day: *"From God can nothing move me"* This hymn of trust in God's guidance and protection was written during an epidemic of the plague that took the lives of 4000 inhabitants of Erfurt, Germany, where the author was rector of the St. Augustine *Gymnasium*. Ludwig Helmbold (1532-1598) was a Lutheran pastor who served as dean of the philosophical faculty of the University of Erfurt, and later as a parish pastor in Muhlhausen. He was crowned a poet by the Emperor Maximilian II.

Announcements for next week:
    Sermon title: Christ the Divider.
    Sermon theme: Taking a stand for Christ and his way often causes dissension.
    Sermon summary: Discipleship demands making decisions. For any decision to be made, there must be choices. When members of a family or circle of friends make different choices, sometimes conflicts arise. When discipleship demands lifestyle change, these conflicts can divide family and friends. Courage is needed to continue to stand for Christ.

Children's object talk:
What To Do When You're Afraid
Objects: Well used (loved) stuffed animal or blanket.
Lesson: Fear can be overcome by learning to trust.
Outline: 1. Unfamiliar situations cause fear.
         2. Familiar people and things displace fear.

3. Trust in God's promise of his presence and his love helps us overcome the fears of growing up.

HAVE YOU EVER BEEN LOST? Have you ever been separated from one of your parents in a shopping mall? Or at a fair with a large crowd of people? Have you ever slept in a strange house, and been afraid?

Perhaps when you were lost, you happened to see a person you recognized, or a playmate, or a police officer and you knew you could ask them to help you find your family. Then your fear disappeared. Sleeping in a strange place, can you remember that one of your parents would say, "Don't be afraid, I am here with you. I will be close by."

Knowing that someone you love is close by takes away the fear. The place is strange, and yet you can go to sleep.

Many situations in life—going to new schools, meeting new people, moving to new homes, and just growing up in God's world sometimes makes us fearful. Knowing that God is present—even when we cannot see him—makes the fear go away. Knowing that people like you, and knowing that other boys and girls want to make new friends helps take away any fear.

God is the creator of love and helpfulness. He helps us by providing friendly people and helpful neighbors, and shows us his presence by sending them to us. We do not have to be afraid of new things and new people.

The sermon:

Have No Fear...

Hymns:
Beginning of worship: Lord, Keep us Steadfast in your Word
Sermon Hymn: Have No Fear, Little Flock
End of worship: Your Kingdom Come, O Father Hear our Prayer

Scripture: Luke 12:32-40

Sermon Text: *"Fear not, little flock, for it is your Father's good pleasure to give you the kingdom."* vs. 32

FEAR is one of the most basic and common emotional conditions of all humanity. (Please check that out with your own experience.)

August 30, 1992
(Epis/Pres/Meth/UCC - August 9, 1992)

I believe God recognizes that with the very frequent use of the expression, "Do not be afraid," or "Have no fear."

Consider the message of the angels to the shepherds on the night of Jesus' birth; or the message to the women at the tomb on resurrection morn; or the words of Jesus to Peter on the occasion of his attempt to walk on the water. They all begin, "Be not afraid..."

The text for today is part of Luke's Gospel in the midst of the familiar words usually identified as the "Sermon on the Mount." They are unique to Luke and add to our insight concerning his care and concern for people as seen in the ministry of Jesus.

Why are people afraid? Of what are people afraid?

Among other reasons I might suggest three—the unknown; rejection; and loneliness. Death, changing jobs, new people, new surroundings all seem to cause fear by degrees. All of us want to please, and be accepted. Rejection, or the fear of rejection causes great anxiety. And the fear of loneliness causes people to do or imagine strange things. Guilt and insecurity are closely related to fear.

How many of us have felt like Ol' Man River: "...tired of living, and scared of dying"?

It was not enough for Jesus simply to say we shouldn't be afraid. He tells us why we shouldn't fear. "It is your Father's good pleasure..." He might have said, Your Father has chosen, or it is your Father's plan. I wonder if the disciples caught the full meaning of these words in relation to the previous message of Jesus, "Your Father knows that you need (these things)." These things of course are food in the stomach and clothes on the back. These are words of comfort and security.

Our needs are known to our heavenly Father; therefore we should not be afraid that we will be denied the basics of life.

Thus the comforting words of the song, "He's got the whole world in his hands ... he's got you and me sister ... you and me brother."

In my mother's kitchen directly above the sink, was a plaque with these words, "There is no problem I have that is bigger than God." Thus the words of Jesus, "Fear not little flock, for it is the Father's good pleasure...

"...to give you the kingdom." Not heaven, or the created earth, but the kingdom of God. Now comes to mind the words of the Lord's Prayer, "Your kingdom come ... on earth as it is in heaven." And the words of Jesus just before this sequence in Luke's Gospel, "Instead seek his kingdom," remind us of the nature of discipleship. The reign of Christ on earth is the kingdom of God. He is not referring to death, heaven, or the future. Life with Christ is in the eternal present.

So what does this mean for you and for me? How does this translate to an antidote for our fears? Three words focus our faith:

1. Courage, which comes from discipline as disciples — as followers of Christ. It is the result of learning, sharing, and communication. It must be worked at regularly.

2. Commitment, which comes from finding a purpose in life, a reason for living. When parents share and live out their commitment to the Christian values and relationships, then children will "catch" as well as "learn" the basics of life. When the Bible stories are read with "purpose" in mind, then it becomes easier to translate, and transfer the message to daily living in the 20th century. Paul the Apostle and Jesus himself make the meaning of commitment clear.

3. Confidence, which comes from trusting the relationship we have with God, through our baptism into Christ. How exciting is the story of Shadrach, Meshach, and Abednego. Their courage came from their confidence in God, that no matter what happened to them, their relationship to him would stand. "Our God is able to save us" they told King Nebuchadnezzar, "...*but if not*, we will still not bow down and worship."

In Victor Hugo's story of *Les Miserables*, the central character, Jean Valjean, is converted by a simple act of forgiveness by a committed Christian. That change in one person brought life and hope to a myriad of others.

For you and me, the words of Jesus are clear and most helpful. I suggest that much of our anxiety is brought about by trying to live out our faith in the present day when we feel caught between our guilt of the past and our fear of the future. Only when we are freed by forgiveness and have a joyful vision of the kingdom which is promised us — now — can we live with meaning and fulfilled service — today.

Thus courage, commitment, and confidence become the antidote for the fears we experience. Christians are not fearless people. That is not the promise. We overcome fear and channel the energy it creates into helpful service by taking Jesus at his word and living in God's kingdom — now. "Fear not little flock, for it is the Father's

August 30, 1992
(Epis/Pres/Meth/UCC - August 9, 1992)

good pleasure to give you the kingdom." I believe he was speaking to us.

T.A. Youngquist
Redemption Lutheran Church
Wauwatosa, Wisconsin

SEPTEMBER 6, 1992

Lutheran: Thirteenth Sunday after Pentecost
Roman Catholic: Twentieth Sunday of the Year
Episcopalian: Proper 15 (August 16)
Pres/Meth/UCC: Tenth after Pentecost (August 16)

Lessons:

Lutheran:	Jer. 23:23-29	Heb. 12:1-13	Luke 12:49-53
Roman Catholic:	Jer. 38:4-6, 8-10	Heb. 12:1-4	Luke 12:49-53
Episcopal:	Jer. 23:23-29	Heb. 12:1-7, (8-10) 11-14	Luke 12:49-56
Pres/Meth/UCC:	Jer. 20:7-13	Heb. 12:1-2, 12-17	Luke 12:49-56

Introductions to the Lessons

Lesson 1

(1) *Jeremiah 23:23-29* (**Luth/Epis**). In chapter 23 of Jeremiah God takes to task the prophets of the day. Except for Jeremiah, the prophets tell lies to the people. Under the guise of dreams, they falsely say they are speaking God's Word. True prophets faithfully speak God's Word, which is powerful like a fire and a hammer.

(2) *Jeremiah 20:7-13* (**Pres/Meth/UCC**). It is not easy to be a faithful preacher of God's Word. Because of the people's sin, Jeremiah's message from God was one of judgment. Because the people did not want to hear this, Jeremiah became immensely unpopular. He was ridiculed, scorned, and his death was plotted. He is tempted to stop preaching, but a divine necessity will not allow it.

Lesson 2

Hebrews 12:1-13 (**Luth**); *Heb. 12:1-4* (**Epis**); *Heb. 12:1-2, 12-17* (**Pres/Meth/UCC**). In Hebrews 11 we were given a long list of faithful people. In this 12th chapter, we find ourselves surrounded by a host of faithful men and women who cheer us on in the race of life. To win the race we must drop whatever hinders us, look to Jesus as our model, discipline ourselves, and live holy lives.

Gospel

Luke 12:49-53 (**Luth/Epis**); *Luke 12:49-56* (**Pres/Meth/UCC**). Jesus is a controversial figure. He came to set the world on fire, the fire of division. People are either for or against him. This leads to division even in family relationships. There is no middle ground; it is all or nothing. As we can tell what the weather will be, we need to know the meaning of the present time. Jesus is here and we must take sides.

September 6, 1992
(Epis/Pres/Meth/UCC - August 16, 1992)

Theme: Taking a stand for Christ and his way often causes dissension.

Thought for the day: Christ calls us to renewed discipleship today. He commands us to love and serve all his brothers and sisters. Obedience to Christ is costly, but he never commands without providing resources.

Prayer of meditation: Lord, help me to pray, to desire to pray. Make all my supplications joyful with faith, joyful with hope, joyful with love. May these words be joyful with your Spirit interceding for me, urgent with prodding behind my inattention, generous with wisdom behind my dim sightedness, burning with fire behind my lukewarmth; joyful in the fellowship of the prayers of all believers, of your whole church including those who surround me, and those who have gone before me. I ask this through your Son, Jesus Christ our Lord, who makes intercession for us at your throne. Amen.

Call to worship: Come thou almighty King, help us your name to sing; help us to praise. Father all glorious, o'er all victorious, come and reign over us, Ancient of Days. Let us worship the Lord in the beauty of holiness. Come with open hearts and open minds to receive the God of creation who offers himself to you, now.

Prayer of adoration: Glory be to you, O God, for all your mighty acts: for calling this world into being, and for bringing order and beauty out of chaos; for awaking in your people a desire and thirst for you. Glory be to you, O God, for sending your Son in the fullness of time; for his life, death, and resurrection in order that we might be redeemed. Glory be to you, O God, for the gift of your Holy Spirit, ever working in the hearts of all humanity; building up your church throughout the world; comforting and counseling us in our daily lives. For all these gifts we give our thanks with adoration. Amen.

Prayer of confession: Let us come before our Lord, Jesus the Christ, in repentance and humbly confess our sins: Our failure to believe in the reconciliation of all humanity to you and to each other through your passion and death; our indifference and complacency, our ignorance and prejudice against one another, our lack of humility and unwillingness to learn from one another; our erecting barriers of race and class, nation and culture among your people; our lack of love and prayer for one another, and our unwillingness to rely on your strength alone. O Lamb of God, who takes away the sin of the world, have mercy on us. Regard not our sins, but the faith of your church, and grant her that peace and unity which are in accord with your will, who lives and reigns with the Father and the Holy Spirit, One God, now and forever. Amen.

Prayer of dedication of gifts and self: Remember, O Lord, what you have wrought in us, and not what we deserve; and as you have called us to your service, make us worthy of that calling. We acknowledge that only in you do we live and move and have our being. We offer and present ourselves, our souls and bodies, our thoughts and desires, our words and our deeds, to be a reasonable, holy, and living sacrifice. Accept, we pray you, this offering of ourselves and our gifts for the service of all humanity. Use, we beseech you, our being and our doing, our gifts and our goods for your glory and the well-being of your creation, through Christ our Lord. Amen.

Sermon title: Christ the Divider.

Sermon thesis: Discipleship demands making decisions. For any decision to be made, there must be choices. When members of a family or circle of friends make different choices, sometimes conflicts arise. When discipleship demands lifestyle changes, these conflicts can divide family and friends. Courage is needed to continue to stand for Christ.

Hymn for the day: *"Jesus calls us"* A native of Ireland, Cecil Frances Alexander (1818-1895) spent much of her life in caring and concern for others. Before her marriage to William Alexander, who later became bishop of Ireland, she established a school for the deaf. Later she was known to walk miles ministering to the sick and taking food to the poor. She wrote a number of hymns, her most important publication being *Hymns for Little Children*. The call to discipleship asks us to "turn from home and toil and kindred, leaving all for his dear sake."

Announcements for next week:

    Sermon title: Where Are You Coming From?

    Sermon theme: According to Jesus, few will qualify for entrance into God's kingdom.

    Sermon summary: Jesus states clearly that there will be a time of judgment concerning who will enter the kingdom of God, i.e. "be saved." Name dropping and complaining will not help. Discipline, commitment, and right priorities are the standards for entrance.

September 6, 1992
(Epis/Pres/Meth/UCC - August 16, 1992)

Children's object talk:
Making The Right Choices

Objects: Facsimile or used ticket from an amusement or theme park, *and* a Church School lesson sheet from 1st or 2nd grade.
Lesson: Making choices about where to go and what to do are sometimes difficult for a Christian.
Outline: 1. Having fun is an important part of life.
2. Learning About God is also important.
3. We need to use Sundays for worship and Church School.

HOW MANY OF YOU have been to Great America (Or whatever fun park is close — holding up the ticket)? Do you like to go to the park, and have picnics and play games?

Fun and recreation are healthy for all of us. God wants us to enjoy living in his world. Fun, parks, picnics, rides with family and friends are exciting. By doing all these things we learn to play together, to share, and to grow up being happy in God's world.

We also need to learn about God, even as we enjoy his world. He has given us brains and intelligence so we can learn about his goodness, his help to our ancestors in the past, and how he shows his love to all people today. To do that, to learn about his ways, we come to worship, and to our Church School.

When you are tempted to miss worship and just enjoy your personal recreation, you miss learning some helpful things. Every Sunday is important, because God gives you life every day. To think that you will not be missed is like thinking that God would skip loving you one day, because there are 364 other days when he can do that.

As you worship regularly, you appreciate God and his ways more and more. You invite your friends to come with you, and you remind yourself, and them, that there will be plenty of time for fun and games after Sunday morning. The more you learn about God, the more you can appreciate his wonderful world.

See you ... in church ... next week.

The sermon:
Christ the Divider

Hymns:
Beginning of worship: How Firm a Foundation
Sermon Hymn: God of Grace and God of Glory
End of worship: O Jesus, I have Promised

Scripture: Luke 12:49-53

Sermon Text: *"Do you think that I have come to give peace on earth? No, I tell you, but rather division."* vs. 51

HOW MANY OF US ASSOCIATE CHRIST WITH PEACE? Peacemaker, peace-giver are thoughts we have of Jesus. How different the words of our text sound in our ears. What could he possibly mean?

The context for these words is interesting. Two Sundays ago we heard the rather harsh words, "Tonight your soul is required of you. And the things you have prepared, whose will they be?" Last week the comforting words, "Fear not little flock, for it is your Father's good pleasure to give you the kingdom" were connected to Christ's words of "For where your treasure is, there will your heart be also." Today the concern is not about the divisiveness of things but of relationships.

Discipleship means decisions. Joshua called upon the people to choose; Jesus confronted the disciples and asked, "Will you also go away?" The rich young ruler was asked to make a choice; and the young man who wanted to follow Jesus, but asked *first* to go and bury his father was refused.

Not only is a choice called for, but a total and complete commitment is the order. "Hear, O Israel, the Lord your God is one Lord ... you shall love the Lord your God with *all* ..." In the parable of the pearl of great price, the merchant sold *all* that he had to obtain the one piece. The saying is true, "It doesn't take much of a person to be a Christian, but it takes *all* of that person."

But why is this passage so difficult, almost offensive?

Permit me to suggest two concerns: 1. We have culturized our Christianity—compromised God himself. 2. We have deified our blood family.

Jesus does not make a general attack on family ties, but an appeal

September 6, 1992
(Epis/Pres/Meth/UCC - August 16, 1992)

to the true source of peace and security. He was concerned about lasting relationships in the face of competing loyalties. The family is not an end in itself, but a means to developing the relationship which each person has with his/her creator. Do you remember how Jesus said, "Whoever loves father or mother more than me is not worthy of me"? Or again, "Who is my mother, and my brother? Whoever does the will of my heavenly Father is my brother and mother."

Now perhaps a warning is needed. Almost any concept can be stretched to its absurdity. A principle can usually be extended to its point of destruction. Thus "Peace at any price" can be nothing but a prelude to war. A person can be "right" to the point of being "dead right," and one can be proud of one's humility.

So the concept of God's gift of family can be placed above God himself, and thus be a divisive influence.

Division comes when commitment and discipleship run counter to family ties and pressures. When loyalties are challenged and time, energy, and money are channeled away from the blood family, then stands are taken, and divisions arise. This is the concern of Jesus.

Following Jesus demands change. He talked frequently about the contrast of the way of the world and the way of the Kingdom of God. The first and the last, the greatest and the least, the master and the servant are a few of the contrasts which he made.

That's what is meant by culturizing Christianity—that is, taking our value system from the world, placing the family first—at all costs—and still trying to be a disciple of Jesus Christ.

When Jesus said he was not bringing peace, I believe he was thinking that peace meant compromise, and he felt there was no place for that in the kingdom. The saying may be true, "Some people are so tolerant that they even tolerate the devil."

For many, peace means having a condition where I can do what I want to do, when I want to do it. My advantage is foremost. When my family comes first, and my excuse for not having time, money, or energy for God's work is my family—then the line must be drawn. Luke records the story of the young man who said he wanted to follow Jesus, but asked first to go and say good-bye to his family. Jesus replied, "No one who puts his hand to the plow and looks back is fit for the Kingdom."

When family becomes a priority, discipleship is questioned.

Thus I understand the words of Jesus. In summary:

1. Make the commitment to Christ — totally.
2. Let the chips fall where they may.
3. Trust and believe that God will take care of you, and that your reward will be in your serving.
4. Enlarge your family concept to include all those who follow the Christ, and if any in your blood family turn their back on him, make your stand with the Savior himself.

May our prayer be in the spirit of the sermon hymn, that God would grant us the "wisdom to know" and the "courage to do."

T.A. Youngquist
Redemption Lutheran Church
Wauwatosa, Wisconsin

SEPTEMBER 13, 1992

Lutheran: Fourteenth Sunday after Pentecost
Roman Catholic: Twenty-first Sunday of the Year
Episcopalian: Proper 16 (August 23)
Pres/Meth/UCC: Eleventh after Pentecost (August 23)

Lessons:

Lutheran:	Is. 66:18-23	Heb. 12:18-24	Luke 13:22-30
Roman Catholic:	Is. 66:18-21	Heb. 12:5-7, 11-13	Luke 13:22-30
Episcopal:	Is. 28:14-22	Heb. 12:18-19, 22-29	Luke 13:22-30
Pres/Meth/UCC:	Jer. 28:1-9	Heb. 12:18-29	Luke 13:22-30

Introductions to the Lessons

Lesson 1

(1) *Isaiah 66:18-23* (**Luth**). The book of Isaiah closes with God's promise of a new heaven and earth. He will gather all nations in Jerusalem where they will worship him. He promises that he is coming to do this.

(2) *Isaiah 28:14-22* (**Epis**). In contrast to the drunken prophets and priests of Judah who have a contract with death, God will lay a foundation of justice, faith, and honesty. Hard times are ahead for a nation that defies God and luxuriates in sin.

(3) *Jeremiah 28:1-9* (**Pres/Meth/UCC**). This is the last of the series from the book of Jeremiah. We have two opposing prophets, Jeremiah and Hananiah. Jeremiah has a message of doom and captivity for the nation. In contrast, Hananiah declares that in two years Babylonia will be defeated and the exiles and temple treasures will be returned. Who is the true prophet? Jeremiah says that the true prophet is one whose predictions come true.

Lesson 2

Hebrews 12:18-24 (**Luth**); *Heb. 12:18-19, 22-29* (**Epis**); *Heb. 12:18-29* (**Pres/Meth/UCC**). Last Sunday we considered the first half of Hebrews 12. Today we read the second half of the chapter. There is a contrast between two mountains: Sinai and Zion. God's people are warned not to ignore God's voice which shakes heaven and earth. However, Christians have a Kingdom that cannot be shaken.

Gospel

Luke 13:22-30 (**Luth/Epis/Pres/Meth/UCC**). On his last trip to Jerusalem, Jesus is asked whether only a few will be saved. Whether few, many, or all depends upon entering the narrow door of Jesus. Moral obedience is required to enter the Kingdom. Outsiders will weep bitterly when they see who is enjoying the feast in the Kingdom.

Theme: According to Jesus, few will qualify for entrance into God's kingdom.

Thought for the day: Discipleship demands discipline which many followers of Jesus are unwilling to commit. As we think about the easy road of "getting by" and self indulgence, we are reminded by Christ that life is a struggle, worth the effort for the faithful.

Prayer of meditation: Lord, I believe in you; help my unbelief. I love you, yet not with a perfect heart as I would like. I long for you, yet not my full strength; I trust in you, yet not with my whole being. Accept my faith, my love, my longing to know and serve you, and my trust in your power to keep me in the time of trial. What is uninspired in me, kindle; what is lacking in my spirit, make up. I await your blessing through Jesus Christ, our Lord. Amen.

Call to worship: This is the day which the Lord has made; let us rejoice and be glad in it. Enter his gates with thanksgiving, and his courts with praise! Give thanks to him and bless his name! Come let us worship him in the beauty of holiness.

Prayer of adoration: Eternal God, before whose face the generations rise and pass away; age after age of the living seek you and find that of your faithfulness there is no end. You are the inspiration of every true prayer; the giver of all wisdom; the source of all truth. Look, O God, upon this congregation of your people. Let it ever remain faithful to you, and to the truth as we have come to know it in your Son, Jesus the Christ. Hear our prayer, as in praise and thanksgiving for all that we have and hold, we pray in the name of Christ, our Lord. Amen.

Prayer of confession: O God, our Father, we bless you for the Gospel of Christ which you have given us. We rejoice that you have called us by him into a great fellowship, your church. We acknowledge with shame that we have received these things and kept them to ourselves. We have not even made known the good news to our neighbors, much less the entire world, and we have been shamefully content that it should be so. We ask to be forgiven for our selfishness and blindness, and beseech your blessing on any and all who make known your saving grace — wherever they are. We do

September 13, 1992
(Epis/Pres/Meth/UCC - August 23, 1992)

not offer our prayers only for others. In humility and contrition we offer ourselves, and pray that we may be used and numbered among those who serve and proclaim your love. Help us to that end, through Jesus Christ, our Lord. Amen.

Prayer of dedication of gifts and self: Eternal God, you are the light of the minds that know you; the joy of the hearts that love you; and the strength of the wills that serve you. We thank you for the time that has been given us, for the privilege of worship, and for the opportunity to concentrate our minds and wills on you. We also bring and dedicate to you offerings of money. It comes from the work which we do every day to stay alive in your world. It represents our faith and trust in you as the giver of our lives, and sustainer of our spirits. Help us to increase our faith, and increase the gifts of time and money for the work of your kingdom. Thus we offer ourselves and dedicate the fruits of our labor to you and your kingdom's work, through Christ our Lord. Amen.

Sermon title: Where Are You Coming From?

Sermon thesis: Jesus states clearly that there will be a time of judgment concerning who will enter the kingdom of God, i.e. "be saved." Name dropping and complaining will not help. Discipline, commitment, and right priorities are the standards for entrance.

Hymn for the day: *"All my hope on God is founded"* This hymn reminds us that our hope is to be found in God alone; all else will "betray our trust." The final lines speak of discipleship and commitment. The hymn, written by Robert Seymour Bridges (1844-1930), is based on an earlier German hymn by Joachim Neander (1650-1680). Neander (for whom the Neanderthal valley was named) wrote some 60 hymns as well as some tunes before his life was cut short by tuberculosis. Several of his hymns and tunes are in use today, the most famous of which is "Praise to the Lord, the Almighty." Robert Bridges also gave us the translations of "Ah, holy Jesus" and "When morning glids the skies." He was an English poet laureate. For the first part of his adult life he was a physician, but he later gave it up to use his exceptional gifts as a poet.

Announcements for next week:

Sermon title: On Being Humble and Hospitable

Sermon theme: True humility and hospitality always consider the well being of the other person first.

Sermon summary: Humility, as a mark of discipleship, is a lifestyle, not a reasoned act for each situation. A humble Christian naturally focuses on other persons, in all situations. Jesus' message was twofold: (1) to the invited guests, and (2) to the host about who should be the invited guests.

Children's object talk:
Growing Up To Be Christ-Like

Objects: Pictures of adults, some in common work situations and some like pastors and missionaries.
Lesson: Study, practice, and persistence (sticking-to-it) are needed as disciples of Jesus Christ.
Outline: 1. What we do affects other people.
2. The Bible tells us what is important and what is unimportant to do with our life.
3. As baptized children of God we must practice every day, doing the right things for God.

HOW MANY OF YOU did something nice for somebody yesterday or today? What was it? How did you know it was nice? How did it feel?

I have here pictures of people who earn their living doing various things. What are they doing? This one? That one?

No matter what they do, or what kind of clothes they wear to work, they all do something that affects other people. If someone helps make a machine, someone else will buy and use that machine. If it is not made right it could hurt or make life difficult for the person who bought it.

God wants us to use our life in ways that help him and his creation. Since he gave us our life, the best thing we can do is please him by showing our love and concern for all of his children. Sometimes this will cost us money or time. Then we remember that Jesus gave us his life, and it cost him money and time, also.

Every kind of work needs practice to do the work well. Some jobs take more education and practice than others. But all of us need practice to do helpful things for others, not only in the work we do to earn a living, but in our daily life at home, at school, and on our way to and from work and play. When we are disciples of Christ, we will work hard every day to please him by studying the Bible, and finding helpful deeds toward any and all of his people. That's why I asked you at the beginning whether you had done something nice for someone recently. Practice doing nice things for others because God has done nice things for you.

September 13, 1992
(Epis/Pres/Meth/UCC - August 23, 1992)

The sermon:
Where Are You Coming From?

Hymns:
Beginning of worship: O God, our Help in Ages Past
Sermon: All Who Would Valiant Be
End of worship: Lead on, O King Eternal

Scripture: Luke 13:22-30

Sermon Text: *"When once the householder has risen up and shut the door, you will begin to stand outside and to knock at the door, saying, 'Lord, open to us.' He will answer you, 'I do not know where you come from.'"* vs. 25

WHAT A SIMPLE, DIRECT, AND APPROPRIATE QUESTION, "Will those who are saved be few?" It came in the setting of Jesus' remarks about the kingdom of heaven and the mustard seed; the healing of the crippled woman on the sabbath; and the parable of giving one more year to the fig tree to show its fruit.

Three emphases seem to stand out:

1. "Strive to enter by the narrow door." Another translation says, "Keep on striving, so that you may enter..." Jesus seems to recognize that life is a struggle. The flip greeting, "How goes the battle" may have some meaning.

Perhaps the epithet on the mountain climber's grave could apply to others of us, "He died climbing."

Because the door is narrow does not mean it is impossible, but attainable only by discipline and commitment. Matthew says, "Those who find it (the narrow way) are few." Life is a journey, an adventure, and a struggle.

2. The door will shut. There will be an end. There will be a deadline (play on words). How this reminds us of Jesus' parable of the ten bridesmaids — the door was shut then, also.

In C.S. Lewis's *Screwtape Letters* Wormwood says to Screwtape, "Tell them there is time ... there is plenty of time." Procrastination is still the major enemy.

3. Some are last who will be first, and some are first who will be last. Surprise! But not really, since there are no secrets with God. He doesn't need to play games. The plan and directions are set out clearly. Perhaps Jesus was thinking again how he spelled out the

differences between the values of the world, and the values of the kingdom, using contrasts like the master and the servants; the greatest and the least; the pride in this world, and humility in the next world. Perhaps he was anticipating the story he told about the last days, the final judgment. The emphasis seems to be the amazement of the saved. "When did we see you hungry, naked, etc..." they said.

But what is needed is not how to outguess God, but the proper response to his call.

I suggest that the answer, like the question, is quite simple, albeit difficult to implement: Discipline. Commitment. Priority for the kingdom values.

God has already given us *opportunities*: the church, our neighborhood, learning situations, our brains are just a few of them. What is needed is our response to those opportunities and I suggest — discipline. Is there really any excuse for not responding as disciples?

God has given us *time*: 24 hours a day for everyone. We are not granted unlimited time — but enough of it. Today, not tomorrow is the arena. Once again, what is needed is a response to God's gift of time, and I suggest — commitment to the best use of God's time.

God has given us free will to make *choices*: the narrow or the broad way is what Jesus refers to in this scripture. Once we have made the commitment, the next step is to set priorities. Jesus' word was clear, "Seek *first* the kingdom."

Jesus' purpose was to motivate, not to condemn. He set an example, and provided his presence as an incentive. How exciting it must have been to his listeners to hear him talk about feasting in the kingdom of God — with people coming from north and south, east and west. Of course he prefaced it by talking about the weeping and gnashing of teeth, but his motivation was for the disciples to know the rewards of faithfulness.

We need to be reminded: Grace comes before judgment. Thus baptism and acceptance are made clear in the striving to enter the narrow door.

Likewise we need to hear about "Abraham, Issac, Job, and all the prophets" who are enjoying the fruits of the kingdom and setting the examples.

When it came to those who were left out, the reaction was so typical, so timeless. They might have been spoken in 20th century

September 13, 1992
(Epis/Pres/Meth/UCC - August 23, 1992)

America. When will we learn that name dropping is not enough? Past actions—"I was brought up in the church; I used to go to Sunday School; before we got so busy..."—do not hold water.

In paraphrase Jesus replied "I don't know where you are coming from." Thus the ball is in our court. We need to make clear what motivates us, where we stand, what direction we are facing, who is our master and leader.

Jesus made a statement, "I do not know where you come from." Before it is too late we need to form the statement into a question and hear Jesus ask it of us, "Where are you coming from?"

T.A. Youngquist
Redemption Lutheran Church
Wauwatosa, Wisconsin

SEPTEMBER 20, 1992

Lutheran: Fifteenth Sunday after Pentecost
Roman Catholic: Twenty-second Sunday of the Year
Episcopalian: Proper 17 (August 30)
Pres/Meth/UCC: Twelfth after Pentecost (August 30)

Lessons:

Lutheran:	Prov. 25:6-7	Heb. 13:1-18	Luke 14:1, 7-14
Roman Catholic:	Sir. 3:19-21, 30-31	Heb. 12:18-19, 22-24a	Luke 14:1, 7-14
Episcopal:	Ecc. 10:(7-11), 12-18	Heb. 13:1-8	Luke 14:1, 7-14
Pres/Meth/UCC:	Ezek. 18:1-9, 25-29	Heb. 13:1-8	Luke 14:1, 7-14

Introductions to the Lessons

Lesson 1

(1) *Proverbs 25:6-7* (**Luth**). The wise writer of Proverbs warns us not to pretend we are important by taking a high position. If we do, we may be asked to step down to let a more important person take our place. Humility prevents humiliation.

(2) *Ecclesiastes 10:12-18* (**Epis**). In this passage from Ecclesiastes a wise and foolish person is contrasted. A wise person is one who speaks sparsely, does not forecast the future, is moderate in eating and drinking, and works hard.

(3) *Ezekiel 18:1-9, 25-29* (**Pres/Meth/UCC**). The author of today's first Lesson is Ezekiel, a prophet and priest, who lived in Babylon as a Jewish exile. Speaking for God, he teaches us that each person is responsible for his or her own conduct. Parents are not to be blamed for their children's sin, nor children for their parents' sin.

Lesson 2

Hebrews 13:1-8 (**Luth/Pres/Meth/UCC/Epis**). The readings from Hebrews conclude today. The time has come to put our faith into living. We have faith, a cloud of witnesses to encourage us, and a kingdom that cannot be shaken. Now is the time to express our love and shun marital infidelity and materialism. Amid all the changes, Christ is the changeless one.

Gospel

Luke 14:1, 7-14 (**Luth/Epis/Pres/Meth/UCC**). Who is watching whom? When Jesus came as an invited guest to a prominent Pharisee's home for dinner, people watched to see if he would heal on the sabbath. On the other hand, Jesus watched the people

September 20, 1992
(Epis/Pres/Meth/UCC - August 23, 1992)

strive for the chief places at the dinner. He told them a parable which taught that in humility we should take the lower seats. Then the host may invite us to take a more honorable seat. Humility is rewarded with exaltation.

Theme: True humility and hospitality always consider the well being of the other person first.

Thought for the day: Humility is a mark of discipleship. Those who would follow Jesus must consider his love and concern for all sorts and conditions of people. He will recognize us in due season, and bids us serve all his children, whether we know them as our friends or not.

Prayer of meditation: Lord, we beseech you, grant us the Holy Spirit to clear away every cloud of darkness by which our sin obscures our vision. Give us an understanding heart to worship you in beauty and truth. We are met together here, as your community in this world, and we wait for your Spirit. Bring light into our worship and make it acceptable to you and helpful to us. May your strength come into our prayers, that you may teach us, and your goodness direct us. We ask this in the name of Christ, our Lord. Amen.

Call to worship: It is good to give thanks to the Lord, to sing praises to your name, O Most High; to declare your steadfast love in the morning, and your faithfulness by night. O come let us worship and bow down.

Prayer of adoration: Almighty God, you are changeless, though our vision of you changes. We hurry too much in our living, but we pause now to worship you. We thank you for the gift of yourself in your Son, Jesus. Help us to appreciate all that comes from our relationship with him. You have filled the world with beauty. May our eyes be open to behold your gracious hand in all your works. Rejoicing in your whole creation, may we learn to serve you with gladness even as we adore you for your greatness, through Christ our Lord. Amen.

Prayer of confession: Our heavenly Father, we would be men and women who see things as they are, who call things by their right name, whose work is valid. We do not ask to be drawn away from everyday life, but to be in it with integrity and inner clarity. You read the hearts of all people and know that there are many things in our lives of which we are ashamed. There is our foolish pride, our inconsiderate selfishness, our mental laziness, and much more which we hardly dare to admit, even before you. We acknowledge that the root of all our failures lies in our unfaithfulness toward you and our friends. Forgive us, we beseech you, our sin, and be patient with us as your children.

We offer this confession and our supplications in all humility to you, through Jesus Christ, our Lord. Amen.

Prayer of dedication of gifts and self: Almighty God, our Father, without your help labor is useless; without your light search is vain; invigorate our lives with your Holy Spirit that we may by due diligence and right discernment establish ourselves in the true faith. We present before you our offerings of money. They represent the results of our living according to your good gifts to us. When our stewardship of money is weak, we pray you to prod us with sharp memories of your presence and your guidance for our lives, even to this day, without which we could neither earn nor spend. With these gifts we offer ourselves to your service. Make us sensitive to the needs and desires of your people everywhere, that we may support and encourage their strengths and stand beside them in any weakness. This we ask in the name of your Son, Jesus the Christ. Amen.

Sermon title: On Being Humble and Hospitable

Sermon thesis: Humility, as a mark of discipleship, is a lifestyle, not a reasoned act for each situation. A humble Christian naturally focuses on other persons, in all situations. Jesus' message was twofold: (1) to the invited guests, and (2) to the host about who should be the invited guests.

Hymn for the day: *"O Master, let me walk with you/thee"* The first stanza of this hymn speaks of humility and discipleship – of "lowly paths of service." A native of Pennsylvania, Washington Gladden (1836-1918) was ordained a Congregational minister and served churches in New York, Massachusetts, and Ohio. A distinguished preacher, lecturer, and author, Gladden wrote extensively on civic and social affairs. This hymn was composed in 1879.

Announcements for next week:
  Sermon title: Yes or No – But Not Maybe
  Sermon theme: To follow Jesus, each person must make a clear-cut choice.
  Sermon summary: When Jesus spoke of the cost of discipleship, he set before humanity a simple, but stark truth concerning choices. Then and now, there are but two paths in life – God's way and the world's way. Each is distinct; no "middle ground" exists. The Christian discipleship path models the life of Jesus, with both its costs and its eternal benefits.

September 20, 1992
(Epis/Pres/Meth/UCC - August 23, 1992)

Children's object talk:

Always Being First, Or #1

Objects: Party decorations, napkins, balloons, etc.
Lesson: When we go to a party and want people to notice us, we cannot push ahead of others, but must wait for the person who invited us to tell us where to sit or stand.
Outline: 1. Every boy or girl likes to be included in parties.
2. When you are invited to a party it is polite to ask the person who invited you where you are to sit.
3. God has chosen many persons through baptism to come to his heavenly home. When he invites us to a great feast in his kingdom, we will wait for him to lead us.

HOW MANY OF YOU HAVE BEEN TO A PARTY RECENTLY? What was the occasion? How many of you have given a party at your house? What was the occasion? Whom did you invite?

Jesus told a story about a person who decided to have a big party, and invited many guests. Some of the first people to arrive rushed right in past the host (the man giving the party) and sat down at the front table at the best seat. Later, the host came to those people and asked them to move, to make room for some other guests who had arrived. Jesus told the disciples when they were invited to a party, they should be patient, speak to the hosts, and ask them where to sit.

Have you ever been to a party where someone always pushed to the head of the line, wanted the biggest piece of cake, and tried to "boss" everyone about playing games? They aren't nice people to be around, are they?

Jesus told the disciples to be humble, that is, to think of other people first, to be thankful that they were invited in the first place, and to be patient. Jesus reminded them that they would be noticed, and be able to participate and be happy.

He reminded them that God cares for the hungry, homeless and poor people in the world, and that when the disciples gave a party, they should invite them, too. God would be pleased and remember them when they came to his heaven.

The sermon:
On Being Humble And Hospitable

Hymns:
Beginning of worship: Open Now thy Gates of Beauty
Sermon: Lord, Teach Us How to Pray Aright
End of worship: Lord, Whose Love in Humble Service

Scripture: Luke 14:1, 7-14

Sermon Text: *"For those who exalt themselves will be humbled, and those who humble themselves will be exalted."* vs. 11

HUMILITY IS AN ATTRIBUTE CLAIMED BY MANY, but evidenced by few. Humility is hard to describe. We want the attribute because we think others will like us better that way. People do not like those who are pushy, loud, always giving answers, etc.

At the same time many of us believe that "God helps those who help themselves" and humility is not thought of as the way to get ahead in this world.

Jesus speaks about humility in the Gospel today. He considers it a necessary attribute for salvation. He speaks to his followers as if they were both subject and object. They are the object of the invitation to the feast in the first portion, and the subject of his words in the second portion, when he tells them whom to invite and why, when they send the invitations.

Their behavior as guests should include primary consideration for their relationship to the host. They are there at his invitation. Jesus' words, "and he who invited you both" are crucial. My understanding of the Christian faith is that behavior is based on relationship. Put differently we might say, relationship determines behavior. Is it not so in marriage and work situations?

Jesus now extends that concept to neighbors and society in general where we all have a stake.

In the illustration of the feast, Jesus reminds them that because they are there at the invitation of the host, they will be recognized by him whenever and at whatever time it is proper. Then, Jesus says, "you will be honored in the presence of all." So it's not a matter of self-image, or self-pity, but recognition of the relationship, and trust in the one who is in charge.

Their behavior as hosts was outlined by Jesus. It might be sum-

September 20, 1992
(Epis/Pres/Meth/UCC - August 23, 1992)

marized in the classic understanding of the word hospitality. We recognize that the word hospital is basically the same. A hospital is a place where people are cared for, where concern is shown for those who have need.

It is interesting, isn't it, that Jesus said the host should show care and concern for "the poor, the maimed, the lame, the blind." Those whom the world neglects, and would like to forget are the very ones Jesus suggests should be the object of the hosts' generosity in extending invitations.

Jesus was quick to point out that normally most sharing and socializing goes on in and among and between friends and family. It's like exchanging gifts at Christmas — giving to those from whom one expects a gift in return. An entirely different perspective is called for in kingdom behavior.

Once again, Jesus reminds them that this kind of sharing will bring "blessings" and "reward". Blessings from those who participate in the feast, and reward "in the resurrection of the just".

I believe humility and hospitality are connected. These are lifestyle expressions, not reasoned behavior acts. Thus in Matthew's Gospel we read the parable of those who visited the prisons, clothed the naked, fed the hungry, all in the normal course of living. They were amazed when singled out for praise. Service is its own reward in kingdom values.

This lifestyle also applies to the church's concern for the unchurched. It's not only the physically needy (hungry, naked, thirsty), but all who are searching on their journey of faith, or struggling to begin a journey, who need Christian hospitality. It is more than a "Good morning" at the church door, and much different than the overpowering "We want you to join" approach of the zealous.

In the letter to the Hebrews we read, "Do not neglect to show hospitality to strangers." Here the concern is more than a welcome to a worship service, but an actual sharing of food and home. It's the attitude, the lifestyle of the Christian that shows.

We believe that faith is formed in us through relationships and interactions with others. Thus hospitality is an expression of the willingness to establish a relationship in which faith can develop, an openness to all persons to share God's grace. Care and concern are more than hospital functions for the bodily ills.

Permit me to summarize. In the first portion of the gospel Jesus spoke "to those who were invited" and focused on humility — the value of the relationship to the host. Recognition comes from the one "who invited you both," not from politically finding the best place at the feast for the wrong reasons.

In the second portion Jesus spoke "to the man who had invited them" and made clear the concern of our Lord for the outcasts and neglected in society. This is true hospitality. Care and concern are needed by all people, and the outreach of the church is for more than the physically needy. Hospitality is shown to those who enter the church building and to those whom one meets on the street.

When humility and hospitality are lifestyle expressions, the Christian will naturally live out the primary relationship in life — to God through Christ — and to God's people everywhere.

T.A. Youngquist
Redemption Lutheran Church
Wauwatosa, Wisconsin

SEPTEMBER 27, 1992

Lutheran: Sixteenth Sunday after Pentecost
Roman Catholic: Twenty-third Sunday of the Year
Episcopalian: Proper 18 (September 6)
Pres/Meth/UCC: Thirteenth after Pentecost (September 6)

Lessons:

Lutheran:	Prov. 9:8-12	Phil. 1, (2-9), 10-21	Luke 14:25-33
Roman Catholic:	Wis. 9:13-18	Phil. 9b-10, 12-17	Luke 14:25-33
Episcopal:	Deut. 30:15-20	Phil. 1-20	Luke 14:25-33
Pres/Meth/UCC:	Ezek. 33:1-11	Phil. 1-20	Luke 14:25-33

Introductions to the Lessons

Lesson 1

(1) *Proverbs 9:8-12* (**Luth**). Can you take criticism? According to Proverbs, if you are conceited, you will resent criticism. If you are wise, you will profit from it. Who is a wise person? The one who fears God in terms of reverence. Understanding results from knowing God.

(2) *Deuteronomy 30:15-20* (**Epis**). In Moses' final address to his people before they enter the Promised Land, he gives them a choice of doing good or evil, to obey or disobey God, and to keep or break God's laws. To disobey is to die; to live is to obey. Moses pleads with his people to choose life and to love the Lord.

(3) *Ezekiel 33:1-11* (**Pres/Meth/UCC**). In Ezekiel's day there was no siren to warn the people of an enemy attack. In his day a watchman warned the people by blowing a trumpet. If the watchman fails to warn, he is responsible for the death of the people. If he warns them but they ignore the warning, he is innocent. A religious spokesman has the same responsibility.

Lesson 2

Philemon 1,10-21 (**Luth**); *Philemon 1 20* (**Epis/Pres/Meth/UCC**). The book of Philemon has only one chapter of 25 verses. Our Second Lesson contains 20 of them. It is a personal letter to Philemon, a slave owner. One of his slaves, Onesimus, ran away. While in prison with Paul, he becomes a Christian. Paul sends this letter by Onesimus to Philemon asking him in love to receive Onesimus no longer as a slave but as a brother in Christ.

The Minister's Annual Manual

Gospel

Luke 14:25-33 (Luth/Epis/Pres/Meth/UCC). Jesus is on his way to Jerusalem and large crowds are going with him. In Jerusalem he knows he is going to die. Thus, he tells the people the cost of discipleship: a cross, loving him more than even family, and giving up everything. As a builder and as a king going to war must first count the cost, we need to know the price of following Jesus.

Theme: To follow Jesus, each person must make a clear-cut choice.

Thought for the day: Christian discipleship is a difficult choice, both in Jesus' time and today. But it is a choice that must be made by any who would be, truly, called "Christian." The costs of discipleship are high, but the benefits, for those willing to pay the cost, ultimately outweigh them.

Prayer of meditation: As we gather to worship you today, O God, we ask that you would prepare our hearts. Our outward acts will include songs, and readings, and preaching of the Word of God. But these are only outer trappings, while you look upon the heart. So Lord, enter our hearts now. By your Holy Spirit, focus us for the hour ahead upon the things of God. Focus us, and keep us fixed, upon you, that this time of worship may truly be just that — *worship*, in your sight. Amen.

Call to worship:
Leader: Why are you here?
People: We gather to worship the Living God.
Leader: Are you sure? God is a Holy God.
People: Yes. And we would be God's Holy people.
Leader: That is a difficult choice. But so be it.
People: Let us now worship God in spirit and truth.

Prayer of adoration: We love you, O God. We celebrate your love for us in sending Jesus to our world. We bow in awe and humility at your willingness to send Jesus yet further, to the cross. We rise in wonder and amazement at your raising of Jesus from death into life eternal. And we glory in the presence of the Holy Spirit with us now, granting us the wisdom, power and ability to live life as Jesus did, to face death unabashedly, and to rise with him into that same inheritance which he received, life eternal in your presence. Yes, Lord, we really do love you. Amen.

Prayer of confession: Whenever we come into your presence, O God, we are reminded both of who we are, and who we should be. We've

September 27, 1992
(Epis/Pres/Meth/UCC - September 6, 1992)

been blessed, we've been loved—and we've been called to do the same. And Lord, we do try. We try to live up to the standards of perfection set for us by Jesus. But they not only elude us; in truth, we too often miss them by a very wide margin. Lord, forgive us our failings. Forgive us for returning cursing for blessing, hatred for love. Forgive us, and help us, O God. Strengthen us for the future, that we might draw closer to the perfection of our example and redeemer, even Jesus the Christ, in whose blessed name we pray. Amen.

Prayer of dedication of gifts and self: As we present these gifts—tithes and offerings—*to* you, O God—we remember that our very lives are gifts—*from* you. So what we present is merely a token of what we have received, products of the lives you have entrusted to us. Thank you, Lord, for the basic gift of life itself. And thank you for the opportunity to use our lives in the service of God and our fellow persons. These gifts are examples of what we have done with our lives. We trust that, by your grace, they are fitting and acceptable in the sight of our Maker. Amen.

Sermon title: Yes Or No—But Not Maybe

Sermon thesis: When Jesus spoke of the cost of discipleship, he set before humanity a simple, but stark, truth concerning choices. Then and now, there are but two paths in life—God's way and the world's. Each is distinct; no "middle ground" exists. The Christian discipleship path models the life of Jesus, with both its costs and its eternal benefits.

Hymn for the day: *"Let me be yours forever"* This hymn asks God to make us his forever and to preserve us from "the mazes of error and distrust." Nikolaus Selnecker (1532-1592), a favorite pupil of Philipp Melanchthon, was one of the framers of the Formula of Concord. A musician as well as a pastor, he served as an organist in Nurnberg and during his years in Leipzig, built up the Motet Choir of St. Thomas Church which was later conducted by J.S. Bach. His life as a theologian was full of the constant conflicts and disagreements over Communion raging between the Calvinists and the Lutherans at the time, so that he was more than once called to, or removed from pastoral and university posts depending on the leaning of the local rulers.

Announcements for next week:
    Sermon title: Lost—and Found
    Sermon theme: The lost can be found—by God.
    Sermon summary: Spiritual "lostness" is the human condition. Although most are unaware of being lost, the futility of their lives is *prima facie* testimony to this negative

reality. The positive counterpoint is: God is searching for the lost. Because God is God, many lost will be *found*. And that is *good* news, indeed!

Children's object talk:

One Way

Objects: A Road Map
Lesson: There is only one way to follow Jesus — his way.
Outline: 1. There is only one road to certain places.
2. There is only one way to follow Jesus — the way he lived and taught in the Bible.
3. Are you willing to follow the one way to Jesus?

(Note: This children's talk requires advance preparation and, probably, individualized adaptation. Using a road map of your state, locate one or two towns which have only one road shown leading into or out of them. Then be ready to ask the kids to find these towns. I have used New Mexico as the example, since that is where I live.)

KIDS, I NEED YOUR HELP. I'm wanting to visit a little town up in northern New Mexico and I haven't yet found how to get there from here. I have here a road map of New Mexico, and I was wondering if anyone could help me use it? (Open the map and spread it out before them. Let volunteers assist.)

The place I'd like to go is called Cowles, and I know it's located up in the north-central part of our state, not far from Santa Fe. Can anybody find it on the map? (Let them try. Give assistance.) There it is! Cowles, New Mexico. Just a little place, but I've heard there's some good fishing up there, and I'd like to visit it and try fishing the Pecos River there.

Now, can anybody show me how to get from here to there? (Let them try to show the way. Give assistance as necessary.) That's right — we go up the interstate to the turnoff at Glorieta, then take that road east about 10 miles, then turn north on this little road, and it looks like about 15 miles farther — and you're there.

Do you notice anything special about that last little road into Cowles? (Let them try to answer.) No. What's special about that road is it's the only road to that town; there aren't any others. If you want to go to Cowles, you've got to take that road. There's

September 27, 1992
(Epis/Pres/Meth/UCC - September 6, 1992)

just no other way to get there.

The Bible says that, if we want to follow Jesus, there's only one way to do it. In fact, Jesus himself says what the way is, in Luke 14:27: "...whoever who does not carry the cross and follow me cannot be my disciple."

What Jesus means is, if we want to be called Christians, we have to live our lives the way Jesus lived his life. Sometimes that means going in a direction that nobody else is going. Sometimes it means taking a path, or a road, that is harder than some other ways we might go. But it's the only way to follow Jesus.

Do you want to follow the one way — the one right way, to Jesus? I hope so, and I wish you God's guidance and blessing in following it.

The sermon:

Yes or No — But Not Maybe

Hymns:
Beginning of worship: Christ for the World We Sing
Sermon: Take Up Thy Cross
End of worship: Are Ye Able?

Scripture: Luke 14:25-33

Sermon Text: *"Whoever does not carry the cross and follow me cannot be my disciple."* (Vs. 27, NRSV)

AS A TEENAGER WHO RATHER IRREGULARLY ATTENDED a small church in suburban Baltimore, Maryland, it seemed that for about four years straight, in the fall, I happened to hit just the particular Sunday when the pastor was preaching a sermon entitled, "The Cost of Discipleship." It was a message based upon the text we just read, Luke 14:25-33, and it was preached in conjunction with that church's annual stewardship drive. I've never figured out just how he got away with preaching the same message four years in a row, but maybe he was one of those pastors who felt his congregation needed to hear the same sermon over and over again until they began to really *live* what it said.

Now, those of you who are holding your breaths can let them out, and you people who have death grips on your wallets can relax — this isn't a financial appeal message. But I do want to talk with you today, as that pastor did with his congregation annually, about *the cost of discipleship*. If you're a regular church attender, or even a sporadic one, like I was as a teen, I'm sure you've heard one or more sermons on the cost of following Christ at one time or another. This text is a powerful one, and Jesus obviously was pulling no punches when he, three times in this short passage, repeated that "No one can be my disciple unless ... unless they are willing to give up everything else in order to follow me."

I'd like to approach the subject of the cost of discipleship today by coming at it from what I hope is a fresh perspective. Might we first of all consider, for a few moments, the cost of *no* discipleship?

Let me illustrate, using a subject that isn't the most popular in the world—funerals. A pastor soon learns that there are two kinds of funerals he or she must perform, and they're very different. When a person dies whose obvious faith in Christ has been known to all, a funeral is a time of celebration. There is fulfillment, peace, confidence. A few tears may be shed, but everyone realizes that those are only a normal, temporary human grief reaction. Unfortunately, those funerals are not the majority of funerals I'm called upon to perform. For when a person dies whose lack of commitment to Christ is obvious, or whose faith or lack thereof is unknown, the funeral is a very different sort of experience. As a pastor, I try to offer hope, help, comfort. I read the same scriptures, often say the same words concerning the Christian hope of life eternal—for I am speaking to the living, not the dead. However, no one is fooled at a funeral. The friends and relatives know that death has come as a thief in the night to take their loved one away—forever. There is remorse, guilt, weeping, wailing, and gnashing of teeth. Nowhere else is there a starker illustration of the cost—of *no* discipleship.

There are many other illustrations of the cost of *no* discipleship in our society. You can chart on a graph the inverse relationship between church attendance in neighborhoods and violent crime in those same neighborhoods. Or consider the well-publicized, and often controversial, statistic concerning divorce in America today. Among persons with no church affiliation, the divorce rate stands at 50% each five years. But among those relatively few families where both parties of a newlywed couple attend the same church together on a regular basis, the divorce rate is 1/12th that—just 4% after five years. Thank God we are now in the midst of at least a minor revival of religious interest in the USA of the 90s. I'm not

September 27, 1992
(Epis/Pres/Meth/UCC - September 6, 1992)

sure our society could have withstood much more of the cost — of *no* discipleship.

Now for the other side of the matter — the so-called "high cost" of Christian discipleship. What does it cost you to accept Jesus Christ as your personal Savior and Lord, and to live your life as his disciple? First of all, it costs you your ticket to Hell: you can't go there anymore — God simply will not let you! You've lost your damnation. And it costs you the burden of your accumulated sins — Jesus Christ takes them away from you. All those stored up lies, perverse thoughts, acts of infidelity, disobedience, hatefulness — those closets full of past evils that you've kept hidden for so long — Jesus Christ takes them out of your life! They're gone — no longer weighing on you, no longer dragging you down. The costs of discipleship — what you have to "give up" to be a Christian. What a terribly high price!

Well, you might say, isn't the cost of discipleship really a lot higher than that? Didn't Jesus tell us that we would be reviled and persecuted because of our belief in him? Haven't Christians had to pay, sometimes with their very lives, for their faith in Christ? Yes — that's all quite true, and in certain parts of our present world, the cost of Christian discipleship, more than ever before, is martyrdom.

But for American Christians today, I'm not sure the costs of discipleship are all that formidable. For some of you, you'll be invited to fewer cocktail parties or beer busts. For others, your swinging friends may drop you out of the "key swap" club, and you'll find yourself going home to the same old wife or husband every night of the week. Some of your suave, intellectual friends will tell you how foolish your faith is, and try to argue you out of it. Yes — and I suppose those are very real persecutions from the point of view of modern, secular American society. But there will most likely be no lion's den for you, no firing squad, no torture chamber.

Now that we've considered the costs of *no* discipleship for Christ, and the costs *of* discipleship for Christ, let's consider one more important issue. Be assured that you will pay one or the other of these costs. There is not a third option, a middle road between these two alternatives. There's no gray area between being a Christian disciple and not being one.

Our present-day culture hates dealing with clear-cut choices. We don't like black-white, either-or, right or wrong alternatives. We prefer to play mental games with decisions that are multi-faceted, multiple-optioned, with many shades of gray. To have to make a clear-cut, either-or *decision*, for or against something, goes against the grain for many of us. We want to explore the options, blur the distinctions, water-down the differences.

But that is exactly what *can't* be done with Jesus Christ. With Christ, it's yes or no, for or against. Jesus himself said so, on more than one occasion: Matthew 13:20—"He who is not with me is against me." Luke 12:51-53—"I have come to bring division." Matthew 25:31-46—The parable of the sheep and the goats. Rev. 3:14-16—The stunning rebuke to Laodicea, the lukewarm church. And of course, our text today, Luke 14:27, "Whoever does not carry the cross and follow me cannot be my disciple."

Repeatedly, from beginning to end, the New Testament highlights the necessity of making a clear-cut choice—for or against Jesus. Even if you choose not to choose, you've still chosen. Any response other than "yes" to Jesus is a negative response. If you do not choose God's Son, either deliberately or by inaction, then you have chosen Satan. If you do not choose Heaven, they you have chosen Hell. If you do not choose eternal life, then you have chosen everlasting death. The cost of discipleship—or the cost of no discipleship. You will, I will, we will each pay one or the other.

The cost of discipleship. Yes, this is one of the "hard" teachings of Jesus. Jesus knew it, too. At the conclusion of this discourse, in Luke 14:35, he said simply and directly, "Let anyone with ears to hear listen!"

David Z. Ring III
Paradise Hills United Methodist Church
Albuquerque, New Mexico

OCTOBER 4, 1992

Lutheran: Seventeenth Sunday after Pentecost
Roman Catholic: Twenty-fourth Sunday of the Year
Episcopalian: Proper 19 (September 13)
Pres/Meth/UCC: Fourteenth after Pentecost (September 13)

Lessons:

Lutheran:	Ex. 32:7-14	I Tim. 1:12-17	Luke 15:1-10
Roman Catholic:	Ex. 32: 7-11, 13-14	I Tim. 1:12-17	Luke 15:1-32
Episcopal:	Ex. 32:1, 7-14	I Tim. 1:12-17	Luke 15:1-10
Pres/Meth/UCC:	Hos. 4:1-3; 5:15-6:6	I Tim. 1:12-17	Luke 15:1-10

Introductions to the Lessons

Lesson 1

(1) *Exodus 32:7-14* (**Luth/Epis**) Because Moses was on the top of Mt. Sinai for 40 days receiving from God the Ten Commandments, the Israelites concluded that Moses deserted them. Sensing their need for a god, they asked Aaron to make one. With the people's contribution of gold, he fashioned a golden bull, Amon-Re, an Egyptian god. The Lord intended to destroy his wicked people, but due to Moses' intercession, he changed his mind.

(2) *Hosea 4:1-3; 5:15-6:6* (**Pres/Meth/UCC**) The first Lessons for the remaining Sundays of the Pentecost season are derived from the Minor Prophets, Hosea to Malachi. Today we hear from Hosea. Yahweh has a bone to pick with Israel. There is no faithfulness nor love in the land. How can God bring Israel back to him? He will send suffering and the threat of judgment. The people say that though God hurts, he will heal.

Lesson 2

I Timothy 1:12-17 (**Luth/Epis/Pres/Meth/UCC**) The coming series of seven second Lessons are taken from the Pastoral Epistles, I and II Timothy. According to tradition, Paul wrote these letters to his spiritual son, Timothy. Paul tells Timothy that he is grateful to God for calling him to be an apostle even though he persecuted the church. He affirms that Christ died for sinners of whom he is chief.

Gospel

Luke 15:1-10 (**Luth/Epis/Pres/Meth/UCC**) Luke 15 is known as the "Lost Chapter" because Jesus gives three parables dealing with the lost sheep, coin, and son. In to-

The Minister's Annual Manual

day's Lesson we have only the lost sheep and coin. These parables were given in response to the criticism of religious leaders that Jesus was associating with sinners. When sinners repent, all heaven breaks loose with rejoicing. *neither earth, nor hell rejoice.*

Theme: The lost can be found — by God.

Thought for the day: Being lost is never enjoyable. Many in contemporary society, however, either do not realize, or will not admit, that a source of their life's problems is spiritual "lostness." On the positive side, God is hard at work, helping the lost to be found — sometimes even before they realize their need. *always*

Prayer of meditation: Lord, we are about to seek you in worship. Often, we do not know exactly what we mean by "worship," but only that we sense a need to reach beyond ourselves, and touch that which is solid, trustworthy, and eternal. So much in our lives is fleeting, changing, transitory. We do not reject the principle of change, Lord, but occasionally we need to pause, and rest, if only for a few moments, upon a solid rock. Here and now, we would find that solid rock. Be near — be here, O God, and guide our attempts at worship. Amen.

Call to worship:
Leader: Draw near to God, and God will draw near to you.
People: Come, O Lord, gather with us now.
Leader: Assemble God's people from the four corners of the earth.
   Search the highways and hedges, and bring them in.
People: For it is God's will that none be left behind nor lost.

Prayer of adoration: Lord, you are worthy. We're beginning a time of worship now, and that's one of the basic things we mean — you are worthy. One of the foci of our worship today is the celebration of Worldwide Communion, which calls to remembrance the words of the apostle, John, who said, "Worthy is the Lamb, who was slain, to receive power and wealth and wisdom and strength and honor and glory and praise!" In all our acts of worship today, we would clearly communicate that wondrous truth. Beyond any and all others, Lord, you *are* worthy. Amen.

Prayer of confession: Earlier, we prayed the glorious truth, "You are worthy, Lord." But calling to mind your perfect worthiness also reminds us, in sharp contrast, of our unworthiness. You created us to share in your perfection, O God, and we have settled for far less. You call us to excellence, Lord, and we are content with mediocri-

October 4, 1992
(Epis/Pres/Meth/UCC - September 13, 1992)

ty. You exhort us to righteousness, and we live with half-truths. Here and now, Lord, we would seek a fresh start. Forgive us our checkered pasts. Wash us clean of our failures, individual and collective. Place us back on the path of light. And keep us, by your Holy Spirit, upon the straight and narrow way for the future. May the worthiness of God draw us to replicate your likeness. Amen.

Prayer of dedication of gifts and self: Today as we make offering to you, the theme of Worldwide Communion reminds us of your offering for us and for our world. You gave yourself, Lord, fully, without reservation. You offered your body and your Spirit, to secure our redemption. You didn't hold back in any way, O God — you gave your all.

The offerings that we present today are far less, in both quality and quantity, than your offering for us. But they are tokens and signs of what we would, given opportunity, like to offer in return. Consecrate these gifts to the work of your Kingdom in this world, the world that you love so much. And consecrate us, Lord, to the spreading of the Kingdom's good news. Amen.

Sermon title: Lost And Found

Sermon thesis: Spiritual "lostness" is the human condition. Although most are unaware of being lost, the futility of their lives is *prima facie* testimony to this negative reality. The positive counterpoint is: God is searching for the lost. Because God is God, many lost will be *found*. And that is *good news*.

Hymn for the day: *"Amazing grace."* John Newton (1725-1807) was seven years old when his mother died. Four years later he went to sea with his father. For many years he was involved in slave trade, which became more and more distasteful to him, until he finally gave it up in 1754. After meeting George Whitefield and the Wesleys he entered the ministry and became curate of Olney. Together with William Cowper, he prepared *Olney Hymns*, 1779, which contained this text. The lost-and-found theme of today's selections is clearly stated in this hymn.

Announcements for next week:
  Sermon title: True to Form
  Sermon theme: People reveal their inner selves by their outward acts.
  Sermon summary: People run true to form. Those who are wedded to this world, with its values and standards — or the absence thereof — reveal this by their actions. Those whose allegiance is the Kingdom of God, with its very different norms and values, likewise reveal this by their actions.

Children's object talk:
Pointing Toward Jesus

Objects: A compass and a Bible
Lesson: The word of God points us toward Jesus.
Outline: 1. We need knowledge of directions in order not to become lost.
2. A compass shows us directions in the world we live in.
3. The Bible directs us toward Jesus in the spiritual realm.

HI, BOYS AND GIRLS! DOES ANYONE KNOW WHAT THIS IS? (Hold up the compass and show it off. Let them answer.) That's correct — it's a compass. What is a compass used for? (Let them answer.) Again, you're right. A compass is used to tell directions. If we know our directions, we can travel all over the neighborhood, or even all over the world, and not get lost. So a compass is a very useful item.

Does anyone here know how to use a compass? No? Let me show you. Do you see this blue needle here, and the big letter "N" on the face of the compass? If I can get those two lined up, then we'll know which direction north is.

(Align the compass needle.) Now, I've got it. North out that way. (Point.) That means south is in the opposite direction, back there. (Point.) And east is that direction, over there — and west there. (Point out all the directions.)

Now we know our directions. If we want to travel south, which way should we go? (Let them answer.) How about if we want to travel east? (Again, let the children reply.) My, you've learned fast!

Here's a tougher question. What if I, or you, want to travel toward the Lord Jesus? Which direction should we go? (Let the children try to give some answers.) Jesus isn't to the north, is he? How about to the west? Actually, Jesus isn't to be found in any direction that this compass can show us.

Here, though, I've got another familiar object. (Hold up the Bible.) It's a Bible. And it's a kind of compass, although a very different one. Everything in the Bible points toward Jesus. If we read and study the Bible, we'll know which direction to go, spiritually, in order to find, and follow after, Jesus.

It's important to be able to find our way in this world, and this compass can help us do that. It's also very important to be able to find our way to Jesus, and the word of God, found in the Bible,

October 4, 1992
(Epis/Pres/Meth/UCC - September 13, 1992)

will help us to do that. So, I encourage you to read, or get your parents to read to you, the Bible — each and every day.

The sermon:

Lost and Found

Hymns:
  Beginning of worship: Guide Me, O Thou Great Jehovah
  Sermon hymn: Savior, Like a Shepherd Lead Us
  End of worship: Amazing Grace

Scripture: Luke 15:1-10

Sermon text: *"Which one of you, having a hundred sheep and losing one of them, does not leave the ninety-nine in the wilderness and go after the one that is lost until he finds it?"* vs. 4, NRSV

HAVE YOU EVER BEEN LOST — really lost? It's a frightening experience, to say the least. When I was 19 years of age, in the summer between two college years, I and a friend from Baltimore named Gerry set out on the "great American odyssey." We were going to see the whole country from a Volkswagen "beetle." At that time, neither one of us could ever remember having traveled west of the Mississippi River. So when we reached Denver, we started looking for the Pacific Ocean, believing it was just over the next hill. We were amazed to be told that it was yet more than a thousand miles farther westward.

I guess we didn't really believe that, so when we camped early that afternoon in Rocky Mountain National Park, we decided to climb Long's Peak, marked as the tallest spot on our maps. We thought maybe from up there we could get a glimpse of the Pacific. Neither of us had ever done Rocky Mountain hiking before, but that didn't stop us. It was early summer and, wearing only tennis shoes and short-sleeved shirts, we started out, up the marked trail. By dusk, we were probably only at the 9,000 foot level, so we decided we'd better turn back.

Ten minutes later, it was as though someone had switched off a light bulb. It got pitch black, and we didn't even have a flashlight. At first, we thought we could follow the trail by starlight, but we soon realized we were kidding ourselves. For a while, we laughed about our predicament — it was exciting to be lost in the wilds of the Colorado mountains. But soon it ceased to be funny. We shivered as the temperature dropped into the 40s. Every noise was a mountain lion on the prowl, every patch of blackness a thousand-foot drop into oblivion. Finally, we just sat down on a rock and yielded to despair, sadly agreeing that neither of us would live to tell about our foolish adventure. We huddled there all night, not daring to move.

About five a.m., just as the first glimmerings of dawn were changing the sky from jet black to only dark gray, we spotted two flashlight beams heading toward us. Park rangers, learning from someone at the campsite that our tent hadn't been slept in, had come searching for us. When they found us, they weren't particularly friendly, to say the least. They led us back down to the camping area, then ordered us to pack up our tent immediately and get out of the park — and never again do such a stupid thing. We didn't even protest — we were just so glad to be found, alive and well.

As I read this week's gospel lesson concerning the lost sheep and the lost coin, that experience, almost forgotten, sprang back vividly into my mind. I thought first about the sheep in Jesus' story, foolishly wandering away from safety, with no thought of what might happen to it. Just like Gerry and I, starting up that mountain, totally unprepared and unaware of what the consequences of our action might be. And then I thought of the many people I know, foolishly wandering into all manner of danger, sin, and heartbreak; not knowing, or not believing, the grave consequences in store for them.

The longer I serve as a pastor, the more convinced I become that most men and women are not all that evil or depraved in nature. Very few people actively seek to hurt others. No, most of us are just a little foolish, just prone to wander away from the right. We dabble in a little sin here, a little wrong there, never realizing how far away, little by little, we're moving from God.

The Bible says that all of us, "like sheep," have gone astray. A shepherd, asked just how sheep go astray, said this: "They just nibble themselves lost. They put their heads down, wander from one green patch to another, and by the time they look up, they're miles from where they started." Does that sound like human beings — us?

One of the strangest parts of being lost, however, is that it's so hard to admit it. Somehow, we all feel like we have to put up a

October 4, 1992
(Epis/Pres/Meth/UCC - September 13, 1992)

brave front, and not let anyone else know we're off the track. Many times, when I'm driving in a strange place, my wife will say, "We're lost, aren't we?" And I'll reply, "Of course not. I know exactly where we are." If I'm lucky, a sign or familiar landmark will appear soon, so I can get my bearings. But if not, I'll eventually have to swallow my pride, pull over, get out the map, and admit it — "Yep, we're lost!" But that's really tough on the old ego.

And of course, if there's anyone else remotely connected with the situation of our getting lost, maybe we can blame it on them. "It wasn't me who picked that apple, Lord! It was Eve — she gave it to me!" I was working in a church booth a few years ago at the New Mexico State Fair in Albuquerque, when a little boy came up, looking very confused. "Have you seen my parents?" he asked, even though I'd never before seen him. "Are you lost?" I asked in return. He replied, "No! I'm not lost! My parents are lost!"

The scriptures tell us what we already know from human experience. It's hard to admit it when we're on the wrong track. It's much easier to put up a front, blame someone else — or blame God. "There is a way which seems right to a person, but its end is death." — Proverbs 14:12. Psychologists claim that half the battle in overcoming a problem is admitting you've got one. Every one of us is a lost sheep, strayed from God. And the first step in getting found is to admit it, because that's reality.

If you've ever read a book about hiking in the wilderness, one of the things most often said is, if you think you're lost, don't panic. don't start running about in every direction trying to find your way out, because you'll probably only succeed in getting more lost. And, unless you're an experienced woodsman, or unless it would be too dangerous to remain where you are, your best bet on getting found is to stay put, right where you are, and let someone else find you. This is amazing, but reportedly true. When sheep get lost from the flock, and realize it, most of them just sit down and wait for the shepherd to find them. They know from experience that they'll be found if they stay put. Only those few sheep that keep on wandering until they fall off a ledge, or get into country inhabited by predators, are permanently lost. Sheep go astray almost every day in an average-sized flock, but a good Mideast shepherd finds all of his lost sheep. He'd soon go out of business if he didn't!

Herein lies the key to the Bible's teaching about lost sheep and lost coins — and even lost people, like us. We're lost, yes. Whether

Key point

The Minister's Annual Manual

we're willing to admit it or not doesn't change the fact of our condition. But the other side of the matter is this: Before we even know we're lost, God is already out looking for us.

A good shepherd doesn't wait one unnecessary minute when he realizes a sheep is missing from the flock. He makes sure the others are safely cared for, then immediately begins searching for the lost one. He doesn't wait for the sheep to find itself, for he knows that it wouldn't be able to even if it tried.

The Bible puts it this way, "God showed his great love for us, in that while we were yet sinners, Christ died for our sins." Before we know God, or care about God in any way — God is working to find us. And God never gives up — no sheep of the heavenly Father's is ever so hopelessly lost as to be "written off" by God.

The parable of the lost sheep says the the shepherd goes out and searches — and searches — until he finds his sheep, no matter how long it takes. It is not God's will that any of his precious human-sheep should ever be permanently lost. And God is already at work, doing his utmost to see that we are found — and quickly.

Both the parable of the lost sheep and of the lost coin end with celebration — with joy at the finding of that which, formerly lost, is now found. I would invite you, if you're among the lost, to share in and to increase the celebration and the joy expressed in today's scriptures — by allowing God to find you the more speedily. You can call out to God, even now. "Here I am, Lord. I'm lost. But I want to be found."

Be assured, God will find you. *+ all heaven will break loose with rejoicing*

David Z. Ring III
Paradise Hill United Methodist Church
Albuquerque, New Mexico

OCTOBER 11, 1992

Lutheran: Eighteenth Sunday after Pentecost
Roman Catholic: Twenty-fifth Sunday of the Year
Episcopalian: Proper 20 (September 20)
Pres/Meth/UCC: Fifteenth after Pentecost (September 20)

Lessons:

Lutheran:	Amos 8:4-7	I Tim. 2:1-8	Luke 16:1-13
Roman Catholic:	Amos 8:4-7	I Tim. 2:1-8	Luke 16:1-13
Episcopal:	Amos 8:4-7 (8-12)	I Tim. 2:1-8	Luke 16:1-13
Pres/Meth/UCC:	Hos. 11:1-11	I Tim. 2:1-7	Luke 16:1-13

Introductions to the Lessons

Lesson 1

(1) *Amos 8:4-7* (**Luth/Epis**) The prophet Amos cries out for social justice. In this pericope the merchants of Israel cannot wait until the religious observances are over so they can cheat their customers and enslave those who cannot pay their debts. God declares he will never forget their wickedness.

(2) *Hosea 11:1-11* (**Pres/Meth/UCC**) Chapter 11 of Hosea is the John 3:16 of the Old Testament. Yahweh loves Israel as a good parent loves a child: teaching, hugging and feeding. In spite of this, the child is rebellious. How can God give up his wicked child? Love will not let him destroy his people. He still hopes his people will return to him that he may forgive them.

Lesson 2

I Timothy 2:1-8 (**Luth/Epis**); *I Timothy 2:1-7* (**Pres/Meth/UCC**) Paul calls upon Timothy as a leader of the church to offer prayers to God for all people, especially for our rulers, that we may live in peace. This would please God, for he desires every person to be saved through Christ our Mediator. Prayers are to be offered in every worship service.

Gospel

Luke 16:1-13 (**Luth/Epis/Pres/Meth/UCC**) By means of a parable Jesus teaches his disciples how to handle finances. A rich man decides to fire his incompetent manager and notifies him of the decision. At once, to make friends for his future well-being the manager reduces the amounts owed the owner. The unjust steward is commended for his shrewdness in making the best of a bad situation. Jesus is not applauding the dishonesty but urges his followers to be equally wise in handling material possessions for future spiritual welfare.

Theme: People reveal their inner selves by their outward acts.

Thought for the day: Our contemporary world is overfull with competing religions, philosophies, ideas, and schools of thought. Careful discernment is required. One useful and telling criterion for such, taught by Jesus, is to pay close attention not to the words of others who would convince us of their position, but to their actions.

Prayer of meditation: It's Sunday again, Lord. We're about to gather together for that which we call worship. It's something many of us do with regularity virtually every Sunday. But as we assemble, Lord, we ask that the enlivening, emboldening power of the Holy Spirit of Almighty God be released in our midst. Release it, O God — pour it out upon us. Renew us; renew our worship, that it be fitting, acceptable, and exciting — both to us and to the God whom we worship — even Jesus Christ, our living Lord. Amen.

Call to worship:
Leader: Rejoice, people of God! Sing praises, make melody!
People: Why? What cause have we for such merriment?
Leader: What cause, indeed? Only that God has chosen you and adopted you into his own dear family!
People: That is very good news. We will rejoice and be exceeding glad. Thanks be to God!

Prayer of adoration: It hasn't been very long ago, Lord, when each of us here present lived in a very different realm. We were secular people — willfully lonely, limited and unsure, fearing the inevitable end of a transitory existence. But somehow, Lord, your grace found us. Your love broke through our barriers of selfish isolation. And now, we live in the dawning of a new reality and a new realm — the Kingdom of God. We praise you, Lord. We thank you for moving us out of the darkness and into your wondrous light — the light of eternity. Amen.

Prayer of confession: When you found us in sin, Lord, and accepted us into your family, you promised to forgive us our many sins and shortcomings. And you did just that, releasing us from the burden of accumulated wrongs which we don't even wish to try to remember. We were clean then, O God. We were fresh, new creatures.

October 11, 1992
(Epis/Pres/Meth/UCC - September 20, 1992)

But since that time we've been out in the world again, and its marks have been left upon us. We've tried to be faithful; we've tried to follow the way of Jesus, but our failures have outnumbered our successes.

And so we come to you again, Lord, asking for forgiveness. Cleanse us once more, that we might be pure and holy in your sight. Freshen and renew us, that we may continue to fight the good fight — and this time, that we may succeed, to your glory. Amen.

Prayer of dedication of gifts and self: So often, Lord, you put before us the opportunity — the opportunity to give, to love, to serve God and our fellow humans. And we respond, Lord — a little, occasionally, when it's convenient for us.

But then we remember your sacrifice of Jesus on the cross for our redemption, and we are challenged to do more, much more. We know that we are capable of giving, loving, and serving much more fully than we are now doing.

Today, O God, we would re-dedicate ourselves — all that we have and all that we are — to responding, in fullness, to the opportunities you set before us. What we offer today is but a token of what we shall offer tomorrow, and each day ahead, as we respond, in faith, to the call of God upon us. Help us, Lord, to be fully and truly faithful now and forever. Amen.

Sermon title: True To Form

Sermon thesis: People run true to form. Those who are wedded to this world, with its values and standards — or the absence thereof — reveal this by their actions. Those whose allegiance is to the Kingdom of God, with its very different norms and values, likewise reveal this by their actions.

Hymn for the day: *"We give thee but thine own"* The author of this hymn, William Walsham How (1823-1897), was an English priest who served several parishes of the Church of England. He was known as the "poor man's bishop" because of his work for the poor in the East End of London. Other hymns by How include "For all the saints" and "O Word of God incarnate." The focus of this hymn is not on serving money but on using our wealth to serve those in need.

Announcements for next week

Sermon title: One Powerful Parable
Sermon theme: The spiritual "law of recompense" is effective — for eternity.
Sermon summary: The parable of the rich man and Lazarus, one of Jesus' most power packed teachings, by stark realism challenges hearers to rouse from complacency

The Minister's Annual Manual

and take action to remedy the plights of the poor. It clearly implies that our status in God's sight is intimately linked to our response to the needy of this world.

Children's object talk:
Is Bigger Always Better?
Objects: Two U.S. coins — a nickel and a dime
Lesson: Don't judge value by size (nor outward appearnces.)
Outline: 1. A dime, although smaller than a nickel, is worth more.
2. Sometimes, a smaller person may be a better person than someone bigger.
3. Learn to value people by their actions, not how they look.

TODAY, CHILDREN, I WANT TO TALK WITH YOU ABOUT SIZE — AND VALUE. Let me show you what I mean by looking at these two coins. You're all familiar with coins like these, aren't you? What is this one? (Hold up the nickel and let them answer.) How about this other one? (Hold up the dime and allow them to answer.) Right again, it's a dime. Now which one is worth more — that is, which one will buy more at a store? Some of you older kids may have to help the younger ones with this answer. (Let them respond.) That's right, the dime is worth more. In fact, it takes two nickels to equal the value of one dime.

Did you notice, however, that the dime is smaller than the nickel? Isn't that interesting — the dime, although smaller, is worth more. It's lesser in size, but greater in value.

Often, in our world, we get the idea that "bigger is better." If my family lives in a bigger house than yours, then we must be better people. If you're taller than me, you're more important than I am. Aren't some of you wishing that you could grow up quickly, so you'd be big and important like adults are?

In God's sight, however, things aren't judged by how big they are, nor by their outer appearance at all. Do you remember the Bible story of how David, the small, young shepherd boy, defeated the nine-foot tall giant, Goliath? Do you remember how, when Jesus was on the earth teaching, he invited the little children to come and sit with him, just like we're doing here? He even said to the adults who complained that, by the standards of the Kingdom of God, these little children were more important than they were.

The Bible even says, in I Samuel 17:7, this, "Man looks at the

October 11, 1992
(Epis/Pres/Meth/UCC - September 20, 1992)

outward appearance, but the Lord looks at the heart." God sees what's inside people — not how big, nor how beautiful, nor however they may appear outwardly. God sees people for who they really are.

None of us is God, of course, but we can see people on the inside, too, if we consider the right clues. People's actions — what they do — show us what these same people are like on the inside. Someone may be big — and handsome, too — but if you see them stealing someone else's property, they're not a very good person, are they? The prettiest girl around may have a dirty, gossipy mouth that diminishes her value in the eyes of those who know her.

On the other hand, even though you are children, and others here are adults, the biggest person in this room — in God's sight — might be one of you. That's because God considers what you do, not your size. If you act like a child of God, you can be ten feet tall — spiritually. Be sure to follow his way, and you'll be a giant in the sight of our Lord!

The sermon:

True To Form

Hymns:
Beginning of worship: How Firm A Foundation
Sermon hymn: Tell Me the Stories of Jesus
End of worship: Truehearted, Wholehearted

Scripture: Luke 16:1-13

Sermon text: *"Whoever is faithful in a very little is faithful also in much; and whoever is dishonest in a very little is dishonest also in much."* vs. 10, NRSV

A FAVORITE STORY I'VE HEARD, WHICH HAS BEEN REPEATED with so many variations over the years that I have no idea of its origin, is that of a policeman who catches an orphaned youth stealing railroad ties. Instead of making the boy suffer a penalty for his crime, the man takes him into his home, cleans him up, adopts him, and sends him to school. The youth proves to be highly intelligent, goes on to college and eventually completes law school. But the policeman who raised the lad bemoans the fact that, as an adult with a top-notch education, the former boy has not changed inwardly. The only difference in his behavior is that now, using his knowledge of the law, he steals whole railroads.

On the other side of the scale, in a former congregation I served, a member came up to me after church one Sunday and told me she had just found a quarter under one of the seats. She asked me to let her see the pew registration pads for the section of the congregation around where she'd picked up the coin. Then, she spent two hours that Sunday afternoon calling people, until she finally found a family who said, "Yes, the quarter is probably ours. Our seven-year-old daughter lost the quarter she was planning to put in the Sunday School offering." Only then was this woman satisfied, having worked two hours to locate the rightful owner of a lost twenty-five cent piece.

The parable which constitutes our text today is often considered one of the "difficult" teachings of Jesus. The story of the dishonest steward, or of the shrewd manager, depending on your translation, may, at first glance, seem to be teaching that Jesus condones, or even approves, dishonesty. After all, the master commends the obviously dishonest actions of his subordinate, and, in many of Jesus' parables, the master is like unto God. But not here.

This parable *is* a "difficult" teaching, but only because it requires, unlike some of Jesus' other parables, more than a surface consideration. Jesus, ever the master analyst of human nature, is, as usual, teaching a significant truth about such via this parable. The truth to be garnered here is not about honesty nor dishonesty *per se*, but about how human nature is, for better or worse, predictably consistent. Worldly people will always respond in worldly ways. Dishonesty — provided you get away with it — is more often than not admired in the secular world, increasingly so today. The dishonest steward impressed his worldly boss with his ability to increase the short-term cash flow in his master's business. That his method was dishonest was of little consequence to his master, who was also, in Jesus' words, one of the "children of this age." Dishonesty was "in character" for them both.

Kingdom people — the citizens of the Kingdom of God — have totally different standards. To kingdom people, faithfulness, trustworthiness, and honesty are values. In this parable, neither the steward nor his master understood nor held these values. But kingdom people, by contrast, must understand and hold to them.

October 11, 1992
(Epis/Pres/Meth/UCC - September 20, 1992)

As they observe the world's deviousness, they must learn to carefully and scrupulously avoid it. For if a purported citizen of the Kingdom of God cannot be trusted to manage with integrity the perishable, transitory items of earth, then, using the words of Jesus, "who will entrust to you the true riches?"

"Whoever is faithful in a very little is faithful also in much; and whoever is dishonest in a very little is dishonest also in much." This verse is Jesus' own summation of the point made by the parable of the dishonest manager. People run true to form. If you observe someone stealing railroad ties, they probably would, given opportunity, steal whole railroads. If you observe someone scrupulously searching for the owner of a lost quarter, they probably could be trusted to handle a million dollars. If you encounter someone whose lifestyle conforms to the standards — or lack of standards — of the world, he or she is probably a worldly person. And if you encounter someone whose actions bespeak the righteousness of the Kingdom of God, you're probably observing a citizen of that Kingdom. People will run, according to Jesus, true to form.

Beyond its descriptive point, that people run true to form, there is also a thinly-veiled prescriptive point, if not an overt command, from Jesus to be found in this parable and its associated commentary. In stating that "whoever is faithful in a very little is faithful also in much; and whoever is dishonest in a very little is dishonest also in much," Jesus is challenging those who hear his teaching. Prove yourselves. By your behavior, here and now — in the short-term, limited arena of earthly life — show which of these two kinds of persons you really are. Are you honest or dishonest in seemingly trivial matters? Are you a citizen of the Kingdom, with God as your master, or are you a citizen only of this world, with the things thereof controlling you?

Jesus often ended his teaching sessions by speaking words to this effect: "Whoever has ears, let them hear the teaching of God." In keeping with the point of the parable of the dishonest steward, I would end this message by adding, "And let them live it as well."

David Z. Ring III
Paradise Hills United Methodist Church
Albuquerque, New Mexico

OCTOBER 18, 1992

Lutheran: Nineteenth Sunday after Pentecost
Roman Catholic: Twenty-sixth Sunday of the Year
Episcopalian: Proper 21 (September 27)
Pres/Meth/UCC: Sixteenth after Pentecost (September 27)

Lessons:

Lutheran:	Amos 6:1-7	I Tim. 6:6-16	Luke 16:19-31
Roman Catholic:	Amos 6:1a, 4-7	I Tim. 6:11-16	Luke 16:19-31
Episcopal:	Amos 6:1-7	I Tim. 6:11-19	Luke 16:19-31
Pres/Meth/UCC:	Joel 2:23-30	I Tim. 6:6-19	Luke 16:19-31

Introductions to the Lessons

Lesson 1

(1) *Amos 6:1-74* (**Luth/Epis**) There is no future for a nation that is morally corrupt. Amos describes conditions in decadent Israel. The people indulge in luxury, leisure, wine, and song. At the same time they are unconcerned about the nation's welfare and ignore the danger of coming disaster. Is Amos speaking of modern America also?

(2) *Joel 2:23-30* (**Pres/Meth/UCC**) In Joel's time, about four centuries before Christ, Israel was devastated by drought and swarms of locusts. The nation responded to a call for all to repent. There followed good crops and prosperity. Best of all, Yahweh promised to send his Spirit on his people. This promise was fulfilled on Pentecost.

Lesson 2

I Timothy 6:6-16 (**Luth**); *I Tim. 6:6-19* (**Pres/Meth/UCC**); *I Tim. 6:11-19* (**Epis**) Paul continues to advise Timothy in his first letter. It is good to have money but not good to love money. The love of money leads to covetousness and greed. If God gives money to Christians, they are to do good with it and share with others. Rather than love money, love truth, goodness, faith, and love. Obey God's commands and make a good confession of faith.

Gospel

Luke 16:19-31 (**Luth/Epis/Pres/Meth/UCC**) The 16th chapter of Luke deals with material possessions. Last Sunday we learned in the parables of the unjust steward that we need to be wise in handling our finances. The Pharisees who loved money made fun of Jesus for what he said. He goes on to tell another story about a rich

October 18, 1992
(Epis/Pres/Meth/UCC - September 27, 1992)

man, Dives, who fails to help a pathetic beggar, Lazarus. What will motivate a person to share? According to Jesus, a person returning from the dead will not accomplish it, but only the power of God's Word.

Theme: The spiritual "law of recompense" is effective — for eternity.

Thought for the day: Jesus once said, "You will always have the poor with you." The presence of the poor among us is a challenge to act on their behalf, showing mercy, compassion, and love, just as God manifested these blessings to us.

Prayer of meditation: Quiet us now, Lord. Take from us feelings of being pushed, harried, burdened. Replace them with calm assurance of your presence. We would disengage, for a brief time, from the world about us, and link up with the power and love of our source of being, even Almighty God. For the hour of worship ahead, we would set aside the material, and enter the realm of the Spirit. Knowing, however, that you love our world very much, Lord, we do this only temporarily, in order to be renewed — that we might again re-enter the world, carrying the gospel with us. Amen.

Call to worship:
Leader: This is the hour of worship!
People: And we are the people of God!
Leader: What assurance have you of this?
People: We know the love of God's Son, Jesus Christ.
Leader: That is more than enough! Let us proceed.
People: May God be glorified in our worship!

Prayer of adoration: Father, with joy and gladness we approach you in this worship setting. For the opportunities, the challenges, and the alluring spiritual goals which have drawn us here, we give you thanks. You have placed within each of us yearnings and hungers which can never be fully satisfied with the mediocre and the mundane. Time after time our lives have been enhanced with meaning and excitement as we have become involved in worship — and then sent forth to share the cause of our excitement with others. We bless you, Lord, and we seek more of your empowering excitement — today. Amen.

Prayer of confession: Lord, although you challenge us to excellence, in love and charity, by the supreme example of your Son, Jesus, we confess that too often we have settled for far less. You meet our needs in fullness and abundance, and we live as misers, barely willing to release even token amounts of the love and mercy of God to those in desperate need all around us.

Forgive us, O God, for hoarding the gracious gifts you have bestowed upon us. Free us from attitudes of doubt, fear, and unfaith which cause us to grasp too tightly your blessings to ourselves, rather than bless others in turn. Help us to understand, in truth, that your love is endless, its supply never exhausted. In the words of a popular song, help us ever to "pass it on." Amen.

Prayer of dedication of gifts and self: You have given yourself to us, Lord, in abundance. Now, we have the opportunity to give, from our abundance, to meet the needs of others. As we prepare to give, remind us, O God, of who we are, of whose we are, and of what we have received. We, who have been blessed, are now faced with the possibility of becoming blessings. Remind us, Lord, and reconsecrate us, that in our giving, we bless with that same quality of abundance which we have received from your generous hand. Amen.

Sermon title: One Powerful Parable

Sermon thesis: The parable of the rich man and Lazarus, one of Jesus' most power-packed teachings, by stark realism challenges hearers to arouse from complacency and take action to remedy the plight of the poor. It clearly implies that our status in God's sight is intimately linked to our response to the needy of this world.

Hymn for the day: *"The church of Christ in every age."* Written in 1967 at the request of the committee for the English *Hymns and Songs* (1969), this hymn speaks of our mission of service to those in need. Frederick Pratt Green, born in 1903, entered the Methodist ministry in 1924 and served various churches until his retirement in 1969. He began to write poetry later in life (at the age of 40) and wrote his first hymn when he was over 60 years old. Since then he has written numerous hymns, which appear in hymnbooks of many denominations.

Announcements for next week:

Sermon title: Only What We Ought To Do

Sermon theme: Faith is not simply a matter of believing, but a matter of doing the will of God.

Sermon summary: It is easy for even dedicated Christians to believe that we deserve special recognition or accolades when we have behaved in a faithful manner. Faith, however, should be our daily work as people of God. It is only what we ought to do. Faith is not only belief in the face of life's crises, it is daily commitment to make all our choices in the light of God's will.

October 18, 1992
(Epis/Pres/Meth/UCC - September 27, 1992)

Announcements for next week: (Reformation Sunday)
   Sermon title: Written On Our Hearts
   Sermon theme: God has re-formed us, writing God's law and covenant in our hearts as part of the promise that we are made (formed) in God's image.
   Sermon summary: God's freedom is born out of the divine image within us which enables us to work in assurance for the coming of the kingdom. We need to remember that God's image is not a static picture, but a growing and maturing truth: as we mature in our faith, God's image within us changes and matures, renewing us and empowering us.

Children's object talk:

Beggars All

Objects: An empty wooden bowl (or similar bowl-like object)
Lesson: Being dependent on God's charity, we should show charity to others.
Outline: 1. Beggars are not looked upon very kindly in our society.
   2. We are all "beggars" who desperately need the mercy of God.
   3. Since we have received God's charity, we should treat others with similar kindness.

GOOD MORNING, KIDS. AS USUAL, I HAVE SOMETHING TO SHOW YOU. Does anyone know that this is? (Let them respond.) Yes, it's a bowl. Yes, it's made of wood. No, it's not a soup bowl, although I guess you could use it for that if you wanted to.

What this bowl is intended to represent to us today is a "beggar's bowl." Have you ever seen a beggar on the streets, maybe downtown? (Let them respond.) Yes, most of them are dirty. Some of them look pretty awful, with scars and missing arms or legs. And some of them will even walk right up to you and ask for — or demand — money. Often, though, you'll see a beggar who just sits there, with a bowl like this, or maybe a box, in front of them. They want you to put money into their bowl. That's why it's called a "beggar's bowl."

Actually, the word "beggar" isn't used much anymore in our day. We usually call people who live on the streets, seeking handouts, "homeless." These are persons who, for many different kinds of reasons, find themselves poor and without a place to live. So they roam the streets of our cities, begging for charity from others.

What do you think of "homeless" people who beg for money from others? (Let the children give their own answers. This may take a minute or two.) Yes, I realize that "homeless" beggars can seem bothersome, and sometimes they make us feel guilty — especially when we don't have any money to give them. But beggars are God's children, too. In fact, Jesus even told a story about a beggar whose name was Lazarus. Lazarus the beggar was so loved by God that he wound up in a wonderful place called Paradise when he died.

When we stop to really think about it, every one of us is a beggar, a "homeless" person, in relation to God. The Bible says that we are all sinners, disobedient persons who have "run away from home," away from the household of our heavenly Father.

And yet, God still loves us. He offers us the riches of his love, freely. The gospel, the Good News of God's love revealed for us by his Son, Jesus, is sometimes described as "one beggar telling another beggar where to find bread." All we have to do is ask for God's mercy, and he'll gladly give us everything we really need to make our lives full and abundant, now and forever.

It's pretty hard, I realize, to show kindness to modern-day beggars, especially when they're dirty, and maybe smelly, and very demanding. But when we remember that we, ourselves, are really "beggars all" in God's sight, maybe we can show a little more compassion for the homeless and the beggars. Will you try to show kindness to everyone, because God has been kind to you?

The sermon:

One Powerful Parable

Hymns:
  Beginning of worship: Christ for the World We Sing
  Sermon hymn: What Does the Lord Require
  End of worship: God of Grace and God of Glory

Scripture: Luke 16:19-31

Sermon text: *"He said to him, 'If they do not listen to Moses and the prophets, neither will they be convinced even if someone rises from the dead.'"* vs. 31, NRSV

JESUS WAS A MASTER STORYTELLER. He required very few words to weave profound tales which communicate significant teachings. We find about fifty of his mini-stories preserved in the

October 18, 1992
(Epis/Pres/Meth/UCC - September 27, 1992)

gospels. These we call *parables*. The occasion for the telling of a parable by Jesus was usually the raising of a difficult question, either as the result of something Jesus said elsewhere in his teachings, of just spontaneously by one of his hearers. In some cases, we have the question preserved with the parable, as, for example, when a man asked Jesus, "Who is my neighbor?" His reply, "A man was going down from Jerusalem to Jericho — and he fell among robbers, who stripped him and beat him . . ." is the universally-known parable of the "Good Samaritan." Its point is clear: Everyone is my neighbor in the eyes of God. Jesus could have answered the question by saying just that, but his answer is far better remembered in its parable form.

Today's gospel lesson is the parable of the rich man and Lazarus. Every time I read this story, my first response is "Wow!" This narrative is stark, vivid, pointed, incisive — and unforgettable. It's one *powerful* parable! We don't know what question, if any, prompted Jesus' telling of the parable of the rich man and Lazarus, but I suspect it was directed at his particular audience that day. As we are told earlier in the same chapter of Luke's gospel, that audience was made up of Pharisees and Sadducees. These two groups liked to argue with each other about the nature of life after death, so it's likely that one among them asked Jesus, "What will it be like for us after we die?" or words to that effect. That's always a popular question to ask. It's one that folks especially like to use when they want to play "stump the preacher."

The parable of the rich man and Lazarus, brief though it is, contains three major sections, and each of the three sections makes a singular, profound point — about life, and about life after life. The first section highlights a particular sin — possibly the most widespread of all sins, both then and now — the sin of *neglect*. We are presented with two men whose lives are intertwined. One lives, literally, on the other's doorstep, and yet the second never sees the first.

The rich man was not necessarily an evil man. Perhaps he was even a just man under the laws of his society, which forbade killing, adultery, theft, and the like. The rich man probably did none of these — he had no cause to commit the petty sins of those around him. Nor did the rich man sin simply by being rich; it is no crime in God's eyes merely to be wealthy. Solomon, highly regarded among God's chosen kings, was one of the richest men who ever lived. Nor, further, did the rich man sin by active cruelty to the poor beggar at his gate. Lazarus was allowed to remain there, at the entrance to the rich man's estate, day in and day out. Possibly he was even thrown a crumb of bread from time to time. No, the rich man was not cruel; I suspect he was more lenient than you or I might be under the same circumstances. Would you allow a dirty, diseased "bum" to sit in front of your house for very many days?

The rich man did nothing in the way of overt sinning against poor Lazarus. His sin was simply that of neglect. Right before his eyes, every day, another human being lay in dire need, and he did nothing about it. His brother-human, poor Lazarus, was in want, and he didn't even notice his presence. The sin — the horrible sin — of *neglect!*

When you and I come to the place and time where God exercises judgment over us, I strongly suspect that our major sins will be of like nature. I know very few people who are actively cruel, overtly malicious — evilly sinful. Most of our real sins are more subtle. A thousand Africans die of starvation each day, while I struggle to get into 38-inch pants that will barely accommodate my expanding waistline. I complain about the high cost of medical insurance for my family, while my Hispanic sisters and brothers die of easily curable diseases, because there is no doctor who will treat their ills at a price they can afford. Fifteen or twenty old person slowly waste away from loneliness and neglect in my very church, while I praise God daily for the comforts of my home and family. In this parable of our Lord Jesus Christ, who are we more like: Lazarus — or the rich man?

The second section of the parable brings a shift of scene. Both men have died, and we follow them to realms beyond the grave for a rare look behind the curtain of death. Although many Christians like to highlight Heaven and Hell, the fact is that our Lord Jesus taught relatively little about life after death; his primary focus of teaching was on human life here and now. But this parable provides one important glimpse of those realms beyond this life. Not surprisingly, the two very different men have met very different fates. Lazarus, the poor, neglected beggar, now lies in comfort in Paradise with Abraham, the forefather of all God's children. But the rich man now suffers the torment of hellfire, punished for his lack of human compassion while on earth.

It's puzzling for me to try to understand many contemporary

October 18, 1992
(Epis/Pres/Meth/UCC - September 27, 1992)

Christians who say they believe in the truth of the Bible, in the divinity of Jesus, and in the reality of Heaven, but they don't believe, there's a Hell. It's puzzling: I mean, if you believe in Jesus — and Jesus taught about Hell — was he lying? Chew on that for a while, please!

Back to the story. The focus of this, the mid-section of the parable, is upon *justice*. God is a just God. On earth, we often question God's justice, when we as Christians observe crooked, immoral, people living it up, while humble, honest folks are trampled upon. It's even harder to see God's justice in natural disasters, capricious diseases like cancer, or babies born hopelessly malformed and retarded.

However, we must acknowledge that we are not in possession of all the data. Our brief span of 70 to 80-plus earthly years is but an eyeblink on the face of eternity. Jesus' parable of the rich man and Lazarus makes it clear that God *is* just — that the "score" is even by God in the world to come for each and every human. Have no fear, people; God knows what he's doing. And we might as well start trusting him now, since he's going to be in charge of our lives for many, many countless years to come. Our God is a *just* God.

The final portion of the parable is, I believe, the most significant for you and me, here and now. The rich man asks that Lazarus be sent back, from the dead, to warn his brothers to change their ways, lest they, too, fall into the torment of Hell. But Abraham, the man of faith, points to the Scriptures. "It's all there already," says Abraham. "There's more than enough of God's will revealed in the Scriptures to bring them to salvation." The rich man protests: " People don't really read Bibles; they don't care to listen to sermons; they don't take warnings from preachers seriously. But . . . if someone were to pull off a *miracle* — a fantastic, mind-boggling extravaganza like coming back from the dead . . . then my brothers would surely sit up and listen." And Abraham responds, "No, I don't think so. Even if someone were to rise from the dead, it wouldn't make an impact. It wouldn't change those who just plain don't want to be reached by God."

And, people of God, that's exactly where much of the world is still sitting today. I hear, in effect, the words of the rich man from someone in this city virtually every week. "Aw, preacher, I'm just not much on church goin'. The people aren't friendly enough, the pews are too hard, the heater's up too high, and the sermon is too long. And I just don't get much out of readin' the Bible — I can't understand most of it. If God wants me to believe in him, why doesn't he just come out and tell me so? Let Jesus show himself — or have him write his name in the stars one night next week — then I'll believe!"

The rich man sought a miracle, something people are always asking for. If someone were to rise from the dead, then men and women would be shocked out of their complacency and turn to God. The people of old had the Scriptures, the writing of Moses and the prophets, the preachers and teachers of God's Word, but it wasn't enough for them. There was still room for excuses. But if someone were to rise from the dead . . .

Jesus Christ rose from the dead! He performed the fantastic miracle the rich man sought! Today, we still have the writings of Moses and the prophets, we have preachers and teachers, we have the Church. And . . . we have the *miracle* — the resurrection of Jesus!

In the parable of the rich man and Lazarus, Abraham, normally renowned as a man of faith, was skeptical. Even a man rising from the dead wouldn't be enough for some people.

And now, the question of the ages. Is the Resurrection of Jesus Christ *enough* — for *you*?

David Z. Ring III
Paradise Hills United Methodist Church
Albuquerque, New Mexico

OCTOBER 25, 1992 (1)

Protestant: Reformation Sunday

Lessons:
Protestant: Jeremiah 31:31-34   Romans 3:19-29   John 8:31-36

Introductions to the Lessons

Lesson 1

(1) *Jeremiah 31:31-34* (**Protestant**) A new covenant is promised for Israel. The old Mosaic covenant was broken by Israel's faithlessness. This new covenant will be different from the old one. The Law will be an internal as well as a personal possession. Through this covenant the people will receive forgiveness. Christians believe that Jesus is the mediator of this new covenant.

Lesson 2

Romans 3:19-29 (**Protestant**) How does a person get right with God? By works? Paul is emphatic when he writes that we are made right with God only by faith in Christ who died and rose again for our sins. By grace are we saved through Jesus Christ.

Gospel

John 8:31-36 (**Protestant**) As long as we remain in the truth of the word of Christ, we will be his disciples. As disciples we will know the truth. This truth will set us free. Therefore, faith in Christ makes us free to embrace the truth and to love and serve Christ.

Theme: God has re-formed us, writing God's law and covenant in our hearts as part of the promise that we are made (formed) in God's image.

Thought for the day: It is only through our formation in God's image and in our willingness to be re-formed again and again when we become bruised and battered by the world, that we are freed to be most fully ourselves. When we are properly shaped to our tasks, we are able to meet them in confidence rather than always being tense and uncertain about our ability to answer our call as God's people.

Prayer of meditation: Beloved God, who formed me in your image: Re-form me this day, so that every atom of my being is conformed to your will. And grant me the faith and courage to be as true a reflection of your love and grace as was my brother, Jesus. Amen.

Call to worship:
Leader: O God, who formed us in your holy image,
People: Re-form us in this holy time and place.
Leader: O God, who formed us in the fertile darkness of our mother's wombs,
People: Re-form us in the empty darkness of a broken world.
Leader: O God, who formed an ordered universe from chaos and void,
People: Re-form us from splintered fragments to a living whole, at one with all creation.

Prayer of adoration: O you who are all righteousness and all grace, O you whose mercy and justice make us heirs with Christ of your kingdom through no righteousness of our own, but through your love alone: Hear our gratitude, our praise, our adoration, this day. We offer gratitude because you formed us in your image. We offer praise because you sent us teachers and prophets to remind us of that image within us. We offer adoration because you are in your fullness so much greater than even your most fully realized image in your children. Amen.

Prayer of confession: We have not lived fully in your image in which we were created, O God. We have shaped our own lives to our own agendas, obscuring your beauty in us. Give us strength to re-turn to you and to submit *our* wills to being re-formed to *your* will so that your kingdom will truly be present among us and your will shall live again on earth in us, as it did in our Savior, Jesus. Amen.

Prayer of dedication of gifts and self: Accept, O Lord, this day, my offerings. Accept the gifts of my hand and the gift of my life. Shape me, transform me, mold me so that I become a gift for all people, an instrument of your will, reflecting your image in the world. Take the small gifts of my hands and use them to meet the needs of your kingdom, showing me where more is necessary and inspiring me to open my hands and heart to meet your great plan. Amen.

Sermon title: Written On Our Hearts

October 25, 1992 (1)

Sermon thesis: God's freedom is born out of the divine image within us which enables us to work in assurance for the coming of the kingdom. We need to remember that God's image is not a static picture, but a growing and maturing truth: as we mature in our faith, God's image within us changes and matures, renewing us and empowering us.

Hymn for the day: *"On my heart imprint your image."* This hymn prays that the image of Christ crucified — the foundation of our life and hope — be printed on our hearts. Thomas Hansen Kingo (1643-1703) was Denmark's first great hymnwriter. Grandson of a Scottish tapestry weaver who had emigrated to Denmark, Kingo was a Lutheran pastor. In 1677 he was consecrated bishop of Odense. Kingo discouraged the use of translated hymns and created a body of Danish hymns. Kingo was appointed by King Christian V to prepare a new hymnal for the Danish Church. The resulting hymnal contained some 130 hymns by Kingo. It met with strong disapproval. A second hymnal, prepared by another committee, contained none of Kingo's hymns. It was also rejected. A third hymnal, approved in 1699, contained 85 of Kingo's hymns. Known as "Kingo's Hymnal" it served the Danish church for over 100 years.

Announcements for next week
Sermon title: Being A Samaritan
Sermon theme: Those who are closest to God can always expect to be regarded as Samaritans (foreigners) in the world.
Sermon summary: We need to admit not only that God *can* change us, but allow God *to* change us, and then to be willing for that to draw us away from worldy agendas into God's immediate presence.

OR

Announcements for next week: (All Saints Sunday)
Sermon title: Blessed Are They
Sermon theme: Being a saint does not depend on extraordinary accomplishments, it confers extraordinary accomplishments.
Sermon summary: Being Christian is not easy, but God promises that if we are faithful in our desire (if we really hunger and thirst for righteousness), we will be filled with the power to be strong and fruitful Christians.

Children's object talk:
Formed In God's Image
Objects: 1. A bowl or vase
 2. Some modeling clay
Lesson: We are not only formed in God's image, but as we get battered and pushed around in the world, we need to be re-formed in God's image.

Outline: 1. Why Reformation?
2. Something happens to us.
3. God is working in my life.

[You can begin to work with the clay as you talk, shaping it so that it looks as much as possible like the bowl or vase.] TODAY IS REFORMATION Sunday. Do any of you know what the word "reform" means? [Give them a chance to answer.] Usually when we say we want to "reform" something, we mean that we are trying to correct the flaws or mistakes in it. But "reform" has another meaning: it also means to make something new or to give it a new shape.

When we talk about the Reformation, we are talking about a time almost 500 years ago when a group of men and women set out to correct some of the mistakes they believed had become part of the church. They wanted to make the church new. If we think that reformation is something that happened way-back-when in history, it's hard to get very excited about it. After all, it was over before our great-great-great grandparents were even born!

But one of the reasons we celebrate Reformation Sunday every year, is to remind ourselves that re-formation is something that is happening to every one of us every day. The prophet Isaiah said once that we are a little bit like clay and God is a potter. God *forms* us into beautiful souls, beautiful vessels for God's spirit, just like I am trying to form this clay into a bowl [or vase.] And, like the clay, we can be pushed out of shape by the things that happen in life. [You can invite one of the children to help demonstrate how the clay can become mis-shapen.]

But God is always trying to reshape us, to re-form us. Remember what it says at the beginning of the book of Genesis? It says we are formed in God's image. And God is always trying to help us stay close to that image. God wants us to *look* like God and to *act* like God in this world: to be loving, creating, helping people.

There are times when I can feel God's hands working in my life just like my hands are working with this clay. God is shaping me to be a good representation of God's image. So Reformation Sunday is an important day for all Christians because it is a day when we think about how God is forming us and how, no matter what happens to us in the world, God keeps working to re-form us so that we will each be the most beautiful person we can be.

The sermon:
Written On Our Hearts

Hymns:
Beginning of worship: O Come and Dwell in Me
Sermon hymn: Have Thine Own Way, Lord
End of worship: A Mighty Fortress is Our God

Scripture: John 8:31-36

Sermon text: *"If you continue in my word, you are truly my disciples; and you will know the truth, and the truth will make you free."* vs. 31b-32

IN HER BOOK *The Young Unicorns* author Madeleine L'Engle says, "Freedom does not necessarily mean disobedience; it can also mean the freedom to obey." Those words have hung over my desk for many years. In an era and a society in which freedom is so often understood to be the right to do whatever we want, whenever we want, with whoever we want, it is critically important for Christians to remember that God's freedom is not license, but an abundant power that enables all God's creatures to work, each in his or her unique way, for the coming of God's kingdom.

To fully understand that power within us, we need to go all the way back to the story of Genesis and the forming of humanity in God's image. Female and male, we were called into being to reflect God by being namers and wise stewards and creators in our own right. But it isn't enough to know that once upon a time we were formed to reflect the love and power and creativity of God. It is too easy, then, to let ourselves assume that *anything* we choose to do automatically reflects the Holy Spirit moving in our spirit; and if we are honest, we know that simply isn't so.

"If you continue in my word, you are truly my disciples; and you will know the truth, and the truth will make you free."

We reflect God's image, God's form with us, only by continuing in God's word. It is in rooting ourselves in the word that we are set free of slavery to conflicting demands, to sin, to false gods. In the book of the prophet Jeremiah, the LORD says, "I will put my law within them, and I will write it on their hearts." And the purpose of this law within us, God goes on to say, is so that "[we] shall all know [God], from the least of [us] to the greatest." It is comforting to know that God does not leave us alone to try to know God, alone to try to form ourselves in God's image. God does not leave us alone to find the truth that will set us free. God writes that law, that word, that truth in our hearts where it is present to us every second of every day.

It is not always easy to see or to follow that truth or to know and follow that law. Our choices are not always choices reflecting God. We are human beings, and we are fallible and broken and given to self-importance. We seek goals, we establish agendas that are unhealthy or selfish. For these reasons, we need not only to be formed, but to be re-formed.

Too many of us understand our formation in God's image as a once-and-forever act which leaves a static imprint on our souls. When we see ourselves as engraved printing plates which, if properly inked, will always turn out an invariable picture, we shut ourselves off from the dynamic power of God's ongoing dialogue with us and from God's ongoing presence in our lives.

Those of us who own photo albums are well aware that, much as we cherish them and the pictures they contain, the photographs are not people, but only dim reflections of moments caught out of the web of time, fleeting shadows of people. We would never believe we know a person from looking at a picture of the person. But many of us allow ourselves to be content with knowing God only as a photographic representation. Of course, it is always easier to deal with a fixed caricature than it is to deal with a living entity. It is easier to love our fellow human beings from a distance where we are untroubled by their very real idiosyncrasies. And it is easier to love a photograph of God which never changes, never makes demands, never challenges us or confronts us, than it is to love the living God who does all those things.

However, being formed in God's image is *not* being imprinted with an immutable likeness. It involves being engaged in a continual revelation, an epiphany, a development of mind and heart and soul which deepens us and broadens us. It is not only a formation, it is a constant re-formation. Simply because God's image resides within us does not mean that we reflect it clearly. We need to grow in maturity and understanding, we need to put ourselves in the way

October 25, 1992 (1)

of the word day after day in order to be ready for its fulness to be revealed in us.

When we are first formed in God's image, we are infants. If we wish to be mature in our Christianity, it is not enough to continue in that infant understanding of God and God's law. A child will obey rules (the law) because he is afraid of punishment or the withdrawal of her parents' approval and affection. A mature adult will obey the same law because she understands the freedom inherent within it, understands that without the law, society would be held hostage by the maladjusted, the selfish, the immature, the brutal. In the same way, as we grow we are offered a deeper understanding of God's will for the world, a broader perspective, the chance to make a more profound commitment to being active participants in the work of the kingdom. As we grow, we are offered the opportunity to be re-formed daily to reflect a fuller and more complete image of God.

When we choose to allow God to work such re-formation, we are choosing life over death, truth over lies, and freedom over slavery. There can surely be no better day on which to commit ourselves to being true to the law written in our hearts and to the word of truth which makes us disciples, than the day on which we celebrate the ongoing desire of faithful men and women to keep the church pure in the teaching of Jesus. It is entirely appropriate that Reformation Sunday should find us examining not only the gathered community of faith, but our individual souls, for the clear image of God which will be our witness and offering in a broken world.

"If you continue in my word, you are truly my disciples; and you will know the truth, and the truth will make you free."

Our freedom is a freedom to be obedient to that clear divine image within us so that in all we do and all we are, we are released from the restraints of doubt and fear and pessimism. When we stand firm in our desire to be of God and allow ourselves to be formed (and re-formed) by God into that divine beauty, there is within us no room for trepidation and anxiety, but only for assured action, for conviction, for trusting and faithful discipleship.

On this glorious day, may we join in the prayer expressed by Adelaide Pollard in her hymn:

Have thine own way, Lord! Have thine own way!
Hold o'er my being absolute sway.
Fill with thy Spirit till all shall see
Christ only, always, living in me! Amen.

Andrea La Sonde Anastos
The First Church of Deerfield
Deerfield, Massachusetts

OCTOBER 25, 1992 (2)

Lutheran: Twentieth Sunday after Pentecost
Roman Catholic: Twenty-seventh Sunday of the Year
Episcopalian: Proper 22 (October 4)
Pres/Meth/UCC: Seventeenth after Pentecost (October 4)

Lessons:

Lutheran:	Hab. 1:1-3; 2:1-4	2 Tim. 1:3-14	Luke 17:1-10
Roman Catholic:	Hab. 1:2-3; 2:2-4	2 Tim. 1:6-8, 13-14	Luke 17:5-10
Episcopal:	Hab. 1:1-6 (7-11), 12-13; 2:1-4	2 Tim. 1:(1-5) 6-14	Luke 17:5-10
Pres/Meth/UCC:	Amos 5:6-7, 10-15	2 Tim. 1:1-14	Luke 17:5-10

Introductions to the Lessons

Lesson 1

(1) *Habbakuk 1:1-3; 2:1-4* (**Luth/Epis**) In the time of the prophet Habbakuk, cruel Babylonians were oppressing God's people with violence and destruction. Habbakuk cries out to God for help but gets no answer. He decides to go up a tower where he can be alone with God and get God's answer. The message comes: evil people will perish but they who are faithful to God will live.

(2) *Amos 5:6-7, 10-15* (**Pres/Meth/UCC**) Amos tells it like is: go to God and live; do not go and die! Wicked people are doomed. Therefore, our goal in life should be to hate what is evil and to cleave to what is good. God is merciful to those who repent and return to him.

Lesson 2

2 Timothy 1:3-14 (**Luth**) *2 Tim. 1:6-14* (**Epis**); *2 Tim. 1:1-14* (**Pres/Meth/UCC**) Paul continues his instruction to Timothy in 2 Timothy, from which we will have four selections. Paul is grateful for Timothy's faith which is similar to his mother's and grandmother's faith. Timothy is urged to keep alive the Holy Spirit received at his ordination by the laying on of hands. As Paul suffers for the Gospel, Timothy is to take his share of suffering. Above all, Timothy is to proclaim the Good News just as Paul has done.

Gospel

Luke 17:1 10 (**Luth**); *Luke 17:5-10* (**Epis/Pres/Meth/UCC**) This selection consists of four unrelated subjects. Jesus is teaching his disciples: (1) It is a terrible thing to cause another person to sin; (2) if a person repents, we are to forgive even seven times; (3) even a little faith can perform miracles; (4) a person who does his/her duty does not deserve thanks.

Theme: Faith is not simply a matter of believing, but a matter of doing the will of God.

Thought for the day: It is extremely difficult for Christians in the 20th century to turn away from the enticements of the world and worldly definitions of success; we find it hard to make the community of faith the central community in our lives. It is easy to think that our work toward God's kingdom (when we manage to fit it in our schedule) is deserving of special reward, but it is "only what we ought to be doing."

Prayer of meditation: As I prepare to pray and preach with your people, O God, fill not only my words with the power of your Holy Spirit, but make my every deed a witness to your will. Rekindle your gifts within me so that my testimony may be faithful and true. Amen.

(Inspired by 2 Timothy 1:6-8)

Call to worship:
Leader: Fill your people with the spirit of holy power.
People: Increase our faith, O God.
Leader: Fill your people with the spirit of love.
People: Increase our faith, O God.
Leader: Fill your people with the spirit of self-discipline.
People: Increase our faith, O God.
Unison: Not by our works, but by your grace, increase our faith, O God.

Prayer of adoration: In thanksgiving we lift our voices. We chant aloud a song of praise for all your gifts to your people. In joy we come before you, filled with your grace. As we grow in faith, O Lord, help us grow in gratitude until our every breath is worship. Amen.

Prayer of confession: We have not always been loving servants, O God; nor have we always been motivated by holy power and self-discipline. We have sometimes been silent in the face of injustice or oppression, ashamed to testify to your will. Forgive us our weakness and uplift us with your strength so that, with Timothy

October 25, 1992 (2)
(Epis/Pres/Meth/UCC - October 4, 1992)

and Paul, we may be filled with your grace and sincere in our faith. Amen.

Prayer of dedication of gifts and self: You have poured out upon us, Gracious God, a renewing stream of gifts, abundance beyond measure. Seeking to grow more deeply into your image within us, we return to you, for your use, these gifts earned by the labor of our hands. Lift us above self-satisfaction, lift us above contentment with the little we do. Raise us to such maturity and generosity that we will accept from ourselves nothing less than all offered back to your service. Amen.

Sermon title: Only What We Ought to Do

Sermon thesis: It is easy for even dedicated Christians to believe that we deserve special recognition or accolades when we have behaved in a faithful manner. Faith, however, should be our daily work as people of God. It is only what we ought to do. Faith is not only belief in the face of life's crisis, it is a daily commitment to make all our choices in the light of God's will.

Hymn for the day: *"Forth in the name."* This hymn by Charles Wesley (1707-1788) was included in his *Hymns and Sacred Poems,* 1749. Wesley, one of the first group of "Oxford Methodists," was ordained in the Church of England. After spending some time in America as a missionary in Georgia, he returned to England and spent many years as an itinerant preacher, and later as a minister to Methodist Societies in London. One of the great hymnwriters of all ages, he composed some 6000 hymns. This hymn asks the Lord to be with us in our daily work, resolved to know him alone in all we think or speak or do.

Children's object talk:

Increase Our Faith

Objects: 1. A jump rope, a pair of ice skates or roller skates, a violin or other instrument [you can use the organ or piano if you need to in order to make the point]
2. [If possible] some pictures of handicapped athletes performing or a handicapped artist at work

Lesson: We often say that something is impossible when it is only difficult. Faith is like practice: it makes what *looks* impossible, possible.

Outline: 1. What can you do?
       2. Is anything impossible?
       3. If you have faith.

I'VE BROUGHT SOME THINGS with me this morning and I'd like to hold them up and see how many people in the congregation know how to use each one. [Hold up the jump rope] Raise your hand if you can jump rope. [Leave time after each question for people to raise their hands.] How about ice (or roller) skating? How many people can skate? And violin? How many people in the church can play the violin [or other instrument]?

Would you say that it is *impossible* to jump rope or skate or play the violin? Of course not. You know that it *can* be done because there are people right in this church who can do all those things. [Pick someone who DOESN'T play the instrument and ask her,] Would you say that it is difficult to play the violin? Yes, it is. Especially if you have never done it. [Pick someone who DOES play the instrument and ask her,] Do you remember the very first time you picked up the violin and tried to play it? Did you believe you would ever play it well?

[You can show the pictures of the athletes or artists now if you have them.] Sometimes we say — or even think — things are impossible when we haven't learned how to do them yet or when we have to work very hard to overcome a handicap of some sort.

Jesus' disciples are always wondering whether something is possible, and Jesus is always telling them that they need to have *faith*. Faith for religious people is just like practice for athletes or musicians or artists. We can strengthen our faith just like athletes strengthen their muscles, but we need to *use* our faith in order for it to become strong. A dancer or a baseball player or a gymnast will tell you that when they go on vacation, they lose their "edge." And it takes them several days of practice when they come back to get in shape.

Jesus says, "If you have real faith, you could tell a mountain to move into the middle of the sea and it would." What he is saying is that when any of us has faith, something that seems impossible, becomes possible — just like playing the violin or doing a back flip on the balance beam. But we need to practice faith just like we practice back flips. In the beginning, we won't be very good. But if we give up just because it is *hard*, we will never learn — whether it is cartwheels or rollerskating or playing the violin or being faithful people of God.

October 25, 1992 (2)
(Epis/Pres/Meth/UCC - October 4, 1992)

The sermon:
Only What We Ought To Do
Hymns:
  Beginning of worship: Jesus Calls Us, O'er the Tumult
  Sermon hymn: Master, No Offering Costly and Sweet
  End of worship: Trust and Obey

Scripture: Luke 17:1-10

Sermon text: *". . . we have done only what we ought to have done!"* vs. 10b

WE LIVE IN A SUCCESS-oriented society. In fact, it could be argued that we are addicted to success. Most of us spend a great deal of our lives expecting a constant affirmation, often of a material nature, for what we do. How many of us would be content to remain in a job year after year without a raise or promotion? It is not enough for many of us to have meaningful labor with decent wages and reasonable vacation time; we feel that a whole menu of "perks" is our **right**, that without such benefits we are being taken advantage of, our talents and skills are being undervalued.

Our culture influences us to want the best for ourselves and our children with "the best" defined in terms of material possessions and measurable achievements. We push ourselves and our children to excel not for the the sake of stretching ourselves and being all that God has called us to be, but far more we seek excellence for its rewards. Being a good soccer player is okay; being the captain of the team brings a shine to a proud parent's eyes. "Captain" is an honor. Being the best salesperson with a company, trusted by your customers, valued for your integrity, courtesy, and unparalleled service, is okay; being Vice-President in charge of Sales makes us worthy in the world's eyes. Status is so important that we willingly buy into worldly attitudes that make it respectable to describe our job as "food service technician" rather than "waitress", or "communications facilitator" rather than "telephone operator".

This attitude can be particularly dangerous for the Christian seeking to mature his or her faith. There are few, if any, material rewards for seeking to know and follow God's will because it runs so often counter to society's definitions of success. The God who said, "The first shall be last," the Savior who knelt to wash his disciples feet, is not at all concerned with whether the disciple is the president of a corporation or "only" a janitor in the same company. Indeed, worldly success can often be a handicap to the serious disciple because it brings a competing set of demands to his or her life. And the more ingrained the world's criteria become, the more difficult it is to see clearly beyond them to our responsibility as servants of the living God.

As Christians we need to step back from the constant worldly pressures, messages and agendas, and put ourselves in the place where our Christianity provides the context in which we make all our decisions: familial, political, professional, economic. When we commit ourselves to tithing, it is a choice consonant with our Christian faith. It is not something that deserves a pat on the back; it is "only what we ought to be doing." When we volunteer to work one evening a month in a soup kitchen, we should not need public recognition of that choice: it is "only what we ought to be doing" as people who seek to follow the way of Christ. When we make the decision to be faithful to our spouse in spite of temptation, to treat our children and our parents with respect and love in spite of their needs which interfere with our personal desires, to give up a promotion which will mean that we need to work on the Sabbath, it is "only what we ought to be doing" to be in line with God's will for the people of God.

With the disciples we often pray, "O Lord, increase our faith," but too often we are unwilling to participate in that spiritual growth. Faith is increased, becomes stronger and more vital, only with constant use. Faith is not something that can be increased *for* us and then presented to us by God, by Christ, or by a spiritual mentor. Faith is the daily practice of being in God's presence intentionally with every choice we make. Faith is "doing only what we ought to be doing."

The world's expectations get in the way of our faith because they cause us to compromise, first in small ways and then, gradually, in larger and larger ways until God recedes from the center of our life to a convenient distance where we can feel comfortable with God's demands. Our faith is irrevocably scarred and weakened when we behave as faithful women and men of God only when it is convenient for us to do so. Those people who are serious about keeping themselves in good physical shape do not only exercise when they think it will be convenient, they make exercise a habit and do it in good weather and bad, when they are feeling positive and when they just want to sit with their feet up. The responsible diabetic does not attend to her insulin injections and watch her diet only once in a while; she makes her blood test a morning habit and her diet a daily discipline.

Those people who are serious about growing from spiritual childhood to spiritual maturity make "doing what they ought to be doing" a daily, hourly, commitment. They are people of faith not because they are people of belief only, but because they are people of action in God's name. The employee who resists the temptation to take home a box of pens from the office, the person who says "no" to a party invitation which conflicts with a prior commitment to work at the homeless shelter, the parent who turns off the TV with its images of violence and revenge, and the customer who returns the excess change given by the cashier are all people of faith. They grow in their faith not by confronting immense challenges occasionally, but by making small and steady choices day after day after day.

When Jesus speaks about faith being able to move mountains, he is not only speaking about geological occurences. He is speaking about the seemingly impossible becoming possible through choice and practice. The infant whose legs are not strong enough to support her, gradually, first crawling, then standing up and falling, standing and falling, tottering one step and then two, gradually gains strength and balance and stamina. The faithful Christian, still an infant in things spiritual, learns how to be faithful in much by being faithful in the smallest, most mundane ways first, making faith a cherished companion. Gradually the little things become habits, one is honest because to be anything else is unthinkable; one is generous because one sees oneself as a steward of God's gifts, a channel of God's grace; one is courteous because love is our mandate as Christians.

By "doing only what we ought to be doing," we come to reflect purely that incomprehensible mystery of being created in God's image. Our faith, strengthened and renewed by daily use, enables us to reach beyond the probable into the miraculous. The Missionaries of Charity have become a power of light and compassion in the world not because Mother Teresa had a great idea one day, but because she was faithful to that call day after day after day after year after decade. So, too, the daily practice of our faith, our intentional commitment to live and act in consonance with God's will, the simple choice to "do what we ought to do" in God's name, will make God's kingdom not only possible, but actual; not in some future heaven, but on earth in these days.

Andrea La Sonde Anastos
The First Church of Deerfield
Deerfield, Massachusetts

NOVEMBER 1, 1992 (1)

All Saints' Sunday

Lessons:

Lutheran:	Is. 26:1-4, 8-9, 12-13, 19-21	Rev. 21:9-11, 22-27 (22:1-5)	Matt. 5:1-12
Roman Catholic:	Dan. 7:1-3, 15-18	Eph. 1:11-23	Luke 6:20-26
Episcopalian:	Ecc 2:(1-6) 7-11	Eph. 1: (11-14) 15-23	Luke 6:20-26 (27-36)
Pres/Meth/UCC:	Dan. 7:1-3, 15-18	Eph. 1:11-23	Luke 6:20-36

Introductions to the Lessons

Lesson 1

(1) *Isaiah 26:1-4, 8-9, 12-13, 19-21* (**Luth**). Isaiah gives us a picture of the city of God, a strong city of salvation. In this city dwell the righteous who long for God and trust in him. God's people will be safe in this city while the earth receives God's judgment.

(2) *Ecclesiastes 2:7-11* (**Epis**). What is the best way a person can spend his/her life? The Philosopher of Ecclesiastes tries pleasure, wealth, and women. When he reflected how hard he had to work for these things, he realized they all added up to nothing.

(3) *Daniel 7:1-3, 15-18* (**Pres/Meth/UCC**). Daniel was an exile in Babylon at the time Belshazzar was king. He had a dream of four beasts coming out of the sea. The four beasts represent four empires. But the people of God will receive divine power to overcome the beasts.

Lesson 2

(1) *Revelation 2:9-11, 22-27* (**Luth**). Heaven is described as the new Jerusalem that came from God. The city has the glory of God, for God himself is in it. Because of his presence, there is no light in the city and no temple. The gates of the city are always open but nothing unclean may enter it. The citizens of this city are those whose names are in the book of life.

(2) *Ephesians 1:15-23* (**Epis**); *Eph. 1:11-23* (**Pres/Meth/UCC**). Christians are God's chosen people because they accept the Gospel. Paul prays that the church in Ephesus may have the Holy Spirit, who will make God known to them, and receive power, the same power that raised Jesus from the dead and exalted him to be Lord over all things.

Gospel

(1) *Matthew 5:1-12* (**Luth**). Jesus begins the Sermon on the Mount with the Beatitudes.

They say how and why believers are happy. The Beatitudes describe the condition and qualities of those in heaven.

(2) *Luke 6:20-26* (**Epis**); *Luke 6:20-36* (**Pres/Meth/UCC**). This passage constitutes the opening section of Luke's version of the Sermon on the Mount. Jesus teaches the people what blessings and woes come to believers or non-believers. One of the blessings is to endure persecution for Christ's sake. In spite of the persecution a follower of Christ is one who loves the enemy and extends mercy.

Theme: Being a saint does not depend on extraordinary accomplishments, it *confers* extraordinary accomplishments.

Thought for the day: We are enabled to do wonderful things in the world because we first were willing to be committed Christians. Without Christ's power in us, all our talents and achievements (however worthy) are ultimately small and weak because they are limited by our human strength.

Prayer of meditation: Beloved God, you have called me to be a pastor and teacher in order "to equip the saints for the work of ministry." I do not ask for perfection, but for such wisdom, compassion, and obedience as I may need to do your will. Lead me this day, I pray, to greater maturity in Christ so that in all I do I teach not only by word, but by deed. Amen.

Call to worship:
Leader: Across the generations, you have called all people to be one people, to become one living and holy temple, one Body of Christ, one community of saints dedicated to the coming of your kingdom.
Response: Through the power of your Holy Spirit, you have poured upon us those gifts we need to be worthy to be called saints: wisdom, faith, knowledge, healing, prophecy, discernment, and holy fear.
Leader: Raise us to be one with that company of witnesses which compasses us around.
Response: Make us saints not in name only, but in deed.

Prayer of adoration: Before your throne, the angels and archangels continually sing your praise. Before your throne, the elders cast down their crowns and sing your praise. Before your throne, the four living creatures sing your praise, day and night, without ceasing. Holy, holy, holy God, grant that we may so live our lives in wisdom and in faith that our voices will be voices of grace and beauty, worthy additions to that great harmonious symphony of praise. Holy, holy, holy God, praised be your name. Amen.

Prayer of confession: O Loving God, who has named us your children, we confess that we have not always lived as we have been taught to live: as true saints of your church. We have caused harm or sorrow or pain where we should have healed; we have been unwise in word and deed; we have been tentative in our faith. Grant us renewed vision and confidence so that we may grow more deeply into the holiness to which we are called. Amen.

Prayer of dedication of gifts and self: O You who have showed us that it is more blessed to give than to receive: Lead us to the place where we become true channels of your gifts, hoarding nothing and sharing all. Receive the fruits we return to you and bless them to holy use; receive also the greater gift of our minds and hearts and make them fit for your service. Amen.

Sermon title: Blessed Are They

Sermon thesis: Being Christian is not easy, but God promises that if we are faithful in our desire (if we truly hunger and thirst for righteousness), we will be filled with the power to be strong and fruitful Christians.

Hymn of the day: *"Blest are the pure in heart"* This hymn, based on the Beatitudes, is the work of two authors, John Keble (1792-1866) and William John Hall (1793-1861). Keble graduated with high honors from Corpus Christi College, Oxford, and became a priest of the Church of England. His famous *Assize Sermon,* preached at Oxford in 1833, has been credited with starting the Oxford Movement. Keble is best known for his religious poetry. *The Christian Year,* 1827, was a classic that went through many editions. The church at Hursley, where Keble became vicar in 1836, was restored from the profits of the book. Hall, also a priest of the Church of England, served successively at St. Paul's Cathedral; the Chapel Royal, St. James'; and Tottenham, Middlesex. He edited *Psalms and hymns adapted to the Services of the Church of England,* 1836, and for many years edited *Christian Remembrance.*

Announcements for next week:

Sermon title: Persistent — Persuasive — Powerful

Sermon theme: Jesus gives us permission to be continuously in prayer, constantly making our petitions known to God.

Sermon summary: Through the telling of the parable of the Unjust Judge, Jesus acknowledged that we are beset by many problems over which we feel powerless. It is permissible constantly to petition God to hear our needs and grant us a solution. God who is merciful and compassionate will listen and answer.

Children's object talk:
The Saints of God

Objects:
1. A number of pictures of people engaged in different tasks. The pictures should show a variety of races, ages, clothing styles, and should not be gender-stereotyped. The pictures should include several of well-known saints such as Francis, Mary, Nicholas, etc.
2. A hand-mirror.

Lesson: The job of every Christian is to be a saint of God. No one is exempt from that expectation.

Outline: 1. All people are saints.
2. Is that scary?
3. You are a saint.

(Interleave the pictures so that the saints are mixed in with the "regular people" and begin to show the pictures one at a time as you speak.)

DO YOU KNOW what all these people have in common? [Give them time to make a few guesses.] Well, let's see if we can figure it out. Are they all men? No. Are they all grown-ups? No. Are they all women? No. Are they all light-skinned? No. I'm not going to tell you just yet; I'd like you to do one more thing first. [Give the mirror to someone in the front row and invite them to look in it and pass it to the person next to them. After it has passed several people, you cay say:] Is there anything in common between the person you see in the mirror and the pictures I showed you?

[You can leave a little time for response or leave some silence and then continue:] All these people, the ones in the pictures and the ones in the mirror, all of these people are saints of God. Did you know that? Did you realize that *you* are one of God's saints? Just like Saint Francis and Saint Nicholas and Saint Mary? The apostle Paul tells us that every faithful Christian is called to be a saint. That means *every*body: all the babies and the little children, all the teenagers, all the grown-ups, all the women and all the men, and the light-skinned, dark-skinned, and medium-skinned people, single people and married people, healthy people and sick people, poor people and rich people and in-between people.

I don't know about you, but I find that a little scary. It means

November 1, 1992 (1)

that I can't do just anything I want to and then hope that someone else will be good and faithful and do the things God needs to make this earth a loving place. It means that God depends on me to do my part and to be as good as I can possibly be every minute. That doesn't mean that we won't make mistakes. Did you know that Saint Francis was a pretty selfish person when he was a boy and a young man? He wasn't perfect, but once he knew that God depended on him, he was willing to *try* to be the best person he could be.

So the day we are celebrating today, All Saints' Day, is not really a day about *other* people, it's a day about *you*, about each one of you. Maybe we should all get in the habit of putting the word "saint" before our name in our own minds to remind us that God needs every one of us to make God's kingdom here on earth. There is a wonderful hymn by a woman named Lesbia Scott that ends with the words, "The saints of God are just folk like me, and I mean to be one, too." Happy All Saints' Day, all you saints of God!

The sermon:

Blessed Are They

Hymns:
   Beginning of worship: For All the Saints
   Sermon hymn: For the Brave of Every Race
   End of worship: I Sing a Song of the Saints of God

Scripture: Matthew 5:1-12

Sermon Text: *"Blessed are those who hunger and thirst for righteousness, for they shall be filled."* (v. 6)

THE BEATITUDES are the mandate of the Matthean community, the charter around which that faithful group of men and women gathered. They have articulated for Christians across the ages what it means to be followers of the itinerant rabbi of Nazareth. The wisdom they contain is not the wisdom of the world. They are not prescriptions for getting ahead, or for influencing people, or for success in any of its myriad secular guises. Indeed, any sane, responsible 20th century adult might easily be excused for considering them ambiguous at best and, at worst, lunacy.

Yet, they have been cherished by generation after generation of religious seekers because they contain such profound promises. They are beloved because they describe (in concrete, concise terms) what it means to be a saint in the sense in which Paul uses that word. A saint is not an extraordinary human being, someone with talents and abilities greater than the norm, but an ordinary person who has made choices which have led him or her to extraordinary empowerment. We are all called to be saints in the household of God: women and men whose life choices are so close to the will of God that we are able to bring the kingdom a little closer. The Beatitudes give us honest hope that being a saint is within reach of every one of us.

On All Saints' Day, the day we honor all those who have gone before us who have held true to the faith they were given, it is also appropriate to look at how each of us is called to sanctity, to saintness, as members of the Body of Christ. It is not easy to hold to the charter we have been offered in the Beatitudes, but we have been promised that it is possible. Sanctity should not be limited to those who have taken religious vows, or to pastors, or to deacons, or to prophets. It is part of the vocation of every Christian in every age and it behooves us to ask not, "Who me?", but "How, Lord?"

The Beatitudes speak to many human conditions and they speak of sanctity in many forms and expressions. At different times, each of us finds resonance in one or another of the verses: we sense God's will manifest in our own lives or we see it manifest in the lives of others.

I think of a woman in the parish who is in her late 60s. Her life is simple, pure, gracious. Many of us deplore worldly busy-ness; we complain and moan about our lack of time, but we do not willingly change. This woman took the risk and became poor in spirit. I watch her move through her days with serenity and radiant wonder because the world is filled with gifts from God for those who will stop and look. Wherever she goes, she carries a small piece of the kingdom to others in her joy and confidence and excitement. Poor in spirit, possessing the kingdom here and now, she is a saint of God.

Tom was a man I knew as a child. He continually surprised me, indeed, amazed me, because his tolerance seemed to know no limits. In every soul, he saw the wounds and the hidden gifts. I never heard him speak with impatience or scorn, never heard him speak ill of anyone. There was a family in my childhood church who were, effectively, outcasts. They came on Sundays and to church activities,

November 1, 1992 (1)

but they were disliked heartily by almost everyone. In fairness to the community, they were difficult people, hostile, frequently rude, loudly opinionated. But in them (and in others over and over during the years I knew him), Tom found God's image. I realize now that he was one of the pure in heart and he *did* see God, and he saw the face of Christ in the woundedness of the human spirit and in its strength and potential to love. Pure in heart, blessed with daily revelations of God, he was a saint.

I have been blessed in knowing more than one of God's peacemakers. When I arrived at my current parish, I heard frequently the name, Rachel Garber. I have never met her, but we have corresponded steadily in the past five years. When the time came for Rachel to retire from teaching, she chose to spend her first year of retirement in a Quaker retreat center. It changed her irrevocably. At the end of that year, she heard her call and is now one of the small band of faithful souls who plot the routes of trains carrying nuclear weapons. She and her friends work passively to stop the trains—always by non-violent means, usually by sitting on the tracks. They work actively in Congress, lobbying to stop weapons of horror, to stop all weapons. They teach where and when they are invited, seeking to pass to the younger generations a vision of a world where negotiation is honored more highly than might and where the use of force is seen as *losing*, not winning. Whether you agree with her particular stand or not, she is seeking to follow the pacifist teachings of Jesus who chose a suffering servant Messiahship rather than a warrior king Messiahship. A peacemaker and a child of God, she is a saint.

"Blessed are those who hunger and thirst for righteousness, for they shall be filled."

These are women and men, each of them, who have hungered and thirsted for righteousness. In their hunger, in their thirst, they were filled. They were filled with the power of God which enabled them to act on God's behalf to begin to reveal the kingdom where Jesus told us it was and is: here, now. This is the desire within the human soul that creates saints: the desire, the passion, the hunger and thirst for righteousness.

So often we think of righteousness as outside us: it is equity and justice in human relations, enforced by just laws; it is love and nurturance of the created order (the environment, other species, the rain forests, the ozone layer) as practiced by societies or companies or institutions; it is the cessation of war and bigotry and hatred so that there is peace between nations. But the Beatitudes are not about nations, societies, cultures and legal systems, they are about individual people. And right in the middle of them, Jesus has made this statement about righteousness. He is not talking about righteous societies, righteous countries, righteous institutions; he is talking about righteous souls. There is no such thing as a righteous country if the people who live within its systems are unrighteous.

The power that has enabled men and women to become saints of God is the hunger and thirst for righteousness *within*, a consonance with the will of God implanted and expressed in the spirit and soul. When the hunger and thirst for righteousness become unbearable, when we truly realize that we will die as spiritual beings without it (as surely as we will die as physical beings without food and water), God acts to fill us with an abundance of divine grace. Then, then, O saints of God, we become saints not only in name, but in truth.

Name we sing of others, then, O then, others will sing of *us*:
O blest communion, fellowship divine!
We feebly struggle, they in glory shine;
Yet all are one in thee, for *all* are thine.
Alleluia! Alleluia!

Andrea La Sonde Auastos
The First Church of Deerfield
Deerfield, Massachusetts

NOVEMBER 1, 1992 (2)

Lutheran: Twentyfirst Sunday after Pentecost
Roman Catholic: Twenty-eighth Sunday of the Year
Episcopalian: Proper 23 (October 11)
Pres/Meth/UCC: Eighteenth after Pentecost (October 11)

Lessons:

Lutheran:	Ruth 1:1-19a	2 Tim. 2:8-13	Luke 17:11-19
Roman Catholic:	2 Kings 5:14-17	2 Tim. 2:8-13	Luke 17:11-19
Episcopal:	Ruth 1:(1-7) 8-19a	2 Tim. 2:(3-7)8-15	Luke 17:11-19
Pres/Meth/UCC:	Mic. 1:2; 2:1-10	2 Tim. 2:8-15	Luke 17:11-19

Introductions to the Lessons

Lesson 1

(1) *Ruth 1:1-19a* (**Luth**); *Ruth 1:8-19a* (**Epis**). Here is a tragic story of a wife, Naomi, and her two daughters-in-law, Ruth and Orpah, whose three husbands die. It is also a beautiful account of filial love and faithfulness. Ruth refuses to go back home and vows to embrace Naomi's nation, home, people, God, and even death. While Orpah goes back to her family in Moab, Ruth and Naomi set out for Bethlehem.

(2) *Micah 1:2; 2:1-10* (**Pres/Meth/UCC**). Micah, like Isaiah, preaches to Judah, the southern kingdom, in the 8th century before Christ. He exposes their wickedness and assures them of divine judgment. The people respond to his preaching: "Don't preach at us. God is not going to disgrace us." Speaking for Yahweh, Micah declares that their sins have doomed them to destruction.

Lesson 2

2 Timothy 2:8-13 (**Luth**); *2 Tim. 2:8-15* (**Epis/Pres/Meth/UCC**). Though Paul writes while he is chained in prison, he answers Timothy that the Word of God is not chained. He endures suffering that people may receive salvation through the Gospel he proclaims. Timothy is warned not to deal with words that ruin people, but to rightly explain the Word of truth.

Gospel

Luke 17:11-19 (**Luth/Epis/Pres/Meth/UCC**). In this instance only one out of ten was grateful for being cured of leprosy, an incurable skin disease. On his way to Jerusalem, Jesus passes close to the border of Samaria. Ten men cry out for mercy. Jesus told them to go to the priests for verification of their healing. Only one, a Samaritan despised by the Jews, came back to say thanks. In amazement and disappointment Jesus asks, "Where are the nine?"

Theme: Those who are closest to God can always expect to be regarded as Samaritans (foreigners) in the world.

Thought for the day: For Christians, the trusting step into the unknown is a step into the miraculous transforming power of God. Our faith is not mature until we are willing to submit ourselves to the abundant miracles God works within each of us.

Prayer of meditation: You have called me this day to lead my brothers and sisters in praise and worship: Grant me such compassion and wisdom that my words may exclude no one here present and that my every act may be a true reflection of your love poured out to all in need. Amen.

Call to worship: Judge me worthy, O Lord, for I have walked in trust before you. The strength of your steadfast love, has made it possible from me to live in faith. In joy, I dance before your altar, singing songs of thanksgiving, telling of your miracles and offering blessings before the great congregation. (Psalm 26, freely adapted)

Prayer of adoration: Healing, holy God, you have worked your power in my life, in our lives. We were born in a miracle of creation, we live in an unending stream of daily miracles, we die into the glorious miracle of your presence. With every breath, you offer us faith to walk into the grace of your abundance. We lift our voices and our hearts in praise this day as did the Samaritan before Jesus, giving thanks, body and soul, for your love. Amen.

Prayer of confession: O compassionate God, in brokenness we have come to you to be made whole. We have allowed our disease and unhealth to separate us from the community of faith. We have walked in unclean ways. Now, in our need, we turn to you to be made one again: one with your holy image within us, one with our sisters and brothers, the strong body of Christ. Renew us, O God, redeem us so that when we are called the holy people of God, we will reflect not our own weakness, but your pure beauty. Amen.

Prayer of dedication of gifts and self: You have not shamed me before the great congregation because I am not perfect and my gifts are not perfect. In age after age, you have accepted the small, flawed offerings we bring to you and you have transfigured them, making

November 1, 1992 (2)
(Epis/Pres/Meth/UCC - October 11, 1992)

them channels of your love to those in need. Accept, beloved and patient God, accept not only the fruit of my labor, but the fulness of my life as a gift this day. Accept the weakness and the strength, the sorrow and the joy, the broken and the whole into your service. Amen.

Sermon title: Being a Samaritan

Sermon thesis: It is not enough for Christians to know the stories of miracle in the Bible; we must be willing to name the miracles within our own lives and to acknowledge the power of God to heal us from all that separates us, whether that is separation from our own souls, from our sisters and brothers, or from God. More: we need not only to admit that God *can* change us, but to allow God *to* change us, and to be willing for that to draw us away from worldly agendas into God's immediate presence.

Hymn of the day: *"When in the hour of deepest need"* Paul Eber (1511-1569), considered to be second only to Martin Luther among the Wittenberg hymnwriters, was a professor at Wittenberg University and preacher at the Castle Church. This beautiful hymn of repentance and forgiveness is based on an earlier Latin hymn. The lepers called on Jesus in their deepest need; one remained to give thanks. Our hymn also remains to give thanks in the final stanza.

Announcements for next week:

Sermon title: Persistent – Persuasive – Powerful

Sermon theme: Jesus gives us permission to be continuously in prayer, constantly making our petitions known to God.

Sermon summary: Through the telling of the parable of the Unjust Judge, Jesus acknowledged that we are beset by many problems over which we feel powerless. It is permissible constantly to petition God to hear our needs and grant us a solution. God who is merciful and compassionate will listen and answer.

Children's object talk:

Love Is Greater Than Fear

Objects: A small hand-held bell
Lesson: Jesus had such love that he could reach out beyond his human fear to those in need.
Outline: 1. Story of the lepers.
         2. Jesus reached out to them.
         3. We can reach out to others.

MANY YEARS AGO, people who had a disease called leprosy carried little bells like this. They had to ring them wherever they went to warn people that they were coming. Other people, healthy people, would get out of the way because they were so afraid that they would catch leprosy. Leprosy was a very serious disease and it was very frightening.

One of the things that made it serious was that people did not understand what caused it; many people believed it was a way that God punished sinful people. Leprosy isn't nearly as frightening to us now because we know it is a disease and that diseases are caused by germs and viruses and bacteria and, through the work of medical researchers and doctors, God has taught us how to cure many of them.

In the story from the gospel today, Jesus does something very loving and very courageous: he meets ten lepers (ten people with leprosy) and he doesn't run away from them. He speaks to them and he tells them how to be healed. Remember that Jesus didn't know about germs and viruses; he grew up at a time when people were scared of lepers. But Jesus loved human beings so much that there was no way for the fear he might have felt to be stronger than the love.

So instead of doing what someone else might have done (run away), Jesus did just the opposite: he reached out to these people who were feeling so alone and so rejected. As we grow as Christians, one of the qualities that will set us apart is our love. We, too, need to grow to the place where we won't let our fear be stronger than our love and where we have hearts big enough to reach out to those who are ignored or shunned by the rest of the world.

The sermon:

Being A Samaritan

Hymns:
    Beginning of worship: Heal Us, Emmanuel, Hear Our Prayer
    Sermon hymn: Your Hands, O Lord, in Days of Old
    End of worship: O Master, Let Me Walk with Thee (You)

Scripture: Luke 17:11-19

Sermon Text: *"Then one of them, when he saw that he was healed, turned back, praising God with a loud voice. ... And he was a Samaritan."*

November 1, 1992 (2)
(Epis/Pres/Meth/UCC - October 11, 1992)

THIS IS A DIFFICULT STORY for the 20th century Christian, especially for those in the industrialized societies. Our culture has encouraged us to value what is rational, logical, explicable, scientific, and factual. We have for generations demeaned the emotional, symbolic, mysterious, intuitive and faithful. The result is that we spend a lot of time in Bible study, in prayer, and in the pulpit explaining away the miracles of Jesus. We operate from the assumption that our rational minds must control our faith. If a passage is not scientifically probable, we would be better ignoring it than asking our brothers and sisters in Christ to take it on faith, to respond to it from a different stance than the one that dominates our worldly agendas. To be valid, our Christianity must never contradict our established world view.

But that entire house of cards is built on a false premise, and I have come to the conclusion that there is nothing a pastor can give her parishioners more conducive to their growth as Christians than a healthy dose of miracle stories. It is time we stopped forcing God to bow to our narrow-mindedness and, instead, expected ourselves to mature in all areas of our lives to meet that divine image that was created in us.

There isn't a hospital in the world, or a doctor's office, or a single medical study that does not accept the validity of the "spontaneous remission." That is to say, there are healings that cannot be explained by scientific principles or attributed to medical intervention. The medical establishment is just beginning to catch up to what the faith community has known for years. Medical researchers are just beginning to record what the faith community has been recording at places like Lourdes for decades. Even the most rational among us accept that from time to time, people are going to get well from even the most serious illnesses.

What makes the story in the gospel today so hard to take is not that a leper, somewhere, at some point in history, was cured of his leprosy. What pushes the story beyond the bounds of reason is the fact that *ten* lepers were healed simultaneously. And so most of us quietly dismiss the story as a primitive (and, therefore, inaccurate) record of an historical event.

What if we were to stop worrying whether the *actual* event was the healing of ten or fifteen or two? What would happen to our faith if we were to consider the height and breadth and depth of the miracle of a single soul healed of what separated him from the rest of humanity so that he was no longer alienated, outcast, alone in his pain? How would we grow in our Christianity if we were to accept (accept from the bottom of our hearts, with every fiber of our beings) that Jesus has the power to heal *us* of what alienates and separates *us* from our fellow human beings? The power to heal *us* of the pain of loneliness? The power to bind us into a holy and faithful community? The power to redeem us when we have shut ourselves away from God's presence? The power to bring us back to that healing and renewing grace?

Miracle stories are not about some long-dead person or group of people or event in ancient Palestine; they are about us and the power God has to work in our lives to transform barrenness to abundance, dis-ease to health, weakness to strength. When we stop needing miracles to be happenings that defy scientific explanation and stop worrying about their size we can begin to welcome and accept God's power to work miraculous change in our own lives: change so profound and at levels so deep that we often do not *see* the change for weeks, months, years. The first aspect of the story today invites us to step into the place where God's transformations can work in each of us individually.

The second aspect of the story is a reminder. The passage tells of ten people requesting healing. It continues with all ten going to the priests and, on the way, being cured. And it tells of one who was so changed by this experience that his praise became a gift to Christ himself.

"Then one of them, when he saw that he was healed, turned back, praising God with a loud voice....And he was a Samaritan."

The fact that the story identifies this man as a Samaritan (an outcast not only by the fact of his leprosy, but by his heritage) tells us something about the life of a mature Christian. First, it tells us that our faith must always be lived on the cutting edge. The other nine lepers presented themselves to the clergy in their place of worship, before their faith community, the community from which they had been alienated by the horror of their disease. What joy they must have felt to be able to return to worship once again! We cannot dismiss them as ungrateful wretches; they did exactly what Jesus told them to do. BUT — one leper was so transformed that he could not contain himself even in a house of worship or a community of the faithful; *one* leper recognized God's power incarnate in the channel of Jesus and he chose to put himself personally, immediately, directly in that presence. And he risked everything to turn back to Jesus in praise and worship.

This one person knew alienation intimately, but when healing and connectedness were offered, he was not content to be connected primarily to the social structure (even the religious social structure). He wanted to be connected first and foremost to God. He did not look to the prevailing world view (even the view of the church) to confirm his experience, to validate his miracle. As Christians in a 20th century world, we, too, are foreigners in the world, we are sisters and brothers to the Samaritan in the story. And we must choose which is more important to us: worldly affirmation and acceptance or renewal and growth in God's presence.

If we choose (as the Samaritan did) *not* to acknowledge the world's ultimate power and authority, we will run the risk of being dismissed and our maturity in God being seen as meaningless. We need to accept that we will remain foreigners to the world when we choose citizenship in God's kingdom. As Christians, our Christianity must come first and it will always involve a stepping out in faith into the unknown transforming power of God. There are times that it will be very lonely, but when we act in such confidence, we can expect to be accompanied on our path by the comforting and challenging words of Jesus, "Get up and go in peace; your faith has made you whole."

Andrea La Sonde Anastos
The First Church of Deerfield
Deerfield, Massachusetts

November 8, 1992

Lutheran: Twenty-second Sunday after Pentecost
Roman Catholic: Twenty-ninth Sunday of the Year
Episcopalian: Proper 24 (October 18)
Pres/Meth/UCC: Nineteenth after Pentecost (October 18)

Lessons:

Lutheran:	Gen. 32; 22-30	2 Tim. 3:14-4:5	Luke 18:1-8a
Roman Catholic:	Ex. 17:8-13	2 Tim. 3:14-4:2	Luke 18:1-8
Episcopal:	Gen. 32:3-8, 22-30	2 Tim. 3:14-4:5	Luke 18:1-8a
Pres/Meth/UCC:	Hab. 1:1-3; 2:1-4	2 Tim. 3:14-4:5	Luke 18:1-8

Introductions to the Lessons

Lesson 1

(1) *Genesis 32:22-30* (**Luth**); *Gen. 32:3-8, 22-30* (**Epis**). Jacob and his brother Esau were enemies because Jacob stole Esau's birthright and his father's blessing. Because Esau was out to kill him, Jacob fled to his uncle Laban's farm. With his two wives and eleven children Jacob decides to return to his homeland. But, he hears that Esau with a band of men is coming to meet him. Scared for his life, he spends the night in prayer wrestling with God's messenger until he is blessed.

(2) *Habbakuk 1:1-3; 2:1-4* (**Pres/Meth/UCC**). In the time of the prophet Habbakuk, cruel Babylonians were oppressing God's people in Judah with violence and destruction. Habbakuk cries out to God for a reason for this, but gets no answer. He decides to go up a tower where he can be alone with God and hear his answer. The message comes: evil people will perish but the righteous will live because they are faithful to God.

Lesson 2

II Timothy 3:14-4:5 (**Luth/Epis/Pres/Meth/UCC**). Paul instructs his spiritual son, Timothy, to faithfully proclaim the truth of God. To do that he needs to be equipped with the divinely inspired Scriptures which are all-sufficient for teaching and preaching. Timothy is to preach the Word persistently even though some people may prefer to hear legends.

Gospel

Luke 18:1-8a (**Luth/Epis**); *Luke 18:1-8* (**Pres/Meth/UCC**). Be not discouraged in prayer! That is what Jesus is saying in his parable of the widow and the judge. He gave her

November 8, 1992
(Epis/Pres/Meth/UCC - October 18, 1992)

the justice she asked because she never gave up appealing. If this works for a human, how much more it is true of God! If we persist in our prayers, we need also to persist in believing. Jesus asks, "Will the Son of Man find faith on earth when he comes?"

Theme: Jesus gives us permission to be continuously in prayer, constantly making our petitions known to God.

Thought for the day: All of us are constantly troubled by many problems and anxieties in life. We pray about these matters so often that we become guilty, feeling we are trying the patience of God. Jesus reassures us that it is all right to continuously petition God.

Prayer of meditation: Dear heavenly Parent, we gather together this day with many troubles and uncertainties. We are often concerned about our lack of money to pay bills, anguished about the health of our parents, worried that our children will be safe through the day, confused regarding an important decision. These problems we lift up to you in this hour of worship, knowing that you shall hear our plea and bless us with the peace of the Holy Spirit.

Call to worship:
Pastor: Praise the Lord!
People: Praise God in his sanctuary; praise him in his mighty firmament!
Pastor: Praise him for his mighty deeds; praise him according to his exceeding greatness!
Pastor: Praise him with trumpet sound; praise him with lute and harp!
All: Let everything that breathes praise the Lord! Praise the Lord!
(Psalm 150)

Prayer of adoration: Heavenly Parent, the one who breathed into us the breath of new life, the one who formed the stars overhead and carpeted the earth with flowers, to you we give our thanks. May we always worship and adore you, great God of creation.

Prayer of confession: Oh Lord, we are ashamed of how we have denied you in the week gone past. We have failed to witness to your great and glorious name. We have failed to share the Gospel message with someone who needed to hear the word of salvation. We selfishly spent our money of the desires of our hearts rather than on the desire of your heart. We have turned the other way when we saw another person in trouble. Forgive us our disobedience. Strengthen us to do better in the week to come. Amen.

Prayer of dedication of gifts and self: Jesus said, "He who finds his life will lose it, and he who loses his life for my sake will find it." Let us now surrender ourselves and our gifts before you dear God, that we may know a life lived in the spirit of Jesus. Amen.

Sermon title: Persistent — Persuasive — Powerful

Sermon thesis: Through the telling of the parable of the Unjust Judge, Jesus acknowledged that we are beset by many problems over which we feel powerless. It is permissible constantly to petition God to hear our needs and grant us a solution. God, who is merciful and compassionate, will listen and answer.

Hymn for the day: *"Christians, while on earth abiding"* . This hymn reminds us to pray without ceasing. Sweden's first important hymnwriter, Jesper Svedberg (1653-1735), was a Lutheran pastor. He served for a time as court preacher to King Karl XI and later became theological professor and dean of the cathedral at Uppsala. The king appointed Svedberg to prepare a new hymnbook for Sweden. Although the book was approved by the archbishop and the theological faculty, it met with violent criticism from other quarters. It was subsequently withdrawn and sent to the Swedish colonists along the Delaware River, who used it for many years. The revised edition of Svedberg's hymnal still clearly bore his stamp, and remained in use in Sweden for over 100 years.

Announcements for next week:
   Sermon title: The Contrite Heart
   Sermon theme: We must always approach God with a humble and contrite attitude.
   Sermon summary: Two men approached God — a Pharisee thinking he had done no wrong and a publican convicted of his sins. One came before the throne of God haughtily, the other humbly. The prayer of the Pharisee was not received by God, the prayer of the publicans was. We are to learn from this lesson always to be an individual with a contrite disposition.

Children's object talk:

God Allows Us To Pray

Objects: People from the congregation.
Lesson: God will hear and answer our prayers.
Outline: 1. God gave permission to pray.
   2. Prayer is how we talk to God.
   3. Demonstrate prayer.

TELL THE CHILDREN how Jesus taught that God as our heavenly Parent gave us permission to pray. As a loving and caring parent God will hear and answer our prayers. Then explain that prayer is how we talk to God, and how God is able to answer and help

November 8, 1992
(Epis/Pres/Meth/UCC - October 18, 1992)

us. Demonstrate this: ask each child to call an adult from the congregation that she/he finds easy to talk to, or an adult of a particular profession (doctor, policeperson, school teacher) that she/he may go to in time of trouble. Explain as these adults are willing to listen and help you, so much more will your Parent in heaven listen and help you.

The sermon:
Persistent — Persuasive — Powerful
Hymns:
Beginning of worship: All Praise to Our Redeeming Lord
Sermon hymn: Guide Me, O Thou Great Jehovah
End of worship: Dear Lord and Father of Mankind

Scripture: Luke 18:1-8a

Sermon Text: *"And will not God vindicate his elect, who cry to him day and night? Will he delay long over them?"* v. 7

IN SEPTEMBER, 1969, Bob was admitted to MacNeal Memorial Hospital in Berwyn, Illinois. He had cancer and was not expected to live. As his parents drove to the hospital to visit their son, they were in a terrible automobile accident. His mother was also admitted to MacNeal Hospital. Learning the plight of his family, television celebrity Mike Douglas rushed to Berwyn. Mike was confident that his money and notoriety would allow him to secure the best physicians and health care possible for his loved ones. As Mike stood in the hospital corridor, his mother on one floor, his brother on another, he realized how powerless he really was. Fame and fortune were of little consequence. Pacing the long, antiseptic hall, Mike began to pray, something he had not done since he was a child. It was a fumbling prayer, but in desperation Mike was seeking the comforting presence of Jesus.

In that hospital corridor Mike Douglas had changed. He realized that the only real authority and power on earth was Jesus Christ. On that day Douglas became a man of prayer. Every day since, he has said his prayers, and prior to each television appearance he goes off into a corner alone for a moment of silent meditation.

Prayer is the most persuasive and powerful force known for

humanity; and, as we learn from our lesson, we are to persist in prayer. Recorded in Luke 18:1-8 is the Parable of the Unjust Judge. Jesus expounded upon the character of a judge who had no regard for people or God. He was a selfish and belligerent old codger. A widow came to him one day seeking justice, but the judge would not be inconvenienced by someone as insignificant as she. Undaunted, the widow continued to petition the judge. Exasperated, the judge reluctantly gave into her demands. If an unjust judge will care for the needs of a persistent widow, Jesus exlaims, "...will not God vindicate his elect, who cry to him day and night? Will he delay long over them? I tell you, he will vindicate them speedily."

The teaching of this parable by our Lord is enlightening and comforting for those of us who believe in intercessory prayer. Jesus tells us that God is a good and righteous diety who cares for each one of us. In his parable he emphasizes that in the eyes of God none of us are unimportant; each is special and never forgotten. Speedily, Jesus taught, God will answer our prayer. God will not tarry, leaving us in spiritual anguish. Instead, Jesus gives us the assurance that God will immediately act to bring us spiritual solace.

Jesus offers another lesson: that it is all right to persist in prayer. I think as Christians we often feel guilty when we constantly plead with God regarding some trauma or adversity in our lives. But in this parable Jesus says it is okay, it is all right, to continually rend our souls before the throne of our heavenly Parent. Jesus removed any guilt or hesitancy we may have in badgering God regarding the anguish that besieges us.

Jesus has given us permission to pray. More than that, Jesus has told us God will hear and answer our prayers. What a blessing and assurance we have received from this parable taught by our Savior.

In an interview, Barbara Bush explained that she and her husband say their prayers out loud each evening before retiring. This is a practice all of us ought to consider adopting. Remember, Jesus said we are to call upon God day and night. Some time each day we must pause to be in conversation with our Creator. What a privilege we have been granted, the ability to converse with the Supreme Being of the universe. Bestowed upon us is the ability to summon a higher power, seeking divine intervention for the many problems that beset us.

Harmon Killebrew, of the Minnesota Twins, was covering first base in the 1968 All-Star game being played in the Houston

November 8, 1992
(Epis/Pres/Meth/UCC - October 18, 1992)

Astrodome. A hard, fast ground ball was hit to shortstop Jim Fregosi, who scooped up the ball and fired it to first base. The throw came in low and Killebrew leaned way down on his outstretched leg to trap it. As the ball slammed into his glove, Killebrew's left foot slipped on the infield dirt. Suddenly there was excruciating pain as a muscle popped in the back of his thigh. Killebrew was carried off the field to the clubhouse where the team's physician told him he might never play ball again.

Baseball had been Killebrew's life ever since he was a boy growing up in Payette, Idaho. The thought of not playing again was devastating. As the weeks went by and the injury persisted, Killebrew requested the elders of his church to visit his home for a service of healing. The two men came, anointed Killebrew with oil, then laid their hands on the ball player and prayed. At the conclusion of the prayer a strange sense of calm came over Killebrew, who immediately discarded his crutches. Though the pain persisted, Killebrew knew God would heal his leg. The following season, Killebrew joyfully walked onto the spring training field in Orlando.

Prayer is powerful. Receive from Jesus permission to persist in this spiritual activity day and night.

Ronald H. Love
Summit United Methodist Church
Erie, Pennsylvania

NOVEMBER 15, 1992

Lutheran: Twenty-third Sunday after Pentecost
Roman Catholic: Thirtieth Sunday of the Year
Episcopalian: Proper 25 (October 25)
Pres/Meth/UCC: Twentieth after Pentecost (October 25)

Lessons:

Lutheran:	Deut. 10:12-22	2 Tim. 4:6-8, 16-18	Luke 18:9-14
Roman Catholic:	Sir. 35:12c-14, 16-18b	2 Tim. 4:6-8, 16-18	Luke 18:9-14
Episcopal:	Jer. 14:(1-6)7-10, 19-22	2 Tim. 4:6-8, 16-18	Luke 18:9-14
Pres/Meth/UCC:	Zeph. 3:1-9	2 Tim. 4:6-8, 16-18	Luke 18:9-14

Introductions to the Lessons

Lesson 1

(1) *Deuteronomy 10:12-22* (**Luth**). What does God require of his people? Moses should know because on Mt. Sinai he received God's ten commands. In this final address to his people, Moses sums up the Law. We are to fear, love, serve, and obey God's laws. They were given for our benefit, because God loves us.

(2) *Jeremiah 14:7-10, 19-22* (**Epis**). Judah is afflicted with a terrible drought. The people ask why God does not end it. Through Jeremiah the Lord explains that the drought is caused by their wickedness. The people acknowledge their sin and beseech God to bring rain because they are his people of the covenant. Their hope is in the One who alone can bring showers.

(3) *Zephaniah 3:1-9* (**Pres/Meth/UCC**). The prophet Zephaniah preached before King Josiah made reforms in the 7th century. Godlessness and immorality abounded. Because of this Zephaniah declared that Jerusalem and the nation were doomed. Though other cities were destroyed, Jerusalem did not take heed and reform. In desperation God is going to destroy the nation with fire. Out of the ashes will come people who will turn to God and obey him.

Lesson 2

2 Timothy 4:6-8, 16-18 (**Luth/Epis/Pres/Meth/UCC**). The time comes for every person to die. In this passage from II Timothy Paul shows how a Christian faces death. He reviews his past and has the satisfaction that he kept the faith. Then he looks to heaven where he will receive a crown of righteousness. Though he writes that he was saved from a death sentence, according to tradition Paul was executed in Rome around 60 A.D.

November 15, 1992
(Epis/Pres/Meth/UCC - October 25, 1992)

Gospel

Luke 18:9-14 (**Luth/Epis/Pres/Meth/UCC**). In the parable of the Pharisee and the tax collector, we have a study of two men at prayer in the temple. They are a contrast. The one is arrogant and proud of himself, and has no requests to make of God. The other, mindful of his sin, is humble and asks only for mercy. Because of his humility, the tax collector went home being right with God.

Theme: We must always approach God with a humble and contrite attitude.

Thought for the day: God desires us to have a good, healthy, positive self-image. What God forbids us to have is an attitude of self-righteousness. Therefore, we should always be humble in thought, word, and deed.

Prayer of meditation: Heavenly Parent, it is our privilege and honor to be able to gather together in this sacred and holy place to worship and praise you. Bless our time together that we may be renewed in the spirit, so we may approach the coming week empowered to serve you. Allow us to enjoy the fellowship of our friends during this hour together, and may we continue to be a blessing one to another throughout the days ahead.

Call to worship:
Pastor: Lift up your heads, O gates! and be lifted up, O ancient doors! that the king of glory may come in.
People: Who is the King of glory? The Lord strong and mighty, the Lord mighty in battle!
Pastor: Lift up your heads, O gates! and be lifted up, O ancient doors! that the king of glory may come in.
People: Who is this King of glory? The Lord of hosts, he is the King of glory!

(Psalm 24:7-10)

Prayer of adoration: Great heavenly Parent, we worship and adore you. May we always honor you and keep your name holy and sacred. We are thankful for the constant care that you have given us. We are thankful that we are forever in your protective custody. We are thankful for the countless blessings that you have bestowed upon us. May we ever be mindful of you.

Prayer of confession: Dear Lord, you have given us so much, and we have returned so little. You have kept us constantly in your thoughts, and we have so often forgotten you. You have never failed us, but each day we have failed you. You have never denied us, but each day we have denied you by failing to speak your name. You have given us wealth, and we have called that wealth our own. Forgive us for forsaking you. Convict us, that we shall never forget you again.

Prayer of dedication of gifts and self: Dear Lord, we give you thanks for the bountiful blessings that you have bestowed upon us. We offer you now a tithe of those blessings to be used for the ministry and mission of this your church. Through our gifts may all come to know the message of salvation.

Sermon title: The Contrite Heart

Sermon thesis: Two men approached God—a Pharisee thinking he had done no wrong and a publican convicted of his sins. One came before the throne of God haughtily, the other humbly. The prayer of the Pharisee was not received by God, the prayer of the publican was. We learn from this lesson always to have a contrite disposition.

Hymn for the day: *"To you, omniscient Lord of all"* Each stanza of the hymn of the day ends with the publican's prayer, "O God, be merciful to me!" The author, Magnus Brostrup Landstad (1802-1880), was one of ten children born to a Lutheran pastor in the extreme north of Norway. Magnus also became a pastor and served a number of churches in Norway, including nine years at his father's church. Landstad was keenly interested in Norwegian folk songs and folk lore. He also edited the *Kirkesalmbog,* 1869, which became the official Norwegian hymnbook.

Announcements for next week: (Proper 26)

  Sermon title: The Seeking Soul
  Sermon theme: No matter how bad we have been and no matter how much others disapprove of us, Jesus is willing to accept and forgive us.
  Sermon summary: All of us share in the life of Zacchaeus. We have done things for which we are ashamed. We have done things that continue to plague us with guilt. And there are people who will never let us forget our transgressions. This is why, like Zacchaeus, we need to be forgiven and accepted by Jesus.

OR

Announcements for next week: (Christ the King. Last Sunday after Pentecost)

  Sermon title: Today! In Paradise!
  Sermon theme: With the completion of the church year, the cycle of telling the Gospel is complete, the love of God revealed by Jesus is fully revealed.
  Sermon summary: On this day the cycle of the revelation of God's word through Jesus is complete. Even as we rejoice to the fullest, we are also aware of our responsibility.

November 15, 1992
(Epis/Pres/Meth/UCC - October 25, 1992)

Children's object talk:

Good At Some Things But Not All Things

Objects: A baseball and bat
Lesson: The children will learn that they cannot do everything well, but they can do some things well.
Outline: 1. Baseball game.
2. Do your best.
3. Don't make fun of someone who cannot do as well as you.

TELL THE CHILDREN we are going to play baseball. Then have the children spread themselves throughout the sanctuary as fielders. The pastor is to try to hit the ball out of his hand, but keeps missing. The pastor calls the children back, saying she/he has a problem—I can't hit the baseball. Then have the children look at the congregation, as the pastor asks if she/he should be embarrassed by not hitting the ball—not doing well—in front of so many people. Then the pastor explains that she/he is not embarrassed because she/he tried to do her/his best. Then the pastor will explain that she/he may not be good at baseball, but there are other things she/he can do well at.—So if I tried my best to hit the ball, I should not feel ashamed. I am not a failure for not hitting the ball, for there are other things I am good at.—Explain that it is the same for the children. Also, explain the children that should never make fun of someone because she or he cannot accomplish a certain task, for there are many other things that person can succceed at.

The sermon:

The Contrite Heart

Hymns:
Beginning of worship: All Hail the Power of Jesus' Name
Sermon hymn: At the Name of Jesus
End of worship: All Creatures of Our God and King

Scripture: Luke 18:9-14

Sermon Text: "...for every one who exalts himself will be humbled, but he who humbles himself will be exalted." v. 14

PROFESSIONAL GOLFER Billy Casper believed Sundays were for golf, and if not golf, then relaxation. It never bothered him that on Sundays he would be on his way to the golf course as his wife and three children were dressed and on their way to church. Then one Sunday as each was prepared to go their separate ways, the oldest child, Linda, said to her father, "Sundays are days for mommies and children to go to church and for daddies to play golf." The remark was casual and innocent, but it hurt Billy Casper's feelings. The comment made him feel guilty for ignoring his responsibility toward God, and made him realize how his absence from church separated him from his family. That morning Billy Casper changed direction in his life, established new priorities, and now worships the Lord the first day of every week.

What are Sundays for? It is so easy to feel that with the busyness of the week, Sunday is "my" day. The day for me to relax. The day for me to go golfing, fishing, swimming, skiing, or whatever other activity I choose. It is the only day I have to cut the grass, trim the hedges, paint the fence, or accomplish some other household chore. It is so easy to attest to the supremacy of God, but then justify one's absence from his holy and sacred sanctuary.

It is so easy to be filled with one's own self-importance. Yes, we affirm that God is the creator of heaven and earth, the one before whom the angels sing their hymns of praise. Yes, I am a good person. I break no laws. I hurt no one. I do what is expected of me. And in our self-righteousness we come to believe that we are better than most other people, even persons who go to church.

In the story of the Pharisee and the publican (Luke 18:9-14), Jesus condemns this kind of thinking. Jesus dispels any excuse one may have for being too busy for God, and he censures anyone who thinks she or he is better than another individual. Jesus tells of the proud and haughty Pharisee who struts into the temple in self-admiration, expounds upon the fact that he is the perfect religious person, and boasts that he is better than any other individual, especially the publican.

Then Jesus turns the listener's attention to the publican, a man who is conscious of the fact that he is a sinner. A man who is too ashamed even to look heavenward. A man who pleads for God's mercy and forgiveness.

Jesus shocks his audience by saying of the two, the publican is the more honorable worshiper. If we could step into the culture of

November 15, 1992
(Epis/Pres/Meth/UCC - October 25, 1992)

the audience to which Jesus addressed this teaching, we would know that the people held the Pharisees in great esteem, for they were the learned religious leaders of the community. No one would ever question a Pharisee's religious perfection. On the other hand, a publican was held in disdain. A publican was a Jewish man who collected taxes from his Jewish compatriots for the occupying Roman government. Worse yet, the publican made his wage by overtaxing the people. Now Jesus says of the two the publican is the more honorable. Jesus offers his reason with these often quoted words. "For every one who exalts himself will be humbled, but he who humbles himself will be exalted."

Jesus places importance upon the individual who has a contrite heart. Before God no one can boast. This is something the Pharisee, with his sanctimonious attitude, could not entertain; but the publican, recognizing his imperfections, could. Jesus calls us all to be humble, for before God no person can stand.

Each night after Ozzie Nelson put his two sons, David and Ricky, to bed, he would kneel between the beds, place a hand on each of the boy's chests, and sing the Lord's prayer. We are to be submissive before God, willing to kneel before the Deity in admiration and praise. We are to join in the heavenly chorus, glorifying the name of our Creator.

Let us guard ourselves against the behavior of the Pharisee, thinking we are too important to kneel before God. Instead, let us imitate the publican, a man who was so aware of his unworthiness that he dared not look into the face of God. Despite how good we may think we are, all of us when pressed would have to confess to countless sins of commission and omission.

President Jimmy Carter recited the same verse of Scripture every morning as he walked to the Oval office: "Let the words of my mouth and the meditations of my heart be acceptable in thy sight, O Lord, my strength and my Redeemer." We must live our lives acknowledging that Christ is present every moment. Never once should we think of ourselves as being self-sufficient enough to journey forth without the blessing of Christ. We must be certain that every thought, every word, every action, truly reflects that Christ is at the center of our lives.

Dolores Hope, the wife of comedian Bob Hope, had a chapel built adjoining their Palm Springs home. The chapel allows Dolores to go to Mass every day. She reasons: "We eat three times a day. Why shouldn't we go to church once a day?"

Let us kneel before our Lord out of respect, and awe, and love, seeking forgiveness and a divine blessing.

Ronald H. Love
Summit United Methodist Church
Erie, Pennsylvania

Proper 26

Lutheran: Twenty-fourth Sunday after Pentecost
Roman Catholic: Thirty-first Sunday of the Year
Episcopalian: Proper 26 (November 1)
Pres/Meth/UCC: Twenty-first after Pentecost (November 1)

Lessons:

Lutheran:	Ex. 34:5-9	2 Thess. 1:1-5, 11-12	Luke 19:1-10
Roman Catholic:	Wis. 11:22-12:2	2 Thess. 1:11-2:2	Luke 19:1-10
Episcopal:	Is. 1:10-20	2 Thess. 1;1-5(6-10) 11-12	Luke 19:1-10
Pres/Meth/UCC:	Hag. 2:1-9	2 Thess. 1:5-12	Luke 19:1-10

Introductions to the Lessons

Lesson 1

(1) *Exodus 34:5-9* (**Luth**). Again Moses is called to go to the top of Mt. Sinai to receive from Yahweh another copy of the Ten Commandments, because in his righteous anger Moses broke the original tablets of stone upon which the commandments were written. The Lord comes to Moses and assures him that he is a God of compassion, love, and faithfulness. He keeps his promises and forgives sin.

(2) *Isaiah 1:10-20* (**Epis**). Judah is compared to the sin cities of Sodom and Gomorrah. Yet in their wickedness they are very religious. But God hates their assemblies and ceremonies. He calls upon them to seek justice and do what is right. In spite of their wickedness, God assures them that if they repent, he will forgive and bless them.

(3) *Haggai 2:1-9* (**Pres/Meth/UCC**). Cyrus the Great defeated the Babylonians who forced the Jews into exile. Then Cyrus allowed them to return to Jerusalem to rebuild their temple. Haggai the prophet was among the returnees. He encouraged the leaders and people to start rebuilding the temple which he said would be more splendid than Solomon's.

Lesson 2

2 Thessalonians 1:1-5, 11-12 (**Luth/Epis**); *2 Thess. 1:5-12* (**Pres/Meth/UCC**). In this first of three readings from II Thessalonians we learn that the church in Thessalonica is enduring persecution. Paul assures his people that God's judgment will come upon

The Minister's Annual Manual

their persecutors and that God will relieve their suffering. Prayers are offered that their faith may prevail.

Gospel

Luke 19:1-10 (**Luth/Epis/Pres/Meth/UCC**). Jesus was on his final trip to Jerusalem. Jericho was the last town he passed through before triumphantly entering Jerusalem on Palm Sunday. As he was passing through Jericho, Jesus saw a short man up a tree. Jesus called Zaccheus to come down and they went to his home for dinner. The result was that Zaccheus became a repentant and believing man.

Theme: No matter how bad we have been and no matter how much others disapprove of us, Jesus is willing to accept and forgive us.

Thought for the day: All of us have done things for which we are ashamed. No matter how hard we try to correct what was done, some people will never let us forget the wrong we committed. Jesus recognizes a penitent heart and will forgive you of all wrongdoing.

Prayer of meditation: Dear Lord and heavenly Father, parent of us all, we are thankful for your vigilant care and protection. Knowing that you are with us each moment of the day gives us a sense of calm and assurance. When confronted with a crisis or an uncertain situation, we find solace that you are our guardian. We know the promises of the Scriptures are our promises, and we claim those words of truth this very day. We know the miracles of the Scriptures are our miracles, and we claim that authority this day.

Call to worship: (unison prayer) As we gather together to worship your holy name, let your spirit dwell among us, resting upon us, empowering us. Through this service of worship may we once again be encouraged to go forth into the world as your faithful and obedient disciples.

Prayer of adoration: Let our prayers be lifted to your throne as sweet incense of love and adoration. May our voices join with the voices of the angels and archangels who surround your heavenly throne, that in one voice we may sing praises unto you. Allow our steps to walk the path of disciples of old, that we may be an ever present witness for you.

Prayer of confession: Dear Lord, receive from us the confession of Zacchaeus who spoke these words, "Behold, Lord, the half of my goods I give to the poor; and if I have defrauded anyone of anything,

I restore it fourfold." And may we in turn hear the pronouncement of Jesus, "Today salvation has come to this house."

Prayer of dedication of gifts and self: Jesus spoke, "Unto whomsoever much is given, of him shall be much required." Dear Lord, we who have been given so much now return joyfully unto you a part of our blessings. We do so not grudgingly, but gratefully, acknowledging our indebtedness to you.

Sermon title: The Seeking Soul

Sermon thesis: All of us share in the life of Zacchaeus. We have done things for which we are ashamed. We have done things that continue to plague us with guilt. And there are people who will never let us forget our transgressions. This is why, like Zacchaeus, we need to be forgiven and accepted by Jesus.

Hymn for the day: *"Chief of sinners though I be"*. This hymn reminds us that Jesus came to seek and save those who are lost. The author, William McComb, was born in Coleraine County, Londonderry, Ireland, in 1793 and was for many years a bookseller in Belfast. He died in 1870.

Announcements for next week: (Proper 27)
   Sermon title: Children of the Resurrection
   Sermon theme: We have no fear of death because of the promise of the resurrection.
   Sermon summary: All of us have many questions regarding death and the life hereafter. The thought of death brings with it the fear of the unknown. Jesus dispels our fears by sharing with us the promise of the resurrection and the glory and serenity of God's heavenly paradise.

Children's object talk:

Zacchaeus

Objects: None required
Lesson: To understand what it means to be forgiven and accepted by Jesus.

HAVE THE CHILDREN select different parts from the story of Zacchaeus to act out. Some will need to be the crowd, one person Zacchaeus, another person Jesus. The upper step in the sanctuary can be the sycamore tree. As the pastor recites the story of Zacchaeus the children are to act it out. The crowd is to keep Zacchaeus from the street. Zacchaeus must climb a tree to see Jesus. Jesus comes along and calls Zacchaeus down from the tree and goes to his home. When the play is completed, explore the feelings of the children as they acted each part. Demonstrate how a person feels when she/he is excluded. Discuss how a person feels when she/he is accepted and forgiven.

The sermon:
The Seeking Soul

Hymns:
Beginning of worship: O For a Thousand Tongues to Sing
Sermon hymn: Amazing Grace! How Sweet the Sound
End of worship: Come, Thou Fount of Every Blessing

Scripture: Luke 19:1-10

Sermon Text: *"Today salvation has come to this house."*

IN FILMING THE MOVIE "Jesus of Nazerath", Ernest Borgnine played the role of the centurion who stood at the foot of the cross, looking up into the face of the crucified Jesus of Nazerath. Since this was a movie, actors only came on the set when needed; so instead of having the actor portraying Jesus before him, Borgnine stared at an "X" chalk mark. In such a sterile setting, Borgnine had a difficult time capturing the emotions that the Roman soldier must have experienced at that tragic moment. In order to feel the part, Borgnine asked someone to read Luke's account of the crucifixion. As the words were being read, Borgnine felt more and more uncomfortable, ashamed that like the first centurion he failed to acknowledge the Son of God in his own life. Then something miraculous happened—the chalk mark suddenly was transformed into the face of Jesus, lifelike and clear. Captivated by the revelation, Borgnine realized how the centurion who first stood at the foot of the cross must have been affected; in all sincerity he repeated the soldier's words: "Certainly this man was innocent!"

To look into the face of Jesus, to touch the hem of his garment, to listen to his teachings, to be invited to share a meal at his table, to be touched by his hand, and to receive the comfort of his blessing will change a person forever. If you choose to come into the presence of Jesus, you will be empowered by his grace and mercy, your sins will be forgiven, strength will be restored to your weary body, your self-esteem will be enhanced, and you will have the assurance that the promises of the Gospels are for all believers.

Zacchaeus understood. Zacchaeus was not a popular man in Jericho. He was despised by all the citizens, for he was the tax collector; demanding money from his Jewish neighbors to finance the occupying Roman army—purposely overcharging for his own personal gain. Eventually Zacchaeus became frazzled with his occupation, and desired to change from his life of debauchery. When he learned Jesus of Nazareth was visiting the city, Zacchaeus knew the chance for a new life awaited him. Being small of stature and not well liked, he was unable to elbow his way to the front of the crowd to greet Jesus with an outstretched hand. Refusing to surrender his one chance to meet Jesus, Zacchaeus climbed a sycamore tree to see his Lord.

As Jesus walked along the dust-covered street, he looked up and saw Zacchaeus perilously balanced on the limb of a tree. With the ability to understand the plight of any troubled soul, Jesus cried out with compassion, "Zacchaeus, make haste and come down; for I must stay at your house today." Zacchaeus quickly climbed down out of the tree, confused and humbled, yet ready to receive Jesus as a guest in his home. The crowd was astonished, murmuring among themselves, for they could not accept Jesus going to the home of a tax collector. And as they gossiped, the point of Jesus' teaching went unnoticed, that acceptance and forgiveness will be bestowed upon any sinner who confesses her/his misdeeds. As the two men broke bread together, Zacchaeus was made aware of his sin; he repented and made arrangement for restitution, and experienced the joy of forgiveness. (Luke 19:1-10)

Everyone of us has the need to join Zacchaeus in the sycamore tree, for not one of us lives without blemish. We too need to look into the face of Jesus and know that we are forgiven.

In the October, 1739, edition of "Poor Richard's Almanac", Benjamin Franklin made this astute observation: "Sin is not hurtful because it is forbidden but it is forbidden because it's hurtful." This is the message that the Scriptures convey to us in each reading: God wants to protect us from self-destructive acts and prevent us from behaving in ways that will be disrespectful of others. Christ wants it to be known throughout the land that all people are loved, accepted, and forgiven.

All of us need a second chance, and that is the message that is taught to us from the life of Zacchaeus. We are sorry for the transgressions of our past, guilt ridden by presently indulging in many immoral acts, and uncertain if the future will bring any relief from our decadent behavior. It is reassuring to know that Jesus will call us by name, beckoning us to accept him as our Savior. In an old New England cemetery, this epitaph is chiseled on a stone marker: "Here lies the body of Ichabod. Pardon his soul, oh gracious God — He would yours if he were God and you were brother Ichabod." All of us who seek the grace of God desire to be blest with his benevolent spirit.

One day Archbishop Fulton J. Sheen was dining alone in the Statler Hotel in Boston. Looking up from his meal he saw a shoeshine boy in dirty tattered clothes. When the headwaiter spotted the youngster he was immediately ushered out of the building. Sheen, unable to finish his meal, left the restaurant in search of the lad. Sheen soon found the youngster and in the resulting conversation discovered the boy was expelled from his Catholic school for repeated acts of misbehavior. The Archbishop promised to get the boy back into school, while the boy protested that his expulsion was final. No one, the boy asserted, would be able to convince the Mother Superior to open the doors once more for a disobedient student.

Archbishop Sheen visited the Mother Superior and shared this with her: "I know of three boys who were thrown out of religious schools: one because he was constantly drawing pictures during geography class; another because he was fond of fighting; and the third because he kept revolutionary books hidden under his mattress. No one knows the valedictorians of those classes, but the first boy was Hitler, the second Mussolini, and the third Stalin. I am sure that if the superiors of those schools had given those boys another chance, they might have turned out differently in the world. Maybe this boy will prove himself worthy if you take him back." Unable to dispute the wisdom of Fulton Sheen, the Mother Superior reinstated the boy. Upon graduation, the young man accepted the calling to be a missionary among the Eskimos.

There is a place for all of us in the Kingdom of God. We need only to focus our attention on Jesus as Zacchaeus did on that special day in Jericho; then we too shall hear for ourselves the same words our Savior pronounced on Zacchaeus: "Today salvation has come to this house."

Ronald H. Love
Summit United Methodist Church
Erie, Pennsylvania

Proper 27

Lutheran: Twenty-fifth Sunday after Pentecost
Roman Catholic: Thirty-second Sunday of the Year
Episcopalian: Proper 27 (November 8)
Pres/Meth/UCC: Twenty-second after Pentecost (November 8)

Lessons:

Lutheran:	1 Chron. 29:10-13	2 Thess. 2:13-3:5	Luke 20:27-38
Roman Catholic:	2 Macc. 7:1-2, 9-14	2 Thess. 2:16-3:5	Luke 20:27-38
Episcopal:	Job 19:23-27a	2 Thess. 2:13-3:5	Luke 20:27(28-33) 34-38
Pres/Meth/UCC:	Zech. 7:1-10	2 Thess. 2:13-3:5	Luke 20:27-38

Introductions to the Lessons

Lesson 1

(1) *I Chronicles 29:10-13* (**Luth**). At the close of King David's 40 year reign, he appealed for funds for the temple to be built by his son, Solomon. The response was tremendous: 190 tons of gold and 380 tons of silver. Instead of thanking the donors, David leads the people in praising God who made it possible.

(2) *Job 19:23-27a* (**Epis**). Job is in the depth of his suffering: physical health gone, family lost, despised by friends. Out of this condition Job expresses his faith that one day he will see God, who will be his vindicator.

(3) *Zechariah 7:1-10* (**Pres/Meth/UCC**). The Israelites have returned to Jerusalem from Babylonian captivity. For many years they fasted for a month in mourning the destruction of the temple. The people asked whether the fast should be continued. Through Zechariah the Lord answered: It is better to do justice and show kindness and mercy to each other.

Lesson 2

2 Thessalonians 2:13-3:5 (**Luth/Epis/Pres/Meth/UCC**). Pastor Paul prays for his people in Thessalonica. He thanks God that they were called through the Gospel and sanctified by the Spirit. He prays for their comfort and well-being in the faith. They also are asked to pray for him that God's Word may spread and conquer.

Gospel

Luke 20:27-38 (**Luth/Epis/Pres/Meth/UCC**); *Luke 20:27, 34-38* (**Epis**). During the last week of Jesus' life, the Sadducees, who do not believe in the resurrection of the dead,

(Epis/Pres/Meth/UCC - November 8, 1992)

tried to trap Jesus with a tricky hypothetical question. If a woman had seven husbands, which one would be her husband in the resurrection? Jesus pointed out that in heaven there is no marriage, but the resurrected ones are like angels.

Theme: We have no fear of death because of the promise of the resurrection.

Thought for the day: For many of us death seems like a dark curtain, hiding us from a scary forbidden zone. We fear death because of its uncertainty. Our fear has now been cast aside as we live in the knowledge and promise of the resurrection.

Prayer of meditation: Dear Lord, let us acknowledge this day that you are the potter and we are the clay. Mold us and form us into vessels worthy to hold your spirit. We are aware that we are vessels with clay feet, imperfect, easily broken, flawed, but still beautiful enough and important enough and unique enough to be called your special creation. May we allow ourselves to be used to bring forth your kingdom on earth as it is in heaven.

Call to worship:
Pastor: O give thanks to the Lord, call on his name, make known his deeds among the peoples!
People: Sing to him, sing praises to him, tell of all his wonderful works!
Pastor: Glory is his holy name; let the hearts of those who seek the Lord rejoice!
People: Remember the wonderful works that he has done, the wonders he wrought, the judgments he uttered.
(I Chronicles 16:8-13)

Prayer of adoration: The angels of heaven sing: "Holy, holy, holy is the Lord God Almighty, who was and is and is to come! Worthy are you, our Lord and God, to receive glory and honor and power, for you did create all things, and by your will they exist and were created." We join the angels in their song of triumph, declaring the majesty and power of our God. May we fall prostrate before your throne in humble submission to your nobility.

Prayer of confession: Dear Lord, we are ashamed of our actions. We have spoken words that were unkind. We have shunned the very person we were to befriend. We have entertained thoughts of lust and passion. We have failed to witness to those who have no faith. We did not invite into your home those who are lost and lonely.

Worse yet, in the coming week we may act in the same ungodly manner. We ask now to be forgiven of these our transgressions, and seek from you the strength of spirit to be more Christlike in the days ahead.

Prayer of dedication of gifts and self: Dear Lord, you have taught us that we "cannot serve God and mammon." Our coming before your altar this morning is our declaration that we have chosen to serve you, and have forsaken the material gains of this world. We affirm the heavenly kingdom and its precious blessings, and allow not the objects of this earthly paradise to blind us from that which is sacred in the heavens.

Sermon title: Children of the Resurrection

Sermon thesis: All of us have many questions regarding death and the life hereafter. The thought of death brings with it the fear of the unknown. Jesus dispels our fears by sharing with us the promise of the resurrection and the glory and serenity of God's heavenly paradise.

Hymn for the day: *"Jesus Christ, my sure defense"* Although this German hymn has been described as "of first rank" and "an acknowledged masterpiece of Christian poetry," we do not know who wrote it. It was published in Berlin in 1653, in a hymnal directed by Luise Henriette von Brandenburg. The preface to the hymnal states that she contributed four hymns. It has been suggested that she included them because they were favorites or perhaps she wrote them in Dutch and they were translated to German for the collection. (She herself did not have command of enough High German to have written them as they stand.) Luise Henriette (1627-1666), daughter of the Prince of Nassau-Orange, was married to Elector Friedrich Wilhelm of Brandenburg. One of her four sons became King Friedrich I of Prussia. The hymn is a marvelous statement of our confidence in eternal life.

Announcements for next week: (Proper 28)

Sermon title: Proclaiming the Love of God or Whistling in the Dark?

Sermon theme: You are called to obedience, but you are not left alone.

Sermon summary: A Christian cannot expect to be exempt from the same hate by the world which resulted in the death of Jesus. Our fate may not be a martyr's death, but Christians must remember that they are called to obedience even if it means the cross.

(Epis/Pres/Meth/UCC - November 8, 1992)

Children's object talk:
The Meaning of the Resurrection

Objects: Enough paper butterflies for the entire congregation to color.
Lesson: The butterfly is a symbol of the resurrection.
Outline:
1. Discuss the life cycle of a butterfly.
2. Compare the butterfly to the concept of resurrection.
3. Have the children pass out butterflies to the entire congregation to be colored.
4. Have the colored butterflies returned the following week and displayed in the sanctuary.

RELATE HOW A BUTTERFLY makes the transition from a caterpillar to a cocoon to a beautiful, colorful butterfly. Explain how the butterfly is a symbol of the resurrection because it demonstrates the birth of new life. Then have the children distribute among the entire congregation — persons of all ages — paper butterflies to color. Instruct the congregation to color the butterflies in a bright and beautiful way. Then next week the children will collect the butterflies and they will be posted on the walls of the sanctuary as a symbol and remainder of the resurrection.

The sermon:
Children of the Resurrection

Hymns:
Beginning of worship: Come, Thou Almighty King
Sermon hymn: Jesus Christ Is Risen Today
End of worship: Come, Ye Faithful, Raise the Strain

Scripture: Luke 20:27-38

Sermon Text: *"...for they cannot die any more, because they are equal to angels and are children of God, being children of the resurrection."* v. 36

JOHN JAY WAS A RESPECTED POLITICIAN, best remembered for his signature on the Constitution. He was also a man of sincere religious faith, once serving as the president of the American Bible

Society. When John was 58 his beloved wife Sally became gravely ill. He and the children kept a vigilant watch over wife and mother, and all were present when she died on May 20, 1802. Shortly after her passing, John escorted the children into the adjoining room where he bade them to sit. John somberly walked over to the stand where the family Bible rested. With great care he picked up the sacred book; he slowly and respectfully turned the pages until he found his desired passage, I Corinthians 15. Affectionately he read Paul's account and interpretation of the Resurrection, concluding with these words: "When this mortal body shall have put on immortality, then shall be brought to pass the saying that is written, 'Death is swallowed up in victory. O death, where is thy sting? O grave, where is thy victory?' " Tenderly he closed the Bible and placed it on the stand. Walking over to the window, he gazed upon the hills which sloped westward. There John stood, comforted by the promise that Sally was dwelling in the kingdom of heaven.

Death is something that we all fear. The fear of our own death — when it will come? Will it be painful? What will it be like in the realm beyond? We fear the death of one we love — how will I deal with my grief? How will I deal with my loneliness? How will I ever manage on my own? Death is something we know is in the near or distant future, so all of us seek solace for this terrifying enigma.

Jesus was asked about the mystery of death. Would the relationships on earth be the same as in heaven? What would the life beyond be like. To that inquiry Jesus offered this response: "The children of this age are given in marriage; but those who are accounted worthy to attain to that age and to the resurrection from the dead neither marry nor are given in marriage, for they cannot die any more, because they are equal to angels and are children of God, being children of the resurrection." (Luke 20:27-38)

What a beautiful, wonderful, and reassuring answer Jesus offers us who fear the uncertainty of death. In heaven we will be equal to angels. In heaven we will take on an angelic countenance. In heaven we will be the children of the resurrection. Upon death, you and I, our friends and loved ones, will join the heavenly throng surrounding the throne of God. There will be a place for us at the bosom of our heavenly Parent.

George Washington believed in life after death. When his mother died in 1789 he wrote a letter to his sister expressing the gratitude he had that his mother lived a long and healthy life. Washington concluded his letter saying, "Under these considerations, and the hope that she is translated to a happier place, it is the duty of her relatives to yield due submission to the decrees of the Creator."

As difficult as it is, we must yield death to the Creator of life. We must believe that the God who has a plan for our earthly pilgrimage has an equally appropriate plan for our heavenly pilgrimage. In the promise of the resurrection we know that death is not the final stage of living, but it is merely a transition point into a more glorious and peaceful existence.

As President Hoover was concluding his banquet speech commemorating the fiftieth anniversary of the discovery of the electric light, the inventor, Thomas Alva Edison, collapsed. Gravely ill, Edison was taken back to his home in West Orange, New Jersey. He grew steadily weaker from uremic poisoning. On October 17, 1931, Edison spoke his last words: "It's very beautiful over there." A man of science, Edison knew only how to report factual information. With a glimpse into the afterlife, he indeed told us that it is beautiful in God's heaven.

Jesus succinctly told us that in heaven we will join with the angels, those magnificantly white-robed children of God. Could there be a more beautiful sight than seeing God enthroned, surrounded by an angelic chorus? But the beauty is more than physical; it is spiritual. It is a beauty of spirit where one feels serene and at peace.

Many of us can remember the tragedy of December 13, 1977, when the DC-3 carrying the University of Evansville basketball team crashed shortly after takeoff. Because it was a drizzling night, it has often been called "the night it rained tears." Ten years later the college dedicated a memorial plaque to Coach Bobby Watson and the 14 players who perished. During his address at the dedication service, Professor Philip Ott recalled that night: "It rained and rained the next two days. And that rain was symbolic of the tears that fell on our campus, and it was not until Sunday that the sun came out."

The thought of death ... the experience of death ... can bring tears to all of us. Be comforted by the teaching of Jesus that in three days the sun will shine, for there is a resurrection.

Ronald H. Love
Summit United Methodist Church
Erie, Pennsylvania

Proper 28

Lutheran: Twenty-sixth Sunday after Pentecost
Roman Catholic: Thirty-third Sunday of the Year
Episcopalian: Proper 28 (November 15)
Pres/Meth/UCC: Twenty-third after Pentecost (November 15)

Lessons:

Lutheran:	Mal. 4:1-2a	2 Thess. 3:6-13	Luke 21:5-19
Roman Catholic:	Mal. 4:1-2a	2 Thess. 3:7-12	Luke 21:5-19
Episcopal:	Mal. 3:13-4:2a, 5-6	2 Thess. 3:6-13	Luke 21:5-19
Pres/Meth/UCC:	Mal. 4:1-6	2 Thess. 3:6-13	Luke 21:5-19

Introductions to the Lessons

Lesson 1

Malachi 4:1-2a (**Luth**); *Mal. 3:13-4:2a* (**Epis**); *Mal. 4:1-6* (**Pres/Meth/UCC**). The last book of the Old Testament, Malachi, tells us of the final day of judgment. Evil people will be burned up but the obedient will receive healing, freedom, and joy. Until that day comes the people are to remember the Law given by Moses and they are to look forward to the coming of Elijah, who will prepare for Messiah's coming.

Lesson 2

2 Thessalonians 3:6-13 (**Luth/Epis/Pres/Meth/UCC**). The Thessalonian church has a problem. Some members are too lazy to work and they meddle in other people's business. Some of them are Gnostics who believe they did not need to work because they are already in heaven. Others expected Jesus to return any day now and thus there was no need to work. In no uncertain terms Paul told the idlers they had to work if they wanted to eat, just as he worked to earn his living.

Gospel

Luke 21:5-19 (**Luth/Epis/Pres/Meth/UCC**). With his disciples Jesus is spending the last week of his life in Jerusalem. Often they were at the temple. The disciples remarked how beautiful it was. Jesus predicted that some day the temple would be rubble. (This happened in 70 A.D. when the Romans destroyed the edifice.) Jesus forecast hard times ahead, but he assured them of his support and protection.

Theme: You are called to obedience, but you are not left alone.

(Epis/Pres/Meth/UCC - November 15, 1992)

Thought for the day: The destruction which comes through disobedience to God is not God's choice but is the inevitable result of disregarding the will of God as revealed in Jesus Christ.

Prayer of meditation: Almighty God, whose creative word brought us into being and who desires nothing but good for us, strengthen us that we might be obedient to your Word, your will, and thus be your agent in preventing the destruction and disorder which always fill the vacuum and folllow when your children (and creatures) are disobedient. We pray for this strength in the name of Jesus, your Son and our Lord. Amen.

Call to worship:
The Lord is here!
　The Lord is everywhere, including this place.
The Lord wishes us to respond in love, obedience, and worship!
　We hear the voice of God whenever we listen.
Come, let us worship the Lord our God.
　We worship in song, prayers, the hearing of scripture, and in our daily lives!

Prayer of adoration: Most gracious and ever-loving God, who created and creates us as does a father and a mother and who created and creates all that is; we bow before you at this hour to glorify you and to worship your holy name. Open our eyes that we may see you, free our ears that we may hear your word, release our fears that we may follow you, and give voice to sing your praises as we commit our souls to you. We pray in the name of Jesus, your son and our risen Lord. Amen.

Prayer of confession: Hear my prayer, Almighty God: I confess I have failed to love you enough to serve you with a single mind, I have failed to be obedient and have followed my own desires; I have failed to treat all your children as my neighbors and as my brothers and sisters; and I have failed to acknowledge that you alone are worthy of worship. Hear my prayer of confession, cleanse me of my guilt, help me to understand that you have received me again into your arms. I pray for this gift in the name of Jesus Christ, my Lord. Amen.

Sermon title: Proclaiming the Love of God or Whistling in the Dark?

Sermon thesis: In today's world, as in the ages past, a Christian cannot expect to be exempt from the same hate by the world which resulted in the death of Jesus. Our fate may not be a martyr's death, but Christians must remember that they are called to obedience even if it means the cross.

Hymn for the day: *"Lord, keep us steadfast in your word"* Martin Luther (1483-1546) was born in Eisleben, Germany, and ordained a priest in 1507. While on the faculty at Wittenberg University he became aware of some of the corruptions in the church of his time. From there the story of the Reformation is well-known. A musician himself, Luther encouraged congregational hymn singing and wrote a number of fine hymns. This hymn is a prayer that God will be with us and support and sustain us. It was written in 1541 when the threat of a Turkish invasion of Germany seemed very real. The Elector requested the pastors to offer prayers for the country's protection, in response to which Luther prepared a special service which included this hymn.

Announcements for next week: (Proper 29)
  Sermon title: God Really Does Trust Me
  Sermon theme: God offers you trust; how will you use that greatest of gifts?
  Sermon summary: Serving God in today's world means doing the will of God. Our profession of our love of God means nothing if we ignore God's will.

Children's object talk:
There's Safety in Following Jesus

Objects: A simple toy tent, or a handkerchief and twigs and some putty which can be used to make a "tent," perhaps with some of the children helping.
Lesson: When you are with Jesus, Jesus protects you from fear.
Outline: 1. We all know what it means to be afraid.
  2. When we hold our parents' hands, our fear does not rule us.
  3. In the past, someone's tent provided safety.
  4. Jesus' presence can take away our fear.

I STRONGLY SUSPECT YOU ARE A GOOD BIT LIKE ME; there are times when I am afraid. Are you sometimes afraid? What are some of the things that frighten you?
  (After the children have had a chance to think about it and perhaps two or three will actually answer the question if you have them gathered about you, continue the narration:)
  Sometimes I'm afraid for no reason, sometimes I'm afraid of what I don't understand; sometimes the fear is of something that is real. In all of these times, when I was a child I felt much better if my

father or mother was with me and held my hand. Even when I was walking down the darkest of streets, I felt much better if one of my parents was with me and perhaps was holding on to me ... I simply felt more safe in their presence.

Here, let's make a little tent. Let's put these little sticks in some of this putty to make them stand up by themselves. We'll put this longer stick in the center of the four corners. Now, we'll put this handkerchief over the sticks and we have a little tent, or at least something we can imagine to be a tent. Oh yes, let's roll up one side of the tent.

Now we need to imagine that we have been chased across the desert and the owner of the tent has invited us in. According to the old law of the desert, if we are in someone else's tent, the one who has been chasing us cannot come in. Even though we're having dinner in this tent, and our enemy can see us because this side of the tent is rolled up, he/she can't come in to harm us. We can relax because we are protected by our host.

Well, that's the way it is when we are with Jesus and Jesus is with us. We are not afraid because Jesus is with us. No matter what makes us afraid Jesus is with us and that is what counts.

The sermon:

Proclaiming The Love of God or Whistling in the Dark?

Hymns:
   Beginning of worship: "Holy, Holy, Holy, Lord God Almighty"
   Sermon hymn: "Must Jesus Bear the Cross Alone"
   End of worship: A Charge to Keep I Have

Scripture: Luke 21:5-19

Sermon Text: *"This will be a time for you to bear testimony."* v. 13

MANY YEARS AGO NOW, during the Vietnam war, a minister friend of mine together with his church's high school group wrote a cantata which was published by a national publisher. A part of the cantata included a newsboy's cry of the headlines which mentioned various kinds of tragedies.

The cantata was written as a testimony in the world of that day and effectively gave witness to the Christian message. In re-reading this cantata a short time ago, I realized every one of the "headlines" used in that song were as valid today as when first written.

You see, my brothers and my sisters in Christ, there are catastrophes in the world today, and there have been for centuries. The message of Jesus in the Gospel lesson read this morning is that it is in the face of catastrophe that we are to bear witness. The most effective time to bear testimony to the presence of God through Jesus Christ is not when all is peace and harmony; it is in the darkness of despair and destruction that the light of Christ is most clearly seen.

Did you catch it when we read the gospel lesson? In the talk of the destruction of the temple, the earthquakes, and the wars — did you catch what Jesus said?

Jesus said that in the midst of all this destruction, wars, earthquakes, and when you who are faithful will be brought before the synagogues and the courts, that will be the time for you to bear testimony. In this time of great tribulation, Jesus said, will be the time when you can be most effective in your testimony about the love of God and the demands of God.

Jesus said, and is saying, that at the very moment when panic will be gripping the world and by human standards you have every reason to be frightened, that is the very time when you must, and can, bear witness and testimony.

Not only that, but you will not be alone; God is with you! You don't even have to worry about what you will say; you only have to be willing to say what God will give you to say! After all, the message is from God; you are the messenger.

That little old lady who dropped two copper coins in the temple offering in Jerusalem didn't realize the testimony and witness she was making, nor could she have understood the great controversy she ignited.

It was her offering of an amount so small that almost all of us today in our society could lose without being aware of it, that was the catalyst for the discussion which follows.

After Jesus had made his comment on the greatness of her offering in contrast to the little if any sacrifice involved in the huge sums given by the rich, some of the people around began to look at the beauty of the temple. Perhaps some of the people around Jesus took a kind of vicarious pride over the appearance of the temple and may have been thinking something like: "What this rabbi says may have some truth in it, but unless there were those with the ability to give huge sums of money, the beautiful temple raised to the glory of God would not be a reality."

Then, as often happened in his ministry, Jesus looked far deeper and he looked much farther down the road of life on which they were all walking. With sadness in his heart, he said terrible days were coming and this temple, with all its beauty and with all its mighty strength, would be destroyed and not one of the stones would be left one upon the other. In effect, Jesus was saying: the destruction will be so immense that you will not realize that the temple was ever here.

To understand the impact of what this outburst would have on the minds and hearts of those of his listeners who really "heard" him, we must remember that the temple was the very heart of Jewish worship. In a way we Christians cannot fully comprehend, the temple represented the very presence of God. A synagogue could be destroyed with little effect on the People of God as a whole, but the destruction of the temple was unthinkable.

Yet, it was in this context, plus the other calamities of which Jesus spoke, that he said they would be called upon to be faithful witnesses.

However, we must understand that this passage has little relevance for us if we merely see it as a historical reference and of the ability of Jesus to see into the future. Actually, there might have been a good many knowledgeable people of the era who would have been so able to read the course of historical events that they could have predicted the total destruction of Jerusalem, including the temple.

The importance of this passage for us is that we are to understand that in the days of our lives, the days we have been assigned, there will be terrible times of catastrophe. There may well be persecution when the people called Christians will, in the eyes of the world, be alone and outnumbered.

It is in these kinds of days when our witness is most needed and will be most effective — and we will not be alone. God through Christ is with us!

I believe Jesus was so sad because he realized his message would not be heard by the people, that his message would be ignored. Even today, when the Christian makes true testimony, the world will say that we are whistling in the dark, searching hopelessly for strength in a faith that world history has passed by.

Christians understand, however, that as we bear true testimony to the love of God revealed by Jesus Christ, we are walking hand-in-hand with the Son of God, the Savior of the world — we are not alone!

Miles Walter Jackson
United Methodist Church
Bow, Washington

Proper 29

Lutheran: Twenty-seventh Sunday after Pentecost
Roman Catholic: Thirty-fourth Sunday of the Year,
Christ the King (November 22)
Episcopalian: Proper 29 (November 22)
Pres/Meth/UCC: Christ the King (November 22)

Lessons:

Lutheran:	Is. 52:1-6	1 Cor. 15:54-58	Luke 19:11-27
Roman Catholic:	2 Sam. 5:1-3	Col. 1:12-20	Luke 23:35-43
Episcopal:	Jer. 23:1-6	Col. 1:11-20	Luke 23:35-43
Pres/Meth/UCC:	2 Sam. 5:1-5	Col. 1:11-20	John 12:9-19

Introductions to the Lessons

Lesson 1

(1) *Isaiah 52:1-6* (**Lutheran**). Yahweh speaks directly to His people in Babylon. They are hostages without freedom and without nationhood. His message is one of hope. Things will get better. The nation shall be restored.

(2) *2 Samuel 5:1-3* (**RC**); *5:1-5* (**Pres/Meth/UCC**). Similar to the age of Jesus, David was 30 years old when the people came to Hebron to anoint him king. His past leadership affirms his kingship

(3) *Jeremiah 23:1-6* (**Epis**) What is the difference between a true and a false prophet? A false prophet scatters the sheep, while a true prophet gathers the people. When David becomes king, his people will then be secure.

Lesson 2

(1) *1 Corinthians 15:54-58* (**Luth**) When this physical body dies, what kind of body shall we be given? A person is never left without a body, which is needed for identification and communication. Our new body will be one sculptured for a spiritual world: imperishable and immortal.

(2) *Colossians 1:11-20* (**Epis/Presb/Meth/UCC**); *1:12-20* (**RC**). Christ is absolutely preeminent in every way. The universe was created through him. In him we see the full nature of God. Through him we see the Redeemer who restores a fallen world to himself through the cross. As a result, grace has come in the relationship between God and humanity.

The Minister's Annual Manual

Gospel

(1) *Luke 19:11-27* (**Luth**). Jesus tells the parable of the pounds. Each person has received a gift; whether it is ten, five, or 1 pound. Upon returning from a journey, he asks for an accounting. The man with one pound was condemned for not investing it.

(2) *Luke 23:35-43* (**RC/Epis**). While hanging on the cross, Jesus was asked to save himself. But, what if he did? The world would have been forever lost. Out of the horrible mess on Good Friday came a saved sould in response to the thief's plea, "Remember Me."

(3) *John 12:9-19* (**Pres/Meth/UCC**). Jesus is at Bethany, just outside Jerusalem. The next day he triumphantly enters the city to the shouts of "Hosannas". However, the Pharisees were jealous of his popularity, "Look, the whole world is following him."

Theme: God offers you trust; how will you use that greatest of gifts?

Thought for the day: Each day is an opportunity to prove (test) our faith in God. Our actions each day of our life are to reflect God's gift of faith!

Prayer of meditation: Almighty God, who has loaned us our days on earth and who has loaned us the use of this planet, strengthen me that I may prove to be faithful in your service. As my faith is tested each day by events which could overwhelm me, help me to be faithful in that which you have entrusted to me. I pray for this strength in the name of Jesus, your Son and my Lord. Amen.

Call to worship:
The Lord is creator of all and everything.
  The Lord is the one who has given us breath and life and love.
The Lord has entrusted us with much of his creation.
  We are accountable only to God through Jesus Christ his Son. Come, let us worship the Lord our God.
  We worship the God of creation in many ways and especially in the way we treat and care for his creation.

Prayer of adoration: O most holy and creative God who, just as a loving parent offers us greater and more abundant life by granting us more responsibility and trust, so you have also entrusted us with your creation. We love you and adore you; you alone are worthy of worship. Help us to prove worthy of your trust; we pray in the name of Jesus, your Son and our risen Lord. Amen.

Prayer of confession: Hear my prayer of confession Almighty God, for I have failed to express my love for you in the ways I treat your creation; I have consumed but have failed to help replace what I have used. In my eagerness to be happy, I have failed to remember that true happiness is worshiping and glorifying you. As I offer my prayer of confession, O Lord, help me to remember true confession leads me to a changed life, one which will be lived in the light of Jesus Christ, my Lord. Amen.

Prayer of dedication of gifts and self:

Sermon title: God Really Does Trust Me

Sermon thesis: Serving God in today's world means doing the will of God. Our profession of our love of God means nothing if we ignore God's will.

Hymn for the day: "The clouds of judgment gather" This hymn and "Jerusalem the golden" are translations of portions of Bernard of Cluny's *De Contemptu Mundi*, a poem of nearly three thousand lines, describing the evils and vices of his time. Bernard was born in France of English parents some time early in the twelfth century. It is generally assumed that he remained at Cluny until his death. This hymn calls on all "true disciples" to do the will of God, "to let wrong give way to right..."

Announcements for next week: (Christ the King. Last Sunday after Pentecost.)

    Sermon title: Today! In Paradise!

    Sermon theme: With the completion of the church year, the cycle of telling the Gospel is complete, the love of God revealed by Jesus is fully revealed.

    Sermon summary: On this day the cycle of the revelation of God's word through Jesus is complete. Even as we rejoice to the fullest, we are also aware of our responsibility.

Children's object talk:

Remembering the Source of Everything

Objects: Little bags, each of which contain ten pennies. Be sure to have more bags than the number of young children who normally come to worship service.

Lesson: Everything we have comes from God; we are faithful to God in the way we treat his gifts.

Outline: 1. All we have comes from God.
          2. Our offerings to God are a portion of what he gave us.
          3. Being faithful over pennies prepares us to be faithful over more of God's creation.

ONE OF THE THINGS God wants us to remember is that all we have comes as a gift from God. What are some of the gifts God has given us?

(Depending on the age of the children you're working with, you may give them a moment or two to answer. If there is no response, or if the children are too young to respond, you may need to give some answers.)

God gives us air to breath, the sun to warm us. God gives us our mothers and fathers to love us and care for us, and the food we eat comes from the work of God. God made everything, even the stars in the night's sky, the moon, and of course the sun which is so bright it's not good for us to look directly at it.

It's hard, isn't it, to describe or to illustrate all the ways that God's love helps us.

So we need to remember that everything we have comes, one way or another, from God. Also, we are responsible to God for the way we treat his gifts.

In the Bible lesson this morning, Jesus tells of a man who gave some of his servants money to take care of for him. Today I want to give you a couple of ideas of how we can think about this.

Here are some envelopes with something in them. Don't look yet until every one of you has a little bag. Now, open the bags and see what your gift is ... that's right, each of you has been given ten pennies. What will we do with your ten pennies? Many times in the Bible, we are told we are to give back to God one-tenth of what God has first given us. So let's do that. We'll ask the treasurer of the church to come and receive one penny from each of us for the work of God.

(It is likely one or more of the children will not want to give back a penny; if this happens, you might say something humorously about some children being just like some adults.)

But giving God one-tenth (we call it tithing) is not all there is to being a Christian. Jesus says we are to use all of God's gifts in a way that will please God.

So, as you go back to your seats with your nine pennies left, think about how you can use the rest of God's gifts to please God. Maybe you could talk with your parents about this later on today.

The sermon:
God Really Does Trust Me

Hymns:
  Beginning of worship: I'll Praise My Maker While I've Breath
  Sermon hymn: Be Thou My Vision, O Lord of My Heart
  End of worship: Trust and Obey

Scripture: Luke 19:11-27

Sermon Text: *"Trade with these till I come."* v. 13b

IT IS AN EXTRAORDINARY TEACHING, extremely extraordinary if we stop for a moment to really think about it, that we can learn from the Gospel lesson we have just heard: *God trusts us, God trusts even me!* with important work that God wants to be carried out.

The idea that God trusts me to do important work is a vast step beyond the reality that God loves me, as important as is the teaching that God loves us. If God wanted to, God could just simply love me, want the best for me, and desire me so to live in right relationship with my creator that we could spend eternity together.

But for God Almighty, King of the Universe, Creator of all that is, who continues to create, to entrust me with important work is even more difficult to imagine!

I believe God's Holy Spirit this morning wants us to understand, to comprehend, that we are more than recipients of God's love; we are God's agents, stewards who have had entrusted to us work that is essential. As the writer of the book of James says, we are not hearers of the word only; we are to be doers of the word. We need to realize that in this parable Jesus is telling us that we go beyond being doers of the word; we are also trusted stewards with responsibility to proclaim the word to others.

In telling this parable in the way he did to the people who were ready to listen, Jesus was continuing his method of using everyday current (or at least recent) history to give important truths. In this story, in all likelihood, Jesus used a recounting of how Archelaus (son of Herod the Great) was confirmed by the Roman emperor in his ruling of Judea in spite of local opposition who did not want him to be confirmed as King. This was a recounting of events, with a twist that would have been readily understood.

Today's Gospel lesson is a perfect illustration of what many biblical scholars say we need to bear in mind while we're studying scripture. In a nutshell, we are told, most biblical stories have three meanings: 1) what it meant at the time it happened, 2) the meaning the author had in mind when he wrote it down many years later, and 3) the meaning the story has for us today.

This way of looking at the meaning of scripture helps us; it certainly helps keep me from assuming Jesus had some deep hidden meaning behind every word, story, or parable he spoke. Jesus was a practical man and he spoke in ways that the people of his day could clearly understand, particularly if they wanted to "hear" what Jesus was saying/teaching.

When Luke wrote down his account of the life and teachings of Jesus, there would have been many stories about Jesus. Why did Luke remember this story, and why did he include it? I believe it was at least for two reasons: 1) the original group of followers who had been commissioned to carry on the message of God's work through Jesus were dying off, and thus 2) the new followers needed to understand that they too were stewards, they too were responsible for so proclaiming the love of God through Jesus that others might hear the gospel and believe.

God's work needed to be done, and the listeners of that day were the ones to carry it on. They were presented with a God-given gift of trust and responsibility.

Can there be any more important message for us today than that we are called to witness to Jesus, who is the perfect revelation of God?

In this day the Chuch of Jesus Christ, the Body of Jesus Christ, is scorned by so many of our society. This is true not only in our country but in other countries as well. In a recent year-long local church ministry in England, I was struck by the devotion and commitment to Christ on the part of most of the members of the local churches, but I was astonished at how much society is anti-church and anti-Christian.

And this is the important meaning of this Gospel lesson for us: In this day, at this moment, God is calling us to be faithful stewards.

God's Holy Spirit is telling us that God does indeed trust us and is giving us great responsibility. We are not spectators merely observing what is going on about us; we are responsible to God to help God's kingdom to increase. When we are faithful in a little, we become aware of greater responsibility in larger circles.

(Epis/Pres/Meth/UCC - November 22, 1992)

It is my testimony that Almighty God's trust in us is a gift; as we make good use of this gift and are faithful to God, we become aware that we have received even greater responsibility. God is giving us the gift of even greater trust.

The only question now is whether you, and I, will step forward and accept the gift and the responsibility. In our prayers, let us not only thank God for this trust expressed in us but also pray that we may be faithful in carrying out this trust!

Miles Walter Jackson
United Methodist Church
Bow, Washington

NOVEMBER 22, 1992

Last Sunday after Pentecost. Christ the King.

Lessons:

Lutheran:	Jer. 23:2-6	Col. 1:13-20	Luke 23:35-43
Roman Catholic:	2 Sam. 5:1-3	Col. 1:12-20	Luke 23:35-43
Episcopal:	Jer. 23:1-6	Col. 1:11-20	Luke 23:35-43
Pres/Meth/UCC:	2 Sam. 5:1-5	Col. 1:11-20	John 12:9-19

Introductions to the Lessons

Lesson 1

(1) *Jeremiah 23:2-6* (**Luth/Epis**). Through Jeremiah the Lord accuses the shepherds (rulers) of the day of scattering the sheep (people). However, God promises to gather his people under righteous rulers. He will send a king, a son of David, to rule. Then the nation will enjoy peace and security.

(2) *2 Samuel 5:1-5* (**Pres/Meth/UCC**). Since the death of King Saul, Israel needed a new king. The leaders of the Israelite tribes gathered in Hebron and crowned a thirty-year-old man named David to be their next king. After an agreement was made, they anointed David as king who ruled for 40 years.

Lesson 2

Colossians 1:13-20 (**Luth**); *Col. 1:11-20* (**Epis/Pres/Meth/UCC**). Christians belong to the kingdom of Christ. The King is God's Son. The universe was created through him. He is also king of the church. By means of his death he reconciled the world to God. Christ is not only a king but King of kings, absolutely pre-eminent in every way.

Gospel

(1) *Luke 23:35-43* (**Luth/Epis**). Jesus was king until his last breath on the cross. His enemies acknowledged his kingship saying, "If you are the king of the Jews." In writing the title above Jesus' head, Pilate admitted Jesus was ing—"Jesus of Nazareth King of the Jews." The repentant criminal on a nearby cross asked Jesus to remember him when he came into his kingdom.

(1) *John 12:9-19* (**Pres/Meth/UCC**). This is John's account of Jesus' triumphant entry into Jerusalem as king. A great crowd gathered to meet him as he entered the city. They sang praises to him as king of Israel. His coming was interpreted by the church as fulfillment of Zechariah's prophecy that their king was coming in the person of Jesus.

November 22, 1992

Theme: With the completion of the church year, the cycle of telling the Gospel is complete, the love of God revealed by Jesus is fully revealed.

Thought for the day: Jesus has now been fully revealed to us, from his birth through his death and resurrection, and the Good News has been proclaimed completely. Now, what will I do about it?

Prayer of meditation: Almighty God, the message of your love has been fully revealed in the gift of your Son to be our Savior. As I prepare for this worship service, may my mind be completely open to you that I may accept your gift of salvation more completely than ever before. With that acceptance, may I be committed completely to doing your will and sharing the Good News of your Son. I pray in the name of Christ my Lord. Amen.

Call to worship:
Jesus Christ, the Son of God, sits upon his throne.
  Jesus Christ, Savior of the world, has been fully revealed.
Let us enter into the very presence of Almighty God.
  We come to worship God in spirit and in truth.
Come, let us worship the Lord our God.
  We worship our God with timbrel and dance, lute and harp.

Prayer of adoration: O most holy and loving God, our God who loves us so greatly that you have given your only begotten child in the person of Jesus to be our Lord and Savior, we rejoice on this day when the telling of this revelation is complete. O Holy God, help us to see the magnificence of your gift that we may rejoice in every possible way. We pray in the name of your Son, our risen Lord. Amen.

Prayer of confession: It is with contrite hearts, Almighty God, that we your children come before you to confess our sin, to admit our guilt, and to acknowledge we have failed to respond to you by being totally committed to you. Sometimes we have sinned consciously, sometimes our sin is expressed by not doing and by not realizing that we have failed to live up to your glory. On this day of celebration of Christ as our King, help us to begin anew our life of service in the name of Jesus Christ, our Lord. Amen.

Prayer of dedication of gifts and self:

Sermon title: Today! In Paradise!

The Minister's Annual Manual

Sermon thesis: On this day of the Festival of Christ the King which is also the last Sunday after Pentecost, the cycle of the revelation of God's Word through Jesus is complete. Even as we rejoice to the fullest, we are also aware of our responsibility.

Hymn for the day: *"The head that once was crowned with thorns"* The author of some 750 hymns, Thomas Kelley (1769-1855) was to Ireland what Isaac Watts was to England in the transition from the exclusive use of Psalm paraphrases to the use of hymnody in worship. Originally ordained to the Church of England, Kelly later became an independent preacher. A man of high scholastic achievements who daily read the Scriptures in their original languages, Kelly was also a great friend of the poor, especially during the Irish potato famine of the 1840s.

Announcements for this week: (Thanksgiving U.S.)

Sermon title: Remembering to Give Thanks
Sermon theme: Human nature seems to be that we cry out for help and, when help is received, we too often forget to express our gratitude. A Christian expresses thanksgiving to God.
Sermon summary: On this day of Thanksgiving, we are reminded of the gifts of God to us, his children. We are not merely to receive, a major part of our worship is to give thanks to God.

Announcements for next week:

Sermon title: Watch!
Sermon theme: To be ready for the Lord's advent, be alert.
Sermon summary: Christ is to come again one day. Christians may trust in the Gospel and look forward to that advent with joy rather than numbing fear.

Children's object talk:
Celebrating The Good News

Objects: Something obviously of a party nature, perhaps a balloon and one of the "snap crackers" that pop and have something inside, also a real or a toy hoe or rake, plus a Bible.
Lesson: There are many ways to rejoice; sometimes we have a party and sometimes we rejoice by doing what others consider to be work.
Outline:
1. The Story of Jesus which "began" at Christmas has been completely told.
2. It is a great cause for rejoicing, being very happy.
3. Sometimes we want to throw a party; other times we may rejoice by doing work.

November 22, 1992

YOU KNOW, I FEEL LIKE THROWING A PARTY! Perhaps I might say I feel more like celebrating. But, come to think of it, it would be more exact to say that I feel like rejoicing! Yes! That's it; I feel like rejoicing.

Did you know this is a very special day in the life of the church? This is the last Sunday after Pentecost, it is also the last Sunday of the Church Year. Of course, you know that our regular New Year according to our calendar is January 1, but here in the church where we measure things according to the life of Jesus, the first Sunday of the Church Year is four Sundays before Christmas. The first Sunday of the new church year will be next Sunday!

However, back to today! This is the last Sunday of this Church Year and this means that the entire story of Jesus has been told. Now, the complete story of Jesus has been told. In today's reading from the Gospel, Jesus makes clear that God loves us no matter what we have done. Now what are we going to do because of the good news of God's love?

We could have a party with balloons *(blow up the balloon)*, or we could have crackers *(here, pull the tab on the cracker and take out the party hat that's usually inside)*. We might even have cake and ice cream.

But you know, I have a feeling that while God wants us to have a good time, it would make God very happy if we rejoiced so much that we would work for him, the kind of work that would show other people how much God loves them.

In this way, we become like a tool, not like this hoe (or rake) is a tool, but by living in such a way that other people will see the love of God in the way we live.

So, how about rejoicing that way, by showing God's love to everyone we meet!

The sermon:
Today! In paradise!
Hymns:
Beginning of worship: This is the day or God is Here
Sermon hymn: Hail, Thou Once Despised Jesus
End of worship: Rejoice, the Lord Is King

Scripture: Luke 23:35-43

Sermon Text: *"Truly, I say to you: Today you will be with me in paradise."*

TRY TO PLACE YOURSELF as the repentant thief on a cross next to the cross where Jesus of Nazareth is nailed. For whatever reason, a reason about which we can only speculate, this repentant thief has asked for mercy from Jesus.

If you can place yourself in this thief's place, imagine the agony he is suffering. Yet, in the midst of all this pain and the seeming hopelessness of your situation, first of all you defend the innocence of Jesus to the other thief on the third cross on that hill. Then you ask to be remembered when Jesus comes into his kingdom.

As nearly as you can, as you are imagining yourself as the criminal next to Jesus, you look directly at the man hanging on the cross next to yours, from all earthly appearances in just as an impossible situation as is yours, and you say: "Jesus, remember me when you come into your kingdom!"

Perhaps it is difficult, if not impossible, for those of us who are living in fairly comfortable circumstances and it is further difficult because we certainly aren't hanging on a cross—but if we can in some way imagine how that criminal would have felt when he heard the words of the one in whom he now had faith: "Truly, I say to you: Today you will be with me in Paradise!"

Perhaps the thief's reaction to Jesus wasn't spontaneous; perhaps he had met Jesus in Capernaum; maybe he was in the crowd of 5,000 Jesus fed on the hillside. It could be he had been in the crowd which welcomed Jesus into Jerusalem during the triumphal entry a few days before. We don't know when, or even if, this thief had come across Jesus before. We do know that Jesus said to him, "Today you will be with me in paradise!"

However, we do have some idea of when we met Jesus. Some of us first became aware of Jesus in a time of personal and dramatic crisis and Jesus was commended to us by a friend. Perhaps some of us got to know Jesus through a process of reason involving God's creation of the universe and wondering about our own part in this total process. Somewhere along the line we took the leap of faith required of all of us when we realize that Christianity is not fully

November 22, 1992

revealed through reason, nor can Jesus the Christ be explained away by "reason."

I suspect most of us are not fully aware of when we got to thinking of Jesus being more than a good man who walked the highways and byways of Palestine nearly 2,000 years ago. Perhaps the revelation came through a process which started with getting ready for Christmas as we did a year ago, and as we will be starting again next week.

Maybe it was during another Epiphany season when we first began to understand that Jesus the rabbi did not simply come to the Jews but also to all people, such as the wise men who came from the east. It could be that in hearing that story we began to realize we had a need for a savior, even if we couldn't articulate our need very well — even to ourselves.

During the season of Lent we began to understand that the approaching death of the sinless Jesus was on our behalf, in a way we couldn't fully understand, he was about to die for us, for me!

Each year during Holy Week there comes to me the great realization of the context of Jesus' life and sacrifice with the entire Biblical story from the very beginning of creation, the story of truth of the rejection of God by all humankind, and of God's work throughout the centuries for us to be restored to right relationship with God.

When, through the Maundy Thursday communion services I soak into my being the gift of God through Christ, I begin to accept anew this great gift. When during the service of Tennebrae the candles are gradually all extinguished I sense the darkness that Jesus entered for me. On Good Friday when we view the cross on which Jesus died I am overwhelmed.

It is with the first service of Easter that the sense of joy is so complete because the darkness has been conquered by Jesus the Christ for all people, including me!

It is then, my brothers and my sisters in Christ, that I more fully understand that Jesus was speaking to me when he said: "Today you will be with me in paradise." It is then that I realize that whereever Jesus is, that place in that time is paradise.

This is why, even as we sit here in our comfortable church, we can have the gift of today being with Jesus in Paradise. This promise is made to each one of you who accept Jesus as Savior!

On this last day of the church year, each one of us has reason to rejoice that Jesus is with us.

Perhaps it's because a loved one is seriously ill, we need to remember that Jesus is with us and with our loved one. Perhaps we feel rejected; and we finally understand that Jesus does not reject us, Jesus is with us!

It could be that a friend has died and some of us are more acutely aware of our own mortality. In the words of Jesus to the thief on the cross we are aware that Jesus is with us, that he has experienced this death and will not let us go this path alone.

All of us have reason to rejoice in the words of Jesus to the thief on the cross: "Today you shall be with me in paradise!"

Miles Walter Jackson
United Methodist Church
Bow, Washington

NOVEMBER 26, 1992

Thanksgiving Day (U.S.)

Lessons:

Lutheran:	Deut. 8:1-10	Phil. 4:6-20	Luke 17:11-19
Roman Catholic:	Joel 2.21 27	1 Tim. 2:1-7	Matt. 6:25-33
Episcopal:	Deut. 8:1-3, 6-10 (17-20)	Jas. 1:17-18, 21-27	Matt. 6:25-33
Pres/Meth/UCC:	Deut. 26:1-11	Phil. 4:4-9	John 6:25-35

Introductions to the Lessons

Lesson 1

(1) *Deuteronomy 8:1-10* **(Luth)**, *Deuteronomy 8:1-3, 6-10 (17-20)* **(Epis)**. In his last message to his people before they enter Canaan, Moses commands them to keep God's laws. They are to remember how good God has been to them since leaving Egypt and now he is bringing them to a wonderful land of plenty.

(2) *Deuteronomy 26:1-11* **(Preb/Meth/UCC)**. When the Israelits settled in the promised land, they were directed to bring to God's altar a basket of thye first fruits of the harvest as an expression of gratitude for being in a good land. Then each family is instructed to worship and celebrate God's goodness.

(3) *Joel 2:21-27* **(RC)**. This book comes out of the fourth or fifth century at the time of drought and invasion of locusts. The people are assured that all they lost will be restored. Their well1being gives them reason to praise the Lord.

Lesson 2

(1) *Philippians 4:6-20* **(Luth)**, *Phil. 4:4-9* **(Presb/Meth/UCC)**. Paul urges the Philippians church to include thanksgiving in their prayers. He has learned to be content with material things whether they be plenty or scarce. For the gift the church aent him, he expresses gratitude. He assured them that God is able to supply every need.

(2) *James 1:17-18, 21-27* **(Epis)**. Every good thing comes from God. In gratitude we should practice our faith. Genuine religion consists of personal purity and social justice.

(3) *I Timothy 2:1-7* **(RC)**. Paul appeals to his spiritual son, Timothy, to pray for all those in authority. We should pray for our superiors because it is God's will that every one be saved. This salvation was made possible by Christ's atoning death on the cross.

The Minister's Annual Manual

Gospel.(1) *Luke 17:1-19* (**Luth**). On his way to Jerusalem, Jesus is met by ten lepers who beg him for mercy. As they go the a priest for examination, all ten were healed, but only one returned to thank Jesus.
(2) *Matthew 6:25-33* (**Epis/RC**). As the Heavenly Father provides food for the birds and clothes the flowers, He also provides for human needs. Isn't a human worth far more than they? Since God will provide, why worry about tomorrow's needs?
(3) *John 6:25-35* (**Preb/Met/UCC**). Jesus had satisfied the hunger of at least 5;000 people. When they followed him to the Galilean Sea, Jesus observed that they came for physical rather than for spiritual bread. He claimed that he is the Bread of Life, the Bread that satisfies hunger forever.

(1) *Luke 23:35-43* (**Luth/Epis**).

Theme: Human nature seems to be that we cry out for help and, when help is received, we too often forget to express our gratitude. A Christian expresses thanksgiving to God.

Thought for the day: God is the source of all that I have, beginning with life itself. Thanksgiving day provides me a reminder to take thought of my dependence upon God and to express true thanksgiving.

Prayer of meditation: Almighty God, the giver and provider of all things, on this day of thanksgiving I am mindful of my dependence upon you. You have given all that I have and particularly you have given your Son as Lord and Savior. Help me to I remember tomorrow the gratitude I feel today; make me truly thankful. I pray in the name of Christ my Lord. Amen.

Call to worship:
Praise the Lord! Praise God in the sanctuary!
　Praise God for God's mighty deeds, praise God according to
　God's surpassing greatness.
Let us enter into God's presence with praise and thanksgiving.
　We worship the holiness and the great providence of God.

Prayer of adoration: O most holy God, in whose presence we only dare to come because you have bid us, how can we who pale in significance glorify you who are so glorious? We dare to honor you, to praise you, and to offer our thanksgiving for the world you have loaned us, for all that you have provided. Most of all, Holy One, we glorify you for the gift of your Son Jesus Christ who came that we might have life and have it abundantly; in his name we pray. Amen.

November 26, 1992

Prayer of confession: O Lord, when we consider all that you are, we marvel that you have created us only a little lower than the angels. We have failed you in so many ways; we have failed to glorify you in our lives, we commit sins of deed and sins of omission. Even though we are not worthy so much as to gather the crumbs under the table of your Son, you have bid us to come to you. In spite of our sin, you love us. Please, help us be aware that as we confess our sins sincerely before you, you do indeed forgive us in the name of your Son and our Savior. Amen.

Prayer of dedication of gifts and self:

Sermon title: Remembering to Give Thanks

Sermon thesis: On this day of Thanksgiving, we are reminded of the gifts of God to us, his children. We are not merely to receive; a major part of our worship is to give thanks to God.

Hymn for the day: *"Sing praise to God, the highest good" "Give praise and glory unto God."* Our hymn of the day is a hymn of praise to the God of creation who has redeemed and sustains us. The author, Johann Jakob Schütz (1640-1690), practiced law in Frankfurt, later attaining the title *Rath* or Counsellor. He published two books of hymns. Influenced by Philipp Jakob Spener and Johann Wilhelm Petersen, he eventually drifted from Lutheranism to Separatism. He had an interest in the Frankfurt company which purchased land in Pennsylvania from William Penn in 1683.

Children's object talk:

God Brings Forth Food From The Earth

Objects: An ear of corn, either field corn or an ear of popping corn.
Lesson: God continues to create and continues to provide us food.
Outline: 1. When we stop to think about it, we remember that God created the world
2. We need to remember that God continues to create and that God continues to feed us.

BOYS AND GIRLS, TODAY IS THANKSGIVING DAY! In a little bit, after worship service this morning, you will be going home and you will have a special meal. Whatever you have to eat it will be a special meal, because as you eat it you will be remembering with great thanks that God has provided all that you have.

In all likelihood before you eat some member of your family will ask you all to be very quiet and you will fold your hands in prayer. In the prayer you will be thanking God for the food that you will soon be eating. Then you will being eating!

What will happen next? Will you play with your brothers and sisters, your cousins, your friends? Will you perhaps watch the football game on television? Will you forget that this is a day of thanksgiving? Will it be easy to forget tomorrow the prayer of thanksgiving you offered today?

You see, that's sort of what happened in the Bible story we read a few minutes ago. Ten people were healed of a terrible disease, but only one bothered to come back to thank Jesus for healing him. The others may have had some momentary time of thinking about thanking Jesus but didn't bother to really do it — perhaps they had many things to do.

One way to help us remember that God continues to create and to provide us with food is to think of an ear of corn, like this one I have here. There are about 600 kernels on this ear *(Note: be sure to get an actual approximate count beforehand or work out a quick system of estimating during the talk)*.

Next spring, if you planted these kernels, God would cause much more corn to grow by using the nutrients in the ground, the heat from the sun, and the water from the rain. This shows us how God continues to create.

Or, take some popping corn like this. With only about a fourth of a cup of corn you will get a whole pan full. God continues to create an increase!

Remember, this is one day to offer thanksgiving to God; we need to remember to thank God every day!

The sermon:

Remembering to Give Thanks

Hymns:
Beginning of worship: Now Thank We All Our God
Sermon hymn: Thanks to God Whose Word Was Spoken
End of worship: Now Thank We All Our God

Scripture: Luke 17:11-19

Sermon Text: *"Where Are The Nine?"* v. 17b

November 26, 1992

THE BACK DOOR BELL RANG. When I opened the door in response, our next door neighbor, whom I didn't know well because we had not lived in the town very long, reported the city water had been shut off and that one way of getting water was to collect snow, melt it and boil the water to be sure it was safe.

"Also," he said, "if you run out of anything to drink I've got plenty of beer you can have." As he left and I began to close the door, at the same time I expressed my thanks for his thoughtfulness for his offer and his suggestion.

Of course my wife and I had a bit of a laugh over it — neither one of us drink alcoholic beverages. But it wasn't a matter of the specific thing being offered; it was a generous response to a neighbor who may be in trouble during a time of crisis.

The evening was one of several spent in the dark. During our recent year-long sojourn in England, there was an unusually great snow fall, extremely wet snow which tore down electric lines. We had no electricity and, because the water pumps couldn't be used, our water was also turned off.

In a few days, the water was back and so was the electric power. After so many days in a house lighted only by candles, we begin to wonder if things would ever get back to normal. My wife and I both uttered sincere prayers of thanksgiving when we could resume life with normalcy.

Being without electricity and water is not nearly the catastrophe of having leprosy. Millions of people around the world never have electric power and clean water from a tap, but for me it was a bad experience.

Once again, I was amazed at how people banded together in this time of crisis; they worked together and worried together. They shared candles and food ... and beer! Many people walked long distances to be sure people in special danger (such as the aged) were okay and were coping. And together they prayed for deliverance.

After the snow melted and the roads were cleared, things did return to normal; and before long the prayers of thanksgiving were forgotten until the snow started to fall again and we wondered how much snow there would be this time.

This experience came to mind as I read the Gospel lesson for today, this day of Thanksgiving. There were ten lepers and they surely formed a kind of brotherhood. They suffered the same affliction and the same prejudices; they were homeless in the worst sense of the word; they had to stay clear away from contact with "normal" humans.

In some way they heard of this Jesus of Nazareth, who was a preacher, a teacher, and a h-e-a-l-e-r! Whether they were believers or not we don't know; perhaps for some of them it was a matter of being willing to try anything.

When they saw Jesus, they called out to him for healing. In response, Jesus told them to go and show themselves to the priests. As the ten went on their way, they were healed. When one of them saw that he was healed, he turned back to give thanks to Jesus; the other ten went on their own way. Perhaps some of the others thought about saying "thank you;" maybe some of the others explained away their healing and talked themselves into thinking they were just healed "naturally."

But one of them came back. Significantly it was a Samaritan. In the Gospel lesson according to Luke, this was been significant because Luke would have been pointing out to the Jewish nation that Jesus, one of them, had healed some of their number but it was only the despised Samaritan which actually expressed gratitude.

On this Thanksgiving Day, we do more than commemorate the first Thanksgiving in the Plymouth Colony when in 1621 our Pilgrim forebears celebrated their thankfulness with a feast, although there will be those of us who will have a feast.

The question that confronts us as we consider the day and its purpose and compare that to the Gospel lesson for today, is, do we truly express our thankfulness for all of God's gifts, or do we just sort of pay lip service to the whole idea?

For many Americans, today is simply "Turkey Day." It is a day of family fun and watching a football game on television — and tomorrow will be the biggest shopping day of the year as we seriously begin to prepare for the "Christmas season."

Are we likened to the one who came back to thank Jesus for healing, or are we one of the nine who for whatever reason did not offer thanks?

We also have to carry it a bit further: Even though we express our thanksgiving to God today, will we remember that in order for our thanks to have real meaning, every day must be a day of Thanksgiving?

Our offering of prayers of thanksgiving must be sincere and not merely mouthed on a particular day. Our true feelings are known

November 26, 1992

only by ourselves and God. May we be truly thankful today and every day!

Lord, help me and strengthen me that I may be one who offers sincere and complete thanks every day of my life!

Miles Walter Jackson
United Methodist Church
Bow, Washington

NOVEMBER 29, 1992

First Sunday in Advent

Lessons:

Lutheran:	Is. 2:1-5	Rom. 13:11-14	Matt. 24:37-44
Roman Catholic:	Is. 2:1-5	Rom. 13:11-14	Matt. 24:37-44
Episcopal:	Is. 2:1-5	Rom. 13:8-14	Matt. 24:37-44
Pres/Meth/UCC:	Is. 2:1-5	Rom. 13:11-14	Matt. 24:36-44

Introductions to the Lessons

Lesson 1

(1) *Luke 2:1-5* (**Luth/Epis/Pres/Meth/UCC**). The new church year begins today (Advent I) with a recipe for world peace. Isaiah, who preached during the reign of four Judean kings, tells about the future when all nations will gather to worship the one true God, who will settle their disputes. Then there will be no more war.

Lesson 2

Romans 13:11-14 (**Luth/Pres/Meth/UCC**); *Rom. 13:8-14* (**Epis**). It may be later than we think. The end of the world and Christ's return may be soon. What are we Christians to do about it? Paul urges us in this passage to stop our sinning and to be clothed with Christ as children of light.

Gospel

Matthew 24:37-44 (**Luth/Epis**); *Matt. 24:36-44* (**Pres/Meth/UCC**). Since we do not know exactly when Jesus will return, we tend to take each day in a routine way, day in and day out. We tend to become smug and complacent. Then Jesus will come as a thief in the night and we will be unprepared. In the light of the uncertainty of the timing, wisdom would have us accept as our motto: "Be prepared."

Theme: To be ready for the Lord's advent, be alert.

Thought for the day: The Christian life is always to have a central focus. As we walk with Christ in life, so we have the privilege of preparing for his second Advent. "Salvation is nearer," says Paul in the second lesson. Watchfulness for the returning Lord is imperative.

Prayer of meditation: Deepen our faith, O Lord, so that we look toward your coming again with anticipation rather than fear.

November 29, 1992

Stimulate within us the eagerness to receive you, so that we prepare well through the Holy Spirit, trust you completely and never wane in our watchfulness. Amen.

Call to worship: "In every way you have been enriched in (Christ), in speech and knowledge of every kind ... so that you are not lacking in any spiritual gifts as you wait for the revealing of our Lord Jesus Christ. He will also strengthen you to the end, so that you may be blameless on the day of our Lord Jesus Christ. God is faithful: by him you were called into the fellowship of his Son, Jesus Christ our Lord."

I Corinthians 1:5, 7-9 NRSV

Prayer of adoration: Gracious Spirit, lead us away from tremulous fears to sensible and sensitive awareness of your love for us, so that we see warnings of judgment as comforting counsel. We give you praise for your generous kindnesses and never-ending patience. Encourage us to take seriously your benevolent words without failing to understand the ultimate joy they direct us to receive, through Jesus Christ our Lord. Amen.

Prayer of confession: It is so easy, O God, to get caught up in the things of the moment — family crises, international news, the economic upturns and down-swings and the soap opera lifestyles of the neighbors — that we fail to look to things that are eternal. Forgive us for side-stepping the most important issue of life by ignoring your beckoning Spirit and putting aside your saving Gospel. Grant us wisdom to value Christ's advent more than we treasure current troubles, so we may see that the greater dimension of eternity alerts us to better responses to apply to the smaller dimensions of present life. Yet, O God, we often focus on the last things so that we may forget responsibilities to right wrong, help the handicapped, provide for the poor, and encourage the despondent. Make us watchful of both the advent to come and advent of Christian compassion needed now for the sake of Christ our Lord, in whose name we seek pardon. Amen.

Prayer of dedication of gifts and self: Accept, dear Father, these offerings, but receive us first. It is when we feel the embrace of your loving arms that we act as your children, sharing generously as you have shared with us. Thus take us into your arms so we may see from your view the needs that our giving supports. Let us see the dollars invested, like water turned into wine and a wasteland irrigated, transform fragmented lives into a whole, reducing this vast planet to a neighborhood of friends, and advancing the mission of the church rather than thwarting it. Accept us, God, so that we may accept the ministry of reconciliation as a joyous opportunity to be fully your sons and daughters. Amen.

Sermon title: Watch!

Sermon thesis: Christ is to come again one day. Christians may trust in the Gospel and look forward to that advent with joy rather than numbing fear.

Hymn for the day: *"Lo! he comes with clouds descending"*. Charles Wesley (1707-1788), one of the first group of "Oxford Methodists," was ordained to the Church of England. After spending some time in America as a missionary in Georgia, he returned to England and spent many years as an itinerant preacher, and later as a minister to Methodist Societies in London. One of the great hymnwriters of all ages, he composed some 6000 hymns. This hymn looks forward to the return of Christ with joy.

Announcements for next week:

Sermon title: Repent!

Sermon theme: Repentance is not just an emotional outburst, but leads to God's renewal from the inside out.

Sermon summary: John the Baptist sought for sincere repentance, but a repentance that was more than weeping and self-abasing. He wanted people to live their repentance in such ways that they would discover the power of the nearing kingdom, the flame and fire of the Holy Spirit, in their lives.

Children's object talk:

Don't Be Late!

Objects: Old theater ducats, sports tickets or an out-of-date mailing from Publisher's Clearinghouse or Reader's Digest. Perhaps last year's calendar, or last month's. Out-of-date material is what we need, plus a calendar for the future — or the new year, 1993. A suitcase could prove useful, one that still has old destination tags on it.

Lesson: It's important to be ready for Jesus' coming, whenever it is.

Outline: 1. Being late for something enjoyable means you lose out.
2. Planning ahead assures you will benefit by being on time.
3. Never put off planning to be ready for Jesus when he comes.

November 29, 1992

HAVE YOU EVER BEEN LATE for something important? Here are tickets for a Giants' game. It would have been a sad disappointment to have missed seeing them play simply because we forgot. Here is last month's parish calendar. See all the things that went on in this church last month. I could have missed (list some important and exciting events) by forgetting to check the calendar. Here's this week's calendar. There are just as many good experiences this week. I plan on attending (list one or two upcoming events of importance) ... and I will be on time. I have it marked on my calendar and I don't intend to forget it. (Holding up the sweepstakes materials) I might as well forget winning $10 million from Ed McMahon. I didn't send the form in on time. Being late doesn't count.

Jesus doesn't want us to miss him when he comes either. While we don't know the date, we do know he's coming. So what can we do to be sure we won't miss him when he comes? (Let the children give some answers)

We can plan ahead. We can be ready to go when he arrives.

That's something that we must not postpone. His love is too wonderful to neglect. Seeing him is too happy an event to miss out on, so making certain you're ready right now for whenever he comes is important.

A few years ago, two friends and I went to Turkey. They were to stop by and pick me up so that we could go to the airport together. I didn't want to be left behind, so I was ready for them with my suitcase (holding up the suitcase) by the door an hour before they were to come. I kept going outside to check to see if they had turned down my street. I wanted to see the cities mentioned in the Book of Revelation as well as visit places the Apostle Paul stayed and other New Testament leaders. I didn't want to be late. I didn't want to miss out.

We can be ready for Jesus' coming when we never forget he can come anytime. He comes to love us into eternity, so keep in touch with him through his Word and prayer.

You will be delighted when he comes, since he comes to give us the kingdom. (Luke 12:32)

The sermon:
Watch!

Hymns:
Beginning of worship: Prepare the Royal Highway
Sermon hymn: O Lord, How Shall I Meet You
End of worship: Come, Thou Long-Expected Jesus

Scripture: Matthew 24:37-44

Sermon Text: *"Therefore you also must be ready, for the Son of Man is coming at an unexpected hour."* v. 4

NOAH WAS ON HIS GUARD. He had an ark to build, animals to assemble, and his own bags to pack. He could not tune into *The Weather Channel.* There was no telling when the sprinkling would start and turn into a stormy and pervasive deluge, pushing his new sea-going ark from its moorings into the churning waves. Thus Noah was on watch.

The others, those who were not members of Noah's family, did not care. They paid no attention. "They were eating and drinking, marrying and giving in marriage," as Jesus says, but they were oblivious to the approaching thunderclouds. Is it unfair to say they were virtually a planet of unthinking apes? They ignored the warnings and sidestepped the telltale signs of a major disaster. They were swept like flotsam and jetsam to their doom as the raging waters flooded the lowlands and the heights and covered the earth. It's a terrifying picture. We tend to wriggle free from its sobering impact by a little humor.

Some wags have wondered about Noah trusting his family and his collection of creatures to a wooden boat that included pairs of termites, woodpeckers and beavers, all a definite threat to the integrity of the ship. Others have jested about the accommodations — and the odor from all those animals! It was never intended to be similar to a Caribbean cruise on the Love Boat. Then there is the grandchild who wondered aloud about his grandfather: Why, if he wasn't on the ark, didn't he drown! Humor, whether pleasant or sarcastic, avoids the serious situations of the Flood, blithely underestimating the need for being serious in dealing with today's sober-

November 29, 1992

ing matters. It blunts the need to be watchful, on guard, ever alert and always aware.

Alexander Solzhenitsyn tells the story of a political prisoner in his novel, *One Day in the Life of Ivan Denisovich*. Ivan is incarcerated in a bleak and barren Soviet camp in Siberia. There, being watchful was a fulltime responsibility. It was taken with incredible seriousness. Guards checked every prisoner as they returned from work or from the clinic to insure they had no contraband. Once before prisoners had managed to sneak handmade knives from one of the shops into the camp itself, and they had no intention of ever allowing that to happen again. In the bleak wintry cold, they even made the prisoners take off their boots to be examined. They were frisked thoroughly. The guards kept watch with calculated seriousness. They took no chances. Nor did the prisoners. They were equally alert. No crumb of bread, no tiny comfort was overlooked, nor did they betray their smallest secrets for fear of punishment. They, too, were fearfully watchful.

Somewhere between the jocularity of those who deal with serious matters flippantly as a zany Steve Martin, and those who are overly watchful and bitterly cruel as was Maureen O'Hara, the stoutly protective mother in *Only the Lonely*, whose lives are locked up in a prison of fear, is a vigilant and cautious watchfulness that Jesus encourages; a spiritual trust that is wary and unwearied. It's a watchfulness based on trusting faith, not fear; sensitive to dangers, but cognizant of deliverance.

Jesus urges us to "Watch!" He insists that we "be ready, for the Son of Man is coming at an unexpected hour." He's not Conan the Barbarian, but Jesus the carpenter's son. He's not a fake Father Christmas in glittering robes, but a Savior born in a stable and borne on a cross.

There are two dimensions to his words, which must not be seen as a threat, but as a considerate warning and even a benevolent, loving invitation: one has to deal with the end of life, death, and the other with Christ's Second Advent, his *Parousia*, when he comes again and the world, as we know it, ends.

During the end of the Pentecost season, the lessons tend to focus on these two aspects of Christianity. Similarly, the Advent lessons pick up the strain. The reason is that we are not only preparing for Christmas, but Christ; not alone for celebrating a festival, but for eternity, and doing so everlastingly. It's the reason Jesus came: to redeem us forever. Therefore, he urges, "Watch!"

It is not possible to make an appointment with death. It comes as we have so painfully learned over the years, often without notice, and too often for those we are unprepared to surrender yet. That's why Jesus lovingly demands that we "keep awake" and "be ready." It is the same for his Second Coming. No one, save the Father himself, knows when that will be, insists Jesus. Instead of quivering in fright, as some do, or calculating by some supposed human means the exact date that only God can devise, we need simply to have a living, ongoing relationship with our Savior. To believe in him is to push aside fear and to be fully prepared for all eventualities. It is not only to be watchful, but to be ready. For not to be on the alert is to allow sin to bombard us like Scud missiles without Patriot Scud-busters to knock them out of existence. Not to be watchful is to leave truth locked up in a book and Christ locked out of life.

C.S. Lewis has pondered the question of why God has chosen to land "in this enemy-occupied world in disguise" as the Messiah, to begin a "sort of secret society to undermine the devil." Others who wonder why God has not invaded this planet by massive force like a General Schwartzkopf zeroing in on Iraq, questions if the King of heaven lacks strength, to which Lewis responds that Christians know he will land in force *one* day, but knowing exactly when is not for us to guess. Then Lewis suggests a reason for the delay of the *Parousia*, the Second Coming. "He wants to give us the chance of joining his side freely," writes the late Christian apologist.

Jesus does not coerce us into his kingdom, but he speaks very plainly about its importance. Instead of being toy soldiers made of lead, who do only what the owner wants, we are human beings created with intelligence, who may choose to trust our Creator or abandon him. Jesus came to mark indelibly the milestones of life with words of hope and love, which he underscores with the reflective paint of warning, so that we will gladly accept the invitation to be his and live forever. "Watch therefore," advises the Lord. "Keep awake," he insists.

Several years ago my wife and I went to a movie. We sat through half of it, but I had a certain uneasiness and asked that we go home before the second half of the film began. Lois was reluctant. I had seen the film before; she hadn't. When we came home, however, it was evident my dis-ease was with reason, albeit unexplained. Our

November 29, 1992

house had been broken into and many valuables had been stolen. We even thought it was possible our youngest daughter had been kidnapped, since the car was gone and she was supposed to have been at home. We evidently surprised the thief who dashed out the back door and through a neighbor's yard, but we didn't realize that until later. Had we been aware we were going to be burglarized, we would never have left home.

Jesus used a parable similar to this to encourage us to be ready for the thief that death is, as well as the surprise that the *Parousia* will be. "If the owner of the house had known in what part of the night the thief was coming, he would have stayed awake and would not have let his house be broken into," argues Jesus for watchfulness. He tells us he will return in a similar way. We "must be ready," as he advises.

We are to be on watch, wary of the signs, but wise in our appreciation of them. That means to be faithful. What do we have to be faithful about?

It is the *person* giving the warning in whom we can easily invest our trust! Jesus is not a camp guard as those Solzhenitsyn says Ivan Denisovich met in his Siberian prison. Jesus' warning is filled with caring love, not fear and hatred. His advice is not imposed, but placed before us as a tray of hearty nutrients whipped up into a delicious stew. It lacks the finesse of pheasant under glass, perhaps, and the caloric sweetness of cheesecake smothered in a sugary sauce, but it provides far more nourishment. It feeds the soul and takes away the spiritual hunger. He gives us strength to face heartache, and energy to contend with doubts. This Lord infuses us with his love so that we see joy ahead as well as experience it presently. He takes away the fear and forboding, so that we can slip into the eternal kingdom unafraid, as well as await his coming again without being jittery fraidycats.

All of this is summed up in the admonition of Advent: "Watch!" "Keep awake!" "Be ready!" It is a priority not to be ignored or put aside, to be laughed at or made fearsome. It is an inivitation that radiates love, so that we might echo faith. That was the intention of the Spanish missionary, Francis Xavier, who, in the sixteenth century, became the apostle to Asia, ministering in India and Japan, while also attempting to enter China. He learned the language of two countries, prepared catechisms for them both, and began teaching countless souls the Gospel of Christ. Many were baptized.

He was one who called to people in a far off part of the world, "Watch!" They had a Lord they didn't even know, a Savior they had never met. Francis Xavier, founder of the Jesuits, always emphasized teaching. As Jesuits were murdered in San Salvador in the 1980s, we are reminded that watchfulness is still an imperative for the 1990s and beyond, not only for Christ's coming again, but for the threats of right now.

This Communion table is our watchtower. From here we may keep a sentinel's gaze for Christ's Second Advent. It is here that we are provided holy rations for our task as we enlist for spiritual guard duty. The old corroding errors are scrubbed away as Baptism's promise is renewed, so that we are not prevented from seeing the signs of his coming. Our souls are fed with Christ himself, his body, his blood, so that we may taste the goodness of his love and know the genuineness of his victory without undue fear. As forgiven people we are prepared once more for keeping watch, for welcoming death as a door to life with Christ, and for greeting his return as a gate to the judgment hall, when the Lord intercedes for the faithful.

Just as a loving father teaches his child to respect the power of a chainsaw, so Jesus teaches us to regard death and eternity with the same kind of watchfulness. A child schooled in the dangers of a chainsaw is apt to keep all his fingers; a soul trained in the Gospel is apt to keep his life forever for having feared wholesomely the warnings God's Word gives and believing the One who gave them.

Noah would have sailed with many more than his own family had others been as alert to God's message as he was.

Friends, "Watch!" "Be ready!" "Keep awake!" Christ is coming!

Richard Anderson
St. Timothy's Lutheran Church
San Jose, California

DECEMBER 6, 1992

Second Sunday in Advent

Lessons:
Lutheran:	Is. 11:1-10	Rom. 15:4-13	Matt. 3:1-12
Roman Catholic:	Is. 11:1-10	Rom. 15:4-9	Matt. 3:1-12
Episcopal:	Is. 11:1-10	Rom. 15:4-13	Matt. 3:1-12
Pres/Meth/UCC:	Is. 11:1-10	Rom. 15:4-13	Matt. 3:1-12

Introductions to the Lessons

Lesson 1

Isaiah 11:1-10 (**Luth/Epis/Pres/Meth/UCC**). A son of David is promised as the world's king. He will possess the seven-fold gifts of the Spirit, will rule with justice, and peace throughout creation will result. Christians believe that this promise was fulfilled in the coming of Jesus.

Lesson 2

Romans 15:4-13 (**Luth/Epis/Pres/Meth/UCC**). Advent is a season of hope. It is symbolized by blue paraments. God is our basic hope. His Word, the Scriptures, is the source of our hope. We have good reason to hope because God fulfills his promises and extends his mercy to all people.

Gospel

Matthew 3:1-12 (**Luth/Epis/Pres/Meth/UCC**). John the Baptist's mission was to prepare the way for Christ. He did it by preaching repentance that demanded a change of lifestyle. The change was symbolized by his water baptism. John witnessed to Jesus as the one greater than he who would baptize with the Holy Spirit. Repentance is necessary to receive Christ.

Theme: Repentance is not just an emotional outburst, but leads to God's effective use of the believer in joyous witness.

Thought for the day: Change is more than picking out a different tie; it's accepting renewal from the inside out.

Prayer of meditation: If I may be ignited with the fire of the Holy Spirit, O God, repentance will lead to more than tears, but also to the cheer of faithful serving. Let the spark of the Spirit spread

The Minister's Annual Manual

throughout the parish rather than sputter in the pew. For the sake of Jesus. Amen.

Call to worship: "The Lord is not slow about his promise, as some think of slowness, but is patient with you, not wanting any to perish, but all to come to repentance."—2 Peter 3:9

Prayer of adoration: We offer you our sins, O Christ, and you give us forgiveness. We give you our hatred and ugliness, our evils and contempt, and you provide us with a holy love. For this wondrous kindness, we revere you. For the manifold sacrifices you have made for us, we worship you. We are grateful that John the Baptizer came to prepare the way, but even more thankful that he was the messenger and not the Messiah. Thank you, Lord, for coming with grace to meet the demands of the Law. To your glory we pray it. Amen.

Prayer of confession: John the Baptist is right. Where we should have borne fruit, we have nothing to show. Prune us. Trim us. By your Holy Spirit, O God, make us fruitful. John the Baptist is right. We have hidden behind the holy... behind Abraham and the Patriarchs, behind Paul and the Apostles. Draw us out of our hiding places and by your Spirit, O Lord, enable us to see in Jesus Christ more than a hiding place, but the answer to our fears. John the Baptist is right. We have sinned. For this we repent that we may be baptized with Holy Spirit fire as faithful followers of Christ. Amen.

Prayer of dedication of gifts and self: John the Baptist calls us not only to repent, but to bear fruit and be wheat to be stored in barns. Here in these offering plates is the fruit of our efforts and the grain of our work. Feed the spiritually hungry with the fruit and sow the grain so those starving for grace will be nourished by it, O God. Make of these seeds harvests yet to come. Through the power of your Holy Spirit we ask it. Amen.

Sermon title: Repent!

Sermon thesis: John the Baptist sought for sincere repentance, but a repentance that was more than weeping and self-abasing. He wanted people to live their repentance in such ways that they would discover the power of the nearing kingdom, the flame and fire of the Holy Spirit, in their lives.

Hymn for the day: *"On Jordan's banks the Baptist's cry."* The distinguished scholar and Latin author, Charles Coffin (1676-1759), was born in northern France. Except for a few years as rector of the University of Paris, he spent most of his life as a member

December 6, 1992

of the faculty of the College of Beauvais. His collected poems filled two volumes. This hymn picks up the themes of John the Baptist: *"Turn from your sins and be baptized"* and *"The Messiah is coming."*

Announcements for next week:
  Sermon title: Look and Listen!
  Sermon theme: The necessity for having eyes opened and ears attuned about spiritual matters is essential.
  Sermon summary: As John the Baptist determined to check again if Jesus was the long-awaited Messiah, so we must both look and listen carefully to the Lord so that our assurance is well-based.

Children's object talk:

Answering The Call

Objects: Sandwich boards made of poster board. "Repent" is in large letters on the front. "Repent" is in large letters on the back.
Lesson: To learn to answer God's call to repentance.
Outline: 1. John wants us to repent of our sins.
  2. Jesus is God's reply to our sins.
  3. We're to answer both calls.

AT ONE TIME, people wore sandwich boards like this to encourage people to "repent!" John didn't wear a sandwich board. He preached so loud and so powerfully that this sign cannot compare with his effectiveness. He got people to listen. Hundreds and thousands of people came from all over Israel to the Jordan River where John was preaching. John could be very hard on people. He didn't speak too kindly. He told it like it is.

He wanted them to change, to give up bad ways and false faith. He pointed to Jesus, who is God's reply to repentance. He came to save us from our sins. He came out of love. He told it like it is also, only Jesus made it clear he would free us from our sins. That's why he came.

You and I still need to repent, not only to say we're sorry for our sins, but to reply to God's gift of Jesus by living for him.

How can our lives reply to God's gift of love? (Let the children suggest some answers)

John says "Repent!" Jesus is God's reply. Now it is for us repeat this over and over again so others know it's not up to us to save ourselves. Instead, being thankful Jesus has done this for us, it is now up to us to let our lives be a reply of gratitude.

The Minister's Annual Manual

The sermon:

Repent

Hymns:
Beginning of worship: Come Ye Disconsolate
Sermon hymn: On Jordan's Banks the Baptist's Cry
End of worship: Just As I Am

Scripture: Matthew 3:1-12

Sermon Text: *"Repent, for the kingdom of heaven has come near."* v.2

"REPENT!" It is an ancient cry, one that lurks behind the early scenes in Theodore Dreiser's *An American Tragedy* of an all-night mission in the sleazy north end of Kansas City. It's the cry for repentance, for renewal, for giving up immoral ways, wine and beer and chasing women. It's a cry that clings to the hope the cross offers. The scene in Scripture is not as Dreiser saw it, however. It was not the rundown tenement districts of the Midwest in which John the Baptist shouted for repentance. It wasn't among the derelicts and the drunks, the prostitutes and the pimps, the drug dealers and the crack makers of modern America. It was among the influential people of Israel, the affluent Pharisees and Sadducees, as well as the poor, the peasants of the desert villages and mountain towns. "Repent!" cried the man of the wilderness. "Repent, for the kingdom of heaven has come near." It was out by the flowing waters of the Jordan, not the Missouri River. It was in the Judean desert, not the slums of Kansas City that John bellowed for repentance. Yet it is in Kansas City and San Jose and Sverdlovsk and Cape Town and every other place that his voice is still heard today. "Repent!"

It's a startling, daring admonition, but one of those admonitions of Advent that we dare not ignore. It's an embarrassing word to many a mainline denomination, and to many a sophisticated cleric caught up in liturgical prancing, who appears immune to the heartbeat of passion throbbing within the call to repentance. But John the Baptizer would strip from us such feeble facades to reveal the essential need. We all need to repent, to be cleansed of sin's corrosive acidity and renewed for the delightful joy of the nearby kingdom, the kingdom of God. It must not be watered down, this kingdom of John's...Baptism or no!

A man was eager to restore the aging wooden church to its original

December 6, 1992

splendor. He had limited funds and therefore limited paint, but he thought he could do it. There remained still one expansive wall and only a few gallons of Gothic Green left after painting several days in the beating sun. He would have to stretch it. He poured in some thinner and painted more, but there was more wall to cover and only a few drops of paint left. He kept adding thinner to the extent the paint turned from a dark forest green to a sickly shade often seen in dying household plants. Suddenly the clouds billowed overhead and a thunderous voice echoed across the whole town: *Repaint! Repaint! And thin no more!*

It's a silly story and yet it captures something of the essence of what happens to repentance when it is primped and fussed over, made dignified and proper. That was not the repentance John sought. He had no intention of thinning down this cry, nor masking it with some kind of sham the way housewives do when they make a frilly cover to hide an old battered and tattered pillow. He cried for repentance for the very purpose that the kingdom was so near that he wanted no one to hide behind respectability and protocol and miss it. They had to be genuine, real, authentic *repenters,* sinners who knew it and wanted to change.

Thus John the Baptist enters Advent, darkening the mood just as the Christmas lights start to come on and Christmas shopping shifts from sluggish to frenzied...or does he?

Jesus is so near that John does not want us to miss him at the gift counter or as we string lights over the eaves.

Repent and bear fruit, he tells us.

Repent and be baptized with the Holy Spirit, he urges us.

It is the cry of one who is preparing the way of the Lord, straightening the crooked paths by correcting corrupt and twisted people, their thoughts and their lives.

John focused on more than emotional repentance. He wanted something to come out of it. Those who repented were to become part of the kingdom. If so, their lives would bear fruit.

That was not what he witnessed in the Israel of the first century. He saw the masquerade that was the lives of the religious authorities. John called them a "brood of vipers." They had hidden behind Abraham too long — behind his name and fame and role in founding the nation of Israel. Hiding was not enough to save them regardless of how important Abraham had been. "Bear fruit that is worthy of repentance," John instructed.

We might examine our repentance. Does it ring hollow? Do we hide behind Christianity as if it is only churchianity? Here is the crunching, grinding demand of the Law! Or is it? If the kingdom is near to us then it is not simply a thing of rules, but something Christ rules with his righteous love. That should prompt us to repent more earnestly and eagerly than did the Pharisees and Sadducees to the snide words of John. If we have been swallowed up in the joy of forgiveness, then our empty branches will leaf out and flower and bear fruit, for love never leaves anyone barren. At least not the love of God-in-Christ.

John calls for an even more radical repentance than fruit-bearing prompted by the will to do good, to be good and be moral. He points to Jesus and acclaims him as "one who is more powerful than I." He is not worthy even to carry his sandals, he says. This Nazarene carpenter will baptize with more than water, but with the Holy Spirit, John tells the crowd. Here is what he means when the kingdom not only comes close, but so near that its sheer energy erupts within those who approach it. It will not be merely do-gooders resulting from approaching the nearby kingdom, but Spirit-filled men and women and youth who will be like wheat separated from the chaff. They will nurture the world. They will feed it, care for it, attend to it.

This word "Repent!" is freighted with more depth than Dreiser could conjure up in the dreary all-night mission for the derelicts of Kansas City's Pendergast era. It has power! God the Holy Spirit empowers the repentant to be lights that fire up joy, wheat that feeds hungry hearts and famished brains.

Do you remember the TV episode when Murphy Brown and the crew at F.Y.I. determined not to buy Christmas gifts for one another, but to take the money they usually spend and give it to a charity? They made a pact, but one they defected from innocently one at a time, until there was no pact and they were back to where they had been before: Christmas shopping, the dreaded scourge of the season. They all repented of it, but they repented of the wrong thing. They hated Christmas. They could not expect the rest of the staff to understand their lack of Christmas spirit. Suddenly what started out as a peaceful Christmas was thrown into open revolt as they all bustled about finding last minute gifts to give so they would not look bad in the eyes of their colleagues.

They missed the mark. They were attempting to be fruitful, but they became frustrated instead. They wanted to blossom, but they blundered. They sought to make merry and they found misery. They

December 6, 1992

wanted to leaf out and instead they left out the meaning of Christmas. Finally, Murphy's painter, the guy who can never finish painting her apartment and evidently not the one who thinned the paint for the church, dropped by. His Christmas was not to be sham gifts and fake greetings. He was going over to the shelter to help feed the hungry. It was then the rest caught the spirit. It was not the Holy Spirit of which John spoke, but it was a better spirit than what they had. John the Baptist calls us to "Repent!" and be baptized with the Holy Spirit that will ignite us with the love and the will to change the world. After all, we're not a TV sitcom, but living people who can hear John still shouting "Repent!" We're people God wants baptized with the Holy Spirit and fire.

Repent means change, and change is not alone an individual thing, but one that provides collective seeds to change the wilderness of our cities and towns and fields and deserts into orchards of fruit-bearing souls and fields of chaffless grain-bearing believers.

No wonder Jesus says the fields are white unto harvest. The Holy Spirit has been doing his job. Others have borne fruit and sowed wheat. Now we need to do ours.

Repent! Bear fruit worthy of repentance!
Repent! be baptized with the Holy Spirit and fire!
Repent and reply with joy because the kingdom has indeed come near!

Richard Andersen
St. Timothy's Lutheran Church
San Jose, California

DECEMBER 13, 1992

Third Sunday in Advent

Lessons:

Lutheran:	Is. 35:1-10	James 5:7-10	Matt. 11:2-11
Roman Catholic:	Is. 35:1-6a, 10	James 5:7-10	Matt. 11:2-11
Episcopal:	Is. 35:1-10	James 5:7-10	Matt. 11:2-11
Pres/Meth/UCC:	Is. 35:1-10	James 5:7-10	Matt. 11:2-11

Introductions to the Lessons

Lesson 1

Isaiah 35:1-10 (**Luth/Epis/Pres/Meth/UCC**). Good news for a people in bondage as the Jews were when this passage was written! God is coming and wonderful things will happen: salvation for the enslaved, health for the handicapped, renewal of nature, and a highway for people to return to God with gladness.

Lesson 2

James 5:7-10 (**Luth/Epis/Pres/Meth/UCC**). Only God knows why Jesus' return to earth has been delayed. Early Christians expected the Parousia in the very near future. In this pericope James addresses the problem of impatience by some expressed in their complaints. He exhorts them to follow the example of patience given by farmers and prophets.

Gospel

Matthew 11:2-11 (**Luth/Epis/Pres/Meth/UCC**). Because of his fearless preaching, John the Baptizer is in prison and facing a possible death sentence. Earlier he declared that Jesus was the Messiah. Was he right? To be certain, he sends his disciples to ask Jesus if he is the Messiah. Jesus answers by pointing to his good works and his preaching the gospel to the poor. Jesus lets John draw his own conclusion. John may have doubts about Jesus, but Jesus is sure that John is the greatest of all prophets.

Theme: The necessity for having eyes opened and ears attuned about spiritual matters is essential.

Thought for the day: Advent is a season that reminds us we need to be alert. John the Baptist was more than cautious, but eager to know if he was hearing and seeing the promised Gospel lived out in Jesus. With him, we need to look and listen carefully.

December 13, 1992

Prayer of meditation: Send, Holy Spirit, your stimulating power to awaken me from the doldrums of life to the excitement of Christ's advent. Empower me to alert others and shake them from the drowsiness that prevents them from both seeing and hearing that the Messiah has come. Amen.

Call to worship: "And the Word became flesh and lived among us, and we have seen his glory, the glory as of a Father's only Son, full of grace and truth."—John 1:14

Prayer of adoration: We lift our voices in praise, singing hymns of acclamation to you, O God. You have stretched beyond the heavens into the lives of humankind and drawn us into your family. We celebrate the wonder of such love, the majesty of such power, and the audacity of such kindness. In adoration we bow before you, O Father. In admiration we seek your embrace, O Christ. In adulation we beg for your guidance, O Spirit. Amen.

Prayer of confession: Empty vessels are we, O Lord, until we discover the corrosion within, the rust caused by sin, and the decay of our disobedience. Scour us clean with the strength of your righteousness, endowing us with the polish of your forgiveness, the sheen of your pardon. Scrub us of our negativism. Bathe from us the filth that contaminates the mind and pollutes the soul. Rinse us again with baptismal grace to the gleaming brightness of your own purity shared with us, Lord of the cleansing cross. Wash us anew in the blood of the Lamb. Fill us, then, with newness, with hope and faith and the courage to be doers of the Word and not hearers only. Inspire us not only to see the truth, but enact it in our world. Amen.

Prayer of dedication of gifts and self: Into the offering plates we have dropped the symbols of ourselves, the coins and currency and checks that represent the labor of our hands, the sweat of our brows, the strength of our backs. You have given us brains to employ, bodies to activate, and unique personalities with which to master life's challenges; thus what we return is something you have first shared with us. Let us, Lord, give with generosity these symbols, and to add to them during the week with a daring witness for Christ that will increase the worth of our gifts by the addition of our selves, for then we give as you do, personally. In the power of the Holy Spirit, we pray. Amen.

Sermon title: Look and Listen!

The Minister's Annual Manual

Sermon thesis: As John the Baptist determined to check again if Jesus was the long-awaited Messiah, so we must both look and listen carefully to the Lord so that our assurance is well-based.

Hymn for the day: *"Oh, praise the Lord, my soul!"* David Frank Wright (b. 1941) wrote this hymn for *Morning praise and Evensong*, published at Notre Dame, Indiana, in 1973. Wright, who holds a Ph. D. from the University of Notre Dame at South Bend, Indiana, has been a member of the Order of Preachers (Dominicans) since 1961), and was ordained a priest in 1968. Since 1974 he has been on the faculty of Aquinas Institute in Dubuque, Iowa. Stanza 5 relates especially to the Gospel, ". . . the blind receive their sight. . ."

Announcements for next week:

Sermon title: Receive!

Sermon theme: The essence of this text is one of acceptance, of being open to the will and the work of God. He transforms crisis into a Christ event, calamity into calm.

Sermon summary: The drama of Nazareth is a prelude to the greater dramas that followed. Within this event, we can learn something of the generosity of God when the willingness of the faithful is open to tackling difficult situations without resistance. To receive a commission from God is to accept a wrapped and secret blessing.

Children's object talk:

Using Common Senses

Objects: A portable television set or the remote control for a TV. A variation would be to have a "boom box" radio.

Lesson: To learn the truth about Jesus.

Outline: 1. We're equipped to discover answers to important questions.
    2. We need to be willing to ask, to research and to discover the truth.
    3. When we do, Jesus' words in Matthew 7:7-8 are fulfilled.

THE DIFFERENCE BETWEEN a radio and a television set is that with the latter you can see what's going on as well as hear it. The radio keeps you guessing. God has equipped us with common senses. Most people cannot only feel and smell and taste, but they canwas sure see and hear as well.

If you smell something burning, you probably should look to see if something is on fire. If your food has a rancid or unpleasant taste, it's best not to eat it even if you're hungry. If you feel an earthquake, head for safety. These are common responses to information the senses feed us.

A television set, when plugged in, provides information for two senses: sight and sound. When John the Baptist was in prison, he had no television available to check up on Jesus. He was sure Jesus was

December 13, 1992

the Messiah at one time, but now, without being able to see and hear it on the 5 o'clock news he had doubts. Jesus told John's followers, "Go and tell John what you hear and see..."

We are often the ones who must take the message of the Messiah to those who have not been able to "hear and see" as we have. We can be living TV sets, especially when we're plugged into Good News. If there are ever any doubts, using these common senses becomes vitally important. Then we know — by sight and sound — that Jesus is truly our Lord and can be the Lord of many others.

The sermon:

Look And Listen!

Hymns:
Beginning of worship: Dearest Jesus, at Your Word
Sermon hymn: On Jordan's Banks the Baptist's Cry
End of worship: Joy to the World

Scripture: Matthew 11:2-11

Sermon Text: *"Jesus answered them, 'Go and tell John what you hear and see.' "* v. 4

MY WIFE OFTEN ECHOES MY MOTHER. When I have failed to give undivided attention to her words, she will tell me I did not listen. The fact is, she is often right. She told me what I needed to know, but somehow I did not let the words penetrate ny ears so that I actually heard what was said.

"You must listen," said my mother when I was a child.

"Pay attention," said my teachers when I was in school.

"It's an order, soldier!" instructed ny commanding officer when I was in the army and did not move quickly enough to what was said.

"Shut up and listen," said my friends when I interrupted their important information.

There are the correlatives that tell us to "watch where you are going" or "look out" for some danger or "open your eyes; it's right under your nose" when we've looked for something and can't find it. Someone is always telling us "look and listen."

There is little comfort in the fact that I am not alone in my inattention. John the Baptist may have had a legitimate excuse, however. He was in prison. He was not able to see and hear what Jesus was up to, thus he sent his messengers to find out.

"Are you he who is to come, or shall we look for another?" they questioned Jesus for John.

The Lord responded, "Go and tell John what you hear and see: the blind receive their sight, the lame walk, the lepers are cleansed, the deaf hear, the dead are raised, and the poor have good news brought to them. And blessed is anyone who takes no offense at me." This was not Robin Hood and his Saddam Hussein stealing a nation and calling it a province. This was the answer to Isaiah prophecy [35:4-6].

That's something to pay attention to, to hear and heed, to see and sense. We need to listen with ears wide open and look with eyes wide awake, for unless we pay attention carefully the wonder of all that Jesus is and does will escape us. That seems to be precisely the predicament in which much of the world is caught. We need more than spouses and parents and commanding officers to stimulate us to use our senses, more than CNN and Dan Rather and Tom Brokaw. That, too, God has taken care of: he has sent his Holy Spirit so that we may both look and listen, see and hear that Jesus is Lord.

The pungent sound of Handel's *Messiah* fills the music halls at this season of the year, and the delightful carols of Christmas resound throughout the shopping malls, but many people are ignorant of the message they convey. They *hear* the music, but they do not see the Master. Or they *see* the creches and the glittering lights, the decorated trees and the sea of gifts under them, but they do not *hear* the words of the Christmas angels clearly enough to respond as faithfully as the Bethlehem shepherds. Jesus would tell them and us all over again to both look and listen, to use our senses to learn the truth that Jesus is God's promised Messiah and to know it's true for us also.

The evidence that Jesus is who he says he is, is not alone in the resonant sound of his voice. It is to be seen in what he did and heard in what he has done for others. Jesus, the ages acclaim, is unimpeachable. If he were only a Billy Crystal, merely the humor would be "mahvalous." Had he been Jose Canseco, we would marvel only at his batting, or Donald Trump at his millions. But Jesus was not merely a super star Savior. Someone has penned that "without the privileges of a prince's palace, he won the homage of kings. Without the army of a Caesar, he captured the hearts of humanity.

December 13, 1992

Without any beauty that people should desire him, he so stimulated human imagination that painters have never tried of depicting his virtue, and musicians have never wearied of composing for his glory. He never wrote a word, except with his finger in the dust of a Palestinian road, yet no one's words have been so widely translated and so frequently quoted. He was mocked and spit upon, yet through the years he has dignified common people, released slaves, emancipated women and freed the oppressed." Surely, he is worthy of our hearing him speak and seeing him act — not only in biblical accounts, but in today's world.

He cured the ailing, those with leprous bodies and even those possessed by demons. He gave blind eyes sight. He unstopped deaf ears and released stuttering tongues. He lifted the dead alive in their grave clothes. Albert Brooks would never have had to put up with *Defending Your Life* had he known. Patrick Swayze would never have wound up a *Ghost* had he believed. The movies distort the truth, while Jesus heals the distraught and the distressed. He fed the hungering with more than food, but love. Storms quieted, water became wine and unbearing fig trees wilted at his command. All around the world, for nearly two thousand years, people have responded to that inspiration, that joy that comes from knowing him, that love that will not let us go, that power defined by his humanity and emboldened by his divinity.

But seeing and hearing, looking and listening, remain our greatest need too, for if Jesus is merely a historical figure, then the past, although glorious, is not enough. He has to live within us now. That's precisely what the Bible claims happens when we are cleansed with the refreshing waters of Baptism. It tells us we are not only buried with him in his death, but resurrected with him in the newness of his life. It assures us, "If Christ is in you, although your bodies are dead because of sin, your spirits are alive because of righteousness." And it further tells us that "if the Spirit of him who raised Jesus from the dead dwells in you, he who raised Christ Jesus from the dead will give life to your mortal bodies also through his Spirit which dwells in you." (Romans 8:9-11)

The implication is remarkable. It assures us that the evidence of the Messiah need not only be one of the past, what was said and done a long time ago, but that he is radiantly active in our world even today. He continues to heal the sick and comfort the sorrowing. He continues to give new life to those who die in him. He still enables us to confront evil and triumph, to know love and share forgiveness. He breaks down dividing barriers now. How else can we understand the great collapse of Communism in Eastern Europe? While the Christian faithful are said to be a minority, they were persistent in wearing away the impregnable might of oppression in Poland and Eastern Germany, in the Baltic States and Hungary via the power of prayer. It is said to be the force that gnawed effectively at the governmental authority in Romania and Czechoslovakia, in Yugoslavia and the Soviet Union to change that part of the world for the better. It will wear away the rock that is Red China and the other totalitarian states, too, just as stone erodes under the persistent pressure of drops of water. This, however, will be drops of prayer.

Why has this happened? Because they've looked and listened, they've seen the power of the Lord Christ, and know the majesty of a love that can sweep forty years of oppression aside peacefully and without rancor.

"Blessed is he who takes no offense at me," says Jesus, who, instead, both looks and listens and is convinced that the ancient evidences of his Messiahship are still readily evident today.

John the Baptist knew his role. He had pointed clearly to Jesus as the Messiah like an Irish Setter hunting quail. Yet, clapped into prison by Herod for words that offended the tetrarch, chained and doomed evidently to Herod's terror, he could not die without assurances he had properly singled out Jesus of Nazareth as the Lord of all, whose sandal he was unworthy to untie. Thus he sent his own disciples to get further word; he was willing to look and listen all over again. Jesus provided the assurances he needed. But then our Lord turned to the crowds that once surrounded the Baptizer and queried them about their understanding of John's role.

"What did you go out into the wilderness to look at? A reed shaken by the wind?" John was no limp-wrist dilettante, no cowering ninny. Jesus knew that the people had not gone to the Jordan, enduring the treacheries of the desert, to see a man wearing silks and satins...not a prince, but a prophet! "Yes," emphasized Jesus, "I tell you, and more than a prophet. This is the one about whom it is written, 'See, I am sending my messenger ahead of you, who will prepare your way before you'." They saw the one God appointed to prepare the way for his long-promised Messiah.

Look and listen, Jesus seemed to be saying. Look at and listen to John for he was no mere entertainer, no second-rate warm-up come-

December 13, 1992

dian for the star attraction, no orator without a message, a candidate without a platform, but the great man God promised who would lead the people from the shock of their sins to the salvation of their souls. We do well to heed our Lord's comments to the crowd, to reevaluate what John means to us, for if we deny him are we then to deny Jesus too?

Friend, look and listen. The Bible provides us something worth seeing and wellworth our listening. It is Jesus the Christ, the Son of the living God, and he has come to claim us for eternity, to take away our sin, and provide us joy that bridges this world and the everlasting kingdom. Look and listen...then go and tell!

This third Sunday of Advent the third candle in the wreath is ignited, the pink one, the rosy one, the one that reminds us that Jesus still is to be heard and seen today in Word and Sacraments, in life and its turbulent issues. And he provides us assurance that we are indeed blessed when we take no offense at him, but rejoice in him to the very toes of our socks. That implies putting our five senses to good use, because it's only common sense to both look and listen before we cross over from this world to another.

Richard Andersen
St. Timothy's Lutheran Church
San Jose, California

DECEMBER 20, 1992

Fourth Sunday in Advent

Lessons:

Lutheran:	Is. 7:10-14	Rom. 1:1-7	Matt. 1:18-25
Roman Catholic:	Is. 7:10-14	Rom. 1:1-7	Matt. 1:18-25
Episcopal:	Is. 7:10-17	Rom. 1:1-7	Matt. 1:18-25
Pres/Meth/UCC:	Is. 7:10-16	Rom. 1:1-7	Matt. 1:18-25

Introductions to the Lessons

Lesson 1

Isaiah 7:10-14 (**Luth**); *Isa. 7:10-16* (**Epis**); *Isa. 7:10-16* (**Pres/Meth/UCC**). Ahaz, king of Judah, is facing a war with Israel and Syria. He plans to go to Assyria for help. Through Isaiah God tells him not to seek foreign aid, but to rely on God's protection. To prove that he will do this, God tells Ahaz to ask for a miraculous sign. Because he would rather trust Assyria, Ahaz refuses to ask for a sign. But God says he will give him a sign any way: the birth of a child, Emmanuel. By the time this child can reason Ahaz' enemies will be gone.

Lesson 2

Romans 1:1-7 (**Luth/Epis/Pres/Meth/UCC**). In these opening verses of Romans, Paul's greatest letter, Paul identifies himself and Jesus to the Roman congregation which he had never visited. He claims to be a slave of Christ and ordained to preach the Gospel. Jesus is identified as a human, a son of David, and as the divine Son of God. Through this God-man comes salvation for humanity.

Gospel

Matthew 1:18-25 (**Luth/Epis/Pres/Meth/UCC**). This is Matthew's account of the Nativity given from Joseph's viewpoint. Being a good man, Joseph planned privately to break the engagement with Mary because she was pregnant. Through an angel God informed Joseph that the child was conceived by the Holy Spirit. He was also told what to name the baby. Joseph obeyed God by going through with the marriage and naming the baby, Jesus.

Theme: The essence of this text is one of acceptance, of being open to the will and the work of God. He transforms crisis into a Christ event, calamity into calm.

December 20, 1992

Thought for the day: Often God gives us a burden to give us a bonanza. Joseph was not saddled with either blame or blight, but a blessing. Unraveling the mysteries given to us often reveals great joy if we will only receive it.

Prayer of meditation: Open my mind and heart to the essence of this text, O God, so that I many follow Joseph more carefully and find in life's many struggles your corrective, blessing hand; through Christ our Lord. Amen.

Call to worship: "Let no one despise your youth, but set the believers an example in speech and conduct, in love, in faith, in purity...Do not neglect the gift that is in you...Put these things into practice, devote yourself to them, so that all may see your progress."
—1 Timothy 4:12, 14a, 15

Prayer of adoration: You who light the stars and give brilliance to the sun and shadow to the night, we thank you that you have seen the darkness of our planet and sent us the Light of the world. Gladly we extol your goodness and grace. Happily we exclaim your unlimited and unmerited love. Heavenly Father, we adore you. Amen.

Prayer of confession: Stunned by difficulty, O God, we cower in fright. Stuck with trouble, we often cave in to its weight, only to discover the strength of Joseph is might enough to meet the catcalls of those who jeer and the sting of those who gossip. We confess that we are more often hesitant to resist than to receive, to reject rightful duties rather than accept demanding responsibilities. Forgive us for our weaknesses. Teach us by means of Joseph, that Nazarene carpenter, to be open to the miracles you make of painful issues. Your plans, O God, are not our plans. Guide us to receive them in the days ahead rather than refuse them as we have so often done in the past; through Jesus Christ. Amen.

Prayer of dedication of gifts and self: Joseph gave more than the sawdust of the carpentry shop; he gave you, O God, the silver of trust and the gold of acceptance. Joseph met more than an angel, but he encountered a holy commission. Give to us, O God of the universe, that trust to see that when we give ourselves, you always make it a sacred journey. If it is not as Joseph caring for Mary and Jesus, it is nevertheless as ones who seek for his Holy Family to be part of our own. Take then our gifts and enable them to be as careful as Joseph in leading the Lord into worlds strange and familiar. Amen.

The Minister's Annual Manual

Sermon title: Receive!

Sermon thesis: The drama of Nazareth is a prelude to the greater dramas that followed. Within this event we can learn something of the generosity of God when the faithful are open to tackling difficult situations without resistance. To receive a commission from God is to accept a wrapped and secret blessing.

Hymn for the day: *"Lo, how a rose e'er blooming/is growing"* Both words and music of this beautiful German carol are believed to date from as early as the fifteenth century. A manuscript from the St. Alban's Carthusian monastery in Trier, written down between 1582 and 1588 is the oldest source. As first printed in the *Alte Catholische Geistliche Kirchengeseng*, Cologne, 1599, the text consisted of 23 stanzas. *Alte Catholische Geistliche Kirchengeseng* is also the oldest source for the melody, although segments of the tune have been noted in other melodies.

Announcements for this week (Christmas Eve)
  Sermon title: Do Not Be Afraid
  Sermon theme: Do not be afraid.
  Sermon summary: The pronouncement of the angels, "Do not be afraid," is echoed in the proclamation of the saints through the ages. It is a word that this world desperately needs to hear. It is a promise that we know through the Savior born this night in Bethlehem.
Announcements for this week (Christmas Day)
  Sermon title: A New Day Dawns
  Sermon theme: A new creation.
  Sermon summary: Jesus' birth is God speaking again the word of hope, "Let there be light." It is the sign of the renewal and restoration of all creation.

Announcements for next week:
  Sermon title: Joseph
  Sermon theme: The promise is fulfilled.
  Sermon summary: Matthew paints a picture of Jesus as the fulfillment of God's promise of deliverance, begun in the exodus from the slavery in Egypt. Joseph serves as God's instrument in the unfolding saga of salvation history.

Children's object talk:

Surprise!

Objects: A gold pan; a spade; a pick or some other tool.
Lesson: Through faith difficult problems can be resolved.
Outline: 1. Problems can be deceptive.
   2. The right attitude can turn troubles into triumphs.
   3. Depend on God to provide good surprises in every struggle.

December 20, 1992

IT'S HARD WORK to pan for gold. The Forty-niners who looked for gold in the Mother Lode of California's Sierra Mountains did not find it easily. They had to dig for it, search in remote and unexplored mountain regions. Many found delightful surprises in their efforts. Not everyone did, mind you, but enough to make us aware that problems can sometimes be gold mines if you have the right attitude and the will to "hang in there."

Joseph had a problem. He was engaged and supposed to be married, but he wasn't sure. It did not appear to be a good thing. God sent an angel in a dream to convince him, however. Joseph dug into the struggle and discovered a wonderful surprise. He found more than gold. He learned that his wife would be the mother of the Messiah, and he would be his guardian.

Joseph had the right attitude. He was open to whatever God wanted. He had the joy of having Jesus in his home.

Mother Teresa of Calcutta could have retired many years ago, but instead she saw in the "poorest of the poor" a struggle filled with blessings. She started helping the dying and the hungry and the neglected. Today there are many who work with her and many places in the world where her work is being carried on in the name of Christ, because she had the right attitude to look beyond the impossibility of the problem to its joy. Many, many people have found the joy of Jesus through her.

She is like Joseph.

You can be like Joseph. Someone might say it's impossible to clean up all the litter people leave on the streets, but we can turn trashy neighborhoods into garden spots if we have the right attitude. Others may think you can't eliminate drugs in some other areas or crime or homelessness. But if you are open to God's power and have the attitude of faith, even these difficult problems can be turned into blessings. It's happening in many places and often it's Christian families who are doing the work because they see blessings in burdens.

The sermon:

Receive!

Hymns:
Beginning of worship: Oh, Come, Oh, Come, Emmanuel
Sermon hymn: Of the Father's Love Begotten
End of worship: O How Shall I Receive Thee

Scripture: Matthew 1:18-25

Sermon Text: "When Joseph awoke from sleep,. he did as the angel of the Lord commanded him; he took [Mary] as his wife---" v. 24

THE FINAL PREPARATORY EPISODE of the Advent Gospel lessons before we launch into the jubilant celebration of Christmas is a four-part drama, just as the *Admonitions of Advent* have come to us in four distinct exclamations. We are enjoined to *"Watch!"*, *"Repent!"*, *"Look and Listen!"*, as well as *"Receive!"* Perhaps that last admonition can be refined to *Accept!* or even *Welcome!* In many ways that's the theme of this little playlet in four parts involving Joseph of Nazareth and a visiting angel, who concern themselves with Mary his betrothed.

In numerous great theatrical pieces from the Greeks and Romans to Shakespeare and Eugene O'Neill, as well as the Bible's own play, *Job*, the dramas begin with **prologues** and conclude with **epilogues**. In between, we find **monologues** and **dialogues**. It is the same for this important one-act play enacted in the hill country of Galilee. There are four distinct aspects clearly defined by Matthew as he helps us ready ourselves for the momentous event of the birth of the long-anticipated Messiah. In one long paragraph are four aspects that mark the beginning of an even greater drama that inevitably changed the world.

When Oscar Wilde was approached by a friend to ask how his new play had gone that opening night, he considered its poor reception for a moment and said, "The play was a great success, but the audience was a failure."

It's true that all too frequently in the two thousand years since this drama was literally acted out in that tiny town of Nazareth as an interested audience we have failed to appreciate the scene of Joseph and the angel. Or Joseph at all, let alone the whole story of Jesus and his Gospel. Yet Joseph remains a key element in the great story

December 20, 1992

of the incarnation, "a just man," who with care provided understanding for Mary and a loving home for Jesus. So, before we inaugurate the celebrative delight of Christmas, let us focus on Matthew's scenario of the man who teaches us what it means to receive, to accept, to welcome God's treasure, and to fulfill humanity's responsibilities. Let us see the success of this playlet as something we must not fail to comprehend. It is the final admonition of Advent: *Receive!*

It is a very simple prologue.

The purpose of a prologue is to set the tone, to reveal the essence of the drama, to clue us into the tension the play seeks to resolve. It is to a play what a preface is to a book or an introduction is to a speech. Thus Matthew very succinctly describes the conflict like an editor of a program guide sharing the content of a television movie.

Matthew puts the plot of the play into a nutshell, yet a nutshell of complications. "Now the birth of Jesus the Messiah took place in this way. When his mother Mary had been engaged to Joseph, but before they lived together, she was found to be with child from the Holy Spirit."

We need to understand, however, that Jewish ways of that time are different from modern American marital and engagement procedures. First, in that time Jewish families arranged marriages for their offspring when they were quite young, possibly only toddlers. At the appropriate age, they were then engaged. Engagement, however, was tantamount to marriage in the eyes of society and religion. Except for conjugal rights, the engaged couple were considered married. The couple lived separately for a whole year before the marriage was consummated, even though they were indissolubly bound. Though only engaged, the bride could not merely give her ring back to break it. She had no rights. The boyfriend, on the other hand, could not simply take the ring back either if he wanted out. He had to go through the legal process of divorce. Albeit considerably less rigorous than divorce today, such an event was a social, if not a religious disaster. It meant scandal for both parties and both families. It was to be avoided if possible. The punishment for infidelity was stoning, which was not always literally practiced. The taint of such a sin stuck with a person, however, so that family and neighbors shunned the guilty adulterer, thus making that attitude almost the same thing in effect as stoning. The guilty never knew forgiveness.

The prologue spells out the conflict. Mary, Joseph's betrothed, is pregnant. He is not the father of the child. The Holy Spirit is, but how do you explain that to nosy neighbors and suspicious relatives? As a righteous Jew, he is put into a dilemma that has to be resolved, a predicament that causes little dis-ease for contemporary people, but was a major problem in Joseph's day, not to mention just twenty-five years ago or less in this society.

So here we have the plot spelled out: an engaged couple who is to be married, who discover a pregnancy that is not due to any impropriety by the groom...or the bride...but the gift of the Holy Spirit. You can hear the tittering of the town gossips at the well on hearing that, can't you? How is this to be resolved? How will Joseph receive this gift, and accept his role, this miracle of the Spirit of God? The prologue states the case.

That's where the monologue comes into play. Like a Shakespearean soliloquy, Joseph must resolve the problem, Matthew says. He has to consider his actions, but here we are given insight into the man. As he ponders within his heart his own actions, he weighs the various consequences. He is "a righteous man" says our playwright. In fact, he is compassionate and tender. He is "unwilling to expose her to public disgrace," we're told. The divorce he is considering will be a private matter. She will not be subject to undue abuse.

One can sense the wheels grinding in Joseph's mind, the pain of his heart whirring within, for it's evident he cares about Mary, as well as is troubled by the anguish within his soul over the awkward predicament, for he is a deeply religious Jew.

There is the need for us to reflect personally and individually on the issues that confront us also, to seriously consider the consequences, and introspectively evaluate an answer, just as there was for Joseph. We cannot escape the responsibility for clearly thinking through our actions either, or for weighing society's demands with our own inner needs. We cannot merely act impetuously. There is too much at stake. Here we see the young carpenter of Nazareth providing us a role model for our own personal struggles. Conscientiously, he considers his actions to accept this as God's plan or not, to receive this as God's gift or evil's burden. It is the admonition of life for him, if not Advent: *Receive! Accept! Welcome!*

It's then that the third ingredient of this drama unfolds. There is a dialogue. God sends an angelic vision to Joseph in a dream (similar to his namesake in the Old Testament family of Jacob), and he is able to hear a response to his troubled soul that confirms what he first understood, what Mary had undoubtedly told him, but for which

December 20, 1992

he had no proof...only the words of his fiancee. The child she carries is the gift of the Holy Spirit, assures the angel, and he is to be named Jesus, *for he will save his people from their sins.* It was the fulfillment of ancient prophecy, of Isaiah 7:14, reminds the playwright, of a virgin conceiving and bearing a son and it is definitely the action of the Holy Spirit. "Joseph, son of David, do not be afraid to take Mary as your wife, for the child conceived in her is from the Holy Spirit", confides the angel. Again we hear the echo of *Receive! Accept! Welcome!* They are the admonitions of this last Sunday of Advent.

Joseph, who is called by name, whose family is identified by the angel, is told to not be fearful. Don't fear to trust, the angel seemed to advise the carpenter. Don't be afraid to risk or be reluctant to commit yourself with radical vulnerability to a plan so fantastic that only God could conceive it, counseled that herald of God, that emissary from the heavens. (no pun intended)

It is evident this angel is not at all akin to the convict masquerading as a priest in one of Hollywood's films. Sean Penn mumbles some inane philosophy that converts a hardened prostitute, and his co-conspirator, Robert DeNiro, bungles into a miracle. It's true they were no angels, these stumbling hoodlums, but this one in Nazareth was real, though it was tucked into a dream. If Joseph had his doubts, they are not voiced. Instead the proof was found in the unfolding drama. Joseph's mind was made up; his attitude formed without reluctance.

While most of us have not had visions of angels, we can all experience the richness of dialogue with God via the means of Christian prayer. It is in the process of sharing our deep feelings with him that the Holy Spirit comes to us with an answer that resolves the dilemma and assures us of his peace. We can learn to accept the most difficult problems of life when we are willing to receive God's angels, his Spirit or his Word as sources of encouragement.

Finally we come to the epilogue, the conclusion, the summary of the results of the drama being acted out in the tumbling hills of Galilee. "When Joseph awoke from sleep, he did as the angel of the Lord commanded him; he took her as his wife, but had no marital relations with her until she had borne a son; and he named him Jesus." Matthew concludes the playlet as briefly as he began it. He tells us Joseph accepted his role and received this event as a gift from God.

It says a great deal to us also about how we are to deal with dif-

whole story becomes prologue
we are the epilogue -
the resolution / conclusion

ficult issues and potentially embarrassing problems. It says we need to look patiently for God before we bail out of a possibly hazardous involvement. It says we need to consider seriously all the implications and to weigh more than the uneasy and awkward overtones and undertones, but the potential blessings. In short, we need to be as receptive to God's messages for us today as Joseph was two millennia ago. We need to accept God's surprises in the midst of human trauma.

Few divorces would occur if both husband and wife trained their minds on the gift God seeks for them to possess, on the miracle he can work in their lives and the blessing he brings to their relationship despite the handicaps they might experience. But this story must not end merely on a note of Biblical morality. There is much more to it. The epilogue looks far into the future.

While Joseph has the male lead in this drama, and the angel has an important part, with Mary given a background role, God is ultimately the Director; the Holy Spirit the Producer, but Jesus is the Star. He has no words to say, no actions to perform...yet...in this play, still clearly his role as Savior resonates throughout the drama.

This, then, was more than some little soap opera that occurred in the tiny village of Nazareth, but the great drama of all the ages for this whole story is a prologue in itself, as is the Old Testament to the coming of Christ and the giving of the Gospel. There is a sequel to follow this scenario of Joseph and the angel. It is going to happen quickly to us, more quickly than for Joseph, for Christmas is before us in four days. For Joseph and Mary who went to Bethlehem to let God's greater drama have its premiere, the months had to pass in Nazareth before they embarked on that journey. For them, it was a drama that covered something like thirty-three years, while for us it is simplified into a phrase of Scripture such as "God with us" or "He will save his people from their sins."

The essence of this story is one of acceptance, of reception, of welcome, of being open to the will and the work of God to see him transform crisis into Christ and potential calamity into the calm peace for which all people hope. The message is meant for us as well as Joseph and Mary, and that is, to be willing to be the instruments of the Holy Spirit to fulfill God's plan and change despair into hope and sadness into joy.

In this little drama we see reverberating throughout the majestic quality of love that Christmas is all about. Forgiveness does not

December 20, 1992

become necessary in this event, since there is no sin by either Mary or Joseph. What was required was the attitude or receptivity to God's will and God's promise. For acceptance to occur, whether it is problem between an engaged couple such as Mary and Joseph or an issue separating you and someone else, a neighbor, a relative, a colleague at work, one needs to exercise the joy of love. Nothing impedes reconciliation or acceptance or reception when love works its miracle, when it forgives and reaches out.

The epilogue is not only a summation of the spirit of the drama, but it provides us with a wonderful reminder that when we waken from our confusing problems, as did Joseph, we need simply to abide by the Lord's commands to us, and discover in the midst of obeying them the Gospel unfolding before our very eyes. Will you receive this gift of God? Will you accept the role he has for you as an obedient Joseph? If you are not a surrogate parent to God's Son, you may nevertheless prove to be the means by which Christ is born in another's life, and turn out to be more of an angel that you thought possible.

Richard Anderson
St. Timothy's Lutheran Church
San Jose, California

DECEMBER 24, 1992

Christmas Eve

Lessons:

Lutheran:	Is. 9:2-7	Titus 2:11-14	Luke 2:1-20
Roman Catholic:	Is. 9:2-7	Titus 2:11-14	Luke 2:1-24
Episcopal:	Is. 9:2-4, 6-7	Titus 2:11-14	Luke 2:1-14 (15-20)
Pres/Meth/UCC:	Is. 9:2-7	Titus 2:11-14	Luke 2:1-14 (15-20)

Introductions to the Lessons

Lesson 1

Isaiah 9:2-7 (**Luth/Pres/Meth/UCC**); *Isa. 9:2-4, 6-7* (**Epis**). A people in the darkness of oppression and war rejoice because they see a great light. It is the light of the birth of a son, the Messiah, who will permanently reign with justice resulting in peace.

Lesson 2

Titus 2:11-14 (**Luth/Epis/Pres/Meth/UCC**). In the birth of Christ the grace of God appeared for the salvation of the world. This results in our living godly lives and in the hope of his return.

Gospel

Luke 2:1-20 (**Luth**); *Luke 2:1-14 (15-20)* (**Epis/Pres/Meth/UCC**). In compliance with a Roman census, Joseph and Mary go to Bethlehem where Jesus is born. The angels of heaven brought the glad news in word and song to shepherds, who then went to the manger to adore the Christchild.

Theme: Do not be afraid.

Thought for the day: Do not be afraid. This word of the angels spoken to the shepherds is given to us and to all the world. Fear no longer holds us in captivity. God has come to save us.

Prayer of meditation: O most gracious God, the holiness of this night is beyond our grasp, even as your love for the world you created is more than we can fathom. Grant to us and to all the earth some sense of the extraordinary nature of your love-gift, as we know it in the birth of your Son, Jesus. Allow us for a few moments to cast

December 24, 1992

all the cares of the world aside and to hear the song of the angels proclaiming the life-giving power that Jesus brings to the earth. Then, fill us with words of praise and thanksgiving like those of the shepherds, that your name might be glorified near and far. Amen.

Call to worship: This very night Mary was called upon to give birth, the angels were called upon to announce the birth, and the shepherds were bid to come and see and then return rejoicing. We, too, are now invited to participate in this joyous event, the once-in-a-world's lifetime birth of the Savior. Come, let us adore him, Christ the Lord.

Prayer of adoration: O most holy God, you have bestowed the most gracious gifts upon this human race. Not only have you given us life, but you allowed yourself to be born in our midst, a human being like us, thereby dignifying all of humanity and honoring the people you love beyond their wildest dreams. Enable us to cherish this most precious gift and to respond with praise and thanksgiving to the giver. Amen.

Prayer of confession: O giver of all good gifts, in this season of joy we are well aware of the temptation to put parties and celebrations, gift exchanges and food, at the top of our list. Guard and keep us from such idolatry. Forgive us our frantic efforts to buy each other's love. Wash away our desire to have everything and more for ourselves. Renew in us, instead, a sense of love sharing, of generosity, and of trust. Allow your Spirit to be born again in us this night that we might follow your star, your will, and your ways, for the sake of the Babe born in Bethlehem.

Prayer of dedication of gifts and self: O holy God, who knows better than anyone what it means to give yourself to your people, our words of praise would never be adequate to thank you for sharing yourself and your love with this planet earth. But bless our humble efforts, as we return a portion of our resources and our selves and dedicate them to the praise and glory of your holy name. Amen.

Sermon title: Do Not Be Afraid

Sermon thesis: The pronouncement of the angels, "Do not be afraid," is echoed in the proclamation of the saints through the ages. It is a word that this world desperately needs to hear. It is a promise that we know through the Savior born this night in Bethlehem.

Hymn for the day: *"While shepherds watched their flocks by night"* This hymn is a quite literal paraphrase of the Christmas story, including the angels' assurance to the shepherds: "Fear not." Included in the New Version of the Psalms by Dr. Brady and Mr. Tate, 1700, this was one of six hymns—as distinguished from paraphrases of the Psalms and canticles—that were permitted to be used in the Divine Worship. Nahum Tate, born and educated in Ireland, went to London, where he made his living writing for the stage. His adaptation of Shakespeare's *King Lear*, which opened in 1681, was his only really successful work, holding the stage until nearly 1840.

Children's object talk:

Do Not Be Afraid

Objects: Night light or flashlight
Lesson: Jesus is the light of the world.
Outline: 1. Being afraid of the dark.
2. Help from someone who loved me.
3. God helps us by sending Jesus.

WHEN I WAS A LITTLE GIRL like you, I was afraid of the dark. Does anyone know what that's like? It is scary, that's for sure.

My parents knew that I was afraid and my parents loved me, so they did things to help me live through my fear. Can you think of something that might help if you were afraid of the dark? Well, my parents gave me a nightlight, and they told me to call them whenever I felt afraid. They would plug the light in at night, and then that little bit of light was enough to take care of the darkness around me and helped me to live through the fear. And if I called to them, they came to me and held me until the fear went away.

Just as my parents gave me a light and someone to call on, so that I wouldn't be afraid, God has given all of us and all the world a light, so that no one would have to be afraid. It was God's way of showing love to the world, just like my parents showed love to me. Jesus is the one God gave to help us live through our fear. Even though Jesus was just a little baby, like my small nightlight, he was enough to take care of the darkness and take away the fear of the world.

December 24, 1992

The sermon:
Do Not Be Afraid

Hymns:
Beginning of worship: It Came upon the Midnight Clear
Sermon hymn: O Little Town of Bethlehem
End of worship: Angels We Have Heard on High

Scripture: Luke 2:1-20

Sermon Text: *"But the angel said to them, "Do not be afraid."*

"I CAN REMEMBER," she began, "when I was just a small child and something would frighten me, my father would come to me and wrap his arms around me, letting me rest against the strength of his body. His love for me was as soft and warm as my security blanket and even safer. He always spoke the same words in the same soothing tone of comfort. 'It's all right. You don't have to be afraid. Papa's here. He'll take care of you.' " Her voice broke as the tears welled in her eyes. She gazed at me tenderly, swallowed a few times, sipped the water at her bedside, and taking her time spoke to me again. "That's what I think of every time I hear the Christmas story. The words, 'don't be afraid,' are so powerful in a time when there is so much to be afraid of."

This was the beginning of the "sermon" that Mabel preached to me that December day. I had come to her bedside in the nursing home to bring her holy communion. She was in her nineties and although she was infirm, I hesitate to call her old. She taught me so much while she lived and as she died.

She continued on, "I'm no longer young, so I have less to be afraid of now. Death itself would come as a blessing at this point in my life. But as I look back, I have come to know the truth of the words spoken by the angel that first Christmas night."

"In those days a decree went out from Emperor Augustus that all the world should be registered   " She spoke now from memory and it was only after she completed the entire birth narrative with ". . . and she gave birth to her firstborn son and wrapped him in bands of cloth, and laid him in a manger, because there was no place for them in the inn," that she had to be prompted to begin the second part of the magnificent story. "In that region there were shepherds living in the fields..." As she recited the words from the depths of her heart, somewhere a connection was made for me between that time long ago and that very day, as if the Savior was indeed being born again in this humble room tucked into a corner of this nursing home. She kept on until she came to the words, "Do not be afraid!" and then she suddenly broke off from the Biblical witness and began her own.

"I remember in the depression, when I was teaching school and they had no more money to pay me. I kept right on teaching and using what little I had to help keep clothes on some of the children who had far less than I did. It was a very cold winter in Cleveland that year." She shook her head helplessly as she said, "Some of them didn't have any shoes at all, and those that did had holes in them. We used to stuff paper in them to try to keep their feet from the frosty pavement. I at least had a little bit coming in so I shared it. God did not abandon me or those little ones in that time of need. I know now that it was God who gave us all strength for the living of those days."

"I remember when my dear husband died, too. It was a terrible time for me. I felt so alone, so empty, so confused. But I kept hearing that word, do not be afraid, and somehow God carried me. I remember feeling especially lonely one afternoon, and just when I felt I could stand it no longer, someone from the church stopped by and invited me to dinner. Church friends are like that. It was as if Jesus himself had stopped in to bring me comfort."

"You know I think about the world today. My problems are nothing compared to the threat of nuclear war, the dire poverty around the globe, the AIDS epidemic and the hopelessness I see in people's faces. Sometimes I'm glad I won't be here much longer to witness anything more terrible than the world wars I lived through. But even as I hear about these things on TV and read about them and see people who suffer, I can't help but repeat the words, do not be afraid. I surely can't say that because I think people will become kinder or that the world's hunger problem will go away or that nations will stop fighting. But I can say those words because they come from God. I know that God loves this earth, as surely as God loves you and me, because of Jesus. God would never have allowed a Son to be born into a world that God hated. So I believe that God is watching over us, that the world is held in the everlasting arms of the Lord as surely as I was held by my father when I was a child. When you get discouraged, when it all looks bleak and overwhelming, remember . . . do not be afraid."

December 24, 1992

There was nothing more to say. After we prayed, I left with this word echoing in my heart and mind, the way it must have echoed through the heavens on Christmas. I share with you the word and the promise that this faith-filled woman shared with me. "Do not be afraid...for to you is born this day....a Savior who is Christ the Lord."

Marie C. Jerge
Evangelical Lutheran Church in America
Buffalo, New York

DECEMBER 25, 1992

Christmas Day

Lessons:

Lutheran	Is. 52:7-10	Heb. 1:1-9	John 1:1-14
Roman Catholic:	Is. 62:11-12	Titus 3:4-7	Luke 2:15-20
Episcopal:	Is. 62:6-7, 10-12	Titus 3:4-7	Luke 2:(1-14) 15-20
Pres/Meth/UCC:	Is. 62:6-12	Titus 3:4-7	Luke 2:(1-7) 8-20

Introductions to the Lessons

Lesson 1

(1) *Isaiah 52:7-10* (**Luth**). Good news for the Jewish captives in Babylon! God is coming to his people to rescue and comfort his people. This is cause for great rejoicing. On Christmas God came in Jesus to save us. It is an occasion for celebration.

(2) *Isaiah 62:6-7, 10-12* (**Epis/Pres/Meth/UCC**). The captive people in Babylon hear the good news that God is coming with the captives to Jerusalem. He is coming to save and rescue. When they return, Jerusalem will be known as the city that God loves. At Christmas God came to the world in Jesus and established the New Jerusalem.

Lesson 2

(1) *Hebrews 1:1-9* (**Luth**). The author of Hebrews begins his letter to suffering Christians by claiming that Jesus is the true, final, and perfect revelation of God. Through him God created the universe. Jesus is the exact likeness of God and is greater than the angels. Heretofore, God spoke at various times through various prophets but now in Jesus God spoke his last word.

(2) *Titus 3:4-7* (**Epis/Pres/Meth/UCC**). Paul writes to Titus, his fellow-worker on his missionary journeys, that Christ's coming brought salvation to us. In no way did we deserve his mercy of forgiveness. It was an act of pure grace. As a result we have new birth and new life.

Gospel

(1) *John 1:1-14* (**Luth**). In this prologue to John's gospel, we learn that the eternal Word of God is God. The Word was with God in the creation of the universe, and is the source of light and life. On Christmas, the Word became human in Jesus, full of grace and truth.

(2) *Luke 2:15-20* (**Epis**); *Luke 2:(1-7) 8-20* (**Pres/Meth/UCC**). In compliance with a Roman census-taking, Joseph and Mary go to Bethlehem where Jesus was born. Angels an-

December 25, 1992

nounced the birth to shepherds who checked out the announcement by going to the manger. Having seen the Christ-child, they returned praising God for what they heard and saw.

Theme: A new creation.

Thought for the day: In the birth of Jesus we can experience once again the miracle of light that shines even in the midst of the darkness.

Prayer of meditation: O most gracious Father, we can't help but begin this day with praise and thanksgiving for the creation you have given and the dawn of the new day you bring every morning. As if that were not enough, you bestowed a new light to pierce our darkness and a new life to bear your love to the world. May we this day bask in the rich abundance of your gifts and may we be truly thankful.

Call to worship: Leader: Jesus is the light of the world,
Response: Who dispels all darkness.
Leader: Jesus is the life of the world,
Response: Who overcomes death and despair.
Leader: Jesus is the Savior Christ,
Response: Who by his presence among us restores and renews all creation.
All: Thanks be to God!

Prayer of adoration: God of all the earth, you visited the world with your Word at the beginning of time, setting in motion the universe. And now you visit the world again, your Word made flesh. It is more than we could ask, more than we deserve and more than we can understand. We offer our profound thanks and our deepest gratitude, which is all we have. Amen.

Prayer of confession: The darkness of the world surrounds us. We are victims of it and we participate in it. We are desperately in need of regeneration, of transformation, of cleansing and of light. Open our eyes to the ways you have been at work in our midst. Fill our mouths with words which affirm what is good and which enlighten all that remains in the shadows. Open our hands to reach out to those around us with your love, especially those who are vulnerable and alone, whom we so often ignore. In all ways recreate us into your people, that this season may indeed be called holy and your people might become beacons radiating your light. Amen.

Prayer of dedication of gifts and self: Blessed are you, O Lord our God, who gave yourself for the people you love. By coming to earth in flesh and blood in the form of a baby born in a manger, you gave yourself fully and completely to us. May your presence invite us to consider the ways we might tangibly offer our thanksgiving to you. We pray that the Babe of Bethlehem inspire us to respond wholly and generously to the work of your church. We offer our bodies: our hands, eyes and feet, that through them you might channel your love to those in need. We offer our intellect, energy and time to the proclamation of your good news. We offer our resources, skills and possessions that you might use them in the ongoing redemption of your glorious creation, for Jesus' sake. Amen.

Sermon title: A New Day Dawns

Sermon thesis: Jesus' birth is God speaking again the word of hope, "Let there be light." It is the sign of the renewal and restoration of all creation.

Hymn for the day: *"Hark! The herald angels sing"* Originally beginning "Hark, how all the welkin rings Glory to the King of kings" (1739), this hymn was altered to its present opening lines fourteen years later in George Whitefield's *Collection of Hymns*. Charles Wesley (1707-1788), one of the first group of the "Oxford Methodist," was ordained to the Church of England. After spending some time in America as a missionary in Georgia, he returned to England and spent many years as an itinerant preacher, and later as a minister to Methodist Societies in London. One of the great hymnwriters of all ages, he composed some 600 hymns. The music by Felix Mendelssohn-Bartholdy (1809-1847) was written to celebrate the anniversary of the invention of printing and was felt by the composer not to be appropriate for a sacred text. It has, however, proved to be a happy combination indeed. The words of this hymn reiterate well the sermon themes of light, renewal and restoration.

Children's object talk:

The Gift

Objects: Some wrapped presents and a baby (if possible)
Lesson: God gave the world a Christmas present of love.
Outline: 1. We give and receive presents at Christmas because we love each other.
    2. God gives us Jesus to show us that God loves us.

I BET THAT SOME OF YOU RECEIVED and gave some Christmas presents last night or today. What presents did you get? What did you give? Why do you think we give presents at Christmas time or

December 25, 1992

any other time? Because it is one way that we can show love for each other.

Well, today is Christmas and God gives us a very special gift of love on Christmas. His name is Jesus and he was a little baby just like this one. Jesus was not born in a hospital like most of us were, but he was born in a barn. Jesus' mother believed that he was truly a gift from God. Babies, just like all children and youth and adults, really all human beings, bring love into the world and at the same time they need love from others. Jesus is the same. Jesus brought God's love into the world and we hope that you will love baby Jesus and want to share his love with everyone you know.

The sermon:
A New Day Dawns
Hymns:
Beginning of worship: O Come All Ye Faithful
Sermon hymn: Of the Father's Love Begotten
End of worship: Joy to the World

Scripture: John 1:1-14

Sermon Text: *"In the beginning---in him was life, and the life was the light of all people---"*

THEY CALLED AT 1:00 A.M. to tell me that my train was going to be four hours late, due to a derailment 500 miles away. I was glad they let me know, but my sleep, for what was left of the interrupted night was restless. As it is, I rarely sleep well when I have a very early day. I guess I'm afraid I will oversleep. This day was scheduled to begin at 4:15 a.m. Now, with the phone call, I had to decide whether to wait for the late train or drive. I decided to drive, but as I got in the car at 5:30 a.m., I figured that this was not going to be one of my better days.

Maybe that's how Joseph and Mary felt. The pregnancy itself had come as a surprise, but Joseph had gotten a call from the Lord through a dream in the middle of the night, urging him to keep this woman and raise this child. He couldn't ignore this clear signal. And then the census was announced. It was terrible timing with Mary so close to delivery. Their travel plans to Bethlehem were shaky at best. They did, of course, manage to arrive in town, but no rooms could be found, despite the onset of Mary's labor pains. No confirmed reservations for late night arrival in those days. Joseph surely had to wonder if this could possibly be a good beginning for any life.

Back to my early morning travel. Although the day began as a disaster, unbeknownst to me God had a surprise "up his sleeve." It began with the deep darkness of night slowly fading from the sky, before the first streaks of light pink began to extend their fingers across the horizon. And then the colors began to deepen, becoming more intense, more pink, then orange, before turning into pure gold. But it was not just the sky that was transformed by the light; the roadway itself became a golden pathway, the yellow brick road to Oz. The haze-covered fields through which the road was winding glistened with dewdrops which honored their creator by reflecting prisms of light everywhere. It was a sunrise. The onset of daylight was no different from yesterday or the day before, yet this dawn somehow birthed a new spirit in me, and the lethargy with which I had dragged myself from sleep was evaporating as quickly as the morning mist. An overwhelming sense of awe rose within me, as if today were the first and last day of the world and I was privileged to be a part of it. As I experienced the dawn, I realized that creation itself was experiencing new birth. Each day was a reenactment of "in the beginning...the earth was a formless void and darkness covered the face of the deep," until God said, "Let there be light," and there was light.

Perhaps Joseph and Mary were just as surprised as I was when the light began to dawn. For it was not just the colorful beauty of creation which they experienced, although that is brilliant enough. It was not just the birth of a newborn, although that in and of itself bears the seeds of the miraculous. But this Child was more than all the children of the earth and all the light of the whole creation. This babe in arms was God's Word in the flesh. The light of the world. In him was life and the hope of the world.

For, in essence, the whole world had become derailed. It lay in the darkness, broken and suffering. The people were desperate in their mourning and their grief. They ached for the day when God would remember the promises made long ago and send the messiah. They prayed for a new day, a day of restoration. They prayed for God to speak again the word of hope, "Let there be light."

God heard the prayers of the people, and on this day which has

December 25, 1992

been named Christmas, God sent the one we call the Christ. This birth signaled the beginning of a new creation, a renewed creation, a world called back into the grand possibilities of God's original design. Even the words of the gospel of John, "In the beginning," echo the words of Genesis, calling upon us to make the connection between the Lord of creation and the Lord birthed in the stable.

But Christmas is not only a day in history. It is also a day in our lives when annually we celebrate the birth of that Savior in our hearts and minds so that the new creation dawns also upon us. As we participate in this celebration and as we experience again that miraculous beginning, we too become children of God, transformed by God's power, as clearly as the sun transforms darkness into daylight.

If I can be inspired and I can receive energy for a day's living from a simple sunrise, can you imagine what it is like to gaze upon the face of the Son of God?

Marie C. Jerge
Evangelical Lutheran Church in America
Buffalo, New York

DECEMBER 27, 1992

First Sunday after Christmas

Lessons:

	Is. 63:7-9	Gal. 4:4-7	Matt. 2:13-15, 19-23
	Sir. 3:2-6, 12-14	Col. 3:12-21	Matt. 2:13-15, 19-23
Roman Catholic:			
Episcopal:	Is. 61:10-62:3	Gal. 3:23-25; 4:4-7	John 1:1-18
Pres/Meth/UCC:	Is. 63:7-9	Heb. 2:10-18	Matt. 2:13-23

Introductions to the Lessons

Lesson 1

(1) *Isaiah 63:7-9* (**Luth/Pres/Meth/UCC**). The love of God came down to earth on Christmas. It is time to recall God's steadfast love for his people. Throughout Hebrew history God in love shared his people's afflictions. In Christ, however, God's full love was personified.

(2) *Isaiah 61:10-62:3* (**Epis**). The promised Messiah filled with the Spirit will bring liberty, comfort, and gladness. Therefore, the prophet rejoices in God for bringing salvation and righteousness to the nations. God's people will be a crown of beauty for the Lord.

Lesson 2

(1) *Galatians 4:4-7* (**Luth**); *Gal. 3:23-25; 4:4-7* (**Epis**). On Christmas, God's Son came to earth to live among people. He came to change us from being slaves of sin to sons of God. Proof of our sonship is the possession of the Holy Spirit, who enables us to call God "Father."

(2) *Hebrews 2:10-18* (**Pres/Meth/UCC**). In the Christmas event, God's Son identified with humanity. In every area he shared our human nature. As a human he suffered, was tempted, and died. He did this to conquer Satan, sin, and death for us.

Gospel

(1) *Matthew 2:13-15, 19-23* (**Luth**); *Matt. 2:13-23* (**Pres/Meth/UCC**). Before he was two years old, the child Jesus went from ecstacy to agony. The ecstacy was the visit of the Wise Men from the East with their gifts. The agony followed consisting of fleeing as refugees to Egypt to escape from cruel King Herod. Later Herod's son succeeded him, but he was no better. To avoid the new king, the Holy Family settled in Nazareth.

(2) *John 1:1-18* (**Epis**). This passage is the prologue to the gospel of John. It tells us who Jesus really is. Jesus is the eternal Word of God. At Christmas the Word became

December 27, 1992

human in Jesus. For the first time humanity was able to see God in Jesus, full of grace and truth. John the Baptist bore witness to him as the Light of the world.

Theme: The promise fulfilled.

Prayer of dedication of gifts and self: Jesus is the new Moses who delivers the people from their slavery to sin, fulfilling God's promise of salvation.

Prayer of meditation: A helpless baby and his parents, ordinary people, taking a trip to Egypt. Yet it is through such as these that you, O Lord, have chosen to accomplish your will for the world's salvation. We give you thanks for your wondrous accomplishments and for the ordinary people through whom you achieve them. Amen.

Call to worship: God calls us from all walks of life to participate in the mighty acts of salvation history: carpenters and homemakers, the unemployed and construction workers, weavers and teachers. Come one and all to witness the fulfillment of God's salvation in Jesus Christ the Lord.

Prayer of adoration: O most holy and gracious God, we offer thanks for your involvement in human history, for your willingness to enter our world in human form, for your love evidenced in the gift of your Son. Enable us to appreciate the extent to which you will go to manifest your devotion to the world. Encourage us to participate fully in the unfolding story of your salvation, for Jesus' sake. Amen.

Prayer of confession: O Lord our God, at this most holy season we are continually made aware of the world's shallowness and greed. The world's festivities are already past history, gifts have been put away and toys tossed aside. Yet your love endures throughout the days and years. Our generosity ends, while your gracious favor persists in showering us with abundant blessing. Grant us, O Lord, freedom from our throw-away society and replace it with insight into your ways, your steadfastness, your eternal glory. Transform our narrow vision into your broad and expansive perspective of all history. Enable us to enter into our world with a strong sense of your kingdom come, through Jesus Christ, our newborn Lord and Savior. Amen.

Prayer of dedication of gifts and self: O Lord and Savior, hope of all creation, we could offer all our hearts, minds, souls and resources

The Minister's Annual Manual

to you and still it would never be enough to thank you for your blessings. And so we ask your grace that we might play our part in your salvation history. Use our ordinary lives as witnesses to your glory. Open our lips to sing your praise. Utilize our skills to provide resources needed by your people. In all things make us responsive to your will for the world, that we might take our places with Joseph and Mary and all the saints as examples of obedient servanthood for your people. Amen.

Sermon title: Joseph

Sermon thesis: Matthew paints a picture of Jesus as the fulfillment of God's promise of deliverance, begun in the exodus from the slavery in Egypt. Joseph serves as God's instrument in the unfolding saga of salvation history.

Hymn for the day: *"Come now, and praise the humble saint of David's house and line"* This hymn was written in 1976 for use at St. Joseph's Episcopal Church, Durham, North Carolina, where the author, George W. Williams, served as choirmaster from 1965-1977. Williams (b. 1922) has been professor of English at Duke University since 1957. His specialties are Shakespeare, seventeenth-century poetry and textual criticism. Among his numerous publications are two children's books and a facsimile edition of John Wesley's first hymn book.

Announcements for next week:
   Sermon title: Silent Night
   Sermon theme: Our emptiness, but God's fullness.
   Sermon summary: The Christmas holiday season is so full of celebrations and festivities that we can easily leave no room for the fullness of God's good news to be received into our hearts and lives. Sometimes empty or even pain-filled moments can open us again to hearing the good news in a new and fresh way.

Children's object talk:

Ordinary People in God's Plan

Objects: A block of wood and something wooden that is carved or crafted (candlestick, statue, etc.)
Lesson: God takes ordinary things and uses them to his glory.
Outline: 1. Joseph was a carpenter and used wood to make useful things for people.
   2. God takes ordinary people, like Joseph, and uses them to do useful things in the kingdom and show love to the people in it.

December 27, 1992

DO YOU KNOW WHAT THIS IS? (Hold up the block of wood.) Do you know what this is? (Hold up the object made of wood.) I am fortunate to have many things in my home that are made of wood. I like wood. But if it were left to me, the wood would look just like this (hold up the block.) I don't have the gifts and skills needed to make something beautiful out of a block of wood. But Joseph did. Joseph was Jesus' father.

When God was searching the earth for a way to show the love that was in God's heart, God decided to work through and use people like Joseph to be part of the plan. Joseph was just an ordinary workman. Mary was just an ordinary teenager. But God used these people to bring Jesus into the world and to help him to grow up to be an adult. God uses all kinds of ordinary things to help people know about love. God uses your moms and dads and their hugs and kisses. God uses pastors and churches to proclaim God's word and to sing God's praise and pray for others. God uses people like you to give hugs and to help out at home and to bring smiles. When we do these things that make God happy, when we listen to God's word, then we are being a good follower of God, just like Joseph was.

The sermon:

Joseph

Hymns:
Beginning of worship: The Bells of Christmas
Sermon hymn: Lo, How a Rose is Blooming
End of worship: Hark the Herald Angels Sing

Scripture: Matthew 2:13-15, 19-23

Sermon Text: *"This was to fulfill what had been spoken by the Lord through the prophet."* (v. 15 and 23)

"WOULD THERE EVER BE ANYTHING ORDINARY about this child?" Joseph was reflecting on the birth of his first-born. In some ways, the preparation he had made was the same as any other expectant father. He was a jumble of fears and trembling, awe and excitement, hopes and dreams. He was a participant in the drama as it was enacted, but he was only in the wings, which was fine, because he surely had a lot to think about. Mary, his betrothed and beloved, had become pregnant without his help. She was the one standing in the spotlight on center stage. "I might have called the whole thing off," he mused to himself, "if my sleep had not been disturbed that night by the angel of the Lord. It was clear that my job was to keep Mary, marry her and care for the child."

Joseph remembered with clarity and some force his own discomfort after that night. He was, after all, only an ordinary man, a carpenter. He was used to working wood. Wood is touchable, tangible. It can be held and shaped and formed into utensils and furniture, items useful for living. The proclamation of the angel was not like the wood. The words came in dreams. They seemed supernatural or extraordinary to his concrete way of thinking. It was difficult to understand where they would lead. There was nothing solid to see or touch, on which to depend.

But he had followed the orders, obeying the angel's command. He and Mary had joined together and even with the journey, the census and the inn with no vacancy, it had all worked out. It hadn't been the best of accommodations. He wished he had been able to provide more for his wife and child, but at least they had found shelter and warmth. The baby had been born, healthy. There had been no complications. As a matter of fact the birth itself—the pains of labor, the pushing and panting, the blood and water—was the only thing that seemed normal about this child. It was a miracle to be part of such an event. "My son or not," he thought to himself with just a hint of pride in his tone, "I was there, participating in the joy of new life." But then the reverie returned, washing over him, as he pondered that never in all his life had he suspected that it would turn out like this.

He realized, now, that he should have known that there would be more to come, but never in his wildest dreams could he have conjured up the image of the wise sages from the east and their mysterious story of the star and the overwhelming generosity of their gifts. This child of his heart, if not his blood, was more than his son. He knew it now, for certain. Even he, an ordinary carpenter could see it. He didn't understand it, but he knew that he was a participant in something even more miraculous than a birth.

So it had not been quite so frightening when the angel came again in his dreams. He had almost expected another visit. "Get up, take the child and his mother, and flee to Egypt, and remain there until

December 27, 1992

I tell you." And suddenly it became clear. He knew. This time it was more than simple obedience to the Lord's command. This time even the simplest of minds could make the connection. Egypt. Egypt, where the people of Israel had been held so long in captivity. Egypt, where God had raised up Moses to bring them out of their bondage to slavery into the freedom of the promised land. Egypt, where God's presence entered human history so that the people would be saved. Emmanuel, God present with us, was the name of his son. The bridge was completed. Though an ordinary man, from a little known town, he recognized the awesome gift and responsibility that had been given unto him. This child was to be the new Moses, the Messiah who would save his people, the fulfillment of all the promises of the prophets.

Marie C. Jerge
Evangelical Lutheran Church in America
Buffalo, New York

JANUARY 3, 1993

Second Sunday after Christmas

Lessons:

Lutheran:	Is. 61:10-62:3	Eph. 1:3-6, 15-18	John 1:1-18
Roman Catholic:	Jer. 31:7-14	Eph. 1:3-6,15-18	John 1:(1-9) 10-18
Episcopal:	Jer. 31:7-14	Eph. 1:3-6, 15-19a	Matt. 2:13-15, 19-23
Pres/Meth/UCC:	Jer. 31:7-14	Eph. 1:3-14	John 1:1-18

Introductions to the Lessons

Lesson 1

(1) *Isaiah 61:10-62:3* (**Luth**). The promised Messiah, filled with the Spirit, will bring liberty, comfort, and gladness to God's people. Therefore, the prophet rejoices in God for bringing salvation and righteousness to the nations. God's people will be a crown of beauty for the Lord.

(2) *Jeremiah 31:7-14* (**Epis/Pres/Meth/UCC**). As a spokesman for God, Jeremiah had the unpleasant task of preaching doom and destruction upon Israel because of their idolatry. Here Jeremiah sees beyond the captivity in Babylon to a glorious return home to freedom and national existence. The day will come when there will be singing, dancing, and feasting.

Lesson 2

Ephesians 1:3-6, 15-18 (**Luth**); *Eph. 1:3-14* (**Pres/Meth/UCC**); *Ephesians 1:3-6, 15-19a* (**Epis**). Thanks be to God for Jesus! Why? Because Jesus has given us spiritual gifts. Because of Jesus, God adopted us as his children, and we are made right with God. In addition, Paul gives thanks for the love of God's people and prays that the Spirit will enable them to know God.

Gospel

(1) *John 1:1-18* (**Luth/Pres/Meth/UCC**). This passage is the prologue to John's gospel. It tells us who Jesus really is. He is the eternal Word of God. At Christmas the Word became human in Jesus. For the first time humanity was able to see God in Jesus, full of grace and truth. John the Baptist bore witness to him as the light of the world.

(2) *Matthew 2:3-15, 19-23* (**Epis**). Before he was two years old, the child Jesus went from ecstacy to agony. The ecstacy was the visit of the Wise Men from the East with their gifts. The agony followed, consisting of fleeing as refugees to Egypt to escape cruel King Herod. Later Herod's son succeeded him, but he was no better. To avoid the new king, the Holy Family settled in Nazareth.

January 3, 1993

Theme: Our emptiness, God's fullness.

Thought for the day: God continues faithfully to speak to us and be present among us. It is important that in the midst of the noise and busyness of our celebrations we allow space for God's voice and room for God's love.

Prayer of meditation: Our bodies are tired from the hustle and bustle of the holiday activities and our minds whirl with remembrances of parties and presents. We thank you for all your blessings in this season, but today we request calm and quietness of spirit that we might be open to your call and to your presence, that we might know the fullness of your grace, as you have shared it in your Son, Jesus. Amen.

Call to worship: The babe, the Son of Mary is born, bearing in his own body gifts of life and light, abundant fullness and gracious love. May we approach our newborn Lord this day bearing gifts which honor his birth: love-filled hearts, prayer-filled lives and praise-filled voices.

Prayer of adoration: Of all the gifts given and received this and every Christmas season, you, O Lord, remain the best. For in you we find our ultimate home and rest, God's own power for living. As we leave this holy season, enable us to continue to seek you and the gifts that you bring above all else, that the love you brought into the world might shine through us to others. Amen.

Prayer of confession: O Lord incarnate, the celebration of your birth has caused us once again to consider the ways that love became flesh in you. Your willingness to live and walk with the poor and the outcast, your voluntary commitment to God's will even though it might mean death are signs for others of what it means to be called God's people. O lover of this earth, we have been remiss in our incarnating of your love. We have not followed your ways, listened to your call or been obedient to your will. We make excuses, and we resist changing our sinful ways. We like our friends and refuse to accept others different from ourselves. We play it safe and neglect opportunities for service that are presented to us. Above all, we call ourselves by your name but ignore you. We turn to you now, because you are our only hope; without your mercy we are lost. And so we pray that you might renew us, shine upon us, fill us and restore us so that we can be your people in this world, serving you and others to the glory of your name. Amen.

Prayer of dedication of gifts and self: O most gracious God, you have showered us with abundant blessings far beyond our merit or deserving. We are full to the overflowing with spiritual and material wealth. We offer now a portion of what we have received from your hand that it might be used in your service and to your glory. It is only a small token of all that you have given to us and for us, and so we ask to be motivated by love to continually grow in our sacrifice for the sake of your church and the proclamation of your word. Make us a generous people, begrudging nothing, but giving instead in the same spirit in which you gave your Son. Help us to dedicate our time, our talents, and our resources as completely as fully and as often as we offer our prayers. Amen.

Sermon title: Silent Night

Sermon thesis: The Christmas holiday season is so full of celebrations and festivities that we can easily leave no room for the fullness of God's good news to be received into our hearts and lives. Sometimes empty or even pain-filled moments can open us again to hearing the good news in a new and fresh way.

Hymn for the day: *"Let all together praise our God"* A contemporary of Martin Luther, Nikolaus Herman (c. 1480-1561) served as a teacher in the Latin school and organist and choir director of a Lutheran church in Gergstadt, Bohemia. The pastor of the church was Johann Mathesius, a pupil and friend of Luther's. Many of Herman's hymns were inspired by Mathesius' sermons. The mystery of the incarnation is the joyful theme of this hymn.

Announcements for this week: (Epiphany, January 6)

Sermon title: Where Are You Going to Find God?
Sermon theme: God came to a troubled world because of love!
Sermon summary: We cannot avoid life's problems. We encounter them just by being human, so God says to us in Jesus, "Let me be with you as you face life's difficulties." God with us — Immanuel! The wise men found him in the most surprising place, poor little Bethlehem, even in the midst of a hard world. Where will we find him?

Announcements for next week:

Sermon title: Touch of the Master
Sermon theme: In baptism we know we are important and valued by God!
Sermon summary: Baptism is an integral part of bringing people into a right relationship with God. It is a sacrament — which is an outward sign of an inner, invisible

January 3, 1993

reality. In baptism, the connection is secured, the link made. God connects with his children. In Christ's baptism Jesus was identified with God, unmistakably. And so are we!

Children's object talk:

We Have All Received

Objects: Anything that symbolizes love to you (wedding ring, photo).
Lesson: God has sent love to the world in Jesus
Outline: 1. Things that help us to know that people love us.
2. Some people don't have these things.
3. Jesus' love is for everyone.

DO YOU KNOW WHAT THIS IS? (Hold up object you have brought, wedding ring.) Do you know why this is important to me? It is important, because whenever I look at it I am reminded that there is someone who loves me, my husband. Can you think of other things that, when you look at them, you are reminded of someone's love?

You know we are very lucky to have all these things. And I think we should remember to thank God for all these love gifts that we have received. But you know that there are some people who don't have lots of things like we do. People who don't have lots of food, people who have hardly any clothes, people who don't have homes. I think it would be hard for them to know that someone loves them. But that's one of the reasons God sent Jesus to the world. For if you know Jesus, if you see his cross in church, or you come to worship, then you are reminded that somebody loves you. Jesus is God's gift to the world, so that everyone would know that God loves them. So when we thank God for love gifts, we will put Jesus right at the top of the list. (Close with prayer of thanksgiving.)

The sermon:
Silent Night

Hymns:
Beginning of worship: What Child is This
Sermon hymn: All Hail to You, O Blessed Morn
End of worship: The First Noel

Scripture: John 1:1-18

Sermon Text: *"From his fullness we have all received, grace upon grace."* (v. 16)

IT WAS CHRISTMAS, 1990. I'll never forget it. It had been a long and difficult fall season. Nothing unusual, just hard work and lots of hours. Then came winter, cold and wet. I was just run down enough that the week before Christmas I picked up a bug that settled in my sinuses, which drained into my throat, resulting in a severe case of laryngitis. My voice totally deserted me on Christmas Eve. I could whisper, but if I tried to speak, no sound at all emerged from my lips. It was awful. I could not sing with the choir or in the trio we had prepared for the evening's service. Not one Christmas carol, nor one angel's song, nor one Gloria in Excelsis. I went to worship, but I could do nothing more than smile, nod my head, shake people's hand in greeting, point to my throat and hope that the person standing next to me would explain. It was devastating for me, for whom Christmas and singing are tied together like love and marriage, horse and carriage, or peanut butter and jelly. Silent night took on a whole new meaning.

Yet that Christmas, although it ranks as one of my all-time most frustrating, will also remain in my memory as one of the most meaningful. For without any way to give of myself in worship, I was forced to remember that Christmas is a gift to be received. I have never listened quite so intently to the pronouncement of God's word spoken by angels and shepherds. I have never relied quite so completely on the rest of God's people in the body of Christ, gathered in worship, to declare God's praise on my behalf. The message came through loud and clear: Christ come to earth is not dependent on my voice or my actions at all, but is God's good work.

It is strange to say, but the holidays when I have heard this message the loudest, are those in which something has gone wrong,

January 3, 1993

or in which there is an emptiness in my heart: my first Christmas away from home or the year of the blizzard when church services had to be canceled. It makes me think that Christmas has sometimes become so busy and so full of joyous celebration and activity that it is difficult to sit quietly and receive. It is so full of food that we miss any sense of hungering for the Savior. It is so full of lights that we are momentarily blinded to the desperate pain and suffering of those who live in our corner of the world and whose need lasts beyond the season of generosity. Perhaps our own material abundance and the good life that we live, compared to so many others around the globe, has become a barrier which keeps us from appreciation for all God's gifts, rather than a blessing.

I have met and have much to learn from people who have far less stuff than I do and who live much more joy-filled lives. They know the grace of God apart from wealth and health. They may be angry and dream about a different life, but they rarely complain about little things, such as which brand of toothpaste gives you more zip, or which brand of jeans we "must" buy to be "in."

Think about those who have through the centuries been persecuted for the faith. Their very lives are in danger for professing that Jesus is Lord. They are sometimes tortured and imprisoned. Their families are harassed, their homes ransacked and their possessions stolen, yet they sing God's praise loud and long. The gift of the Savior and the freedom he offers the world is a reality for these people in ways I have only begun to ponder.

"From his fullness we have all received, grace upon grace." I have so much to learn about the richness of God's grace from those who live in poverty, but whose spirit is full to overflowing in praise to God for gracious gifts of Jesus and love and hope.

The Christmas season is now coming to an end. Most of the festivities are over, the presents have been stored away, the cookies are crumbs and even the leftovers have been consumed. It's time to take down the tree, put away the ornaments and decorations and move on into the new year. Perhaps instead of a letdown, we can turn this end of the holiday season into a blessed new year time, where the resolutions we make are less focused on us and more in keeping with holy days just past. Perhaps we can for a moment feel, with the world, the emptiness, the hunger, the ache and the craving for good news. Perhaps that sense of longing will enrich our lives and leave room for God to act, to speak, to love. For the joyous

The Minister's Annual Manual

good news that is proclaimed, not for one day of the year, or even just for a season, but for all time, is that God has and does fill the empty desolation which plagues us and our world. Jesus Christ is born! The Word has become flesh and lives among us. The light has dawned, overcoming all darkness. "From this fullness we have all received, grace upon grace."

Marie C. Jerge
Evangelical Lutheran Church in America
Buffalo, New York

JANUARY 6, 1993

Epiphany

Lessons:

Lutheran:	Is. 60:1-6	Eph. 3:2-12	Matt. 2:1-12
Roman Catholic:	Is. 60:1-6	Eph. 3:2-3, 5-6	Matt. 2:1-12
Episcopal:	Is. 60:1, 6-9	Eph. 3:1-12	Matt. 2:1-12
Pres/Meth/UCC:	Is. 60:1-6	Eph. 3:1-12	Matt. 2:1-12

Introductions to the Lessons

Lesson 1

Isaiah 60:1-6 (**Luth/Pres/Meth/UCC**); *60:1, 6-9* (**Epis**). Epiphany is the festival and season of light. It is associated with the five-pointed star. A star can be seen only in the darkness. Israel at the time of this writing is in the darkness of the dispersion of her people. Now the light of God is seen and the scattered people will be returned and the glory of God will appear in their midst.

Lesson 2

Ephesians 3:2-12 (**Luth**); *3:1-12* (**Epis/Pres/Meth/UCC**). Paul has a secret. It was hidden for centuries. It was revealed to him that the Gospel is for Gentiles as well as for Jews. This makes Christianity a universal religion, for Christ died for all human beings. By the grace of God Paul was called to proclaim this good news to the Gentiles.

Gospel

Matthew 2:1-12 (**Luth/Epis/Pres/Meth/UCC**). Led by a star, learned men from the East came to worship the king whose star they saw. Since the baby was a child of a king, they naturally went to Jerusalem, the capitol city where they learned that the Scriptures named Bethlehem as the birthplace. Again, the star led them to the holy family where they worshiped the Christchild with gifts.

Theme: God came to a troubled world because of love!

Thought for the day: The birth of Christ was a real event in a real world. It was God's way of saying "Yes" to you and me in whatever predicament we find ourselves facing, even in prisons of all kinds. The birth of Christ and recognizing that, which is what Epiphany celebrates, is not isolated from life nor set apart, but rather set in the heart of living — in the mainstream of life.

The Minister's Annual Manual

Prayer of meditation: Heavenly Father, open our eyes that we might truly see; open our ears that we might genuinely hear; and open our minds that we might honestly understand your love and your care. In the name of the One wise men continue to see. Amen.

Call to worship: "The light shines in the darkness, and the darkness has not overcome it." Welcome into the presence and power of our God, who out of love entered our world as it is, so that it might become what only his love could fashion. Welcome in the name of the newborn King!

Prayer of adoration: Mighty God, out of love for a confused and lonely world, you entered into our midst. Help us to recognize that you have never left us. Encourage us to live out of the love you have given us. Allow our emotions and intellects to be captured by the awe-someness of what you have done for us. Let us tremble at your power and let us bask in the warmth of your compassion. Enable our lives to be filled with gratitude. Amen.

Prayer of confession: Most holy and merciful Father, we confess to you and to one another that we have not fulfilled the hope in which you created us. We have not cared, when we should have loved; we have been indifferent to the cry of need; we have rejected the way of your Son, and we no longer deserve to be called your children. Forgive us. Renew in us the grace and strength of your Holy Spirit for the sake of our Savior King. Amen.

Prayer of dedication of gifts and self: Bless these gifts, O God, that by them we may dedicate our lives to you, and through them we may show the world a measure of your love. This we humbly yet confidently ask in the name of Christ Jesus, your perfect gift and our precious Savior. Amen.

Sermon title: Where are You Going to Find God?

Sermon thesis: We cannot avoid life's problems. We encounter them just by being human. So God says to us in Jesus, "Let me be with you as you face life's difficulties." God with us—Immanuel! The wise men found him in the most surprising place, poor little Bethlehem, even in the midst of a hard world. Where will we find him?

Hymn for the day: *"We three kings"* John Henry Hopkins, Jr. (1820-1891) composed both the text and the tune of this Epiphany carol in 1857. He also wrote the hymn, "Come with us, O blessed Jesus." Hopkins worked as a reporter in New York City while studying law. He later graduated from General Theological Seminary in

New York City and from 1855-1857 served as the first instructor in church music. During the 1850s and 1860s he was active in the New York Ecclesiological Society and edited the *Church Journal*, which he had founded. He was ordained a priest in 1872 and afterwards served churches in New York and Pennsylvania.

Children's object talk:

Looking for God

Object: A flashlight
Lesson: To show how Jesus is God's light for us to follow.
Outline: 1. We need light to move forward in the dark.
         2. This world is often dark and frightening.
         3. God sent his light—Jesus the Christ—so that we could find
            our way.

WHAT IS THIS? (Show them the flashlight) When do you use it? (In the dark to see your way.) Does the dark ever scare you? It does me sometimes, when I can't see what is out there. What do you think the dark and a flashlight have to do with God and the church today? You just heard me read the story of the wise men searching to find the newborn Jesus. Did you hear me talk about the star? They followed the star in the middle of a very dark, scary world. God sent a light for them to follow.

Did you know that God sent a light for you and me to follow? Jesus. He is our light because he shows us the way. Now he doesn't shine like this flashlight; but he leads us by showing us how we should live, by telling us how he loves us, by helping us when we are afraid. Jesus is our light in a world that is very dark at times. He came to shine in our lives, to help us know God better and live good, happy lives in his love.

I am thankful for God's light and I can go with Jesus and not be afraid.

The sermon:
Where Are You Going To Find God?

Hymns:
  Beginning of worship: Brightest and Best of the Stars of the Morning
  Sermon hymn: The First Noel
  End of worship: Good Christian Friends, Rejoice

Scripture: Matthew 2:1-12

Sermon Text: "Where is the child who has been born king of the Jews?" (vs. 2)

I TOOK MY TURN as did the other five pastors in Pierce: On Sunday afternoons we brought devotions, conversation, and prayer to the small county jail in our little town. It was not something I especially looked forward to, nor was it anything I really dreaded. It was just something that needed to be done. This particular Sunday, my turn, was greeted with even less enthusiasm because it was the first Sunday after Christmas, just three days past, and my heart was more with my family.

Nothing seemed unusual as the deputy sheriff unlocked the cell door to let me in. I headed for the cement block picnic table in the center of the sleeping cells, as the deputy announced that the preacher was here for anyone who wanted to talk. I've had better introductions. Eight guys were current residents—all dressed in the bright orange jumpsuits that declared brazenly across the front: Property of Pierce County Jail. Seven of them came and sat at the table with me. It's easy to be the best show in town when you're the only show in town.

We talked for awhile, nothing especially insightful. Then I had a brief devotion and prayer, and we talked again. After a while, I started to get up and one of the guys asked very innocently: "Aren't you going to lead us in singing?" I experienced one of the most amazing emotions in my life, a genuine cross between fear and fascination, to think of me leading group singing with seven other guys, That should trigger fear and fascination in your souls. And — I don't want to lose any credibility — but I honestly believe, out of the eight of us I had the best voice. Now that's close to amazing, but the best of a bad crew.

January 6, 1993

Anyway, we sang — Christmas carols — first verses of all we could think of. Each one started a little rough, like winding up an old Victrola needle, and the accoustics in a jail cell are not musically enhancing. But we sang ... and sang ... and we talked in between. From time to time one of the fellows would tell a story from their Christmas past. Then we sang some more, each time gaining volume and confidence. After more than an hour, I again made preparations to leave, feeling differently about these men, about our time together, about Christmas celebrations. As I put my coat on, one of the men, a quiet fellow I don't remember talking, simply stated: "God cares, doesn't he?" And you know what? That was the most profound Christmas message I heard that year, "God cares, doesn't he?" You see, God was there, and eight of us knew it!

Singing Christmas carols in jail is most appropriate, for the Christ event itself happened in the midst of a troubled world, a world held captive by hurt and disappointment, cruel powers and inhumanity, a world that yearned to hear his message of love. Jesus' birth was not just for people who worship on Sunday morning. He came for people in jails, hospitals, sick at home, in nursing homes. He came for people who have never darkened the door of a church. He came for folks who live in far away lands, places we've never even heard of or will ever see, in Asia and Africa and South America.

The Christmas event happened so that God's message of love for humankind might be available to people in physical pain or isolation; for people facing uncertainty, economical and emotional. The birth of Christ was a real event in a real world. It was God's way of saying "Yes" to you and me in whatever predicament we find ourselves facing, even in prisons of all kinds.

You see, that's the message of Epiphany, the celebration of the wise men coming, the astrologers from a far-off country who followed the star that claimed the birth of a newborn king. WE celebrated today, this twelfth day of Christmas, the meaning of that birth. And we get a glimpse of what that birth *can* mean for us. But we dare not romanticize or sanitize the story of God's coming into a never, never land that has no contact with your life or mine because that's not true! If we do, we end up with a Jesus far away, out of touch with reality. We end up with that which God intended for Good News as old news, cold news, and even no news. We turn it into a mere trivial, fanciful romantic story for children. The birth of Christ is not isolated from life nor set apart, but rather set in the heart of living, the mainstream of life. Right where you and I find ourselves day in and day out. That's where God is — even in the midst of an often hostile world.

The wise men came, dusty and tired, and probably frustrated. Using common sense, they looked where you'd expect to find a newborn king — in the palace in the capital — in Jerusalem, of course. And the current king, Herod, was most interested in their quest. Herod the Great, answerable only to Augustus Caesar in Rome — the kind of man who would kill his own sons if he thought they had their eye on his throne. And visitors from far away come with a tale of hoping to find the new Sovereign? Herod's blood boiled. In fact, history tells us, he murdered not one or two, but three of his own sons for that very reason. Later he had 300 officers disposed of, and finally his own wife and mother were killed at his request.

That was the climate of the times surrounding Jesus' birth — an insecure ruler who becomes furious over the birth of a possible threat to his throne. The times were volatile, to say the least. Five verses from where our Gospel ends for today, Matthew simply states: "He gave orders to kill all the boys in Bethlehem and its vicinity who were two years and under." Pretty ugly times! And yet, where could God be found? The wise men found him in Bethlehem, in the midst of poverty, born in a barn, not where they thought they'd find God's Messiah. But that's where he was. God seems to do that, to be found in unlikely places where we don't always think of looking. Yet he's there!

A fellow named John Garvey was moved by the courageous response of a family in the time of crisis, and he saw God. Garvey was at best an agnostic, questioning the purpose of faith, thinking it only for the weak, doubting it had any power. He asked: "What difference does the Christian faith make?" But now he answers by saying the difference is in the way you respond to terrible times, which brings us to the family who awakened his understanding. They had a child who fell ill while staying with relatives and suffered severe and permanent brain damage. The child needs constant attention now, and the parents give it to him. They have no vacations; they have very little social life; they have lots of reasons to complain and gripe, but they don't and that amazed Garvey. They respond instead only in love. After watching this family, Garvey wrote: "I felt, looking at him and at them, that there are depths here which are

January 6, 1993

holy and a mystery of love which cannot by spoken about very well ... It is the mystery which leads us to baptize infants, which tells us that God's relationship with this person is not as limited as our own ... The moment that this realization begins to be marginal among Christians, we will have begun to betray an essential part of what it is that we have been given as a vocation ... the work of saying and living as if it were so, that the Creation is holy, that what is good, even when it is terribly wounded, is holy, and maybe especially then." And he concludes with this quote: "Love is not consolation. Love is light!" Garvey saw God, even in such a difficult situation. God's yes to humankind was being spoken in the mainstream of life. He was saying on Christmas morn: "I see the problems of the world. I hear the cries of my people. I know the struggles you are facing, and I want to be with you and to see you through them, around them, and over them."

We can't avoid life's problems; we encounter them just by being human. So God says to us in Jesus, "Let me be with you as you face life's difficulties" and that's what the wise men found that first Christmas! God with us — Immanuel! And the wise men found Him in the most surprising place, even in the midst of a hard world, even in a jail cell, even in little, poor Bethlehem.

As you and I head off into 1993, where are you going to find God? He will be there!

David de Freese
Immanuel Lutheran Church
Bellevue, Nebraska

JANUARY 10, 1993

First Sunday after Epiphany, Baptism of our Lord

Lessons:

Lutheran:	Is. 42:1-7	Acts 10:34-38	Matt. 3:13-17
Roman Catholic:	Is. 42:1-4, 6-7	Acts 10:34-38	Matt. 3:13-17
Episcopal:	Is. 42:1-9	Acts 10:34-38	Matt. 3:13-17
Pres/Meth/UCC:	Is. 42:1-9	Acts 10:34-43	Matt. 3:13-17

Introductions to the Lessons

Lesson 1

Isaiah 42:1-7 (**Luth**); *Isa. 42:1-9* (**Epis/Pres/Meth/UCC**). This passage is one of four servant poems in Isaiah. The poem contains a description of God's Servant and his work. On this Baptism of our Lord Sunday, we see the fulfillment of this prophecy in Jesus. Like the Servant, Jesus was given the Spirit and was well pleasing to God. Jesus' work was the same as the Servant's: to establish justice, to mediate a new covenant, and to liberate the oppressed.

Lesson 2

Acts 10:34-38 (**Luth/Epis**); *Acts 10:34-43* (**Pres/Meth/UCC**). Cornelius, a captain in the Roman army, sent for Peter to tell him and his friends gathered in his home about the Gospel. Peter recounted the baptism of John the Baptist and at Jesus' baptism the coming of the Holy Spirit and power. After his baptism, Jesus went about doing good, died on a cross, and rose from death. By the power of his name, sins are forgiven.

Gospel

Matthew 3:13-17 (**Luth/Epis/Pres/Meth/UCC**). John the Baptist was baptizing people in the river Jordan. One day a 30-year-old man came to be baptized, but John did not want to baptize him not because he was non-repentant nor unbelieving but because he was Jesus. John the Baptist thought that Jesus rather should baptize him. Jesus insisted and John yielded to his request. For Jesus this was an intense religious experience in which he received the Holy Spirit and heard God's voice of acceptance and approval.

Theme: In baptism, we know we are important and valued by God!

Thought for the day: In the baptism we share with and in Christ, we can't help but know that we are important, worthwhile, and cared for by God. He has proclaimed us as his very own children — sons and daughters of the Almighty.

January 10, 1993

Prayer of meditation: Dear heavenly Father, awaken us to your touch that lets us know what great compassion you have for us. Sensitize us to your touch that gives comfort and strength and hope. Capture us with your touch that calls us to respond as a different people, valuable and caring. We pray this in the name of our Servant King, the Christ. Amen.

Call to worship: "Bless the Lord O my soul, and all that is within me bless his holy name. Bless the Lord O my soul, and forget not all his benefits." Enter into the presence of God as a baptized people, proclaimed by the Almighty as his very own daughters and sons, children of the heavenly Father.

Prayer of adoration: Loving Lord, we would ask today that every heart here may experience what it means that you came to us for the sake of love. Guide our every effort to speak of the power and hope that you give. Let our lives shout of the gratitude that recognizes the giftedness of each day and of your calling to us to be a people of worth. Thank you. In the name of Christ we pray. Amen.

Prayer of confession: O God, we confess that we have fallen short of the calling you have given us as your children. We have preached what we have not always practiced. We have enjoyed the title "Christian" rather than been humbled by it. We have uncritically accepted the world's idea of success, despite the call to self-giving love like that of Jesus. Forgive us. Empower us anew with your Spirit. Amen.

Prayer of dedication of gifts and self: Creator and Owner of all, we return these gifts to you, acknowledging your priority in and over our lives. Accept, we pray, what we offer as a conscious and intentional expression of our love for you and faithfulness to you. In Christ we pray. Amen.

Sermon title: Touch of the Master

Sermon thesis: Baptism is an integral part of bringing people into a right relationship with God. It is a sacrament—which is an outward sign of an inner, invisible reality. In baptism, the connection is secured, the link made. God connects with his children. In Christ's baptism, Jesus was identified with God, unmistakably. And so are we!

Hymn for the day: *"To Jordan came the Christ"* "When Jesus went to Jordan's stream". Martin Luther (1483-1546) was born in Eisleben, Germany and ordained a priest in 1507. While on the faculty at Wittenberg University he became aware of some of the corruptions in the church of his time. From there the story of the Reformation is well known. A musician himself, Luther encouraged congregational hymn singing and wrote a number of fine hymns. This hymn on the Baptism of Christ was one of Luther's hymns on parts of the Catechism.

Announcements for next week:
  Sermon title: Following the Lead
  Sermon theme: If we follow the leading of God, he can use us.
  Sermon summary: We need to allow our faith to be revitalized with the understanding that we don't need to know why, or exactly what we are doing for God. We don't have to know how he is using us. We, like John the Baptist, just need to follow his leading. For God can use us and he longs to use us, if we but follow.

Children's object talk:

God Connects Us and Uses Us

Objects: Little 4 ounce "dixie cups" and a thermos of water
Lesson: In baptism, God makes us his and he calls us to help in his kingdom.
Outline: 1. What happened in our baptism?
  2. We can be a part of helping God in baptism.
  3. God calls us to share in the mystery and power of his proclamation.

WHAT HAPPENED when you were baptized? (Let the young people tell you everything they know about their baptism — water poured — special day with family, Mom and Dad were happy, whatever.) Did you know, that when you were baptized, God made you his very own son and/or daughter? God said, "You are mine!" You are very special and important to God. He chose you to be his. Now this morning I have something for you. (Pour water into the dixie cups and pass them out to each child.) This is yours to do with as you want. It is a gift for you from God. Did you know that we are having a baptism this morning at this service? You and I are going to be a part of God's making another little person his very own. You know what you could do with your water? You could pour it into the baptismal font where we will baptize the baby. (Go to the font and help those who want to share, pour their water in ... talk as they do it.) What does water do? What can we do with water? (Elicit answers such as: cleans us, drink it, waters the flowers, and we swim and play in it. Relate all these answers to what God

January 10, 1993

does in baptism — forgive us, gives us life, keeps us alive and close to him and makes us happy.) Thank you for helping me this morning, and more important, thank you for helping God. I want you to watch when we baptize the baby and know that you are very important and special. Thank you!

The sermon:
Touch of the Master
Hymns:
Beginning of worship: To Jordan came the Christ, our Lord
Sermon hymn: On Jordan's Banks the Baptist's Cry
End of worship: Lift Every Voice and Sing

Scripture: Matthew 3:13-17

Sermon Text: *"This is my beloved Son, with whom I am well pleased."* v. 17b)

SOMETIMES I WONDER if it wouldn't be wise to ride the elevator all day just to get sermon illustrations. Yesterday following a call at University Medical Center I got on the elevator on the sixth floor heading down to my car. It stopped on fifth floor and in walked a very stylish and faddishly dressed woman. She smiled as she entered and took her place in the front, next to the doors. Again, the elevator stopped after only traveling one floor. Two men rushed at it, but one noticed that it was going down, grabbed the other as he was stepping on, and said, "It's going down and we wanna go up!" They clumsily stepped away. The doors closed and the stylish woman stated, to no one in particular: "Idiots!" Stunned by the quickness and harshness of her judgment, none of us replied. This time the elevator went down several flights, passed the main floor into the basement, the doors opened and out stepped that same woman. The doors were about shut when she noticed she'd gotten off in the wrong place. Lunging back, she caught the door and they automatically opened wide. She smiled and announced, "I guess we're all idiots!"

That's a very simple situation, nothing earth-shattering there, except maybe a profound glimpse at how some people see others and see themselves. "Idiots!" "I guess we're all idiots!" And that's sad!

I am very thankful for the Christian faith, a God-given gift which moment after moment reminds us that we're *not* all idiots. That even though we may do idiotic things, even hurtful and harmful things, we are God's, his creation that he has made into his children. We're loved and valuable in his sight.

This morning, our Gospel is focused on Jesus' baptism, and in that Baptism, we can't help but know that we are important, worthwhile, and cared for — not idiots.

I think the Gospel text this morning, although it is very simple and short, is filled with fascination and questions. Have you ever wondered *why* Jesus had to be baptized? Why he went into the water and received God's word? The Messiah, very God of very God, came to be baptized. And we know that John's baptisms were for forgiveness of sin, because John called for repentance with such intensity and consistency. Yet, that doesn't make sense to us for Jesus, because we believe he was without sin. Was he baptized to *become* God's son? That doesn't fit either, we've just celebrated the angel's announcement at his birth that this babe in the manger was the Christ, only Son of the Father. Did Jesus need it to gain entry into God's family or kingdom? Now that's far-fetched.

So why was Jesus baptized? Puzzling, isn't it? And not just to us. Remember John the Baptist's first words to him? ... "I need to be baptized by you, and do you come to me?" In other words, John says, "What's going on here? Why?"

And then God made it perfectly clear, in a very direct and dramatic way. The Heavenly Father reached down and said to Jesus, "Beloved Son, you are mine! I am acting in you!" Powerfully and without any doubt, God declared this Jesus of Nazareth to be his and that he took great pleasure in who he was and in what he was about! Now this happened a couple of times in the Biblical narrative of Jesus' life. As I said earlier, the angels in the birth announcement stated: "This is the one!" At the end of this Epiphany season, we will commemorate the Transfiguration, where on a mountaintop, God announced to Peter, James and John, "Hear well, you disciples. This is the one!" But this day especially, there is no room for doubt, the Spirit of God reached down, the voice boomed over the desert: "This is the one! Touched by God!" God had his hands on Christ!

Yet still the question can be asked: "But why baptism? Why this ceremonial rite for Jesus?" and that's where you and I come in. You see, baptism is to be an integral part of bringing people into a right

January 10, 1993

relationship with God. It is a sacrament, which is an outward sign of an inner, invisible reality. In baptism, the connection is secured, the link made. God connects with his children.

In Christ's baptism, Jesus was identified with God, unmistakeably. "This is my beloved Son, with whom I am well pleased." And in his baptism Christ identified with us, our human need for that connection. He leads us where he wants his followers to go. Christ makes the connection. He became the bridge between God Almighty and you and me. We are not idiots, but God's children, a connection which is vital, so that we might know the touch of God, so that God might put his hands on us. We are connected!

Back on January 21, 1930, the most far-reaching broadcast up to that time was scheduled. It was King George's message at the opening session of the London Arms Conference. For the first time, the entire world was to be brought together with the sound of the king's voice. However, here in America, we almost missed it. A few minutes before the king was to speak, a member of the control room staff of the Columbia Broadcasting System tripped over a wire and broke it, severing the connection. Harold Vivian, then chief control operator, grasped one of the broken wires in one hand and the other wire in his other hand, and forced them together, restoring the circuit. Two hundred and fifty volts of electricity shot through his arms and coursed through his body, but he held on, and the king's message went out to all America through the tingling body of that technician.

You see, that's what our Christ has done. He connects us, low, simple humans with the Infinite and all Loving. You see, the circuit is broken until Christ makes the connection, with one hand reaching down to a lost and needy world, and the other reaching up to an all-sufficient Creator God. Then the circuit of his healing and grace flow to us, his children, and hopefully through us. Christ has made the link and he has shown us what to do; and out of our obedience in baptism, we can know the touch of God. Now, we probably need to stop there, because we're dealing with some terminology that might not be comfortable, the touch of God. If you hear some say that someone is "touched" it's not usually a compliment, is it? What does it mean to be "touched"? They're off a little — they are not connected with reality? That's not what it means to be "touched by God" Rather it means we're not off, but we're fully on, and that we are *connected* with the very Source of reality. To be touched by God means that God has his hands on us, and we are different, wonderfully different!

I like the way one of our confirmation books talks about the touch of God on his children: "God captures the minds and hearts of many people, and they pit themselves against the evil of the world, striving to share the Good News of God's care." You see, that's what Baptism means, the Baptism we share with and in Christ. It is a sign of this inner, invisible connection with God that acts out in visible, tangible ways. This is one of our first worship services together in 1993. What more powerful entry can we have as individuals and as a community than to remember and live in the hands of God, partnering with his touch leading and guiding, comforting and bolstered. You and I are baptized the sign of the Cross was made on our foreheads, the waters were poured over us, and God said to us: "I want you to be with me for all time. You are my child, heir to my kingdom." That happened to us. We belong to God not because we made it that way, but because he wanted us. We have his touch. We are in his hands! This morning, I began with the confused statement that we humans are all idiots, and that's wrong and sad. I'd like to close with a baptismal understanding that recognizes the touch of God!

'Twas battered, scarred, and the auctioneer thought it scarcely
   worth his while
To waste his time on the old violin, but held it up with a smile.
"What am I bid, good people," he cried, "Who'll start the
   bidding for me?
A dollar, a dollar, now two, only two; Two dollars, and
   who'll make it three" ... but no!
From the room far back a gray-haired man came forward
   and picked up the bow.
Then wiping the dust from the old violin, and tightening up the
   strings
He played a melody pure and sweet, as sweet as
   an angel sings.
The music ceased and the auctioneer, with a voice that was
   quiet and low, said, "What am I bid for the old violin?"
   and he held it up with the bow.
"A thousand dollars, and who'll make it two ... two thousand,
   and who'll make it three?"

January 10, 1993

"Three thousand one, three thousand twice, and going and gone," said he.
The people cheered, but some of them said, "We don't quite understand — what changed it's worth?"
Swiftly came the reply, "The touch of the master's hand."
And many a one with life out of tune, and tattered and torn with sin
is auctioned cheap to a thoughtless crowd; much like the old violin.
He is going once, and going twice, he is going and almost gone, but the Master comes, and the awestruck crowd never quite understand the worth of a soul — and the change that's wrought ... by the touch of the Master's Hand!"
Be reminded today — God's touch is yours. Live in the baptismal love he has given.

David de Freese
Immanuel Lutheran Church
Bellevue, Nebraska

JANUARY 17, 1993

Second Sunday after Epiphany

Lessons:

Lutheran:	Is. 49:1-6	I Cor. 1:1-9	John 1:29-41
Roman Catholic:	Is. 49:3, 5-6	I Cor. 1:1-3	John 1:29-34
Episcopal:	Is. 49:1-7	I Cor. 1:1-9	John 1:29-41
Pres/Meth/UCC:	Is. 49:1-7	I Cor. 1:1-9	John 1:29-34

Introductions to the Lessons

Lesson 1

Isaiah 49:1-6 (**Luth**); *Isa. 49:1-7* (**Epis/Pres/Meth/UCC**). Today we have another servant poem. The people of Israel at this time are in captivity in Babylon. Their nation and temple are in ruins. Israel was chosen as God's servant to restore the people to nationhood. More than that, God intends Israel, his servant, to be a light to the nations that the whole world might be save.

Lesson 2

I Corinthians 1:1-9 (**Luth**); *I Cor. 1:1-11* (**Epis/Pres/Meth/UCC**). During the remaining Sundays in the Epiphany season our 2nd Lessons, in a series of seven readings, will be taken from the first four chapters of I Corinthians. Paul begins his letter with the customary salutation. He is grateful for the grace the church in Corinth received as evidenced in their spiritual blessings and knowledge. While they wait for Christ's return, he is confident that God will continue them in this grace, because God can be trusted.

Gospel

John 1:29-41 (**Luth/Epis**); *John 1:29-42* (**Pres/Meth/UCC**). When John the Baptist baptized Jesus, he saw the Spirit descend on Jesus as a dove. This convinced John that Jesus was the Messiah, the Son of God. Accordingly, he witnessed, "Behold the Lamb of God." Because of this testimony, two of John's disciples left him to follow Jesus. One of them was Andrew who then brought his brother Peter to Christ.

Theme: If we follow the leading of God, he can use us.

Thought for the day: John the Baptist did what he felt called by the Lord to do and only after it was over did he know how God was going to use him and to what purpose. John trusted and followed, without knowing the result. We need to know: it does

January 17, 1993

not matter was much where we are going, as who we are following. God will take care of his results. We need only trust and follow!

Prayer of meditation: Dear Heavenly Father, grant us the power to trust ... to follow ... to live. Give us faith that acts. Help us to overcome our paralysis of analysis, so that we might genuinely serve you. Thank you. In the Name of our Christ who came to us, we pray. Amen.

Call to worship: "Blessed are they whose way is blameless ... who walk in the way of the Lord." As we gather to worship, may we so trust our God of love, that we will walk in his ways.

Prayer of adoration: Lord God, you showed your glory and led many to faith by the works of your Son. As he brought gladness and healing to his people, grant us these same gifts and lead us also to perfect faith in him, Jesus Christ our Lord. Amen. (Lutheran Book of Worship)

Prayer of confession: With yearnings we can not fully identify; with fears too personal to voice; harboring hostilities of which we are ashamed; regretting past acts of misunderstanding; and weighed with a sense of guilt for having done so little with so much; we now are bold to seek your forgiveness. O God, your mercy is ever greater than our sinfulness. Grant us your pardon and a sure knowledge of your love, so that we may serve you in newness of life in Christ Jesus our Lord. Amen.

Prayer of dedication of gifts and self: These our gifts, O God, we offer from our hands and our hearts. Bless them we ask, that they may be multiplied in justice and mercy for your work in this world. We ask this is Christ's name. Amen.

Sermon title: Following the Lead

Sermon thesis: We need to allow our faith to be re-vitalized with the understanding that we don't need to know why, or exactly what we are doing for God. We don't have to know how he is using us. We, just like John the Baptist, just need to follow his leading. For God can use us and he longs to use us, if we but follow.

Hymn for the day: *"When Christ's appearing was made known"* In today's Gospel, John the Baptist recognizes Jesus as the Lamb of God. The third stanza of our hymn makes reference to the baptism of the Lamb of God in the Jordan. The hymn is taken from Coelius Sedulius' *Paean Alphabeticus de Christo,* a poem giving the life of Christ in verse, with each of the twenty-three stanzas beginning with one of the letters of

The Minister's Annual Manual

the alphabet. Sedulius was probably born in Rome, and lived during the early fifth century. From two of his letters we can infer that in his early life he devoted himself to heathen literature, but once he became a Christian, he turned to Christian writings.

Announcements for next week:
Sermon title: Repent — Wow!
Sermon theme: Our souls are restless, until they rest in God.
Sermon summary: Jesus called his disciples to follow him, and they responded immediately. Jesus called his followers to repent, and they did. He told them it was Good News in their lives, and so it was. Each day, we have an opportunity to follow the Christ — Immediately in every decision we make. We too hear his call to repent, and it is Good News for us also!

Children's object talk:

Jesus Says

Objects: None but a willingness to play
Lesson: What voice will we listen to above all the others? We hope Jesus'.
Outline: 1. Play the old familiar game of "Simon Says"
2. In our world, we have so many different voices telling us what to do.
3. God's people listen for God's voice and follow it above all the others.

HAVE ANY OF YOU ever played the game: Simon Says? You know how to play it. Whatever I tell you to do, you only do it if I say "Simon Says" before I tell you. If I say, "Touch your nose," don't do it. If I say, "Simon says, 'Touch your nose,' " then you do it. Ok? Let's play the game for a little bit, and if I catch you doing something Simon didn't say, then you have to sit down. (Play the game ... getting faster and faster, until all the children are out.)

That's fun, isn't it? But tell me, what does this have to do with God and his church? Do you know that there are lots of people and groups who will be telling you what to do? Can you think of any? (Hopefully, someone will talk about advertisers or bullies or some other kind of influence.) I want you to know that as Christians, we want to do what Jesus tells us to do. We want to do what we know he would want us to do, and sometimes that is very different from what others will tell us. I once had a coach who told me, "Don't get mad, get even." Do you think Jesus would want us to get "even"

January 17, 1993

with someone if they hurt us by hurting them back? Does that sound like Jesus? No. Jesus says we should try to forgive, even when that is very hard. Jesus says we shouldn't act bossy with other people, but that we should help them. What Jesus says is good. From now on, whenever you are going to do something, I think it would be a good idea to ask yourself, does Jesus say I should do this? If you don't think Jesus would tell you to do something, it is best not to do it. As Christians, we listen well to what "Jesus says."

The sermon:

Following The Lead

Hymns:
Beginning of worship: "How Good, Lord, to be Here"
Sermon hymn: Hail to the Lord's Anointed
End of worship: O Savior, Precious Savior

Scripture: John 1:29-41

Sermon Text: *"I myself did not know him; but he who sent me to baptize with water said to me, 'He on whom you see the Spirit descend and remain, this is he who baptizes with the Holy Spirit.' And I have seen and have borne witness that this is the Son of God."* vs. 33 & 34

THERE IS A STORY TOLD about a minister who was brand new to a community, and one of his first days there, he came out of the church, and wanted to go to the post office, but he realized he didn't know how to find his way there. So he stopped a little fellow going by and said, "Son, can you tell me how to get to the post office?" The little boy replied, "Sure, you go down this street here to the light, and you take a right, and you take the second left, and the post office is on your left." The minister thanked the young man and said, "I really appreciate your help. You see this church here? I'm the minister of it. Now you come to church next Sunday and I'm going to tell you how to go to heaven." And the little boy sniffed and stated, "Sure!?! How are you going to tell me how to go to heaven, when you can't even find the post office?"

This morning we are going to focus in on something that is wrapped up in mystery, something that is of God and his ways, which none of us understands too fully nor comprehends completely. I as your pastor am more than willing to confess the amazing and mysterious which I cannot totally understand. And yet, I want to invite you to struggle with me, to endeavor to recognize something about our God and his children that, while baffling, is good and wonderful! John the Baptist stated: "I myself did not know him; but for this I came baptizing with water, that he might be revealed to Israel."

The question for today is, "Do we have to know what we are doing, in order to do the will of our God?" And our answer is, "Of course we do!" We have to plan it out, we need to be intentional and we need to know what we are doing, so that we might do his will — right? Could we serve God by wandering around doing things we think are important but really don't understand? That doesn't sound likely, does it? But I submit to you there might be a twist in our God's ways, and that God goes beyond what we even think can and should happen. I hope you noticed some redundancy this week in the Gospel lesson. Remember last Sunday? We heard the story of the baptism of Jesus from St. Matthew's writing, and now today we heard that exact same story told from St. John's perspective. To be honest, it's not much fun preaching two Sundays in a row on the same passage. So when I saw that we were getting the same incident, just different writers, I searched for something different in this second writing.

And I found it! But, I wasn't too excited about what I found because it bothered me! It haunted me! John the Baptist announces to everyone that this Jesus is the Lamb of God, the Messiah. In fact, he states it so that no one can misunderstand: "I have seen and have borne witness that *this is* the Son of God." No questions there! And that feels good and of God. Jesus is the Christ. But John the Baptist also declares twice in this passage, "I myself did not know him." I did not know him; but this is why I came baptizing with water, that this might be revealed to Israel."

In other words, John did what he felt called by the Lord to do, and only after it was over did he know how God was going to use him and to what purpose — John trusted and followed without knowing the result. Now, let's go back to that question for today: "Do we have to know what we are doing in order to do the will of the Lord?" We agreed readily ... of course! Yet, did John know from the beginning why he was led into the wilderness to preach and bap-

January 17, 1993

tize? Apparently not, but because he followed the leading of God, he was used by God to do a powerful work.

In other words, we don't always know what we are doing, but if we will follow the leading of God, he can use us, even sometimes while we don't know what's going on. He uses us to do his will for him. That's a bit bothersome, isn't it? Yet, if John the Baptist didn't know how God was using him, maybe there is a word of liberation in there for us!

Tell me, do you always know how God is using you? I sure don't. And if I always had to know, I'm afraid I'd be so paralyzed by trying to figure it out I wouldn't do anything. In fact, that just frees us up to act, to follow God and not worry about how he will use us. And maybe that's the key to this whole struggle in faith. Possibly what you and I need to hear more than anything else today is that it doesn't matter as much where we are going as who we are following. God will take care of his results; we just need to follow his lead, even when we can't make sense out of it or don't recognize its end purpose. Sometimes we're just not clear as to where God is leading us, nor why. But if we follow what we believe to be his leading, we can safely leave the rest to him.

A while back, I read a quote in a magazine that fascinated me. It was about Mark Rader of Palmra, Illinois, a speedboat driver, who had recently survived a racing accident. He said that he had been near top speed when his boat veered slightly and hit a wave at a dangerous angle. The combined force of his speed and the size and the angle of the wave sent the boat spinning crazily into the air. He was thrown from his seat and propelled deeply into the water ... so deep, in fact, that he had no idea which direction the surface was. He had to remain calm and wait for the buoyancy of his life vest to begin pulling him up. Once he discovered which way was up, he could swim to the surface.

Sometimes we find ourselves surrounded by confusing options, too deeply immersed in our own concerns to know "which way is up". When this happens, we too should wait for God's upward tug to pull us in the right direction, and trust it. Our life vest might be other Christians, scripture, or some other leading from God's Spirit; but the key is recognizing our dependency on God and trusting him. We are to follow his leading, even when we can't make sense of it.

I was inspired by the story of Helen Roseveare, who served as missionary doctor in the Belgian Congo, now know as Zaire. During the civil war in 1964, she was captured by rebel soldiers. During her five month captivity, she was raped, beaten and abused. But after her release and a two year furlough she returned to Zaire to continue her medical work for another seven years. She is now traveling for a mission organization, speaking at conferences and seminars. Listen to her words: "I want people to be passionately in love with Jesus, so that nothing else counts. Maybe God calls me to Africa, in the midst of an area being swept by a killer disease no one knows how to cure. What if I get AIDS ... But if God sent me to Africa with my family, he's going to look after us. That doesn't mean that I'm not going to get that disease; it means that he's in charge of my life, and if I get AIDS, that's because he can use me to witness to others who've got it. How's that for success? I'm a fanatic, if you like, but only because I believe so strongly that nothing counts except knowing your sins have been forgiven by the blood of Christ. We've only got this short life to get others to know the same truth!" She doesn't know where she's going, she doesn't know the end of the story, but she knows who she is following and that God holds the final word of that story!

This morning, allow your faith to be revitalized with the understanding that you and I don't need to know why or exactly what we are doing for God. We don't have to know how he is using us. We, just like John the Baptist, just need to follow His leading, for God can use us, and he longs to use us, if we but follow.

David de Freese
Immanuel Lutheran Church
Bellevue, Nebraska

JANUARY 24, 1993

Third Sunday after Epiphany

Lessons:

Lutheran:	Is. 9:1b-4	I Cor. 1:10-17	Matt. 4:12-23
Roman Catholic:	Is. 9:1-4	I Cor. 1:10-13, 17	Matt. 4:12-23
Episcopal:	Amos 3:1-8	I Cor. 1:10-17	Matt. 4:12-23
Pres/Meth/UCC:	Is. 9:1-4	I Cor. 1:10-18	Matt. 4:12-23

Introductions to the Lessons

Lesson 1

(1) *Isaiah 9:1b-4* (**Luth**); *Isa. 9:1-4* (**Pres/Meth/UCC**). The focus in Lesson 1 and the Gospel for today is upon Galilee. Through Isaiah God promises that Galilee will one day become glorious, because the enemy will be overcome. In today's gospel lesson Matthew quotes this promise and sees Jesus' ministry in Galilee as its fulfillment.

(2) *Amos 3:1-8* (**Epis**). Nation after nation beyond Israel received through Amos God's judgment. Now it is Israel's turn. Because Israel is the only family God knows, God will punish the nation for her sins. This secret has been revealed to the prophets. Since God has spoken, who cannot proclaim his message?

Lesson 2

I Corinthians 1:10-17 (**Luth**); *I Cor. 1:10-18* (**Epis/Pres/Meth/UCC**). According to Paul, the Corinthian church is a divided congregation. Members are quarrelling. There is a party spirit. Their loyalty is divided among Paul, Peter, Apollos, and Christ. But Paul will not be a party to this conflict. He is glad he baptized only a few because he does not want people to follow him but rather Christ.

Gospel

Matthew 4:12-23 (**Luth/Epis/Pres/Meth/UCC**). John the Baptist's arrest marked the end of his ministry but the beginning of Jesus' ministry. Most of Jesus' ministry was in Galilee consisting of preaching, teaching, and healing, with headquarters in Capernaum. One day as Jesus walked along the coast of the Sea of Galilee, he called two sets of brothers to be disciples. In fulfillment of Isaiah's prophecy, Jesus made Galilee glorious.

Theme: Our souls are restless, until they rest in God.

Thought for the day: The first followers of Jesus of Nazareth were very much like us; they too were looking for a sense of meaning in their life. They too wanted to know why they were alive. They heard in Jesus a calling that expected a life-changing decision. Too often, we are dulled to the power of what it means to live with Jesus as our Christ and Master. He needs our immediate response, in everything we do. Will we also follow him?

Prayer of meditation: Heavenly Father, we gather once again in your presence, longing for your help and your care. Our world frightens us and we feel so insignificant. Touch us again with your hope and implant within us a purpose that makes a difference. In the name of our Savior we pray. Amen.

Call to worship: "Happy are those whose strength is in God, in whose heart are the highways to his kingdom." Welcome into the presence and power of our God who cares, who listens, who guides and who hopes. Join with others who long for purpose and joy in the living of our days.

Prayer of adoration: O God, the Creator of all things, we lift up our hearts in gratitude to you this day for the mere joy of living; for all the sights and sounds around us; for family, friends and fellowship; for all things bright, beautiful, and engaging; for work to perform and the skill and strength to perform it. Thank you. With joy in your goodness, we will not forget that we are not here to stay, but only pilgrims in this world on our way to a new place. Thank you for loving us. Amen.

Prayer of confession: Dear God, you know us better than we know ourselves. We confess our pain of alienation, of feelings disconnected from the very purpose for our living. We admit that it is our own fears of the unknown and worries over self-preservation that keep us away from the acceptance and joy you have meant for us. Forgive us and refresh us in your love, your salvation, your acceptance and your hope. In the name of Christ our Lord, we ask. Amen.

Prayer of dedication of gifts and self: "Thy life was given for me. Thy blood, O Lord was shed, that I might ransomed be and quickened from the dead. Thy life was given for me; what have I given for thee?"

Sermon title: Repent ... Wow!

Sermon thesis: Jesus called his disciples to follow him, and they responded immediately. Jesus called his followers to repent, and they did. He told them it was Good News in their lives, and so it was. Each day, we have an opportunity to follow the Christ, immediately in every decision we make. We too hear his call to repent, and it is Good News for us also!

Hymn for the day: *"The Son of God, our Christ"* Edward M. Blumenfield (b. 1927), a minister of the United Church of Christ, has served parishes in Vermont, Illinois and Wisconsin. This hymn of discipleship was written in 1957 and was the first choice of the hymns obtained by the Hymn Society of America at the request of the United Christian Youth Movement of the National Council of Churches of Christ in the USA.

Announcements for next week:

Sermon title: These Are Blessings?
Sermon theme: The world we know is turned upside down by our relationship to Christ.
Sermon summary: Often the scripture tells people truths which seem inane or illogical from the perspective of human reason. When one remembers, however, that in God's logic, grace and mercy rule, our viewpoint becomes radically different.

Children's object talk:

God's Love Frees Us

Objects: Some photographs of the "speaker" doing different things
Lesson: God's forgiveness is real and it sets us free
Outline: 1. The things we do that are hurtful are too often remembered
2. God's forgiveness is real.
3. God's forgetfulness is also very real.

I HAVE SOMETHING I want to show you today. Well, maybe I don't want to show, but I thought it would be helpful for our lesson for this morning. Here are some pictures of me doing some things I am not proud of. (Show the pictures.) Here is one that shows me picking a neighbor's flowers . . I forgot to ask her. Here is another one of me being too stubborn to say I was sorry when I said something mean. And here is another one that shows the time I wouldn't play the game because I did not get to be the leader. Pretty sad and awful pictures, aren't they?

You know what? I really don't like having those pictures around that remind me of how mean and selfish I have been. They make me feel really bad, and I can't seem to get rid of them.

Did you know that some people think God keeps a record of all the bad things we do, just like these pictures. They think God hangs on to them forever.

But do you know what? God doesn't. He forgives. When we ask him to forgive us, he tears up the record and throws it away. (Tear up the pictures)

You and I don't have to carry around these pictures, the record of the hurtful and selfish things we have done. God wants us to be free, so he throws away any memory of what we have done that is wrong, and wants us to start out fresh and new. And he wants us to do what is good and helpful and loving. You and I are free to try, to begin anew. God doesn't keep a record, rather he loves and forgets. I am very thankful that God forgives.

The sermon:

Repent ... Wow!

Hymns:
Beginning of worship: "We Praise You, O God"
Sermon hymn: Son of God, Eternal Savior
End of worship: On Our Way Rejoicing

Scripture: Matthew 4:12-23

Sermon Text: *"...proclaiming good news of the kingdom."* vs. 23

TWO STATEMENTS in today's Gospel have always puzzled me. The first is repeated twice in four verses: "And immediately they left their nets and followed him." A little later we hear: "Immediately he called them and they left their father." What do you think of when you hear the word "immediately"? I think of microwave popcorn, instant replay on TV, push-button read-outs on machines, and high speed photocopying. I think of things that produce an instant response, not people.

As the father of three girls, "immediately" is no longer part of my vocabulary. We don't do anything immediately at our house! Whenever I use such cryptic terms as "Right Now" it is almost always replied: "In a minute" ... "Just a second" ... or my favorite contradiction: "I can't hear you." And going some place is a slow, tedious procedure with car seats that can not be speedily secured. "Im-

January 24, 1993

mediate" just isn't part of my life even here at church. The Church as a body is not something that the word "immediate" would fit. Change takes time. Information must flow. Ideas and concerns must be shared. Very little if anything happens immediately: "We'll bring that up at next month's meeting." "That will have to be discussed by..." In fact, as I thought, the only place I regularly see persons doing anything immediately is at the hospital when the words: "Code blue" or "stat" are heard over the public address system. Well, this morning, Jesus didn't yell: "Code blue!" He simply said, "Follow me," and he received an immediate response.

Tell me, why didn't these four men express hesitation, as did Jonah and Moses and others who have been called? What was it about this Jesus that made Simon and Andrew leave their nets by the seashore? Can you imagine these two men, sweaty and stinking of fish, their hands raw from years of handling nets, tossing their livelihoods aside on the basis of some stranger's call to follow him and be made "fishers of people." James and John leave Dad sitting in the boat with a partially mended net. The hired men watch these two walk into the sunset with some passerby and wonder, "What's gotten into them?" How do you think Zebedee reacts? Do you think he yells, "You guys come back here and help me clean these fish!" or do you picture him shrugging his shoulders and resigning, "Well, they've always had trouble saying no"?

How could this Jesus generate such an immediate positive response? Could they instantly perceive that this man was unlike any other, about to proclaim a message unlike any other? What was it about him? Or what was it about them?

Is it possible that they were just like the rest of us—looking for a sense of meaning, for a reason for getting up in the morning, for being alive? I would suggest to you that the question of God was and is still really the only question in town. Were James, John, Simon, and Andrew searching for meaning in their lives? I bet so ... don't we? As St. Augustine said, "Their souls were restless until they found their rest in God." Could that be why they dropped what was in their hands and responded so quickly to Jesus?

Now this text with its "immediacy" leaves me with mixed feelings, perhaps a combination of intimacy and distance. Intimacy because we have all been there. Haven't we all wanted something more in our lives—wanted to turn in our resignations and find jobs and lifestyles that were more life enhancing, purposeful? Don't most of us wrestle with that question of meaning? Can't you identify with the disciples' desire for a change in direction?

But I also experience distance from the scene at the seashore. I'm jealous of the immediate, life-changing response of those men but wonder if it's not more difficult for us today. "Sure, they could leave their nets — they didn't have to worry about the mortgage payment, the church pledge, the VISA balance, child care or gas prices." Most of us have difficulty seeing ourselves responding totally and quickly to the call of Christ. We'd rather give excuses. I'd like a nickel for every time I've heard: "Sunday's the only day I have to sleep late. We'll become involved in church when our children are a little older." The fact that those first disciples responded immediately has always puzzled me; but yet, wouldn't you agree that each day you make hundreds of decisions, at home, at work, with family, with friends, some small, some big, decisions that have an immediacy to them? I do. I believe the Gospel today is about those decisions. And I believe it is about you and me responding to Christ in those decisions. You see, he stands in front of us *in everything we do* and he says, "Follow me." Follow me in how you treat your co-workers; follow me in responding to your family; follow me in deciding what to do; and how you'll do it. And that is no different or less difficult than it was for those first disciples. It requires our immediate response in each moment. "Follow me," Jesus said, and immediately they did — and so can we!

And that leads to the second statement that has always puzzled me in this Gospel passage. Did you hear at the beginning: Jesus said, "Repent" and then later it says he called it "Good News"?? Now to be honest with you "repent" and "good news" have not always been hooked together in my vocabulary. Usually I think of repenting as being sorry for something, being sad, filled with guilt and regret. But Jesus doesn't say that at all. He says, "Repent and know the Good News!"

You see, repent means stop what you are doing now, stop the way that you are thinking now, and embrace a new way of thinking about our world. Repentance is not some negative, life-denying gesture — repentance means turning to a new way. I love the way theologian Fred Buechner says it: "To repent is to come to your senses." It is not so much something you do as something that happens. True repentance spends less time looking at the past and saying "I'm sorry," than to the future and saying "Wow!" If you want

January 24, 1993

a good picture of that understanding of repentance, it is today's Gospel lesson: Jesus came and said, "The time is fulfilled, and the Kingdom of God is at hand."

Simon and Andrew, old fishermen, hear Jesus saying: "The new age is here, so follow me and I will give you something more significant to do with your lives than standing knee deep in a boat full of dead fish. Follow me, and I will give you life in abundance!" "And they left their nets immediately and followed him." No ifs, ands, or buts, no hemming and hawing, no lame excuses. They just walked into the future and started living the life that God created for them to live. And that was to repent — to turn — and that was Good News, great news!

David de Freese
Immanuel Lutheran Church
Bellevue, Nebraska

JANUARY 31, 1993

Fourth Sunday after Epiphany

Lessons:

Lutheran:	Mic. 6:1-8	I Cor. 1:26-31	Matt. 5:1-12
Roman Catholic:	Zeph. 2:3; 3:12-13	I Cor. 1:26-31	Matt. 5:1-12a
Episcopal:	Mic. 6:1-8	I Cor. 1:(18-25) 26-31	Matt. 5:1-12
Pres/Meth/UCC:	Mic. 6:1-8	I Cor. 1:18-31	Matt. 5:1-12

Introductions to the Lessons

Lesson 1

Micah 6:1-8 (**Luth/Epis/Pres/Meth/UCC**). The Lord has a fight to pick with his people. Why has his people forsaken him? He asks, "What have I done to you that you should treat me so?" He has done them nothing but good. On the other hand, what have the people done for God? What does God expect of them? He wants them to show mercy, execute justice, and live in humble fellowship with him.

Lesson 2

I Corinthians 1:26-31 (**Luth/Epis**); *I Cor. 1:18-31* (**Pres/Meth/UCC**). For the world Christ and his cross constitute nonsense. The wisdom of the world is foolishness to God. Christ is the power and wisdom of God. The foolishness of God is wiser than the world's wisdom. This is seen in the fact that God called the weak and unwise, people the world despises, to be his people through Christ. The lowly, poor, weak, and socially disinherited have Christ as their wisdom.

Gospel

Matthew 5:1-12 (**Luth/Epis/Pres/Meth/UCC**). Today we begin a series of five readings from chapter 5 of Matthew which is the first chapter of the Sermon on the Mount. Jesus gathered his disciples on a mountain top and taught them the nature of life in the Kingdom of God. The Sermon on the Mount is one of five collections of Jesus' teachings in Matthew. The sermon opens with the Beatitudes. Christ wants his followers to be happy. The word, "blessed," means "happy." In the Beatitudes we learn what true happiness is.

Theme: The world we know is turned upside down by our relationship to Christ.

Thought for the day: One's perspective on life is often determined

January 31, 1993

by one's angle of vision. If you don't like your view, get up and move across the room.

Prayer of meditation: O Light to the nations, give to us this day the eyes to see you, the ears to hear you, and the heart to feel you. May your presence fill the sanctuary of our hearts. Amen.

Call to worship:
Trust in the Lord, and do good;
so you will live in the land, and enjoy security.
Take delight in the Lord,
and he will give you the desires of your heart.
(Psalm 37:3-4)

Prayer of adoration: Almighty God, creator of every good and perfect thing, how awesome is your world. To see the beauty of a sunrise or newborn calf reminds us that we live in a world of miracle. You called the earth into being with your word and continue to nurture us by this same Spirit-infusing voice. We live as you speak. Amen.

Prayer of confession: On our way from there to here, O Lord, we have lost our direction. Painfully, we stumble through life, following our own path rather than the one you forged for us. Our path is one fraught with self-destructive objects, while the path you have set before us is one paved by the mercy and grace of our Lord and Savior Jesus Christ. Forgive us our willful neglect of your teaching and put our feet back on the path which leads to you. Your love calls us back into a proper, righteous rleationship to you through your Son, Jesus Christ. It is in his name we confess. Amen.

Prayer of dedication of gifts and self: O God, who gives and gives and gives to your people, here today we bring plates to your altar. In these plates are our tokens of faith in you and the grand life given us by your hand. For some, these gifts represent a full measure of devotion to your heavenly realm. For others, gifts are small but, as we grow in faith and trust, would that we might someday reflect this growth in a true tithe.

O God, accept our lives as you accept our offering, that the realm of God might come upon the earth. Amen.

Sermon title: These Are Blessings?

Sermon thesis: Often the scripture tells truths which seem inane or

The Minister's Annual Manual

illogical from the perspective of human reason. When one remembers, however, that in God's logic, grace and mercy rule, our viewpoint becomes radically different.

Hymn for the day: *"Jesus, thy boundless love to me"* This hymn of Jesus' love and our response to that love is based on a prayer by Johann Arndt. The author, Paul Gerhardt (1607-1676), ranks with Martin Luther as a writer of German hymns. Ordained a Lutheran pastor, he served in churches in and near Berlin until 1666, when his refusal to sign a statement that he would not preach on doctrinal differences with the followers of Calvin resulted in his removal from his post. His last ten years were spent at Lübben on the Spree ministering to a rough and unsympathizing congregation.

Announcements for next week:
  Sermon title: You Talkin' to Me?
  Sermon theme: Jesus continues the work of law and prophecy.
  Sermon summary: People painting divisions between Law and Gospel must be sure they don't paint themselves into corners they really don't want to inhabit eternally.

Children's object talk:

Being Peacemakers

Objects: Dove (picture or cutout)
Lesson: Being a peacemaker is hard.
Outline: 1. Doves reminds us of peace
  2. Jesus blesses peacemakers.
  3. Being peacemakers is our job, too.

HELLO, CHILDREN! Today, in our Bible reading from Matthew, is the sentence: "Blessed are the peacemakers, for they shall be called children of God."

Do you remember the story of Noah's Ark? During a flood, caused by forty days and nights of rain, Noah and his family rode in a boat. In this way they saved their lives. But not only their lives; they saved the lives of two of every kind of animal also. When the water went down, Noah let a dove go to find whether there was dry land. When the dove returned to the Ark, it had an olive branch in its beak. To this day, whenever we see either an olive branch or a dove, we think of peace. For the dove coming to Noah meant God was at peace with human beings and they could begin their lives again — on dry land.

Jesus, in our story today, tells us that peacemakers will be blessed, or peacemakers will be made happy. Notice that we don't try to

January 31, 1993

be peacemakers in order to be blessed or made happy. But, rather, those who are peacemakers are already blessed by doing peace work.

I know you can all think of times when you stopped someone from fussing or fighting. Even very young people can be peacemakers. This is what God wants us to become.

The sermon:
These Are Blessings?

Hymns:
Beginning of worship: Joyful, Joyful, We Adore Thee
Sermon hymn: Blest Are the Pure in Heart
End of worship: Amazing Grace

Scripture: Matthew 5:1-12

Sermon Text: *"When Jesus saw the crowds, he went up to the mountain; and after he sat down, his disciples came to him."* (v. 1)

THE BIBLE, IF IT IS FULL OF ANYTHING, is full of surprises. From beginning to end, scripture's account of God's dealings with human beings takes odd twists and turns. It can be said the Bible is a book which teaches people never to be surprised at what God can and will do. Perhaps we think this when we think about the awesomeness of God and the scripture as a witness to God's work.

For instance, I remember when I fully began to understand the implications of what it meant for Abraham and Sarah to be "with child." Mr. Wiley, in my eighth grade health class, explained the cycle of human fertility. At the same time, my eighth grade Sunday School teacher Mrs. Graveter, was bravely marching us through the book of Genesis. I began to understand why Sarah laughed! The Bible does this to us.

Later we talked about David and Goliath. I don't know about you, but if I were a betting parson, I wouldn't put my filthy lucre on David over Goliath — whether their weapons be knives, spears, or even sling-shots. In the Bible, the hand of God always stacks every deck.

The Beatitudes are no exception, for they, too, surprise those paying close attention. "Blessed are those" in the New Revised Standard Version is translated as "Happy are those" in other versions.

The Minister's Annual Manual

But look at those who are blessed or happy! "Blessed are the poor in spirit"? "Blessed are those who mourn"? "Blessed are those who are persecuted"? These are blessings which make people happy? No doubt, those in Jesus' day were as confused as we are today by these kinds of beatitudes.

There is, however, a key to interpret these sayings of Jesus. All that Jesus says is in light of the coming of God's reign. This reign is ushered in, ironically, by Jesus' birth, death, and resurrection. Thus, only in the light of Jesus as the Christ who inaugurates God's new age, do these blessings make any kind of sense whatsoever.

Gene Siskel reports on the (Jewish) faith of Academy Award winning Marlee Matlin of "Children of a Lesser God" and her deafness: "Specifically, she was asked if she believed in God, a God that could allow an 18-month baby to become deaf." Marlin replied with a sign-language interpreter's help: "Yes, I believe in a greater being and a God that answers prayers, maybe not every prayer. Because if I hadn't lost my hearing, I wouldn't be talking to you now. I wouldn't be going to the Academy Awards." Siskel: "Her eyes glowed as she signed her life-affirming answer…" (a story in the Chicago Tribune).

Blessings in God's realm are of a different order than those in our world. It takes a special discernment and deep faith to understand the world where God rules. God's logic gives us all grace and mercy. This indeed is a miracle. God gives what we need — not what we deserve.

David N. Mosser
First United Methodist Church
Georgetown, Texas

FEBRUARY 7, 1993

Fifth Sunday after Epiphany

Lessons:

Lutheran:	Is. 58:5-9a	I Cor. 2:1-5	Matt. 5:13-20
Roman Catholic:	Is. 58:7-10	I Cor. 2:1-5	Matt. 5:13-16
Episcopal:	Hab. 3:1-6, 17-19	I Cor. 2:1-11	Matt. 5:13-20
Pres/Meth/UCC:	Is. 58:1-9a (9b-12)	I Cor. 2:1-12(13-16)	Matt. 5:13-20

Introductions to the Lessons

Lesson 1

(1) *Isaiah 58:5-9a* (**Luth**); *Isa. 58:1-12* (**Pres/Meth/UCC**). Fasting is something many Christians practice especially during Lent, but here we have the subject in the Epiphany season. Today the question is to fast or not to fast. In Isaiah's time it was a question of the right and the wrong way to fast. Isaiah's point is that fasting without repentance is futile. True fasting calls for putting one's faith into practice by caring for the unfortunate.

(2) *Habbakuk 3:1-6, 17-19* (**Epis**). Habbakuk declares his faithfulness to God no matter what happens. Let God in his glory and power allow suffering and tragedy. He will still keep his faith. If the fields and forests fail to yield, if there are no cattle, if the worst comes to the worst, he will rejoice in the God of his salvation and strength.

Lesson 2

I Corinthians 2:1-5 (**Luth**); *I Cor. 2:1-11* (**Epis**); *I Cor. 2:1-12 (13-16)* (**Pres/Meth/UCC**). When St. Paul came to Corinth to preach, he decided not to use big words of human wisdom. He preached only Christ, the wisdom of God. The world does not know this kind of wisdom. It is from God through the gift of his Spirit.

Gospel

Matthew 5:13-20 (**Luth/Epis**); *Matt. 5:13-20* (**Pres/Meth/UCC**). Jesus describes his followers as genuine people. They are like salt and light. The danger is not being what we are. What good is salt if it is not salty? What good is a hidden light? Christians are to be people of quality that do more than the Law requires.

Theme: Jesus continues God's work of law and prophecy.

Thought for the day: It is often easier for us to look outward on the shortcomings of others than it is to look inward upon our own.

Prayer of meditation: Almighty God, you have built the Body of Christ—the Church—upon the lives of prophetic people down through the ages. As we inherit your shared spirit with and from them, may we too be the salt of the earth and the light of the world. In Christ's name we pray. Amen.

Call to worship:
Leader: The law of the Lord is perfect, reviving the soul.
People: The testimony of the Lord is certain, making the foolish wise.
Leader: The teachings of God Almighty are righteous, they make us rejoice.
People: The commandment of God is pure, enlightening our eyes.

Prayer of adoration: O God, you are our God, not because we have called upon you, but because you, in your infinite compassion have called us out. We worship you this day because you have blessed us with both grace and mercy. May you grant us peace in our day and make us vessels of your peace. Amen.

Prayer of confession: Today, O Lord, we gather as a people who have lost their way. We, to a person, have fallen short of the folk you created each of us to be. In our own insecurity, we have hurt others and ourselves by forgetting that all human beings are created in your magnificent image. Draw us now close to your heart through the teachings of holy scripture and the sacrifice of our worship to you. May we recall the great grace you have showered on our forebears in Egypt, Babylon, and other places of darkness. May the light of Jesus Christ illumine our journey to the place of promise. Grant that we, as a congregation, might become new persons in Christ and do the mighty work of love and reconciliation in our community and in your world. We ask this in Christ's holy name. Amen.

Prayer of dedication of gifts and self: Lord Jesus, for our sake you emptied yourself. Help us be better stewards of the many households over which we are master: our prayers, our spirit, our worldly goods, our time, our compassion. May we pass along to our sisters and brothers the gifts we have received from your gracious hand. Amen.

Sermon title: You Talkin' to Me?

Sermon thesis: People painting divisions between Law and Gospel

February 7, 1993

must beware they don't paint themselves into corners they really don't want to inhabit eternally.

Hymn for the day: *"Come, gracious Spirit, heavenly dove"* In today's Gospel we are told that we are to be the salt of the earth and the light of the world. The hymn of the day seeks light and guidance from the Holy Spirit that we may choose the way of Christ, the living way. Simon Browne (1680-1732) was an independent minister in London. In later years he suffered from depression brought on, no doubt, by the fact that he was attacked by a robber and accidentally killed his assailant in the struggle, after which he lost his wife and soon thereafter, his son. He retired from the ministry but continued to work at translating classical authors, compiling a dictionary, and writing children's books and hymns.

Announcements for next week:
Sermon title: What Does Exceeding Righteousness Look Like?
Sermon theme: The reconciling power of the new righteousness.
Sermon summary: With his coming as Messiah, Jesus not only fulfills Israel's hope. Jesus also demands a new level of righteousness of those who claim God's grace.

Children's object talk:
Light of the World

Objects: A flashlight
Lesson: God's love lights up dark places.
Outline: 1. We all know darkness.
2. God in Jesus is light.
3. Jesus' followers are light, too.

TODAY, WE HEARD these words, "you are the light of the world." Jesus said these words, so let's see what he may have meant by them.

First, all of us know how scary dark places can be. Where I live there is an underground cave called InnerSpace Caverns. Once, in a cave like this one, there was a power failure and the underground lights all went out for about ten minutes. During this time it was absolutely dark. People could not see anything at all. They were afraid to even move.

Second, sometimes in this life there is that kind of darkness. People forget to see and everything seems dark. God sent Jesus into the world to be a light to the nations. In a way, Jesus as the light is like a flashlight in a dark cave or even in our rooms at night. The flashlight doesn't light up everything, but it does light up enough until other light comes. This is what people need when the light of life goes away. Jesus gives people the light they need in their dark world.

Third, Jesus called his disciples, then others, and finally us to help him be the light. Remember back at Christmas Eve when our sanctuary was dark — except for one candle. Then we all lit our candles and there was a beautiful glow in this very room. This is what a dark world would look like when we all remember that Jesus says to us: "You are the light of the world."

The sermon:

You Talkin' To Me?

Hymns:
Beginning of worship: Christ Is the World's Light
Sermon hymn: We Would See Jesus
End of worship: Christ Whose Glory Fills the Skies

Scripture: Matthew 5:13-20

Sermon Text: *"Think not that I have come to abolish the law and the prophets..."* (vs. 7)

PERHAPS, ONE OF THE ELEMENTAL MISUNDERSTANDINGS of the gospel among many church folk is about the relationship of the Hebrew scriptures to the New Testament. Often the former is seen as a testament of judgment, the latter as a testament of grace. This misunderstanding was summarized in a short book by "theologian" Dick Van Dyke when he said, "Jesus is God's answer to God's bad reputation." Today's text, if nothing else, should help Christians understand that Jesus considered his own ministry not as a break from Jewish law and prophecy, but as a continuation of it. Don't miss the Messiah's explicit words, "I have come not to abolish the law or the prophets; I have not come to abolish, but to fulfill" (vs. 17).

Matthew tries to help the early church make this connection between Jesus and Moses. We might note this connection, as well. On the Mount of Transfiguration, Jesus' select disciples see Jesus and Moses and Elijah. Thus, this verse about law and prophets is incarnate on the mountaintop with each prototypical representative: Moses for the law; Elijah for prophecy.

February 7, 1993

Last Sunday we read from the beginning of the Sermon on the Mount the ten Beatitudes of Jesus. These obviously correspond to the Ten Commandments of the Jewish decalogue. Also note that in Matthew, mountains provide the place for God's revelation: Transfiguration, the Mount of this sermon, Calvary. In Hebrew scripture mountains are also a place of divine revelation: Moriah, Sinai, Nebo, Ararat, Horeb.

In these various ways, Matthew establishes Jesus to be the new Moses and Elijah for the Hebrew people. He is to be a leader and prophet of the people. Jesus is to lead the people of a new Israel to a place called the kingdom of heaven. It may not be as geographically explicit as the promised land. It is perhaps more like leading them into a new relationship with their God. The realm of God is now a promise of a new state of being before the Lord.

One of the great hurdles the early church had to overcome was the charge that they, as followers of Jesus, had violated the sacred ritual laws of Judaism. This in fact can be seen in the contentious relations between Jesus and the Pharisees. The Pharisees saw themselves as guardians of the sacred traditions of Judaism. In our day, this debate is usually understood as pitting law and grace against one another. Jesus' statement shows he is serious about the weighty matters of the law.

As we look at the text, we notice, in fact, the absolute seriousness with which Jesus' words undergird the law, or torah, of God. "I say to you, till heaven and earth pass away, not an iota, not a dot, will pass from the law until all is accomplished." To underscore this earnestness, Jesus emphasizes one's very standing in the kingdom of heaven is at stake. So, we must assume these issues are not of a take-it-or-leave-it variety. One's very soul hangs in the balance with regard to the sacred tradition of law (torah) and prophecy.

In this passage, however, the punch-line is saved for the last. Rather than let his hearers, the crowd and disciples, off the hook, Jesus drives home the point in a very plain way. To those feeling smug about listening to Jesus preach at the Pharisees, Jesus adds a final postscript. He says that unless their righteousness exceeds the scribes' and Pharisees', then they will never enter the kingdom of heaven. This is where the rubber of the Christian faith meets the pavement of life.

For all of us, it is a much safer and easier task to sit in judgment over another's relationship with God. The difficult task is for us to grow into a better and more righteous relationship with God. What often looks like an indictment of others can often, from a different perspective, call our own discipleship into question.

David N. Mosser
First United Methodist Church
Georgetown, Texas

FEBRUARY 14, 1993

Sixth Sunday after Epiphany

Lessons:

Lutheran:	Deut. 30:15-20	I Cor. 2:6-13	Matt. 5:20-37
Roman Catholic:	Sir. 15.15-20	I Cor. 2:6-10	Matt. 5:17-37
Episcopal:	Ecc. 15:11-20	I Cor. 3:1-9	Matt. 5:21-24, 27-30, 33-37
Pres/Meth/UCC:	Deut. 30:15-20	I Cor. 3:1-9	Matt. 5:21-37

Introductions to the Lessons

Lesson 1

Deuteronomy 30:15-20 (**Luth/Pres/Meth/UCC**). Moses is 120 years old and will soon die. For 40 years he has led the Israelites out of Egypt to the Promised Land. In his final address to his people, he calls upon them to make a life or death decision: to obey or not to obey God's commands. Not to obey means death; to obey means life. He begs them to choose life by loving the Lord.

Lesson 2

(1) *I Corinthians 2:6-13* (**Luth**). Though Paul will know nothing but Christ and him crucified, he still has wisdom for the Corinthian church. But, it is a wisdom hidden and kept secret from the world. It is God's wisdom revealed by the Spirit. It is not the world's spirit but God's Spirit who enlightens and reveals the truth of God.

(2) *I Corinthians 3:1-9* (**Epis/Pres/Meth/UCC**). Paul is still dealing with the problem of disunity in the Corinthian church. Members are dividing themselves against each other according to leaders. Jealousy and quarreling indicate they are babes in Christ. They need to grow up to understand that church leaders, like Paul and Apollos, are partners working for God.

Gospel

Matthew 5:20-37 (**Luth**); *Matt. 5:21-24, 27-30, 33-37* (**Epis**); *Matt. 5:21-37* (**Pres/Meth/UCC**). Jesus is all for the Law of Moses. His interpretation makes the Law more difficult to obey. It is not only the act but the motive that is involved. The commandment not to kill includes also not hating a person enough to want to kill. The intention is as wrong as the act.

Theme: The reconciling power of the new righteousness.

Thought for the day: God's teaching helps us live with others and ourselves.

Prayer of meditation: God of all glory, on the first day you created the earth and all its fullness. Bringing light out of darkness, you also separated the waters from the dry land. You created plants and animals and have made people to be stewards over them. As we worship, make us ever mindful of the awesomeness of life and our responsibility toward it. Everything in creation praises your name. May we do no less. Amen.

Call to worship: "Arise, shine; for your light has come, and the glory of the Lord has risen upon you" (Isaiah 60:1).

Prayer of adoration: Gracious God, you have given us the Messiah, Christ Jesus, to be the light of the world. We thank you for putting our lives within the sphere of your life. As the baptized, we are called into the ministry of love and reconciliation. Strengthen us for your godly work. Gird us up where we stumble and give us hope where worldly disappointment assails us. May the measure of our devotion to the gospel grow as we sojourn as people of the divine realm. In Christ's name, we pray. Amen.

Prayer of confession: Most merciful Lord, we confess we have done little as disciples to advance the cause of Christ in our world. Often we pray without conviction, sing without enthusiasm, and minister to others without passion. Forgive us our sin of outward obedience, without inward contrition. Rekindle the flame of the spirit of Pentecost within us so we may display not only the smoke of the gospel, but also its fire. Restore the intimacy of our relation to you, so we may be reconciled to those we ought to love as you have loved us. Today is a day of salvation for us all, for today you have placed your kingdom within us. In Christ we pray. Amen.

Prayer of dedication of gifts and self: Eternal God, within our reach you have placed every good gift by which our lives are constantly enriched. As our gifts are received, may we rededicate our lives to the eternal truths of the gospel. Help us live the covenant you have written upon our hearts through the life, death, and resurrection of Jesus Christ, in whose holy name we pray. Amen.

Sermon title: What Does Exceeding Righteousness Look Like?

February 14, 1993

Sermon thesis: With his coming as Messiah, Jesus not only fulfills Israel's hope. Jesus also demands a new level of righteousness of those who claim God's grace.

Hymn for the day: *"Forgive our sins"* The ideas for this hymn on forgiveness came to the author as she was digging weeds in a long-neglected garden. She realized how those deeply-rooted weeds were choking the life from the flowers in the garden. In much the same way, deeply-rooted resentments can destroy Christian joy and peace unless we can learn, with God's help, to forgive. Born of British parents in India in 1905, Rosamond E. Herklots worked for over 20 years as secretary to an eminent neurologist. Although she wrote verse from childhood, she did not begin to write hymns until later in her life. She died in 1987.

Announcements for next week:
   Sermon title: After the Mountain, Then What?
   Sermon theme: God's vision gives us meaning and purpose.
   Sermon summary: Many Christians yearn for the mountaintop experience, but the truth, is most of us live life in the valleys.

Children's object talk:
Telling the Truth is Enough
Objects: None
Lesson: Jesus says, "Tell the truth."
Outline: 1. We want people to like us.
   2. Sometimes we stretch the truth.
   3. Simple truth is all we need.

HAVE YOU EVER SEEN A COURTROOM on television? When people testify in court, and this means they are asked to tell the truth, they put their hand on the Bible. Then a person asks them to raise their right hand and say, "Do you swear to tell the whole truth, so help you God?" This is called swearing in or taking an oath. As my childrens' friends would say, "If I'm not telling the truth, you can stick 1000 pins in my eye."

I think all people want others to like them and respect them. Most of us want to be popular and likable. But sometimes our wanting people to like us will make us do things that aren't really helpful or right.

For instance, people who want others to think that they are really good at fishing will tell stories that make us laugh. These are called fish stories. These stories start, in fact, with very small fish which are really caught, but every time the story is told the fish gets bigger and bigger. This is called stretching the truth. Many people tell these kinds of stories and they don't really hurt people. But when these little stories are used about things more important than how big the fish we caught is, or how many runs we hit, or our golf score, they can hurt other people.

Jesus was telling people, in biblical times, that they don't need to stretch the truth. He said, "Let what you say be simply yes or no; anything more than this comes from evil." In other words, we don't need to tell more than the truth to impress people or have them respect us. Real friends appreciate the simple truth. We don't need to add a thing.

The sermon:
What Does Exceeding Righteousness Look Like?
Hymns:
   Beginning of worship: We, Thy People, Praise Thee
   Sermon hymn: Breathe on Me, Breath of God
   End of worship: Lead on, O King Eternal

Scripture: Matthew 5:20-37

Sermon Text: *"You have heard it said to those of ancient times..."* (v. 21a)

IF ONE ACCEPTS THE IMPLICATIONS OF the gospel, then what would this mean to the way we look at life? More important, perhaps, is what will be required of us? These are questions Jesus addresses to those who hear the Sermon on the Mount. In other words, what does it mean for Jesus as God's Messiah to come and usher in the new era which Matthew calls the kingdom of heaven?

First of all, for Jews who lived before Jesus' time, the promise of Messiah was one of primary promises of God which gave them hope. As we read the history of the Jewish people, we read a tradition filled with stories of enslavement and captivity. Even in those years when these people were not actually in bondage, they were often in war staving off bondage. With only a few respites from external threat, the Hebrews were fed a steady diet of the fear of subjugation. The Egyptians, Assyrians, Babylonians, and Romans were the superpowers which often shaped Israel's destiny. When not in-

February 14, 1993

timidated by world powers, Israel was often in conflict with smaller nations and tribes trying to gain political and economic control over them. The Philistines and Amorites immediately come to mind as among these many smaller nations.

"When the Messiah comes" was the rallying cry, and indeed prayer, raised by the Hebrews to give hope to otherwise despairing situations. The idea of Messiah gave tenuous hope to which Israel clung for the generations between David and Jesus.

Jesus as God's Messiah, however, had another implication beyond the first, for it did more than simply give hope. It, second of all, required something of the people. In Matthew 5:20, Jesus says, "For I tell you, unless your righteousness exceeds that of the scribes and Pharisees, you will never enter the kingdom of heaven." The passage spells out for those accepting Jesus as Messiah what will be expected of them. Four times in today's lesson Jesus contrasts the operative theology and ethics before and after his coming. Jesus does this by saying in various ways, "You have heard it said to those of ancient times...," then Jesus adds a teaching about current relations between people. Not only this, but each teaching echoes verse 20 regarding righteousness which exceeds that of those who hold the law with ultimate esteem: the scribes and Pharisees. This means that those persons in God's new kingdom of heaven must be even more righteous than the righteous ones charged to obey the ritual laws of Judaism.

The first application of this new teaching, verses 21-26, guides people in their relations with others within the assembly. Not only is murder condemned, but even the angry rage which precedes murder is verboten. Persons in this new messianic kingdom are not to hurl insults at brothers and sisters. Rather, reconciliation is now the order of the day in this new kingdom of heaven. Instead of going to court, Jesus commands, "Come to terms quickly with your accuser while you are on your way to court." These are especially good words today.

Second, Jesus teaches about new ways for men and women to relate to one another. Women, this teaching states, are not objects to be used—even the way one looks at a woman betrays one's heart and soul.

Third, in this passage, Jesus deals with the topic of relations within marriage. Even though he speaks of divorce, it is only because divorce signals the end of this most significant human relationship.

In the new age, inaugerated by Jesus' coming, relations between husband and wife are to be reconciling and gracious. Thus, marriage vows are not to be made nor broken because of convenience or whim. Again, people in the new age of righteousness are of ultimate worth.

Last, Jesus' teaching focuses on exceeding righteousness by extolling the simple truth. One need not swear oaths. The truth is just that: the truth. In the messianic kingdom, persons can count on one another to be honest and straight-forward. People merely need to say 'yes' or 'no.' Anything more is motivated by evil intent.

The whole of Jesus' Sermon on the Mount is directed toward what the new kingdom of heaven will look like. It is comforting to know God's promises will protect us from our enemies. Of more comfort, however, is that God's promises can also protect us from ourselves!

David N. Mosser
First United Methodist Church
Georgetown, Texas

FEBRUARY 21, 1993

Transfiguration

Lessons:

Lutheran:	Ex. 24:12, 15-18	2 Pet. 1:16-19 (20-21)	Mat. 17:1-9
Roman Catholic:	Is. 49:14-15	I Cor. 4:1-5	Matt. 6:24-34
Episcopal:	Ex. 24:12 (13-14) 15-18	Phil. 3:7-14	Matt. 17:1-9
Pres/Meth/UCC:	Ex. 24:12-18	2 Peter 1:16-21	Matt. 17:1-9

Introductions to the Lessons

Lesson 1

Exodus 24:12, 15-18 (**Luth/Epis**); *Ex. 24:12-18* (**Pres/Meth/UCC**). For 40 days Moses had a first-hand experience with God on top of Mt. Sinai while the Israelites were camped at the foot of the mountain. In the experience God's presence was a dazzling light and Moses received the Decalogue written on two tablets of stone.

Lesson 2

(1) *II Peter 1:16-19* (**Luth**); *II Peter 1:16-21* (**Pres/Meth/UCC**). Like Moses Jesus had a mountain-top experience with God when he was transfigured on Mt. Transfiguration. Peter assures us that it was a real experience. He and two others were there, saw the transfiguration, and heard God's voice of approval.

(2) *Philippians 3:7-14* (**Epis**). If anyone ever had reason to boast about themselves, it was Paul. He was a top-notch Jew, a Pharisee, a persecutor of the church, and morally blameless. Yet, he considered all of these honors as garbage and readily gave them up for the wonderful knowledge of Christ. Not feeling he was perfect however, Paul pressed on to the goal of oneness in Christ.

Gospel

Matthew 17:1-9 (**Luth/Epis/Pres/Meth/UCC**). Before Jesus sets out for Jerusalem where he is to die for the world's sins, he needs to be sure of his Father's approval of his messianic ministry. He takes three of his closest disciples with him to the top of a mountain. The glory of God's presence causes him to glow physically. Moses and Elijah give their approval. Best of all, God assures Jesus that he is well-pleased with his Son.

Theme: God's vision gives us meaning and purpose.

Thought for the day: Seeing life at the top, from God's perspective, makes life at the bottom worth living.

Prayer of meditation: Gracious God, teach us to notice the many points of grace in our lives and in your world. May we behold the small moments of glory in the laugh of a child, the smile of a friend, or the embrace of a brother or sister. Help us appreciate the wonder of nature in a snowflake, tree bud, or blooming flower. The wonder and beauty of nature are ever before us. We pray that we may heed the many small miracles of this life which make it such a thing of awesome wonder. In Christ we pray. Amen.

Call to worship: "I have set my king on Zion, my holy hill." Ask of me and I will make the nations your heritage, and the ends of the earth your possession. Psalm 2:6, 8

Prayer of adoration: Master of all, we glory in your love which has made us and all the splendor of your garden we are to till and keep. We praise you, for in your infinite wisdom you have made us partners in this marvelous creation. This creation humbles us as it spurs us on to become not only co-creators, but also preservers of the sacred trust over which we are stewards. May we never forget the grace and mercy you pour into each of our lives. Amen.

Prayer of confession: Lord, you have told us that those faithful over a little will later be asked to be faithful over much. Often we want to be slothful regarding our duties and responsibilities. Our drive and passion for the spiritual things wane. Often, we confess, when we do the right things it is not for the right reasons. The joy of discipleship has flagged and we neglect not only our own spirits, but the spirit of the very church which is to proclaim the day of the Lord. Almighty God, send again your spirit of revival and renew our spirit. Send us again that passion to do heavenly work. Shore us up against both pride and despair which often overcome us. We know that the sacrifices which are pleasing in your sight are a contrite heart and a broken spirit. Have mercy upon us for Christ's sake. Amen.

Prayer of dedication of gifts and self: O God, you are the source of all our comfort and joy. Today we rejoice because you love us and people love us, too. Through your holy church we can hear those wonderful words of life. As partakers in these gifts of life, we need to give back out of our bounty. This world teaches us to look

February 21, 1993

out for number one and protect what we have. But through the wisdom of scripture you have taught us that the only life worth having is the one we give away. We vow this day to worship you in our deeds and material blessing, all in the name of Jesus. Amen.

Sermon title: After the Mountain, Then What?

Sermon thesis: Many Christians yearn for the mountaintop experience, but the truth is most of us live life in the valleys.

Hymn for the day: *"Swiftly pass the clouds of glory"* This new hymn on the transfiguration speaks of returning to the valley, to a life transfigured by the Cross. Thomas H. Troeger (b. 1945) studied English at Yale University and theology at Colgate Rochester Divinity School in Rochester, New York. Ordained to the ministry of the United Presbyterian Church, he served as a pastor until 1977 when he was appointed to a teaching post at Colgate Rochester Divinity School/Bexley Hall/Crozer Theological Seminary. He has published extensively, including *New Hymns for the Lectionary*, 1985, for which Carol Doran prepared the musical settings.

Announcements for this week: (Ash Wednesday)
  Sermon title: Return to the Lord.
  Sermon theme: It is time to return to the Lord.
  Sermon summary: In returning to the Lord, we can be honest about ourselves and remove our masks; we can find forgiveness for our sins and wholeness for our brokenness; we can be loved without condition; and we can be given direction and meaning for our lives.

Announcements for next week:
  Sermon title: I Am Not God. You Are Not God.
  Sermon theme: Thank God that we are not God!
  Sermon summary: Sometime we are tempted to play the part of God. But when we accept that God is God and we are humans, there comes a freedom in being able to be ourselves, to listen and raise questions, to be honest and responsible, and to view life and people as precious.

Children's object talk:

Going To The Mountain

Objects: Hiking boots
Lesson: We follow Jesus.
Outline: 1. Adventures are fun.
  2. Jesus took three disciples on an adventure.
  3. We're on an adventure with Jesus, too.

I KNOW YOU ALL KNOW what these are. These are my hiking boots. I like to hike. In fact many people like to go hiking. When you hike you never know what you will see.

This was true for Jesus' disciples. One day Jesus took his disciples on a hike to the top of a mountain. We now call this the Mountain of the Transfiguration. When they got to the top something very strange happened. Jesus became glowing and his appearance was changed before the disciples' eyes.

Then another strange thing happened. The disciples saw Jesus talking to two very old characters from our Bible. Jesus was talking to Moses and Elijah. Then came a voice from a cloud, "This is my Son, the Beloved; with him I am well pleased; listen to him!" This made the disciples afraid because they realized this was the voice of God.

Jesus then came and touched them and told them not to be afraid. As they looked up, only Jesus was with them. Jesus told them not to tell anyone about what they had seen or heard. Then they came down the mountain.

Most adventures are fun because as we explore things, we never know what we'll find. The disciples found this out as they followed Jesus. They saw miracles and healings. They saw his great love for people. The disciples heard Jesus teach many important things.

Today, as Jesus' followers in 1993, we have the chance to see and hear wonderful things if we follow Jesus. Some things will make us glad, some will make us sad and afraid. As long as Jesus is with us, we'll all be okay.

The sermon:

After the Mountain, Then What?

Hymns:
Beginning of worship: Mountains Are Aglow
Sermon hymn: Christ, Upon the Mountain Peak
End of worship: Silence, Frenzied, Unclean Spirit

Scripture: Matthew 17:1-9

Sermon Text: *"Six days later, Jesus took with him Peter and James and his brother John and led them up a high mountain, by themselves."* (v. 1)

February 21, 1993

TODAY IS THE LAST SUNDAY AFTER THE EPIPHANY. As we worship today we do so within the reality of many contexts. Several of these contexts are our church, community, and denomination. Another context we often forget is the context of the liturgical or worship season. For instance, as we look back over the last few months, we remember in Advent we heard the proclamation concerning the coming of the Messiah. At Christmas, we sang of the great gift of Emmanuel, God with us. During this season of Epiphany, we have celebrated God's word as the light to the nations, or Gentiles. We have considered what it means to be baptized and what it means to be Christ's missionaries.

Our worship context, however, also includes where the liturgical calendar will take us next. Ahead of us is the penitential season of Jesus Christ's suffering and death during Lent. This will begin, of course, this Wednesday, as we impose ashes upon our foreheads. Beyond the pain of Lent is the joy and hope Easter affords.

The season of Lent is placed, in something of a geographical sense, between the Mount of the Transfiguration and Calvary. Today we are taken up this high mountain of transfiguration. From here, much like Moses' view from Mount Nebo, we look out beyond Lent, to the place of God's promise.

In the gospels, context is also important. Prior to taking the select disciples up the mountain, Jesus had fed 4000, contended with the Pharisees and Sadducees, and taught his disciples. Peter also makes his confession as to who Jesus is. Then occurs this marvelous story of the transfiguration with these characters from our faith tradition: Jesus, Moses, Elijah, Peter, James, and John. You have already heard this story as told to the children.

The transfiguration story has long been dear to the church. In it Jesus is identified as not only heir to Israel's law and prophecy, he is also explicitly identified as the Messiah. The voice of God from the cloud declares, "This is my Son, the Beloved; with him I am well pleased; listen to him!" I'm sure the disciples, though scared to the point of paralysis, later realized the significance of this revelation. For the church, this ultimate spiritual experience is reflected for believers in the phrase, "I had a mountain top experience." Many of you have described a deeply moving religious experience this way as you came back from a revival, summer camp, or a spiritual life retreat.

In light of this good feeling, in response to a wonderful experience, it is important to note what the disciples came back to after coming down the mountain. Jesus and the disciples, presumably all of them, came upon a crowd (vs. 14-21). A father comes to Jesus and as he kneels he says, "Lord, have mercy on my son, for he is an epileptic and he suffers terribly." In Ronald Knox's translation from the Vulgate the father says, "Lord, have pity on my son, who is a lunatic and in great afflication."

Today we know epilepsy is a disease which, in many cases, can be controlled by medication. In Jesus' time, the term "lunatic" came from the idea that the moon had evil effects on certain people; hence, the word lunacy from "lunar" or moonlike. We know now that epilepsy has nothing to do with mental illness. For people in Jesus' time all they could do was make nonscientific judgments about people's behavior.

All of us want experiences on the mountain. We want to be with Jesus—high, alone, and with the Christ. But the ugly truth is that most of life is lived in the valley. This valley is filled with death, epilepsy, and lunacy. Many things in this world are beyond our help or understanding, yet this is where we are called to ministry. Life in the valley is never easy, nor often pretty. This is why Christ was sent and why we too are called into ministry by virtue of our baptism.

Seeing life from the mountain of God, even if only a glimpse, makes life in the valley not only possible, but bearable. The mountain gives us perspective, meaning, and most of all, purpose. Christ never takes us up to hold the vision for ourselves. We are to share it with a world gone mad. This is our redemption. This is our calling.

David N. Mosser
First United Methodist Church
Georgetown, Texas

FEBRUARY 24, 1993

Ash Wednesday

Lessons:

Lutheran:	Joel 2:12-19	2 Cor. 5:20b-6:2	Matt. 6:1-6, 16-21
Roman Catholic:	Joel 2:12-18	2 Cor. 5:20b-6:2	Matt. 6:1-6, 16-18
Episcopal:	Joel 2:1-2, 12-17	2 Cor. 5:20b-6:10	Matt. 6:1-6, 16-21
Pres/Meth/UCC.	Joel 2:1 2, 12, 17	2 Cor. 5:20b-6:10	Matt. 6:1-6, 16-21

Introductions to the Lessons

Lesson 1

Joel 2:12-19 (**Luth**); *2:1-2, 12-17* (**Epis/Pres/Meth/UCC**). Sound the alarm! A day of doom is coming. Therefore, repent and return to the Lord with fasting and weeping. If you do, your gracious God will have mercy and bless you.

Lesson 2

2 Corinthians 5:20b-6:10 (**Epis/Pres/Meth/UCC**); *2 Cor. 5:20b-6:2* (**Luth**). Ash Wednesday is the first day of Lent, a time to be reconciled to God by faith in Christ. Through Paul God is making this appeal to be reconciled. Accept his salvation today. Do not receive the grace of God in vain.

Gospel

Matthew 6:1-6, 16-21 (**Luth/Epis/Pres/Meth/UCC**). In this section from the Sermon on the Mount, Jesus deals with the practice of piety in giving, praying, and fasting. None of this is to be done for "show" but to be done secretly. By doing these things privately and sincerely, we store up spiritual treasure in heaven.

Theme: It is time to return to the Lord.

Thought for the day: As we begin this journey through Lent, we need to examine our lives honestly and offer our confession. We also need to claim the forgiveness, the love, and the mission that God offers us through Jesus Christ.

Prayer of meditation: Almighty and merciful Lord, create in us honest hearts. During this time of worship, help us to reflect upon our lives and repent of our sins. In your mercy, grant to us your full pardon and forgiveness. Amen.

Call to worship:
P: Seek the Lord while he may be found.
C: Call upon him while he is near.
P: Let the wicked abandon their ways,
C: And the unrighteous their thoughts.
P: Let them turn to the Lord for mercy,
C: To our God, who is generous in forgiving.
(Lenten Dialog, Service of the Word, Lutheran Book of Worship, page 127).

Prayer of adoration: We are humbled, dear Lord, because we know our unworthiness and our frality. We are humbled because you are slow to anger and abounding in steadfast love. We are humbled because you have chosen to look upon us with mercy. Thank you for offering us the forgiveness of sins and the hope of eternal life. In your name we pray. Amen.

Prayer of confession: We confess, dear Lord, that we do not live as we ought. Yet, even as we utter these words, we pray that we are saying them not because it is the proper thing to do, but because it is the truth. We pray that we may rend our hearts and not just our garments. Help us indeed acknowledge our unworthy attitudes and sinful behavior. Help us to turn to the strength of your love and forgiveness. Amen

Prayer of dedication of gifts and self: We offer ourselves to you, O Lord, and ask that you use us to remember the prisoners, the poor, the anxious, the despairing, and the fearful. Use our gifts and our time so that they may know of your love and acceptance of them. Use our lives to give meaning to the lives of others. In your name we ask these things. Amen.

Sermon title: Return to the Lord

Sermon thesis: In returning to the Lord, we can be honest about ourselves and remove our masks; we can find forgiveness for our sins and wholeness for our brokenness; we can be loved without condition; and we can be given direction and meaning to our lives.

Hymn for the day: *"Out of the depths I cry to you"* Martin Luther (1483-1546) was born in Eisleben, Germany, and ordained a priest in 1507. While on the faculty at Wittenberg University he became aware of some of the corruptions in the church of his time. From there the story of the Reformation is well-known. A musician himself, Luther encouraged congregational hymn singing and wrote a number of fine hymns.

February 24, 1993

Psalm 130 was a favorite of Luther's and this hymn is one of the finest German Psalm versifications. Written in 1523, the hymn was sung in 1525 at the funeral of Elector Friedrich the Wise, and also at Luther's own funeral in 1546.

Announcements for next week:
   Sermon title:
   Sermon theme:
   Sermon summary:

Children's object talk:

Why Are We Sorry?

Objects: A piece of candy
Lesson: Be sincerely sorry.
Outline: 1. Story of two boys caught stealing.
   2. Explanation of rending one's garments.
   3. Need to be sincere when we are sorry.

ONCE UPON A TIME, two boys were caught stealing some candy from a local grocery store. Both said that they were sorry, but for different reasons. One said that he was sorry only because he figured he would get off lighter. He was not really sorry for stealing; he was sorry that he was caught! The other said that he was sorry because he truly felt bad for taking something that did not belong to him. Which boy had the right attitude? It is the one who was sincerely sorry for doing something wrong.

Today in our lesson from the Book of Joel, there is a line that says, "Rend your hearts not your garments." Can anyone tell me what the word "rend" means? It is not a very common word. "Rend" means to rip or to tear. Long ago, people would sometimes tear their clothes to show their anguish over the bad things that they had done. Sometimes, they were sincerely sorry, but sometimes they really were not that sorry. They just tore their garments because that is what they were supposed to do. Is that a good idea? No. When we say that we are sorry, God wants us to mean it from the bottom of our hearts!

What are some things we do that are wrong? Our list might include disobeying our parents, hitting a classmate, making fun of someone, telling a lie, etc. When we are caught, most of us will say, "I'm sorry." I hope that when we say these words we sincerely mean them. I hope that these words come from our hearts.

The sermon:
Return to the Lord

Hymns:
Beginning of worship: Jesus, Refuge of the Weary
Sermon hymn: Out of the Depths I Cry to You
End of worship: My Song Is Love Unknown

Scripture: Joel 2:12-19

Sermon Text: *"Yet, even now, says the Lord, return to me with all your heart, with fasting, with weeping, and with mourning; and rend your hearts and not your garments."*

RETURN TO THE LORD! On this day and in the weeks to come, turn from that which hinders you and turn towards him who gives you life. Return to the Lord because we cannot do it on our own. Return to the Lord because we need Jesus Christ in our lives. Yet even now, return to the Lord.

If we are left on our own, many of us tend to wear masks—even if no one else is in the room. We try to hide who we really are—our thoughts, our fears, our dreams. Sometimes we will wear the mask of casualness or indifference to avoid admitting hurt. Sometimes we will wear a smile to disguise the lack of true peace inside. We try to avoid honesty with ourselves and others. We fear that we will not be acceptable if the truth is known. We fear that others might not think highly of us. And so, in our Gospel text today, our Lord talks about those almsgivers who sound the trumpets so that they may be praised by people, those hypocrites who love to stand and pray in the synagogues and on the street corners so that they may be seen by others, and those who disfigure their faces so that their fasting may be seen by others. At some time or another, all of us will try to present an image of ourselves other than what we truly are.

Because Jesus Christ helps us to remove these masks that we wear, we need to return to the Lord. Jesus Christ already knows who we are—with all our shortcomings, pretenses, and failures. That means we can wash off our painted smiles and rosy cheeks and squarely look at our naked face in the mirror and be honest with ourselves. We can be just as we are without one plea. We can admit that we are the sinners that we are. We can admit our mixed motivations,

February 24, 1993

our mixed emotions, our mixed signals. Our Lord already knows them. Return to the Lord. Take off your mask.

As we go through this life, we tend to "mess up" a great deal. Good intentions disintegrate and best efforts become futile. As it says in Romans, "We do not do what we want, but we do the very thing we hate." Then, we end up lashing out even more at others, especially loved ones. Using a phrase from Saul Bellow's book, *The Dangling Man*, we become "nasty, brutish, and short" to those around us. The other day, I was upset with myself for overextending myself once again. But, what did I do? I took my frustration out on my mother over the phone with no justification. So, I compounded my offense with yet another one. Thus, we slouch over more and more because the burden of memories, guilt, and failures continues to grow. We hurt ourselves and others more and more. It becomes a descending spiral and we cry, "Blot out my transgressions! Wash me from my iniquities! Cleanse me from my sins! Purge me! Wash me!"

Because Jesus Christ offers forgiveness, we need to return to the Lord. Jesus Christ can give us the courage to stand up and move forward. Jesus Christ can give us his body and blood so that we might have new life. By ourselves, we are broken toys. With our Lord, we are made whole again. By ourselves, we get stuck looking backwards. With our Lord, we can look forward. God forgets our iniquities, but remembers us forever. Return to the Lord. Receive forgiveness.

There is also a need in each of us to belong. We need to be loved, we need to be embraced. Dag Hammarskjold, in his book *Markings*, once captured the essence of this need. "As a husband embraces his wife's body in faithful tenderness, so the bare ground and trees are embraced by the still, high light of the morning. I feel an ache of longing to share in this embrace, to be united and absorbed. A longing like carnal desire, but directed toward the earth, water, sky, and returned by the whispers of the trees, the fragrance of the soil, the caresses of the wind, the embrace of water and light." We need to be loved. That is part of who we are. That is who I am and who you are.

Because Jesus offers us unconditional love, we need to return to the Lord. We need to turn again to the hearing of his word, to the joining with his people, to the partaking of his sacrament so that we may hear again of his love for us. We need to hear that Jesus Christ accepts us just as we are. For Valentine's Day, my parents sent me a card with the following words on it. In one sense, it is definitely corny. But, in another sense, it conveys their abiding and sincere love for me and, in a broader context, God's steadfast love for us. The card reads, "Love you cheerful, love you scrappy; Love you tearful, love you happy. Love you mopey, love you sweetly; Love you, love you, so completely." Return to the Lord. Hear of his unconditional love for you.

When we are left on our own, we also tend to become more and more self-centered. And when we focus inward, we fail to see the needs, the hurts, the joys, and the concerns of others. We can only see our own. I remember very clearly an incident that happened when I was living in Minneapolis with my four college friends. One of my housemates had broken up with her boyfriend, but it took me an entire weekend to realize that something was wrong! And I lived with her day in and day out! Then, when I finally noticed her subdued demeanor, her strained conversation about him, and her shadowy eyes, I did not even ask what was the matter! I was too busy with myself to notice, to ask, or to give her a chance to tell me.

Because Jesus Christ helps us not to be so self-absorbed, we need to return to the Lord. Jesus Christ teaches us to give of ourselves to others. He asks us to die to our old nature and to choose to lay our lives down for others. Jesus Christ also shows us what it means to live for another and to die for another. He says, "Follow me." Jesus Christ also needs us. As it says in our text from II Corinthians, "We are ambassadors for Christ, God making his appeal through us." Return to the Lord. Find meaning not only for your life, but also meaning beyond yourself.

On this day and in the weeks to come, return to the Lord. Return to the Lord for it is with him that we can be honest about ourselves and remove our masks. Return to the Lord for it is in him that we can find forgiveness for our sins and wholeness for our brokenness. Return to the Lord for it is through him that we are loved without condition. Return to the Lord for it is in him that we are given direction and meaning for our lives. Yet even now, return to the Lord.

Beth Marie Halvorsen
Shepherd of the Hills Lutheran Church
Austin, Texas

FEBRUARY 28, 1993

First Sunday in Lent

Lessons:

Lutheran:	Gen. 2:7-9, 15-17; 3:1-7	Rom. 5:12 (13-16) 17-19	Matt. 4:1-11
Roman Catholic:	Gen. 2:7-9; 3:1-7	Rom. 5:12-19,	Matt. 4:1-11
Episcopal:	Gen. 2:4b-9, 15-17, 25-3:7	Rom. 5:12-19 (20-21)	Matt. 4:1-11
Pres/Meth/UCC:	Gen. 2:15-17, 3:1-7	Rom. 5:12-19	Matt. 4:1-11

Introductions to the Lessons

Lesson 1

Genesis 2:7-9, 15-17; 3:1-7 (**Luth**); *Gen. 2:4b-9, 15-17, 25-3:7* (**Epis**) *Gen. 2:15-17; 3:1-7* (**Pres/Meth/UCC**). In this second account of creation, we are told about humanity's first temptation and sin. In the form of a serpent Satan tempts Eve. He raises doubts in her mind and tells her the biggest lie ever told: "You will not die." The forbidden fruit was so attractive that Eve and then Adam yielded to the temptation.

Lesson 2

Romans 5:12, 17-19 (**Luth**); *Rom. 5:12-19* (**Epis/Pres/Meth/UCC**). Sin came into the world through one person, Adam. Because of his original sin, all of humanity is by nature sinful. The result of sin is estrangement from God, condemnation, and death. But, as sin came into the world by one person, sin went out by one person, Jesus Christ. Through him comes grace which brings acceptance by God and eternal life.

Gospel

Matthew 4:1-11 (**Luth/Epis/Pres/Meth/UCC**). Jesus just said no to the Devil's temptations. He had just been baptized and received the Holy Spirit. Now the Spirit leads him to a desolate place where he is to decide what method to use in carrying out his mission to be the Messiah. His secret of overcoming Satan's temptations was the truth of Scripture. After the battle with Satan, angels comforted and strengthened him.

Theme: Thank God that we are not God!

Thought for the day: Though we intellectually realize that we are not God, there are subtle ways in which we try to assume the role of God. As we become aware of these temptations, we experience freedom.

The Minister's Annual Manual

Prayer of meditation: Dear Jesus, we remember this day that you were subject to many and varied temptations, just as we are. In your compassion, help us when we are tempted. Clear our minds so that we may recognize problems and remember consequences. Soften our hearts so that we may be open to that which is right. Use your spirit and your people to aid us in living a holy life. Remind us to turn to you in prayer; through your Son, Jesus Christ, our Lord. Amen.

Call to worship:
P: When the battle of good and evil rages around us,
C: Keep us steadfast, O Lord!
P: When the battle of good and evil rages within us!
C: Keep us steadfast, O Lord!
P: In time of temptation, be our strength
C: So that we may proclaim your name!

Prayer of adoration: Dear Jesus, we praise you for your victory over Satan! We praise you that, while in human form, you resisted temptation by praying and trusting in God's Word! Grant us your aid, grant us your strength. In your almighty name we pray. Amen.

Prayer of confession: Forgive us, gracious God, when we forget who we are and try to take your place. Forgive us when we pretend to be someone that we are not and when we try to control others. Forgive us when we make excuses for our behavior and when we avoid the fact of our finiteness. Forgive us, gracious God, when we succumb to these temptations. In your name we pray. Amen.

Prayer of dedication of gifts and self: O Master, let me walk with you in lowly paths of service true; tell me your secret; help me bear the strain of toil, the fret of care. Help me the slow of heart to move by some clear, winning word of love. Teach me the wayward feet to stay, and guide them in the homeward way. In hope that sends a shining ray far down the future's broad'ning way, in peace that only you can give, with you, O Master, let me live. Amen.
—Washington Gladden, 1836-1918

Sermon title: I am not God. You are not God.

Sermon thesis: Sometimes we are tempted to play the part of God. But, when we accept that God is God and we are humans, there comes a freedom in being able to be ourselves, to listen and raise questions, to be honest and responsible, and to view life and people as precious.

February 28 1993

Hymn for the day: *"Lord, who (O Lord) throughout these forty days"* Claudia Frances Ibotson (1838-1898), a native of England, was married to the Reverend J.W.D. Hernaman, an inspector of schools. Intensely interested in the religious education of children, she wrote 150 original hymns and translations from Latin for children. This hymn remembers Jesus' temptation in the wilderness.

Announcements for next week:
   Sermon title: Let Go and Walk!
   Sermon theme: We step forth into unknown, but promised lands.
   Sermon summary: We do not know what the journey of life will bring us, but we can step forth in trust because we know who is calling and what is promised. Thus, we respond to the Spirit that moves us, the people that compel us, and the time that passes so quickly.

Children's object talk:
The Forty Days In Lent
Objects: A calendar
Lesson: Understanding Lent
Outline: 1. The number "40".
   2. Number of days in Lent.
   3. Importance of Lent.

HOW MANY FINGERS DO I HAVE ON MY HANDS? Ten. How many times do I have to flash my hands to reach the number "forty"? Four. Ten, twenty, thirty, forty! In the Bible, the number "forty" appears quite often. It rained for forty days when Noah, his family, and all the animals were on the ark. Moses wandered in the wilderness for forty years. Jesus spent forty days in the desert fasting and praying. The number "forty" appears quite often, and something mighty always happens at the end!

We are now in the church season of Lent. Guess how many days it has? Forty! You can see that I have marked these forty days on this calendar. Lent begins with Ash Wednesday which was this past Wednesday. As you look at the calendar, can you tell me what days I skipped? Sundays! We do not count Sundays as part of the forty days of Lent because we consider them to be "little Easters." When does Lent end? I can tell you that something important happens then! Lent ends on Easter Eve, just as we are getting ready to celebrate the resurrection of our Lord. This is what Lent looks like on a calendar.

In the early church, Lent was a time of teaching. People who wanted to become Christian would spend three hours a day in class for seven weeks learning more about our faith. When Lent was over, they were then baptized on Easter Day. Today, Lent is still a time for us to learn more about Jesus and to prepare for the celebration of Easter.

The sermon:

I Am Not God

Hymns:
Beginning of worship: O God, Our Help in Ages
Sermon hymn: O Lord, throughout These Forty Days Past
End of worship: In the Cross of Christ I Glory

Scripture: Genesis 2:7-9, 15-17: 3:1-7

Sermon Text: *"But the serpent said to the woman. 'You will not die. For God knows when you eat of this your eyes will be open, and you will be like God, knowing good and evil.' "* (Genesis 3:4-5)

I AM NOT GOD. YOU ARE NOT GOD. On one hand, this statement can seem quite obvious because we are aware of the frailty and brevity of our lives. From the words of scripture, we know that we are dust and to dust we shall return. From the words of the hymn, we know that "time, like an ever-rolling stream, soon bears us all away." This statement can also seem quite obvious because we know the faults and failings in our lives. Our Old Testament lesson for today captures the essence of sin — the temptation, the disobedience, the consequences. Our attitudes and our choices capture the reality of sin. I am not God. You are not God.

On one hand, this statement can seem obvious. But, on another hand, this statement is maybe not so obvious to you and me. Even though we claim that we are not God, there are indeed times when you and I act or think as though we are God. Today, I would like us to recognize those times when we try to usurp the place of God. Also, I would like for us to hear the freedom that comes with saying, "I am not God. You are not God."

One of the times when we play God is when we try to be someone we are not. This was the temptation that the serpent gave Eve — "You shall be like God, knowing good and evil." The allure is to

February 28 1993

be something other than what we are! Sometimes we try to be someone else by putting on a facade or wearing a mask. Sometimes we try to be someone else by cultivating an image with certain stories or gestures. We can be afraid of standing "just as is." Eve succumbed to temptation by rationalizing that her disobedience was desirable in that it would make her more wise. But God created Eve to be Eve, just as God created me to be me and you to be you! God did not create us to be someone else.

During these times of insecurity when we wish we were someone "other than me," it is good to remember this story about a young rabbi named Zusia. Now Zusia was discouraged about his work. He would preach and his congregation would doze off or look out the window. The young people thought he was old-fashioned and the community seemed indifferent to him. He knew that he was not much of a scholar. He saw himself as a failure. So, Zusia visited an older rabbi and said, "Rabbi, I am so discouraged. What can I do?" The old Rabbi answered, "My son, when you get to heaven, God is not going to say to you, 'Why weren't you Moses?' He's going to ask, 'Why weren't you Zusia?' So, why don't you stop trying to be Moses and just be the Zusia that God made you to be?"

I am not God. You are not God. Thus, we do not have to play God by trying to be someone else. I don't have to be anyone else. You don't have to be anyone else. We can be ourselves because that is the way God made us.

I am not God. You are not God. Yet, there are times when we also play God by trying to control others. Now this can take many forms. In our lessons from Genesis today, the serpent dares to speak for God, dares to speak about what God will or will not do! The serpent tells Eve, "You shall not die. For God knows that when you eat of it, your eyes will be opened..."

Sometimes, we also assume that we know what another person is doing, feeling, or thinking without checking it out first. Unfortunately, presuming to know the full story can happen too often and can cause a great deal of pain and confusion. Rumors can start; stereotypes can be established; and communication can be blocked.

Have you ever heard of the story, "The Blind Men and Elephants," by John Godfrey Saxe? This story points out only too well that each of us has a limited perspective. The story is about six men of Indostan — all of whom who are blind — who go to see an elephant and satisfy their minds. The First man, falling against the elephant's

311

broad and sturdy side, is sure that the elephant is very much like a wall! The Second, who feels the round, smooth, sharp tusk, cries out, "To me 'tis very clear this wonder of an elephant is very like a spear!" From the feel of the squirming trunk, the Third boldly states that the elephant is very like a snake! And the Fourth, after touching the elephant's knee, declares that this beast is like a tree. But the Fifth, who chances to touch the ear, proclaims that the similarity is to that of a fan! Finally, the Sixth seizes on the swinging tail and pronounces that the Elephant is like a rope! This story finally concludes, "Though each was partly in the right, they all were in the wrong!"

I am not God. You are God. We do not have and we do not need to have the definitive answer for everyone and everything! That is quite freeing news! Instead of trying to control others and insist that we are right, we can listen to them and let them be who God made them to be. Maybe that is why God created us with one tongue and two ears. Thus, though we cannot tell a grieving widow how she feels, we can listen to her tell us. Though we cannot tell an adult child how to live, we can listen and raise questions. We do not have to provide all the answers for others and about others. We can listen and learn.

I am not God. You are not God. Yet, there are also times when we play God by thinking that our actions or non-actions have no consequence. Eve clearly knew what God had commanded, but she side-stepped around his command with a whole series of rationalizations. "The tree was good for food ... it was a delight to the eyes ... the tree was to be desired to make one wise." But, the truth is that her disobedience did have consequences, serious consequences. As much as we might like to believe otherwise, that piece of cake we might eat does have calories and that third or fourth drink we might have does alter our judgment and reflexes. That lie we told does make a difference and the time we did not speak up was nonetheless a voice. Even though we do not want to admit it, things do catch up with us.

I am not God. You are not God. We do not have to sneak around about our activities and attitudes. We do not have to create a whole series of excuses. Instead, we can be honest about what we do and what we do not do, as we continue to accept the responsibility for our behavior!

I am not God. You are not God. Finally, there are also times when

February 28 1993

we play God by avoiding the reality of death. I am going to die. You are going to die. And we do not know when that will be. We would like to be able to say, "Not me!" We would like to believe the serpent when he says, "You will not die!" But, that is not the truth. We are frail human beings who will eventually pass away. As I listen to the prayer requests from people in our congregation and community, I realize that there are many people who are grieving or sick or dying. I remember that time here on earth can be much briefer and more difficult than I would like. But that also can help my perspective about life by reminding me how precious it is and by questioning myself about how I am living it.

I am not God. You are not God. Sometimes we try to play the part. But it will never work, because God is still God, and we are still humans. As we accept this, there comes a freedom. There comes a freedom in being able to be ourselves and not be anyone else. There comes a freedom in being able to listen and raise questions without having to provide all the answers for everyone else. There comes a freedom in being able to be honest and responsible rather than trying to rationalize away our actions and non-actions. There comes a freedom in being given a perspective that makes life and people more precious, rather than trying to avoid the reality of our finiteness. I am not God. You are not God. Thank God!

Beth Marie Halvorsen
Shepherd of the Hills Lutheran Church
Austin, Texas

MARCH 7, 1993

Second Sunday in Lent

Lessons:

Lutheran:	Gen. 12:1-8	Rom. 4:1-5,13-17	John 4:5-26 (27-30, 39-42)
Roman Catholic:	Gen. 12:1-4a	2 Tim. 1:8b-10	Matt. 17:1-9
Episcopal:	Gen. 12:1-8	Rom. 4:1-5 (6-12) 13-17	John 3:1-17
Pres/Meth/UCC:	Gen. 12:1-4a	Rom. 4:1-5, 13-174	John 3:1-17

Introductions to the Lessons

Lesson 1

(1) *Genesis 12:1-8* (**Luth**); *Genesis 12:1-4a* (**Epis/Pres/Meth/UCC**) It takes a heap of faith at age 75 for a person to take his family and possessions to go to a strange foreign land. It was faith in God who called Abraham to do just that with the promise he would become a great nation and a blessing. His religious devotion was seen by the fact that wherever he settled, he built an altar to the Lord.

Lesson 2

Romans 4:1-5,13-17 (**Luth/Epis/Pres/Meth/UCC**) In a previous chapter Paul taught that it is by faith in Christ that we are made right with God. Abraham is an example of this truth. It was not his good words by obeying the Law that made God and Abraham friends, because the Law had not yet been given. Abraham's faith was demonstrated in his obedience to God's command and in his trust in God's promise.

Gospel

(1) John 4:5-26 (**Luth**) Jesus was on his way from Judea to Galilee. He had to pass through Samaria. One day at noon he stopped to rest and get a drink from a well. The disciples had gone to the village for food. Jesus was alone sitting by a well. Along comes a Samaritan woman to get water. He initiates a conversation with her by asking her for a drink of water and then leads her to have faith in him as Messiah.

(2) John 3:1-17) (**Epis/Pres/Meth/UCC**) Late at night two teachers have a discussion: Jesus and Nicodemus. Jesus teaches a teacher that spiritual birth is necessary to enter God's kingdom. Moreover, faith is a necessity for eternal life. In today's gospel lesson is the famous verse, John 3:16, which Luther called "The Little Bible". The emphasis is on faith: "every one who believes in him may not perish but have eternal life."

March 7, 1993

Theme: We step forth into unknown, but promised lands.

Thought for the day: God calls each and every one of us into ventures unknown. How do we respond to the uncertain and unfamiliar? Do we back away in fear or do we step forth in faith?

Prayer of meditation: Lord God, you have called your servants to ventures of which we cannot see the ending, by paths as yet untrodden, through perils unknown. Give us faith to go out with good courage, not knowing where we go, but only that your hand is leading us and your love supporting us; through Jesus Christ our Lord. Amen.
(Matins prayer, Lutheran Book of Worship, page 137)

Call to worship:
Leader: Give thanks to the Lord and call upon his name;
People: Make known his deeds among the peoples.
Leader: Sing to him, sing praises to him,
People: And speak of all his marvelous works.
Leader: Glory in his holy name;
People: Let the hearts of those who seek the Lord rejoice.
   (Psalm 105:1-3)

Prayer of adoration: We stand in awe of you, O God, for you stand over all. You stand over both the grandeur and the intricacy of creation. You stand over the stretch of time and the changes of history. Yet, in all your majesty, you choose to embrace us and guide us through this life. We praise you for awesome power and tender care. Amen.

Prayer of confession: Dear God, we confess that sometimes we are afraid — afraid of the unknown, afraid of failure, afraid of success, afraid of change. In fact, we confess that sometimes we let our fears control our lives and dictate our choices. We pray to be freed from this bondage. We pray to be freed to risk and to reach out. In your name, we pray. Amen.

Prayer of dedication of gifts and self: Almighty God, draw our hearts to you, guide our minds, fill our imaginations, control our wills, so that we may be wholly yours. Use us as you will, always to your glory and the welfare of your people; through our Lord and Savior Jesus Christ. Amen.
   (Prayer of Self-Dedication, Lutheran Book of Worship, page 47)

The Minister's Annual Manual

Sermon title: Let Go and Walk!

Sermon thesis: We do not know what the journey of life will bring us, but we can step forth in trust because we know who is calling and what is promised. Thus, we respond to the Spirit that moves us, the people that compel us, and the time that passes so quickly.

Hymn for the day: *"I heard the voice of Jesus say."* The second stanza of this hymn relates directly to today's Gospel, in which Jesus promises living water. Horatius Bonar (1808-1889) was a descendant of a family which had been represented in the Church of Scotland for over 200 years. He followed suit and was ordained by the Church of Scotland ministry in 1837. At the time of the Disruption in the Church of Scotland in 1843, however, he joined with Dr. Thomas Chalmers in the formation of the Free Church of Scotland. For many years he was an editor of the Free Church paper, after which he was minister of Chalmers Memorial Free Church in Edinburgh, and finally, moderator of the General Assembly of the Free Church of Scotland. He was the author of some 600 hymns, and wrote voluminously — nearly one book a year. [NOTE: Churches using the Living Water lection on the 3rd Sunday in Lent should exchange this Hymn of the Day with that for the 3rd Sunday in Lent.]

Announcements for next week:

    Sermon title: Come to the Light
    Sermon theme: The light of Jesus Christ shines.
    Sermon summary: The light of Christ shines, but we respond to it differently. Sometimes we miss it, sometimes we embrace it fully. At other times, we deliberately turn away from it or glimpse it in fear. Yet, the light continues to shine, and the invitation to come to it still stands.

Children's object talk:

A Pretzel!

Objects: A pretzel
Lesson: The pretzel is a symbol of prayer.
Outline: 1. Pretzels!
        2. History of its symbolism
        3. Importance of prayer

WHAT DO I HAVE IN MY HAND? A pretzel! Who here likes to eat pretzels? I know that I do! Can anyone tell me what pretzels taste like? They have a salty taste, don't they? Some pretzels are doughy; some are crispy. Overall, they taste pretty good. I especially like to eat pretzels while watching a football game on television.

Do you know that a pretzel is also a religious symbol? Though not very common, it has been regarded as a symbol of prayer. About 1500 years ago in Southern Europe, a monk used leftover scraps of bread dough to make something a little more imaginative. He formed the scraps into dough-ropes which he twisted into this shape. Someone remarked that the shape reminded them of a child's arms folded in prayer. Imagine that these are our forearms (which are crossed) and our palms (which are on opposite shoulders). This is yet another posture for prayer. In the early church, there was even a prayer that went like this: "Grant us, we pray, that we too, may be reminded by the daily sight of these pretzels to observe the holy season of Lent with true devotion and great spiritual food."

Because Lent is a time of reverent prayer, a pretzel is a good reminder of the importance of prayer. In fact, it is such a good reminder that I think that is how we should close. Let us take this "pretzel prayer position" by crossing our forearms. And let us pray, "Dear God, we thank you for this opportunity to worship you this day. Help us to remember Jesus and his love for us. Teach us to turn to you with our joys, our sorrows, and our worries. In your name we pray. Amen."

The sermon:

Let Go and Walk

Hymns:
  Beginning of worship: Jesus Calls Us; O'er the Tumult
  Sermon hymn: If You But Trust in God to Guide You
  End of worship: Guide Me Ever, Great Redeemer

Scripture: Genesis 12:1-8

Sermon text: *"Now the Lord said to Abram, 'Go from your country and your kindred and your father's house to the land that I will show you.'"* (Genesis 12:1)

HAVE YOU EVER WATCHED A CHILD LEARNING HOW TO WALK? Picture a parent, in close reach and with outstretched arms, calling the child to come, calling the child to take that first tentative step. Then the child (who has been clinging to what is safe and secure) lets go — lets go of what is known, lets go of what is familiar — and steps forth. Now the child steps forth not knowing what the journey will bring. "Will I stumble or will I fall or will I walk?" Yet, the child steps forth   steps forth in trust. It is in trust because the mother is calling and the father is hovering near. It is in trust because there is a promise of being able to walk and, I assume, for someone who has been relegated to dirty floors and dusty carpets, that is a blessing indeed! Now learning to walk does not happen overnight. It takes time; it takes trial and error. But it happens; the child learns how to walk.

The call to step forth consistently comes. It came to Abram and Sarah, the father and mother of us all. And it comes to you and me, the children of faith. Ever feel the Holy Spirit moving within you to say or do something? Ever meet someone or hear of someone that compels your involvement? Ever sense that time is quickly passing? In these examples, God is calling us to respond, calling us to step forth.

Reading again from our text, "Now the Lord said to Abram, 'Go from your country and your kindred and your father's house to the land I will show you.' " God was calling Abram and Sarah to leave what was familiar and certain (their city, their friends, their home) and to go to what was unfamiliar and uncertain (some vague undesignated land). God was calling them from a known land into an unknown land.

I cannot speak definitely for Abram and Sarah regarding their feelings about all of this. But I do know that for many of us, different and powerful emotions arise when we are called into unknown lands — sadness, fear, irritation, maybe even anger. I think there is something in me and in you that can identify with the little girl whose family is moving to another town. "I don't want to move. I like my friends here. And I don't know who I will play with there. Mom and Dad, do we have to move?"

Stepping forth into unknown lands can be unsettling. Our tendency is to cling tightly rather than to let go freely. For what happens when we let go? We can no longer guarantee what will happen. We lose a sense of control. Yet, God continues to call us to respond, to step forth in faith. For the Spirit still moves, the people still compel, the time still passes.

Now a good question might be: Into what area is God calling us to let go, as individuals and as a community? Into what unknown land might we be stepping forth? For me, hearing the stories of people in Third World countries leads me into an unknown land. Many times, I pretend that my world is the only world. But I am reminded differently by the face of a squatter woman lined with dignity and suffering, by the expression of a refugee haunted by horror and

March 7, 1993

fear, by the eyes of a textile worker full of struggle and hope. And I am compelled to be involved, compelled to acknowledge their world. And so, I question how to break down isolating walls and construct connecting bridges. I question how best to preach and talk. It is a journey with many trials and errors — and some successes.

Where are the unknown lands in your life? Where is God calling you? Is it in changing your communication style, maybe by talking more or by not talking so much? Maybe it is by learning when to say "no" and when to say "yes." Possibly, there are unknown areas in your relation with God. Maybe it is baring one's soul to God in prayer or expanding one's image of God. Or are there unknown lands in your family? Is it struggling with the tension of when to care for others and when to care for yourself or is it in figuring out how to deal well with elderly parents or divorced children? Or are there unknown lands within your congregation? Maybe it is assuming more responsibility in leadership or maybe it is confronting some issues with care. Where are the unknown lands in your life? Where is God calling you?

When we hear God call us into an unknown land, some of us will sit; the unknown can be too overwhelming. Some of us might even stand — but, without more details, will just stay put. And some of us will walk, in trust and obedience. How will we answer that call to walk into the unknown land? Do you and I have the courage to let go like a child? Do you and I have the initiative to step forth like Abram and Sarah? How will we answer?

Abram and Sarah choose to walk, even though they did not know what their journey would bring. But, they went out because they knew who had called them — the Lord . . . the Lord who had created the heavens and earth, the Lord who had made a covenant with Noah. And they went out because they knew what had been promised — a promise of receiving land, becoming a great nation, and mediating blessing to other people.

Yes, Abram and Sarah did step forth into an unknown land. But, they also stepped forth into a promised land. For the Lord was with them and before them with blessings to bestow. They walked into an unknown land but also a promised land.

That holds true for us and our unknown lands today. We can step forth in trust because we know who calls us. It is God — God who created us with minds to think, bodies to move, and hearts to feel. It is Jesus — Jesus who redeemed us from that fear, from that self-absorption, and from that grave. It is the Holy Spirit — the Holy Spirit who sustains and strengthens us through the Word, the sacraments, and the community of believers.

We can also step forth in trust because we know what has been promised. It is a promise of presence — "Lo, I am with you always to the close of the age." It is a promise of blessing — "He who began a good work in you will bring it to completion at the day of Jesus Christ." The unknown land is also the promised land.

We can answer God's call by responding to the Spirit that moves us, by engaging the people that compel our involvement, by befriending the time that passes so quickly. We might not know what the journey will bring, but we do know who calls and what is promised.

Let go like a child! Step forth like Abram and Sarah! And walk. Walk into an unknown, but also a promised land. For God is with you and before you with blessings to bestow.

Beth Marie Halvorsen
Shepherd of the Hills Lutheran Church
Austin, Texas

MARCH 14, 1993

Third Sunday in Lent

Lessons:

Lutheran:	Is. 42:14-21	Eph. 5:8-14	John 9:1-41
Roman Catholic:	Ex. 17:3-7	Rom. 5:1-2,5-8	John 4:5-42
Episcopal:	Ex. 17:1-7	Rom. 5:1-11	John 4:5-26 (27-38) 39-42
Pres/Meth/UCC:	Ex. 17:1-7	Rom. 5:1-11	John 4:5-42

Introductions to the Lessons

Lesson 1

(1) *Isaiah 42:14-21* (**Luth**) God makes wonderful promises and declares he will keep them. For a time God was silent but now he speaks. He promises to turn our darkness into light and give us smooth sailing through life. God is for his people and is eager to save them. To this we say, "How great thou art!"

(2) *Exodus 17:1-7* (**Epis/Pres/Meth/UCC**) Under Moses' leadership the Israelites are in the wilderness on their way to the Promised Land. They come to Rephidim where there is no water. They blame Moses and are so angry they want to kill him. He takes their complaint to God who tells him to take his rod and strike a rock at Mt. Sinai. He does and water pours out. The people got the answer to their question, "Is God for us or not?"

Lesson 2

(1) *Ephesians 5:8-14* (**Luth**) Jesus said he was the light of the world. He also taught that his followers are the light of the world. Therefore, the people of God are expected to live in the light as well as be the light in a dark world of sin. To live as light means to practice goodness and truth.

(2) *Romans 5:1-11* (**Epis/Pres/Meth/UCC**) The 5th chapter of Romans begins with "Therefore". It refers to Paul's previous explanation that we are justified by grace through faith in Christ. As a result we have peace with God through reconciliation. The amazing truth is that Christ died for us while we were still sinners.

Gospel

(1) *John 9:1-41* (**Luth**) Jesus gives sight to a man born blind. It is not only physical sight but spiritual insight. Sin and unbelief result in spiritual blindness. Gradually

Jesus brings the man from the darkness of agnosticism to the clear vision of faith that Jesus is the Messiah. Vision came when he said, "Lord, I believe."

(2) *John 4:5-42* (**Pres/Meth/UCC**); *John 4:5-26, 39-42* (**Epis**) Jesus was on his way from Judea to Galilee. He had to pass through Samaria. One day at noon he stopped to rest and get a drink from a well. The disciples had gone to the village for food. Jesus was alone sitting by the well. Along comes a Samaritan woman to get water. Jesus initiates a conversation with her and leads her to have faith in him as the Messiah.

Theme: The light of Jesus Christ shines

Thought for the day: How have we been responding lately to the light of Jesus Christ in our lives? To what degree has ignorance, rejection, or fear been part of our reaction? Whatever our response may be, Jesus Christ still extends his invitation to come to his light, for his light continues to shine.

Prayer of meditation: Dear Lord, teach me to see what you would have me see — in your creation, in your people. Teach me to hear what you would have me to hear — your forgiveness, your challenge. Teach me to speak what you would have me speak — your grace, your hope. Shape and mold me so that I may be an instrument used by you for good. Accept this my petition, dear Lord. Amen.

Call to worship:
Leader: All you who are thirsty, come to the water.
You who have no money, come, receive bread, and eat.
Come, without paying and without cost, drink wine and milk.
People: Praised be God, the Father of our Lord Jesus Christ, the Father of all mercies, and the God of all consolation.
(Lenten Dialog, Service of the Word, Lutheran Book of Worship, page 127)

Prayer of adoration: Lord God, heavenly King, almighty God and Father: We worship you, we give you thanks, we praise you for your glory. Lord Jesus Christ, only Son of the Father, Lord God, Lamb of God: You take away the sin of the world; have mercy on us. You are seated at the right hand of the Father; receive our prayer. For you alone are the Holy One, you alone are the Lord, you alone are the Most High, Jesus Christ, with the Holy Spirit, in the glory of God the Father. Amen.
(Hymn of Praise, Lutheran Book of Worship, page 59)

March 14, 1993

Prayer of confession: Dear Lord, we confess that sometimes we choose the darkness over the light. We choose to stay with that which is unhealthy but familiar to us. We choose to stay with that which is demeaning to others but comfortable for ourselves. Forgive us when we choose the darkness. Let your light break in upon us. In your merciful name, we pray. Amen.

Prayer of dedication of gifts and self: Accept, we pray, our bodies and souls, our hearts and minds, our talents and powers, together with these gifts, as our offerings of praise. Amen.

Sermon title: Come to the Light

Sermon thesis: The light of Christ shines, but we respond to it differently. Sometimes we miss it, sometimes we embrace it fully. At other times, we deliberately turn away from it or glimpse it in fear. Yet, the light continues to shine and the invitation to come to it still stands.

Hymn for the day: *"The great Creator of the worlds."* This hymn, which tells the story of Christ's saving mission on earth, was written probably about 150 A.D., during the time of great Christian persecution. It is taken from a letter by an unknown author written to one Diognetus, who may have been a tutor to the Stoic emperor, Marcus Aurelius.

(NOTE: Churches using the Living Water lection should refer to the previous Sunday for the Hymn of the Day.]

Announcements for next week:

Sermon title: Are You Able to Drink this Cup?
Sermon theme: The call to servanthood: Can you drink the Lord's cup?
Sermon summary: Jesus' question, "Are you able to drink this cup?" is a question addressed beyond James and John to each of us. It is a question that calls us through discipleship to servanthood. It is an ultimate question that resonates with Jesus' death and our own. And it is a question that calls us beyond our death to life with Christ in the kingdom of God.

Children's object talk:
The Sign of the Cross

Objects: The cross around one's neck
Lesson: To understand the sign of the cross.
Outline: 1. Observations about crosses
        2. Sign of cross during baptism
        3. Sign of cross during worship

WHAT AM I WEARING AROUND MY NECK? A cross. This cross reminds me that Jesus Christ loves me. Do you notice any other crosses in the room? Can you point them out to me? There are crosses all over — on the wall, on my stole, on our linens, around our necks, on top of our hymnals! No other symbol is so widely used; the cross of Christ is the core of the Church's story. It tells of the suffering and death and victory of our Lord and Savior.

When you were baptized, your pastor made the sign of the cross on your forehead — just like I am doing now. This action is an announcement that you belong to Christ and that Christ will watch over you. As I make the sign of the cross during a baptism, I will say these words: "Child of God, you have been sealed by the Holy Spirit and marked with the cross of Christ forever." This is very special!

Now we can see crosses, we can wear crosses, we can receive crosses. But, we can also make the sign of the cross ourselves! This can be done by moving the fingers of your right hand from your forehead to your chest, then from your left shoulder to your right shoulder and then to the center of your chest. Try it! We make the sign of the cross when we say, "In the name of the Father, and of the Son, and of the Holy Spirit." Some people make the sign of the cross; some do not. But, it is always nice to know that you can. It is another reminder of God's love for you.

The sermon:

Come to the Light

Hymns:
Beginning of worship: Jesus, Refuge of the Weary
Sermon hymn: Jesus, the Very Thought of You
End of worship: May God Bestow on Us His Grace

Scripture: John 9:1-41

Sermon text: *"As long as I am in the world, I am the light of the world. "* vs. 5

AT DIFFERENT TIMES, I RESPOND TO LIGHT IN DIFFERENT WAYS. Sometimes I embrace it. When I am chilled, I often move so as to bask in the warmth of sunlight brightly streaming through a window. Other times, I turn away from the light — like when someone unexpectedly turns on a light in a dark room. The light glares and I shield myself from its brightness. Light shines. How do we see it? How do we respond to it?

The various people in our Gospel lesson today also respond in different ways to light — whether it be the light of Christ or God's light within each person. Some blossom in this light; others glimpse this light; still others outright choose to turn away from it. Light shines. But, how do we see it? How do we respond to it?

God's light is present within people, but sometimes we fail to recognize it because of our own preconceptions. In our Gospel story today, the disciples did this as they entered the Temple marketplace and looked at the beggars sitting against the wall. As they discussed a man blind from his birth, they automatically assumed that this man was blind as a punishment for sin. They debated: Did God punish the parents for some previously committed sin by causing their son to be born blind? Or, was this man's blindness due to his own sin — a sin committed even while in his mother's womb? The disciples could not see God's light within this man. His affliction and their assumption that intense suffering must be connected to intense sin got in the way of seeing him as a person loved by God.

Today we are called to come to the light and recognize it as such. We are called to let go of preconceptions that get in the way of seeing God's light within a person. Instead of responding to an affliction, we are called to respond to a person. Instead of responding with objectivity and speculation, we are called to respond with compassion. All of us are vessels for God to use, for God to work his glory. Now some of us might not be in the best condition; we might be bent, or cracked, or missing a part. But the issue is not the condition of the vessels. The issue is our ability to function properly as vessels for God. Even in our afflictions — whether physical or emotional — God works in and through us to show forth his grace, his peace, his power.

At other times, light is shining and we respond fully to its brightness. In this story, Jesus physically heals the blind beggar. For the first time in his life, this man can see a smile! A face! A bird! The sky! Imagine! What a gift of grace! But this man responds not only physically to light, but also spiritually. He obeys Jesus and gives witness to him. After Jesus anointed the man's eyes with clay made from his spittle, Jesus tells him to go and wash in the pool of Siloam.

Siloam means "sent" because it receives water which is *sent* from a spring outside the city wall through Hezekiah's tunnel. Now there is a wonderful play on words here. Jesus *sent* the man to wash in this pool of *sent* water. In doing so, the healed man acclaims Jesus as one *sent* from God. This man blossoms in the light of Jesus. In fact, he grows more and more confident in his confession of Jesus. First, he calls him "a man called Jesus," then "a prophet", then "as one sent from God", and finally as "Lord."

Today we are called to come to the light and rejoice in it! We are called to let the light help us to see and grow and confess. Even though there were a lot of things this man did not understand, he still gave witness to the light. Even though there may be a lot of things we do not understand, we are still called to share how the light of Christ gives us an identity, frees us from our bondage, provides us with purpose, and gifts us with a community of believers.

Yet, there are others who choose to turn away from the light. Though some Pharisees saw this healing as a sign of Jesus' goodness, other Pharisees condemned this act of mercy. They chose to concern themselves not with the healing, but with the fact that Jesus had healed on a Sabbath! In their legalistic understanding, making the clay out of spit and earth was similar to kneading. Consequently, this would be work which would be against the Sabbath law. Never mind the healing! Jesus broke the commandment!

Today we are called to come to the light, not to turn from it. We are called to not lose sight of what is truly important. Instead of becoming so caught up in how and what certain things need to be done, we are called to celebrate the light that surrounds us! Instead of concerning ourselves with things that seem urgent at the time, we are called to discern and to hold onto that which is important.

Finally, there are others who glimpse the light, but are afraid to trust it or follow it. Think back to the parents of the formerly blind man. How would you feel if your son, who once was blind, could now see? Elated, I'm sure. But his parents were also afraid. If they claimed that Jesus performed this miracle and that Jesus was the Christ, then they could be kicked out of the synagogue! Though they must have been drawn to Jesus, it was too risky to follow him. They feared what they would lose, feared the changes the light might demand. They glimpsed the light, but were too afraid to trust it or to follow.

March 14, 1993

Today we are called to come to the light, not just to glimpse it. We are called to chose to follow Jesus above all else and to put discipleship before anything else. We are called to let security, convenience, routine be second.

Jesus Christ said, "I am the light of the world." Sometime, we miss the light. Other times, we embrace it fully. Still other times, we deliberately turn from it or just glimpse it through eyes of fear. Yet, the light of Jesus Christ continues to shine. The darkness cannot overcome it! And the invitation is always extended. Come to the light. Let go of preconceptions that get in the way of seeing God's light within a person. Do not lose sight of what is truly important. Let ignorance, fear, or disbelief be transformed. The light of Christ is here to stay. Come. Come to the light.

Beth Marie Halvorsen
Shepherd of the Hills Lutheran Church
Austin, Texas

MARCH 21, 1993

Fourth Sunday in Lent

Lessons:

Lutheran:	Hos. 5:15-6:2	Rom. 8:1-10	Matt. 20:17-28
Roman Catholic:	I Sam. 16:1b,6-7, 10-13a	Eph. 5:8-14	John 9:1-41
Episcopal:	I Sam. 16:1-13	Eph. 5:(1-7) 8-14	John 9:1-13 (14-27) 28-38
Pres/Meth/UCC:	I Sam. 16:1-13	Eph. 5:8-14	John 9:1-41

Introductions to the Lessons

Lesson 1

(1) *Hosea 5:15-6:2* (**Luth**) In desperation God tried everything good to regain the love and loyalty of his people, but failed. Now he decides to abandon them in the hope that in their suffering they will repent. Indeed, the people respond, "Let's return to the Lord."

(2) *I Samuel 16:1-13* (**Epis/Pres/Meth/UCC**) A shepherd boy, David, is anointed king of Israel to succeed Saul, whom God wanted replaced because of his sin. The prophet Samuel is sent to the home of Jesse and his eight sons. Seven were not satisfactory. The eighth was a lad keeping watch over his father's sheep. David was called, and Samuel, under God's direction, anointed him king.

Lesson 2

(1) *Romans 8:1-10* (**Luth**) Christians live above the Law because they live by the Spirit of Christ. Therefore, they are not condemned by the Law. To live by our human nature results in sin, and death follows. To live in and by the Spirit brings peace and joy. Christians live not by their sinful human nature but live with the Spirit of Christ in their hearts.

(2) *Ephesians 5:8-14* (**Epis/Pres/Meth/UCC**) Jesus said he was the light of the world. He also taught that his followers are the light of the world. Therefore, the people of God are expected to live in the light as well as be the light in a dark world of sin. To live as light means to practice goodness and truth.

March 21, 1993

Gospel

(1) *Matthew 20:17-28* (**Luth**) In the face of approaching death, Jesus is faced with a controversy among the disciples over the question of greatness. The mother of two disciples asks Jesus to give James and John the top positions in his kingdom. The request is resented by the other disciples. Jesus settles the problem by stating that a truly great person is a servant, even as he came not to be served but to serve.

(2) *John 9:1-13, 28-38*(**Epis**); *John 9:1-41* (**Pres/Meth/UCC**) Jesus gives sight to a man born blind. It is not only physical sight but spiritual insight. Sin and unbelief result in spiritual blindness. Gradually Jesus brings the man from the darkness of agnosticism to the clear vision of faith that Jesus is the Messiah. Vision came when he said, "Lord, I believe."

Theme: The call to servanthood — Can you drink the Lord's cup?

Thought for the day: The Lenten call to discipleship is a call to servanthood. In our service to one another we are serving the Lord. Matthew 25 is a motif of today's theme: we serve Christ not so much among the great and powerful as among the poor, hungry, homeless and imprisoned to whom we humble ourselves in service.

Prayer of meditation: Gracious God, as I continue my Lenten journey among your people this day, open my ears to hear clearly your word. Open my eyes that I may clearly see you in others whom I serve. Open my heart that I may faithfully believe. Open my hands and my life to servanthood in your home. Amen.

Call to worship:
Come, let us return to the Lord. Our lives have drawn us into the wounds of the world and we ourselves are wounded. Come, let us return that the Lord my heal us. Our ministries have drawn us into the despair of the world. Come, let us return that the Lord may fill us with hope.

Prayer of adoration: God of grace and mercy, Lord of love and peace, we give you thanks and praise that your beloved One was faithful unto death, that he drank the cup of sacrifice. We give you thanks that your beloved One gave his life as a ransom for many — including our own. Have mercy on us. Bind us up. Heal us. Revive us. "Send out your light and your truth, that they may lead me, and bring me to your holy hill and to your dwelling; . . . Put your trust in God; for I will yet give thanks to him, who is the help of my countenance and my God." Amen.
(Ps. 43:3, 6)

Prayer of dedication of gifts and self: Almighty God, you are the creator of the universe, the earth, seas and stars. You give us life and breath, food to nurture us, pure air to breathe, water to refresh and cleanse. You are almighty, all-knowing, all-powerful and all-wise. Yet you bid us to call upon you with the love and intimacy of a parent. Dear Father, in thanksgiving for all that you have given to us, we offer you these modest gifts: money to help those who are in need and to further your kingdom on earth; bread and wine that you may bless them and feed us with Christ's body and blood to strengthen and nourish our faith; and our very selves that we may be your people and serve you as bearers of your Good News, peace and justice. Receive these gifts and us, in Christ's name. Amen.

Sermon title: Are You Able to Drink This Cup?

Sermon thesis: Jesus' question, "Are you able to drink this cup?" is a question addressed beyond James and John to each of us. It is a question that calls us through discipleship to servanthood. It is an ultimate question that resonates with Jesus' death and our own. And it is a question that calls us beyond our death to life with Christ in the kingdom of God.

Hymn for the day: *"O Master, let me walk with you/thee."* A native of Pennsylvania, Washington Gladden (1836-1918) was ordained a Congregational minister and served churches in New York, Massachusetts, and Ohio. A distinguished preacher, lecturer, and author, Gladden wrote extensively on civic and social affairs. This hymn of love and service to others was composed in 1879.

Announcements for next week:
   Sermon title: I Am the Resurrection and the Life
   Sermon theme: I am the resurrection and the life. (John 11:25)
   Sermon summary: The gospel account of the raising of Lazarus is a foreshadowing of Jesus' own rising from the tomb. Unlike Lazarus' resurrection, however, Jesus' is forever. The gospel confronts our world, in which death seemingly reigns, with the promise of life in spite of death.

Children's object talk:

The Cup of Servanthood

Objects: The communion chalice from the altar
Lesson: There are many servants in our worship.
Outline: 1. There are many servants in worship.
   2. We can learn how to serve by watching others.
   3. Look for opportunities to serve.

March 21, 1993

THIS MORNING many servants have helped us in our worship. When you arrived, who was the servant who gave you your bulletin and worship book? (the ushers) Who was the servant who helped us to sing the hymns? (the organist) Who was the servant who lit the candles on the altar? (the acolyte) Who was the servant who read stories for us? (the lector)

Some of the servants you may not have seen. Do you know who the servant was who prepared our Sunday bulletins? (worship planning committee, pastor, secretary — have them all stand up) Do you know who cleaned up the church to get it ready for worship this morning? (the custodian — have him/her stand up) Do you know who provided the flowers for our altar today? (have them stand up) Do you know who set the altar table for communion (the altar guild — have them stand up)

In a few minutes you will see another servant at work. Do you know what this is? (chalice, communion cup) Do you know when we use it? (for holy communion) Who is it that serves it? (pastor and other assistants)

Watch to see who are your servants today during the eucharist. You will see me, the pastor, as one of the servants. I will be serving the bread and/or giving you a blessing when you come forward. Suzanne will be a servant this morning. She will be serving this cup of wine to those who come forward. Suzanne and I will be the servants at holy communion today.

Jesus invites each of us to be servants. You can learn about being a servant within worship as you watch others serve. You can help in serving right now. With your parents you can be a servant some Sunday and serve as an usher. You can help to welcome people, hand out bulletins to help guide in worship, assist in receiving the offering and in bringing the offerings to the altar.

You can also help in the future. When you are a bit older, you can be a servant like Andrew and light the candles. When you are a little older, you can serve as a reader within the congregation. Perhaps one day you will be a musician who can help serve the congregation in music.

Watch carefully each Sunday and give thanks for all our servants in worship.

The sermon:
Are You Able To Drink This Cup?

Hymns:
Beginning of worship: Lord of Glory, You Have Bought Us
Sermon hymn: O Christ, Our King, Creator, Lord
End of worship: In the Cross of Christ I Glory

Scripture: Matthew 20:17-28

Sermon text: *"Are you able to drink the cup that I am about to drink?"* vs. 22

THE PROGRESSION OF LENT has taken us from the temptation of Jesus, through his dialogue on living water with a marginalized woman, through his dialogue with the man born blind to today's encounter with servanthood. How might we — people born again in the living waters of baptism — more clearly open our eyes to see the call to servanthood in today's gospel?

The scene unfolds with a classic Jewish mother, right out of a Woody Allen film. She might be the sort to brag about "my son the doctor"; clearly the type to hover about the kids with the ubiquitous bowl of chicken soup at the ready. She approaches Jesus, seeking not only the well-being and future, but the honor of her boys. Unlike Mark's account of this story, where James and John ask on their own for the honor, Matthew has their mother, Zebedee's wife, intercede for their honor to sit at Jesus' right and left hand in the kingdom.

Jesus' response to this unnamed woman is set in the context of a passion prediction. His response is curious: "Are you able to drink the cup that I am about to drink?" Not realizing that the cup he speaks about is his own coming death, James and John confidently answer: "We are able."

James affirms their answer. They will indeed drink the cup of death with him. For James, the cup he drank would be the cup of a martyr's death (Acts 12:2). For John, the cup he drank would be the cup of discipleship and faithfulness, as he reportedly lived to a ripe old age in Ephesus. It is as Dietrich Bonhoeffer once wrote: "When Christ calls a person, he bids him come and die." Bonhoeffer knew it well. For he, too, would drink the cup on a spring morning in

March 21, 1993

1945 in Germany, when he was executed for his faithful witness against Nazi Germany.

The call to servanthood is the call to live out our baptism. In the Lutheran Book of Worship's order for the Affirmation of Baptism, a question is put to those making their affirmation: "Do you intend to continue in the covenant God made with you in Holy Baptism: to live among God's faithful people, to hear his Word and share in his supper, to proclaim the good news of God in Christ through word and deed, to serve all people, following the example of our Lord Jesus, and to strive for justice and peace in all the earth?" It is a question that embraces all of one's life.

The response is one step on the journey of discipleship and servanthood: "I do, and I ask God to help and guide me." (**Lutheran Book of Worship**, p. 201)

As the community of God's people, we are recipients of God's gift of grace in baptism. Can we, therefore, claim special privilege over against our sisters and brothers in faith? In the living waters of baptism we are re-born as children of God. Can we who are equal in God's sight elbow our way to the top? The rulers of the Gentiles lord it over one another, but it shall not be so among the followers of Jesus. He gently reminds and attests that whoever would be great must be a servant.

"Are you able to drink the cup that I am to drink?" Jesus' question is a call given not only to James and John, but to each of us. It's a call given by Jesus that he accepts for himself. This is not some Moonie or Scientologist who gives orders applicable only to the followers. Jesus himself serves even as he calls others to servanthood. Jesus himself drinks the cup, gives his life on the cross as a ransom for many, and asks, "Are you able to drink the cup that I am to drink?"

We are called, in baptism, to be servants. But it is a mission that we do not undertake alone. For the crucified and risen One who calls us to this servanthood also stands with us to guide and direct us. He offers himself as food for the journey, giving his body and blood to sustain, encourage, empower and direct us — this day and all days, now and forever.

Stephen M. Larson
Evangelical Lutheran Church
Geneva, Switzerland

MARCH 28, 1993

Fifth Sunday in Lent

Lessons:

Lutheran:	Ezek. 37:1-3 (4-10) 11-14	Rom. 8:11-19	John 11:1-53
Roman Catholic:	Ezek. 37:12-14	Rom. 8:8-11	John 11:1-45
Episcopal:	Ezek. 37:1-3 (4-10) 11-14	Rom. 6:16-23	John 11:(1-17) 18-44
Pres/Meth/UCC:	Ezek. 37:1-14	Rom. 8:6-11	John 11:1-45

Introductions to the Lessons

Lesson 1

Ezekiel 37:1-3,11-14 (**Luth/Epis**); *Ezekiel 37:1-14* (**Pres/Meth/UCC**) Ezekiel has a vital message for God's people exiled in Babylon. They are like dead bones because they are discouraged and without hope. The Lord commands him to preach the Word to these dead bones. As a result the bones become live bodies. The Word preached brought the Spirit, who gave them life based on the promise of a return to their Jerusalem homeland. The Spirit identified with the Word is the life-giving power of resurrection.

Lesson 2

(1) *Romans 8:11-19* (**Luth**) As the Spirit brought life to dead bones in Ezekiel's time, the Spirit of God will also cause us to rise out of death. If we live by our sinful human nature, we will die, but if we have the Spirit, we will live. People with the Spirit are assured by the Spirit that they are children of God.

(2) *Romans 6:16-23* (**Epis**) Every person is a slave either to sin or to righteousness, to Law or to grace. If we are saved by grace, should we sin to experience grace? Paul answers negatively. To live by grace is to be enslaved to righteousness. Sin causes death but God gives eternal life to his children.

(3) *Romans 8:6-11* (**Pres/Meth/UCC**) According to Paul, there are two ways we can live: live by our base human nature or live by the Spirit of God. The former way leads to death. We who accept Christ live by the Spirit. We receive peace and joy because Christ has made us right with God the Father. The same Spirit that raised Jesus from the dead will likewise raise us from the death of sin to a life of righteousness.

March 28, 1993

Gospel

John 11:1-53 (**Luth**); *John 11:1-44* (**Epis**); *John 11:1-45* (**Pres/Meth/UCC**) This is not the first time Jesus raised a dead person to life. His raising Lazarus marked the beginning of his passion in Jerusalem and the beginning of the plot by religious leaders to kill him. The miracle put the evil machine of religious bigotry into motion that stopped only at the cross. The story shows us the compassion of Christ for the bereaved and his power over death.

Theme: "I am the resurrection and the life." (John 11:25)

Thought for the day: We live in an age in which, as William Stringfellow phrased it, "death reigns." Amidst the dusty dry boneyard of our age, the one who spoke of living waters comes among us still — the Christ. And he proclaims, "I am the resurrection and the life."

Prayer of meditation: As my Lenten journey nears its fulfillment. I come to worship you this day, O God, aware of death. Death surrounds my life. Friends and family members have died. Acid rain drops death into lakes. Oil coats the life-giving seas with death. Entire species of your creation have died. Can the dry bones of this creation still live? Speak your word of life to me this day. Breathe your spirit of love anew into me this day. Amen.

Call to worship:

"I love the Lord, because he has heard the voice of my supplication, because he has inclined his ear to me whenever I called upon him. The cords of death entangled me; the grip of the grave took hold of me; I came to grief and sorrow. Then I called upon the name of the Lord: 'O Lord, I pray you, save my life.' Gracious is the Lord and righteous; our God is full of compassion." (Ps. 116:1-4)

Prayer of adoration: God of the resurrection and of life: "You have rescued my life from death, my eyes from tears, and my feet from stumbling. I will walk in the presence of the Lord in the land of the living." (Ps. 116:7-8) I will sing your praise and tell the story of your death-destroying, life-giving love all the days of my life. Amen.

Prayer of confession: Have mercy upon us, O Lord. There are occasions in our lives where "death reigns," when the dusty graveyard of our broken hopes and crushed dreams threaten to overwhelm us. There are times when our thoughts and actions even serve death and devastation. We are ensnared in sin and know too well the taste of death, sin's fruit. Purge us of our fear. Turn our hearts toward

The Minister's Annual Manual

you. Breathe into us your Holy life-giving Spirit and let it dwell within us. Amen.

Prayer of dedication of gifts and self: "How shall I repay the Lord for all the good things the Lord has done for me? I will lift the cup of salvation and call upon the name of the Lord. I will offer you the sacrifice of thanksgiving and call upon the name of the Lord. I will fulfill my vows to the Lord in the presence of all God's people, in the courts of the Lord's house, in the midst of you, O Jerusalem." (Ps. 116:10-11, 15-17) Amen.

Sermon title: I Am the Resurrection and the Life

Sermon thesis: The gospel account of the raising of Lazarus is a foreshadowing of Jesus' own rising from the tomb. Unlike Lazarus' resurrection, however, Jesus is forever. The gospel confronts our world in which death seemingly reigns, with the promise of life in spite of death.

Hymn for the day: *"Christ, the life of all the living."* This hymn, which ponders the price of our salvation and eternal life, was written by Ernst Christoph Hornburg (1605-1681). Homburg practiced law in Saxony and was a highly-regarded secular poet. During a time of illness, both his own and his wife's, he turned to God and wrote some 150 hymns intended mostly for his own private use.

Announcements for next week:
   Sermon title: Truly This Was the Son of God
   Sermon theme: Truly this is the Son of God
   Sermon summary: The "old familiar story of Jesus' life and glory" can become new, unfamiliar and startlingly real when told with different media. The sermon describes one such way to experience the Passion narrative with new insights from music, drama and dance.

Children's object talk:

Jesus Cried Like You

Objects: A bowl of salt water
Lesson: Jesus had feelings like you.
Outline: 1. What are the times you have cried?
   2. Tears are a sign of our feelings.
   3. Jesus had feelings like you.

HAVE ANY OF YOU EVER CRIED? I thought so! What happened to make you cry? (I was spanked, I fell on my bicycle, I was sad, I was laughing too hard)

Tears are a sign of our feelings. Sometimes we cry when we are

March 28, 1993

hurt and feel the need to have our father or mother comfort us. Sometimes we cry when we are sad and need someone close by us to comfort us. Once I laughed so hard at something, my eyes started to water.

Have you ever tasted tears? What did they taste like? Here, dip your fingers in this bowl and taste the water. Is that what tears taste like?

Jesus had feelings like you. Once when he was very sad, he cried. His friend, Lazarus, had died and Jesus went to the cemetery where Lazarus was buried. And there he cried for his friend. His tears probably tasted like this.

Did you ever know Jesus was sad? Can you think of a time when Jesus was happy? Jesus knew how to cry. Jesus had feelings like you.

Another feeling that Jesus shares with you is love. Can you think of anybody you love? (Mom, Dad, uncles, aunts, siblings, etc.) Jesus also knows that feeling. Because Jesus loves you.

The sermon:
I Am The Resurrection and the Life
Hymns:
  Beginning of worship: God Loved the World
  Sermon hymn: Christ, the Life of All the Living
  End of worship: Guide Me Ever, Great Redeemer

Scripture: John 11:1-53

Sermon text: *"Jesus said to her, 'I am the resurrection and the life; he who believes in me, though he die, yet shall he live . . .'"* vs. 25

THIS LENTEN SEASON we have had a crash course in the meaning of Holy Baptism.

Historically that was one of the purposes of Lent. It was a time of preparation for baptism at the Great Vigil of Easter. The catechumens, those who were being prepared for baptism, were instructed in the basics and meanings of the faith into which they would be baptized. At the Vigil, they were graciously washed into the kingdom of God, into the family or community of Christ's body, the church. Then in the "week of weeks," the seven weeks of the Easter Season, they were further instructed on the meanings of what

The Minister's Annual Manual

we now call the catechism: the Ten Commandments, the Creed, the Lord's Prayer, the meaning of baptism and eucharist.

The shapers of our three-year lectionary cycle have provided us this year with a mini-course in baptismal theology. Our Lenten season has been a sort of primer in what our baptized life is all about. Review it with me.

On the First Sunday in Lent, we read the account of Jesus' temptation in the wilderness. It was as if to say that our lives, too, are lived out amidst the crucible of temptation. We, too, know the temptor's cunning power. As Luther wrote in his well-known hymn, "A Mighty Fortress."

> The old Satanic foe
> Doth seek to work us woe.

In the midst of temptations we are invited to remember that we have been baptized, that Christ stands with us in our times of temptation to give us faith and strength to withstand. We are reminded of the role of Scripture, that as Jesus used Scripture to respond to the devil's tempting, we also might immerse ourselves in Scripture as a means of withstanding temptation.

On the Second Sunday of Lent we heard the story of Jesus talking with the Samaritan woman at Jacob's well. Amidst the sometimes cryptic conversation about thirst and husbands and worship and the Messiah, there flowed the image of living waters. The imagery of living waters is rich with baptismal nuance: "The water that I shall give will become in one a spring of water welling up to eternal life." (John 4:14) It was a time to remember the gracious waters of baptism, the gift that baptism is for us, that while we were yet sinners, Christ died for us. While we were yet sinners, God called us into faithful relationship through the waters of Holy Baptism.

On the Third Sunday in Lent the wonderful story of the man born blind was read. Did you know that the early church sometimes spoke of baptism as "illumination?" The second lesson that Sunday boldly proclaimed it: "Once you were darkness, but now you are light in the Lord; walk as children of light." (Ephesians 5:8) In baptism we were illuminated; we had our eyes of faith washed open. In the gospel account there again appeared numerous references to baptism: questions linking blindness to sin. Jesus' declaration of himself as the light of the world, Jesus' healing of the man used a baptismal-like washing in the Pool of Siloam. The healed man's ready and faithful witness to the role Christ played in his life reminds us of our own baptismal

March 28, 1993

calling to be witness for Christ. The blind man incarnates the imagery from a familiar hymn:
Amazing grace, how sweet the sound
That saved a wretch like me.
I was once lost, but now am found;
Was blind but now I see.

Last week on the Fourth Sunday in Lent we read the story of James and John's mother who sought a position of prestige and honor for her sons. Here again there is a baptismal emphasis (although it is much more explicit in Mark and Luke where Jesus asks in addition to the question, "Are you able to drink the cup that I am to drink?" — "Are you able to be baptized with the baptism with which I am to be baptized?") The emphasis here is on the ethics of the baptized community. In baptism we are made equal — children of God, equal in the sight of God. There is therefore no calling to prestige and honor in the community of God's family; rather we are called to servanthood, even slavery, in service to others. We read again that Christ came not to be served but to serve and to give his life as a ransom for many. In so doing we were reminded that we also are called to serve like Christ and that we, too, are called to give our life.

This Fifth Sunday of Lent then sums the baptismal teaching in the story of Lazarus and foreshadows next week's Passion narrative of Jesus' crucifixion.

The story of Lazarus is in a way our own story. Who has not known the questions of grief articulated by Mary and Martha? Who has not walked in the dry, dusty graveyard of existence and voiced the lament: "Why? Why now? Where is God in the midst of this catastrophe?" Who has not known the tears that Jesus knew welling up in his eyes and washing down his cheeks? (Could tears be a baptismal image?)

But then in a startling and dramatic shift, the story becomes more deeply our own story. Jesus, deeply moved, stands at the mouth of the tomb and orders the stone to be removed. (A foreshadowing of another stone from another tomb that would be removed.) He then prays to God in thanksgiving and in need, providing thereby a model of prayer for the baptized community. And then Jesus cries out in a loud voice, "Lazarus, come out."

Lazarus emerging from the tomb is a baptismal symbol. For in baptism we, too, have been buried. In baptism we, too, have been called forth to newness of life. As St. Paul wrote: "Do you not know

The Minister's Annual Manual

that all of us who have been baptized into Christ Jesus were baptized into his death? We were buried therefore with him by baptism into death, so that as Christ was raised from the dead by the glory of the Father, we too might walk in newness of life, for if we have been united with him in a death like his, we shall certainly be united with him in a resurrection like his. (Romans 6:3-5)

Jesus declared to Mary and Martha, "I am the resurrection and the life." That same declaration is made to us in our baptism. The same declaration is made to us this day, amidst this watery, baptismal season of Lent. We are thereby called back to the font, back to the baptismal origins of our faith. We are thereby reminded that Christ, the Savior of the world, is with us in our time of temptation. Jesus, the Messiah, speaks to us of living waters that will quench our thirst for life in all its fullness; Jesus, the light of the world, has illuminated our lives. Christ, the servant, has called us to servanthood and to sacrificial living. And Christ, the life of the world, has vowed that nothing, including death, can separate us from the love of God.

Stephen M. Larson
Evangelical Lutheran Church
Geneva, Switzerland

APRIL 4, 1993

Passion/Palm Sunday

Lessons:

Lutheran:	Is. 50:4-9a	Phil. 2:5-11	Matt. 27:11-54
Roman Catholic:	Is. 50:4-7	Phil. 2:6-11	Matt. 26:14-27:66
Episcopal:	Is. 45:21-25	Phil. 2:5-11	Matt. (26:36-75) 27:1-54 (55-66)
Pres/Meth/UCC:	Is. 50:4-9a	Phil. 2:5-11	Matt. 27:11-54

Introductions to the Lessons

(1) *Isaiah 50:4-9a* (**Luth/Pres/Meth/UCC**). This is the third of four servant songs in Isaiah. Because of God's help, the servant can bear the world's ridicule and physical suffering. In this description Christians see Jesus during his passion.

(2) *Isaiah 45:21-25* (**Epis**). God calls the nations who worship idols to come to court to decide who is the one true God. Since Yahweh is the one God, the appeal is made to turn to him and be saved. They who turn to God will experience victory and strength.

Lesson 2

Philippians 2:5-11 (**Luth/Epis/Pres/Meth/UCC**). In this liturgical poem Jesus leaves heaven to come to earth as a human. He takes the form of a servant and is obedient even to death on a cross. Consequently, God exalts his Son to the highest position and authority. In response every person should kneel before him and confess him as Lord.

Gospel

Matthew 27:11-54 (**Luth/Pres/Meth/UCC**); *Matthew 27:1-54* (**Epis**). Here is an account of the tragedy of the ages. Jesus stands on trial for his life before Pilate, a weak judge who gives in to a blood-thirsty mob. A criminal, Barabbas, is preferred to an innocent man. Jesus is tortured by sadistic soldiers. In mockery he is crowned king of the Jews. Feeling forsaken even by his Father, he cries out in agony. The meaning of it all? An unbiased soldier has the answer: "Truly this was the Son of God."

Theme: Truly this is the Son of God.

Thought for the day: This Sunday of Lent opens onto Holy Week. The moods of the texts take wild swings: from the weariness and suffering of Isaiah to the triumphant Philippian hymn, from the palm branch hallelujahs to the sorrow of Jesus' trial, torture and execution. But all are summed up in the awe-filled words of the witnesses: "Truly this was the Son of God."

Prayer of meditation: O God, as I prepare to enter into this holiest of weeks, be my companion. Stay near to me. Sustain me with your word. Give me the grace and the courage to bend my knee at the name of Jesus. Gift me with a tongue able to confess that Jesus Christ is Lord, to your glory. Amen.

Call to worship: Behold, your king is coming to you in humility. Open the gates to receive him. Open your hearts and lives to welcome him. Open your mouths to shout and sing his praise: "Hosanna to the Son of David! Blessed is he who comes in the name of the Lord! Hosanna in the highest!"

Prayer of adoration: Great and gracious God, with praise and thanksgiving we come before you. We sing your praises, for we know that if we were silent, the very stones of your creation would cry out. And yet we come before you in awe as we embark on this holiest of weeks in which we bring to our remembrance the events of your Son's last week on earth. Give us the humility to listen and to learn, that in the re-telling of these awesome events we might know our faith to be deeper, truer. We pray in the name of Jesus. Amen.

Prayer of confession: "Have mercy on me, O Lord, for I am in trouble; my eye is consumed with sorrow.... For my life is wasted with grief, and my years with sighing; my strength fails me because of affliction, and my bones are consumed.... I am forgotten like a dead man, out of mind; I am as useless as a broken pot.... But I have trusted in you, O Lord. I have said, 'You are my God. My times are in your hand; rescue me....'" (Ps. 31:9-10, 14-15a)

Prayer of dedication of gifts and self: Holy God, Mighty Lord, Gracious Father, on this Sunday of the Passion we are reminded of the enormous gift that you first offered to us, your Son, Jesus Christ, our Lord. We are painfully aware that we, your human creatures, rejected and slew him. Open our hearts, minds and lives that we may receive anew your wondrous gift. Mercifully give us the grace and faith to love him and you with our whole heart, body and spirit. We offer you, in thanksgiving, these gifts of money, bread, wine and our selves. Use them and us to your purpose that they and we might, through your grace and power, become instruments of your saving work. We pray in the name of Jesus, whom we confess to be our Lord. Amen

Sermon title: Truly This Was the Son of God.

Sermon thesis: The "old, familiar story of Jesus' life and glory" can become new, unfamiliar and startlingly real when told with different media. The sermon describes one such way to experience the Passion narrative with new insights from music, drama and dance.

Hymn for the day: *"I danced in the morning"* Using an American Shaker tune as its setting, this hymn tells the whole story of salvation in terms of dance. Sydney Carter, born in England in 1915, has taught and lectured for the British Council in Norway, Germany, Poland, and Spain, and has written a large number of radio and television scripts for the British Broadcasting Corporation. Since the 1960s he was written and performed his informal songs, which have been gathered into numerous collections.

Announcements for this week (Maundy Thursday)

Sermon title: To Go In Peace
Sermon theme: The gift of the eucharist and of footwashing are means to remembrance.
Sermon summary: In washing his disciples' feet, Jesus calls them to servanthood. In our call to discipleship and servanthood, Jesus stands with us, present in word and sacraments.

Announcements for this week (Good Friday)

Sermon title: Behold Your Son
Sermon theme: The cross of Christ is our life and our salvation.
Sermon summary: In death, as in life, we are bound to one another in the family of Christian community. The cross of Christ deepens that perception and transforms it into the *koinonia* of God's kingdom.

Announcements for next week:

Sermon title: It Was on Fire When I Lay Down
Sermon theme: The light of the resurrection saves us from self destruction.
Sermon summary: The significance of Easter is not lived, even by Christian disciples, because we fear what our new life in Christ requires of us. We need not fear, though, because in the light of the resurrection we are saved from habits of self-destruction. In the hope of the new life we are freed to experience the revelation of God's mercy in simple words and deeds of love.

Children's object talk:

Hosanna!

Objects: Palm branches — have one big one and several small ones for each child

The Minister's Annual Manual

Lesson: We still shout and sing praise to God today.
Outline: 1. Jesus was greeted by shouts of praise.
 2. We use objects to accompany our praise.
 3. We still shout and sing praise to God today.
IN THE BIBLE LESSON this morning we heard about people who shouted and sang their praise to Jesus. They cut down palm branches to honor Jesus. They waved some of them and laid some on the roadway for Jesus to ride over.

Here is a palm branch for each of you. (Pass out the palm branches) Let's see you wave them.

As you look around the church this morning can you see anything else that we use to honor Jesus, or to show our thanksgiving and praise to God? (Palm branches, flowers, colorful banners, colored paraments or vestments, art work in the sanctuary, etc.)

Like the people in the Bible story, we also use our voices. In the Bible they shouted "Hosanna," a very old word which means "help" or "save us." Let me hear you shout "Hosanna." (hosanna) Oh, that wasn't very loud. I could hardly hear you. Shout it again. (Hosanna) Oh, come on, I know you can shout louder than that. Give it all you've got. (HOSANNA!!)

That's better. We also use our voices in worship to praise God. Can you think of some ways? (hymns, songs, liturgy, prayers, psalms, etc.) In one of the Psalms we sing, "Let everything that has breath praise the Lord."

Tonight when you go to bed, hold on to your palm branch and say a prayer to tell God that you love God.

The sermon:
Truly This Was the Son of God

Hymns:
 Beginning of worship: All Glory, Laud, and Honor
 Sermon hymn: O Sacred Head, Now Wounded
 End of worship: Ride On, Ride On in Majesty

Scripture: Matthew 27:11-54

Sermon Text: *"They were filled with awe and said, 'Truly this was the Son of God.' " v. 54*
 [Note: For a far more powerful Palm Sunday worship, instead of

April 4, 1993

this sermon, arrange to use "The Cry of the Whole Congregation" as a dramatic, narrative reading of the Passion. It is found in Walter Wangerin Jr.'s book, **Ragman and Other Cries of Faith** (New York: Harper and Row, 1984) pp. 28-44.]

ONE PALM SUNDAY MORNING, the congregation I served participated in a profound experience of our Lord's Passion. For many years on Palm Sunday, we had employed several readers in a kind of choral reading of the Passion. One reader would read the part of Jesus, another that of Peter or Pilate and so on. It was a fine experience of hearing the entire Passion narrative from a number of voices at the outset of Holy Week. But it does not compare to this other experience.

On this particular Palm Sunday morning, the entire congregation participated in the Passion narrative. And it was stunning. We made use of Walter Wangerin's adaptation of the Passion narrative entitled, *The Cry of the Whole Congregation.* While this dramatic rendition of the Passion did not involve much acting, it did involve the entire congregation in unexpected ways.

The piece began traditionally enough with two voices reading the account of Jesus' triumphant entry into Jerusalem. The difference was that in their bulletins, the congregation had much of the text, and often had a part to play themselves. So when the part came to challenge the disciples in their appropriation of the donkey, suddenly scores of voices, the entire congregation demanded: "Why are you untying the colt?" Later the entire congregation would join again in song as they sang, "All Glory, Laud and Honor" as if in joyful reception of Christ's entry.

Throughout the piece there was that movement on the part of the congregation. One time they would be faithful followers of Jesus, singing hymns of praise or praying with Jesus. At another time they would be accusing Jesus, or joining their individual voices into a crowded, ugly mob scene in which they were surprised to hear themselves screaming, "Crucify him! Crucify him!" It was a kind of theater piece of human experience in the movement between grace and sin, faithfulness and apostasy. And it was sobering!

At times the congregation would join in sorrowful song to accompany the reading. "Go to Dark Gethsemane" was softly sung or played on a musical instrument as the story described Jesus' agony in the garden.

As the story reached its climax, a drum began to beat a kind of death march cadence in accompaniment. Then most surprisingly, a dancer appeared. The dancer, in our case, was a black American woman. She performed a slow liturgical dance in the chancel and about the altar as another woman sang as a solo, the spiritual, "Were You There When They Crucified My Lord?" These two women, one black and slowly dancing her interpretation of sacrificial death, the other white and slowly singing her account of our Lord's death — these two women in song and dance touched people in ways they had never been touched before. More than a few people had glistening eyes as the story reached emotional depths in them that had hitherto been untouched.

Our people's participation in the drama, song, dance and Passion narrative challenged them in unexpected ways. With their own voices they identified themselves as human beings, simultaneously saint and sinner. At times they were noble, faithful, strong in their witness and discipleship. At other times they were wounded, sinful, accusatory, joining in the throng to shout a death sentence at Jesus.

At the end of the piece, most sat in profound silence. Many were grieving. Others saw themselves with new eyes. Others pondered new insights into the Biblical story of Jesus' betrayal, abandonment, trial, torture and death. The mood and emotion of the morning stayed with us throughout Holy Week as the story unfolded again and again in the liturgies of Holy Week.

Most of us felt in a new way that we stood with the crowd on Golgotha. All felt in an unsettling way that we shared in the crowd's awe and gave voice with them in our own voice: "Truly this man was the Son of God."

Stephen M. Larson
Evangelical Lutheran Church
Geneva, Switzerland

APRIL 8, 1993

Maundy Thursday

Lessons:

Lutheran:	Exodus 12:1-14	I Cor. 11:17-32	John 13:1-17, 34
Roman Catholic:	Exodus 12:1-8, 11-14	I Cor. 11:23-26	John 13:1-15
Episcopal:	Exodus 12:1-14a	I Cor. 11:23-26 (27-32)	John 13:1-15
Pres/Meth/UCC:	Exodus 12:1-4 (5-10) 11-14	I Cor. 11:23-26	John 13:1-17, 31b-35

Introductions to the Lessons

Lesson 1

(1) *Exodus 12:1-14* (**Luth/Pres/Meth/UCC**); *Exodus 12:1-14a* (**Epis**) The Israelites are on the threshold of leaving Egypt. Before leaving, Moses and Aaron are instructed by God to hold the first passover. Each family was to roast a lamb, and its blood was to be put on the doorposts. Seeing the blood, the angel of death would pass over those homes. This was to be done annually in remembrance of their great deliverance from slavery.

Lesson 2

I Corinthians 11:17-32 (**Luth**); *I Corinthians 11:23-36* (**Epis/Pres/Meth/UCC**) Here is the earliest account of the institution of the Holy Communion. The words are known as the Words of Institution. They are spoken when the bread and wine are consecrated as the body and blood of Christ. Paul assures us that these words came from Jesus himself.

Gospel

John 13:1-17, 34 (**Luth**); *John 13:1-15* (**Epis**) *John 13:1-17, 31b-35* (**Pres/Meth/UCC**) Today is Maundy Thursday of Holy Week. It is called "Maundy" because the word means "commandment". At the Last Supper Jesus gives the new commandment to love one another as he loved them. His love was expressed in the upper room where he and the disciples met for the Last Supper. In humble love Jesus washed his disciples' feet. In doing this, he set an example for the disciples to do the same.

Theme: The gift of the eucharist and of footwashing are means to remembrance.

The Minister's Annual Manual

Thought for the day: Themes of old and new covenants intermingle this day to strengthen our faith. The Passover was a formative experience for the people of Israel. A meal of remembrance told the story of God's saving action at the Exodus. At the Passover meal with his disciples, Jesus spoke of a new covenant in his blood. He gave his followers a meal of remembrance which also tells a story: the story of God's saving action in Jesus' death and resurrection.

Prayer of meditation: O God, in days of old you acted with a mighty arm and outstretched hand to save your people from slavery. Now in this day, I pray that you would act again in a small and gentle way: speak to me in this time of worship that I might have my faith renewed and deepened. As I journey now into the climax of Holy Week and the Church Year, be near to me to uphold me with your mighty arm of mercy and your outstretched hand of grace. Amen.

Call to worship:
"How shall I repay the Lord for all the good things the Lord has done for me? I will lift up the cup of salvation and call upon the name of the Lord. I will fulfill my vows to the Lord in the presence of all his people" (Psalm 116:10-12)

Prayer of adoration: God of liberation and freedom, in ancient days you brought forth your chosen people from slavery to freedom, from bondage into a promised land. In the death and resurrection of your beloved Son, you again brought forth your chosen people from slavery to death into life, from bondage to sin into the freedom of forgiveness. We give you thanks and praise you for your mercy and loving kindness, O God. Amen.

Prayer of confession: God of all mercy, you are slow to anger and abounding in steadfast love. As your beloved Son once washed the feet of his disciples, even so we pray that you would this day wash us of our sin. We have fallen short of your expectation of us. We have betrayed you with our lives of disunity and divison. We have not loved you as we ought. Bring to our remembrance our baptism. Help us to understand what you have done for us. As once your gracious waters of forgiveness and mercy washed over us in baptism, let your word of forgiveness wash us anew. We pray in Jesus' name. Amen.

Prayer of dedication of gifts and self: O God, on this very night, the night of Jesus' betrayal, he took bread and gave you thanks. We,

April 8, 1993

too, take our bread and our wine, our money and our very lives and hold them before you in thanksgiving. We thank you for the abundance of your gracious gifts to us. We thank you for the beauty of your creation. We thank you that in your mercy you sustain us and all life. We thank you for your faithful presence in the lives of your chosen people — from the time of Abraham and Sarah through the era of Moses and Miriam, up to our own day and age. You are a God of faithfulness and prodigal grace. We thank you. We praise you. We glorify you. Amen.

Sermon title: To Go In Peace

Sermon thesis: In washing his disciples' feet, Jesus calls them to servanthood. In our call to discipleship and servanthood, Jesus stands with us, present in word and sacraments.

Hymn for the day: *"Love consecrates the humblest act."* This hymn of Christ's footwashing calls us all to servanthood. The author, Silas Bettes McManus (1845-1917), lived in Indiana, where he studied medicine. He never practiced medicine, however, but went on to become an author and a poet. From 1893 to 1895 he was a state senator. Throughout his life he was a devout member of the Methodist Episcopal Church.

Children's object talk:

Try To Remember

Objects: Small birthday cake or cupcake with candles lit
Lesson: (Note: This is not the service to have a children's sermon. Let the children sit near the front and simply hear the story from John and watch the actions. They will learn mightily from watching the pastor take off his/her vestments, put on a towel and wash the feet of some people, including one or two children! But if you must have a children's sermon . . . here is one.) A special meal can help us remember.
Outline: 1. Have you ever had a birthday party?
       2. One of the purposes of a birthday cake is to help us remember.
       3. Jesus gave us a meal to help us remember him.
ANYBODY KNOW WHAT THIS IS? Anyone have a birthday today?

How many of you have ever had a birthday cake at a birthday party?

What do you do at a birthday party with your family? (eat special foods, tell stories of the child's birth, give presents, etc.)

This Thursday is a special day for us to remember. And we are doing much of the things you do at a birthday party.

We are telling stories. We read from the Bible the story of what Jesus did with his special friends the night before he died.

We will eat special foods. This Thursday is a day to remember Jesus' gift of the Last Supper. So we will eat the special food of bread and wine.

We will give presents. How do we give presents to God? In our offerings, we give God a gift to say thank you for all that God has given to us, for all that God has done for us.

This Thursday is kind of like a birthday party. We tell stories to remember Jesus. We give presents to God in our offerings to say thank you. We share the special meal Jesus gave to us. We eat bread and wine, the special foods that Jesus gave us to remember him.

Can you help me blow out these candles now?

The sermon:

To Go In Peace

Hymns:
Beginning of worship: It Happened on That Fateful Night
Sermon hymn: Love Consecrates the Humblest Act
End of worship: Ah, Holy Jesus

Scripture: John 13:1-17, 34

Sermon text: *"When he had washed their feet, and taken his garments, and resumed his place, he said to them, 'Do you know what I have done to you?' "* vs. 12

NEAR THE END of Alan Paton's novel, *Ah, But Your Land is Beautiful,* there is a wondrous scene.

The scene is set in the Holy Church of Zion in Bochabela, a township outside of Bloemfontein, South Africa. It was Maundy Thursday.

The community had been broken and divided yet again by the horrors of apartheid. A black serving man had died and the white authorities forbade his funeral to be held in the white church where he had served. In an attempt to bring healing to his community,

April 8, 1993

Rev. Isaiah Buti, the pastor of the Holy Church of Zion, went to the white Acting Chief Justice, Jan Christiaan Olivier, and asked of him an act of mercy: would he participate in the Thursday evening footwashing at his church?

Later, at that very service, Rev. Buti recounted the story of Jesus washing the disciples' feet. Then he called Hannah Mofokeng forward. She was an ancient woman, brought forward by her 70-year-old son. Rev. Buti knelt, washed her feet, dried them and told her to go in peace. Then Esther Moloi, a crippled child, was called. She was wheeled forward in her wheelchair. Rev. Buti's daughter, Maria, washed and dried Esther's feet.

Rev. Buti dismissed both girls in peace. There followed this scene, which I quote:

—*Martha Fortuin, I ask you to come forward.*
So Martha Fortuin, who thirty years earlier had gone to work in the home of newly married Advocate Olivier of Bloemfontein, and had gone with him to Cape Town and Pretoria when he became a Justice of the Appellate Court, now left her seat to walk to the chair before the altar. She walked with head downcast as becomes a modest and devout woman, conscious of the honour that had been done her by the Reverend Isaiah Buti. Then she heard him call out the name of Jan Christiaan Olivier and, though she was herself silent, she heard the gasp of the congregation as the great judge of Bloemfontein walked up to the altar to wash her feet.
Then Mr. Buti gave the towel to the judge, and the judge, as the word says, girded himself with it, and took the dish of water and knelt at the feet of Martha Fortuin. He took her right foot in his hands and washed it and dried it with the towel. Then he took her other foot in his hands and washed it and dried it with the towel. Then he took both her feet in his hands with gentleness, for they were no doubt tired with much serving, and he kissed them both. Then Martha Fortuin, and many others in the Holy Church of Zion, fell a-weeping in that holy place. (pp. 234-235)

The scene is deeply moving, for it embodies the vision of which Jesus speaks. The highest legal authority in the land kneels in servant humility. The lowly, servant woman, herself literally a piece of the judge's property, is lifted up, enthroned like a queen.

This day brings to our remembrance Jesus' command of servanthood, love and remembrance. We are called to model our lives on Jesus, to be alert for opportunities to serve. Furthermore, we are called to that servanthood in a spirit of love. We are not servants because of a law which dictates the task to us. We are servants out of a spirit of love, for we know that in the person of the one whom we serve, we encounter the Christ.

When in servanthood we visit people in the hospital, we encounter Christ. When in servanthood we take time to serve at a food shelter for homeless people, we encounter Christ. When in servanthood we gather clothing or blankets to provide for victims of flood or fire, we encounter Christ. When in servanthood we open our church, or our home, or our hearts to the stranger in our midst, we encounter Christ. (Matthew 25)

There are times when that call to servanthood can be a burden. There are times when we do not feel capable of serving, or times when we are too exhausted to serve. There may even be times when we are afraid to serve or times when we are too bitter from life's experience to care to serve.

At such times it is well to remember that our call to servanthood does not take place in isolation. We are called to servanthood as a community of God's people. It is a shared ministry of servanthood, it is not always undertaken alone. But more: our call to servanthood comes from Jesus who himself goes with us in our life's journey of servanthood. He does not call us to the task and leave us alone to it. The Christ does not call us to a task and then leave us unequipped for it. The crucified and risen Lord goes with us every step of the way, giving us his very self, his body and blood, as food for the journey to nourish our faith and sustain our servanthood.

From his meal of remembrance we arise refreshed. We have been forgiven and set free. Nourished and sustained by Christ's presence we may go in peace, to serve the Lord. Thanks be to God!

Stephen M. Larson
Evangelical Lutheran Church
Geneva, Switzerland

APRIL 9, 1993

Good Friday

Lessons:

Lutheran:	Is. 52:13-53:12	Heb. 4:14-16, 5:7-9	John 19:17-30
Roman Catholic:	Is. 52:13-53:12	Heb. 4:14-16, 5:7-9	John 18:1-19:42
Episcopal:	Is. 52:13-53:12	Heb. 10:1-25	John (18:1-40) 19:1-37
Pres/Meth/UCC:	Is. 52:13-53:12	Heb. 4:14-16; 5:7-9	John 18:1-19:42

Introductions to the Lessons

Lesson 1

Isaiah 52:13-53:12 (**Luth/Epis/Pres/Meth/UCC**). This is one of the most remarkable, beautiful and beloved chapters in the Bible. Christians see the Savior depicted in these words of Isaiah. Yahweh's servant was abused, despised, and rejected. His suffering and death were for our benefit. Patiently he endured it all that our sins might be forgiven. This was all in accord with God's will.

Lesson 2

(1) *Hebrews 4:14-16, 5:7-9* (**Luth/Pres/Meth/UCC**). Even though Jesus is the Son of God and our high priest, he understands our human condition of weakness. He was tempted as we are but did not sin. Through his suffering he learned to be obedient unto death. To all who obey him he is the source of our salvation.

(2) *Hebrews 10:1-25* (**Epis**). Christ is our supreme high priest. Human priests offered sacrifices for their own sins, but Jesus offered himself as the sacrifice for the sins of the world. A human priest repeatedly offered sacrifices for sin, but Jesus offered himself as the one, permanent sacrifice, the final and perfect sacrifice for sin.

Gospel

John 18:1-19:42 (**Luth/Pres/Meth/UCC**); *(18:1-40) 19:1-37* (**Epis**). These two chapters constitute John's account of the Passion. The story begins with Jesus' betrayal and arrest, continues through the trials and crucifixion, and ends with his burial.

Theme: The cross of Christ is our life and our salvation.

Thought for the day: Far from being a dead end of despair, the cross of Christ leads us to life and is our salvation. The cross draws our own despair, our own cries of "My God, my God, why have you forsaken me?" and turns them toward the crucified One. He, in turn, leads us from the cross to the empty tomb, from death to life, from isolation to community.

Prayer of meditation: My heart is wounded, O God, as I reflect and consider the wounds and sufferings of your beloved One. On this somber and awesome day that we call "Good," I pray that you would open my ears to hear this old and familiar story with new insight. Open my eyes to see your will in my life. Hear my prayer in the name of the crucified One. Amen.

Call to worship: "Praise the Lord, you that fear the Lord; stand in awe of the Lord, O offspring of Israel; all you of Jacob's line, give glory. For the Lord does not despise nor abhor the poor in their poverty; neither does the Lord hide his face from them; but when they cry to him the Lord hears them. My praise is of the Lord in the great assembly; I will perform my vows in the presence of those who worship the Lord." (Psalm 22:22-24)

Prayer of adoration: From the day of our birth you are our God. "You are the one who took me out of the womb, and kept me safe upon my mother's breast. I have been entrusted to you ever since I was born; you were my God when I was still in my mother's womb." (Psalm 22:9-10) To the day of our death you are our God. And from the time beyond our death, you are our God. "My soul shall live for the Lord; my descendants shall serve the Lord; they shall be known as the Lord's forever. They shall come and make known to a people yet unborn the saving deeds that the Lord has done." (Psalm 22:29-30)

Prayer of confession: God of life, have mercy upon us. You reproach us with the question, "What more could I have done for you, O my people?" You gave us the beauty of creation and we have despoiled it. You gave us the brilliance of light and we have preferred darkness. You gave us freedom from sin and we have continued to live in sin through our thoughts, words and deeds. You gave us the law and we have broken it. You gave us your beloved Son, the Christ, and we have nailed him to a tree. God of life, have mercy upon us.

Prayer of dedication of gifts and self: "Create in me a clean heart, O God, and renew a right spirit within me. Cast me not away from your presence, and take not your Holy Spirit from me. Give me the joy of your saving help again, and sustain me with your bountiful Spirit. . . . Deliver [us] from death, O God, and [our] tongue[s] shall

April 9, 1993

sing of your righteousness, O God of [our] salvation." (Psalm 51:11-13, 15)

Sermon title: Behold Your Son

Sermon thesis: In death, as in life, we are bound to one another in the family of Christian community. The cross of Christ deepens that perception and transforms it into the *koinonia* of God's kingdom.

Hymn for the day: *"Nature with open volume stands"* This hymn reflects with awe on the Good Friday story. Isaac Watts (1674-1748) was educated at a Non-conformist academy and served for ten years as minister to the Mark Lane congregation in London. During his stay the congregation grew so that it was necessary to move twice to larger facilities. Watts' first hymn was written on the suggestion that he write something better, when he had complained that the Psalm versions then in use were harsh and uncouth. He went on to write over 600 hymns.

Children's object talk:

The Cross of Death and Life

Objects: Crucifix and a cross from El Salvador (or pictures thereof)
Lesson: [Note: This is not the day, or evening for a children's sermon. Let them simply hear the story and feel the mood of the day. But if you must have a children's sermon, here is one.] The cross symbolizes death *and* life.
Outline: 1. This is a sad day.
2. This is the day we remember Jesus' death on the cross.
3. Be sure to come back to church on Easter Sunday to hear the rest of the story!

YOU ALL KNOW what these are I hope. What are they? (two crosses)

What differences do you see between them?

Look at this one (the crucifix). What color is it? Who is this that we see pictured on the cross? (Jesus) What has happened to him?

This is the day in which we especially remember Jesus' death on the cross. You have heard the story read again about the last events in Jesus' life. It is a sad story and maybe you saw some tears in the eyes of your mom or dad as the story was read. Maybe you felt some tears in your own eyes.

It is important to remember that this sad day was not the end of the story for Jesus!

Look also at this cross (the El Salvador cross). What do you see here? What color is it? It's many colors isn't it! And what do you see painted on the cross in all those colors? There are some flowers and some animals and food crops and people and houses and.... This cross comes from a land that knows tears and sufferings all too well, but look at this wonder! This cross is full of life and hope and possibility.

That is because the cross is a symbol for us of life as well as death.

I want to especially invite you to come back to church tomorrow night for our Easter Vigil and again on Sunday morning for our Easter service. For then we shall again learn the lesson that Jesus' death on the cross was not the end of the story. Then we shall learn again the lesson that the cross is a symbol for life as well as death.

The sermon:

Behold the Son

Hymns:
Beginning of worship: Lamb of God, Pure and Sinless
Sermon hymn: O Sacred Head, Now Wounded
End of worship: Sing, My Tongue, the Glorious Battle

Scripture: John 19:17-30

Sermon Text: *"Woman, behold your son."* (John 19:26)

IN 1968, WORKERS on a construction site in Jerusalem made an astonishing discovery. They had chanced upon some tombs containing *ossuaries,* stone containers bearing the skeletal remains of people long dead. In one of the ossuaries they found the remains of a crucified man and a young child.

According to the doctor who examined the remains, the man was about thirty years old. His legs had been broken, his forearm bones badly scarred by hammer blows. The two heel bones were still joined together by a large iron nail, about seven inches long.

Immediately some cynics claimed that the body of Jesus had been found. But of course, that was not so. Several facts spoke against that claim. In the first place, some argued, the Bible testifies that none of Jesus' bones had been broken. But more tellingly, the man's name was inscribed in Hebrew on the lid of the ossuary. It was John. Also

April 9, 1993

scratched on the outside of the container was the fact that the smaller body was his child. Most poignant of all, they found inside the ossuary the remains of some flowers.

We don't know why this man was crucified. But we know that he was loved by someone.

Death often underscores a sense of community and family that can sometimes be missed in life. Little wonder that at the occasion of a death, the family and community gathers from far and wide to pause, to give recognition with thanksgiving to this life now gone. When my 101-year-old grandmother died, I flew from Switzerland to Iowa to be a part of that family gathering, for I knew that the extended family would not gather again in such a way in my lifetime. And yet, where had I been the previous many, many years? Circumstances and distances had kept me from visiting my grandmother for over a decade.

In some cultures and traditions, the sense of community is alive and well, it thrives, long before death. It is one of the gifts of the ecumenical movement that we can learn from other churches — churches from other Christian traditions as well as from other parts of the world. Consider the church of southern Africa. There exists among those churches a Xhosa proverb: Umntu ngumntu ngabantu. It translates: "A person is a person because of other people." One's very identity is rooted in an awareness of a larger community.

Or consider the churches among the Dene in the northern parts of Canada. There one encounters a sense of community that transcends time and space. The Dene, for example, speak of their land as being held in trust by their generation *from* their long-dead ancestors *for* their unborn descendants. Land is not theirs individually, but belongs to the people.

We, too, as a people of God are a people, a community. From the cross, following betrayal, torture, denial and abandonment, Jesus affirms that fact.

It is from the cross, from the agony and weariness of his torturous death that Jesus reminds his immediate family and his extended family of disciples that they are one community, one people. Among his last words, gasped out from dying lips, Jesus speaks of community. To his mother he says, "Woman, behold your son." And to his friend and disciple, he speaks words that would bind John in a relationship of love and protection with Mary: "Behold your mother."

We are a people — a community. Death teaches us that and life invites a living awareness of that fact.

One of the most moving (in the literal and figurative sense of that word) Good Friday liturgies I ever participated in was held in the inner city area of Edmonton, Alberta. It was an ecumenical liturgy, a gathering of the people of God from across various Christian traditions. The liturgy consisted of a procession through the streets of downtown Edmonton. The procession was led by a Franciscan brother in a brown habit carrying a large wooden cross. We would stop at sites of sorrow and hope in the city. For example, we stopped at a native community center, where to drum beat accompaniment we heard scripture read and sang a hymn. We stopped at an old armory that was no longer used for storing weapons, but now was a depot for the food bank. There we heard Isaiah's ancient words about swords of death being beaten into plowshares of nourishing life.

One of the places we stopped was the city jail. It is a tall building. Among the upper floors the windows are barred. And as we stood there singing, we could see men at the windows behind the bars. My two young daughters were astounded at the sight. "Were those really criminals and bad guys, Dad?" they asked. And then, in the midst of scripture and prayer and song, they waved to the prisoners. And the inmates waved back. Those waves were a sign of community, a sign of connectedness despite the barrier of broken laws and incarceration. That scene stayed with my daughters for a long time. And with me.

"Behold your son. Behold your mother." We are a community as the people of God. And we are a community with the wider world.

From the cross, in his dying moments, Jesus seems to be teaching still: "Love one another as I have loved you."

Stephen M. Larson
Evangelical Lutheran Church
Geneva, Switzerland

APRIL 11, 1993

Easter Day. The Resurrection of Our Lord.

Lessons:

Lutheran:	Acts 10:34-43	Col. 3:1-4	Matt. 28:1-10
Roman Catholic:	Acts 10:34a, 37-43	Col. 3:1-4	John 20:1-9
Episcopal:	Acts 10:34-43	Col. 3:1-4	John 20:1-10 (11-18)
Pres/Meth/UCC:	Acts 10:34-43	Col. 3:1-4	Matt. 28:1-10

Introductions to the Lessons

Lesson 1

Acts 10:34-43 (**Luth/Epis/Pres/Meth/UCC**) In response to a Roman's soldier's invitation, Peter tells Cornelius and his friends the story of Jesus' ministry. The most important item of the message was Jesus' death and resurrection which Peter claimed was the work of God. Along with other disciples, Peter had the experience of eating and drinking with the resurrected Christ.

Lesson 2

Colossians 3:1-4 (**Luth/Epis/Pres/Meth/UCC**) Christ has risen and is at the right hand of God. Likewise, a Christian dies to self and is raised to a new life in Christ. Consequently, Christians keep their minds and hearts not on earthly things but on Christ.

Gospel

John 20:1-18 (**Luth/Epis/Pres/Meth/UCC**) By herself, according to John's account of the Resurrection, Mary Magdalene goes before sunrise to the tomb of Jesus and finds the stone before the tomb rolled away. She reports this to Peter and John who race to the tomb and find it empty. The men go home, but Mary Magdalene remains weeping. Jesus comes and reveals himself to her. Excitedly she returns to the disciples and exclaims, "I have seen the Lord!"

Theme: The light of the resurrection saves us from self-destruction.

Thought for the day: "Far from seeking, like Homer, merely to make us forget our own reality for a few hours (or once a year at Easter) (the Bible) seeks to overcome our reality: we are to fit our own life into its world . . . Everything that happens in (our) world . . . must be fitted as an ingredient of the divine plan" (Erich Auerbach's *Mimesis* as quoted by Hans Frei in *The Eclipse of Biblical Narrative* p. 3)

Prayer of meditation: We love you, O our God; and we desire to love you more and more. Grant us that we may love you as much as we desire, and as much as we ought. O dearest friend . . . come . . . and dwell in our hearts; then you will keep a watch over our lips, our steps, our deeds . . . Give us love, born of your love to us, that we may love others as you love us . . . Let our hearts, frozen in sin, cold to you and cold to others be warmed by this divine fire. So help us and bless us in your Son. Amen. (St. Anselm in *The Communion of Saints: Prayers of the Famous* ed. Horton Davies, Eerdmans, 1990)

Call to worship: O God, who for our redemption gave your only-begotten Son to the death of the cross, and by his glorious resurrection delivered us from the power of our enemy; Grant us so to die daily to sin, that we may ever more live with him in the joy of his resurrection; through Jesus Christ, your Son, our Lord . . . (*The Book of Common Prayer*, Charles Mortimer Guilbert, Custodian, 1977)

Prayer of adoration: O Lord, we praise you, for despite our fear you have given us the power of praise. We worship you, for despite our sin you have suffered death. Despite our despair or denial, in the resurrection you have given us the power of faith and the hope of love. What then shall we give you, Lord, in return?

Praise to you for your birth in poverty.
Praise to you for your love of scripture.
Praise to you for your baptism by John.
Praise to you for your calling the disciples.
Praise to you for your healing the sick and the blind.
Praise to you for your teaching the foolish and wise.
Praise to you for your love of children.
Praise to you for your mercy towards Jerusalem.
Praise to you for your passion.
Praise to you for your suffering, your death,
   and all Praise to God for your resurrection. (After St. Ephraim of Syria) Amen.

April 11, 1993

Prayer of confession: Most merciful God, we confess that we have sinned against you in thought, in word, and deed, by what we have done, and by what we have left undone. We have not loved you with our whole heart; we have not loved our neighbors as ourselves. We are truly sorry and we humbly repent. For the sake of your Son Jesus Christ, have mercy on us and forgive us; that we may delight in your will, and walk in your ways to the glory of your name. Amen. (*The Book of Common Prayer.* Charles Mortimer Guilbert, Custodian, 1977)

Prayer of dedication of gifts and self: Almighty God, you who have made all things for us, and us for your glory, sanctify our body and soul, our thoughts and our intentions, our words and actions, that whatsoever we shall think, or speak, or do, may by us be designed to the glorification of your name . . . and let no pride or self-seeking, no impure motive or unworthy purpose, no little ends or low imagination stain our spirit, or profane any of our words and actions. But let our body be a servant to our spirit, and both body and spirit servants of Jesus Christ. Amen. (Thomas a Kempis in *The Communion of Saints: Prayers of the Famous,* ed. Horton Davies, Eerdmans, 1990)

Sermon title: It Was On Fire When I Lay Down

Sermon thesis: The significance of Easter is not lived, even by Christian disciples, because we fear what our new life in Christ requires of us. We need not fear, though, because in the light of the resurrection we are saved from habits of self-destruction. In the hope of the new life we are freed to experience the revelation of God's mercy in simple words and deeds of love.

Hymn for the day: *"Now all the vault of heaven resounds."* Paul Zeller Strodach (1876-1947) served for 27 years as a Lutheran pastor in New Jersey, Pennsylvania, and Ohio. Thereafter he was literary editor of the United Lutheran Church Publication house in Philadelphia. A liturgical scholar and author he published several works and served on the hymnal committees for the *Common Service Book,* 1917, and the *Service Book and Hymnal,* 1958. The third stanza of the hymn prays, "Oh, fill us, Lord, with dauntless love."

Announcements for next week:
   Sermon title: Something Hidden, Something Pro-found
   Sermon theme: We often do not experience forgiveness because we do not hope in Christ.
   Sermon summary: The mystery of the resurrection is that it is so much more beyond us and so much more present to and within us that we misconstrue both the high

holy majesty and deeply human humility of God. God is with us in Jesus Christ. In this hope we can be assured of completing our high calling through Jesus Christ.

Children's object talk:

Do Not Be Afraid

Objects: A soda bottle (narrow necked), a cup of water, a sauce pan (to catch the water).
Lesson: Jesus tells us not to be afraid; he is our friend.
Outline: 1. What do you want to be when you grow up?
2. What will happen if you are afraid?
3. How will you succeed if you are afraid? A friend can help you. Remember that a friend, Jesus, said to you, "Do not be afraid."

WHEN I WAS YOUNG I wanted to be a fireman. What do you want to be when you grow up? (Permit time for responses) That's great. Let me tell you about wanting to be a fireman. When I was six I received a fire truck for my birthday. I used to dream of driving my truck to a fire, pulling right up to a burning building, extending the ladder, and then I would imagine beginning to climb the ladder to the top . . . but there was a problem. I never could imagine climbing the ladder. I was afraid of high places. I could dream that I was putting on my fire boots, my coat, my fire hat, and I had no fear of fighting the fire. But when I thought of climbing the ladder, I began to shake. I could imagine myself starting up the ladder, but then the ladder began to shake because I was shaking and I had to stop and climb down. Let me show you how this felt. (Take soda bottle and try to pour water into the bottle, pretending to be afraid, with a shaking hand) Can I pour water into the bottle when my hand is shaking? How can it be done? What about if someone helped me, someone held my hand while I poured? (Try it). Helping someone helps them not to be afraid. When we are afraid, do we feel better if a friend helps us? Yes. How then could I imagine climbing that high ladder? Would it work if someone, a friend, climbed with me? Yes. Sometimes when we are afraid it helps to have someone with us. This is what I needed, a friend to say, "Don't be afraid." This is what Jesus says to us today on Easter. "Don't be afraid". Our dreams can become real, when we grow up with a friend, like Jesus, who helps us forget our fears.

April 11, 1993

The sermon:
It Was On Fire When I Lay Down

Hymns:
Beginning of worship: Christ the Lord is Risen Today
Sermon hymn: There's a Wideness in God's Mercy
End of worship: Come, Christians, Join to Sing

Scripture: Matt. 28:1-10

Sermon text: *"Do not be afraid; go and tell my brothers to go to Galilee; there they will see me."* vs. 10

"A TABLOID NEWSPAPER carried the story, stating simply that a small-town emergency squad was summoned to a house where smoke was pouring from an upstairs window. The crew broke in and found a man in a smoldering bed. After the man was rescued and the mattress doused, the obvious question was asked: "How did this happen?" "I don't know", (he replied). "It was on fire when I lay down on it." (Robert Fulghum: *I Was On Fire When I Lay Down On It.)*

"It was on fire when I lay down on it." A lot of us could settle for that on our tombstones. A life-story in a sentence. Out of the frying pan and into the fire. I was looking for trouble and I found it. The devil made me do it the first time; afterwards, I did it on my own. This is not a modern problem. We've got some fine old friends in this deal. Saint Paul bemoaned the fact that "I cannot understand my own behavior. I fail to carry out the things I want to do, and I find myself doing the very things I hate," (Romans 7) and we know the rest of the story.

It Was On Fire When I Lay Down On It. Many of you may recognize the work. It is by Robert Fulghum. It is a simple book about the problem of evil. It answers the question about how we can understand evil. Simple but insightful. It suggests that evil is something we make for ourselves. Like the man who complained "that he had the same damn stuff" for lunch every day, and when asked who prepares his lunch, responded, "I do". We know the rest of the story: same lunch, same complaint, even when he had a choice between tuna and turkey.

God, it is written, warned his first children, Adam and Eve. He made it clear. Don't eat that piece of fruit — it will lead to trouble.

You know the rest of the story. But what is the rest of the story? Adam *and then* Jesus. That's the rest of the story. But do we know it? Do we know the rest of the story, especially on Easter?

My sense is that we do not, not because we have not heard it, not because we can't recite some of it if asked (some Sunday School saint is to be thanked for this). We do not know the story because we have not discovered how we fit into the plot. This is my thesis.

Easter is the time of hope. My thought is that though we may experience and express the hope of Easter we may not really "know the rest of the story", no matter how familiar it is to us, because Easter is something new, something so powerful, that we may be afraid of what it really means for us and for others. This seems to be the position of Mary and Mary Magdalene. In the earthquake of revelation they were afraid. "But the angel said to the women, 'Do not be afraid.' " This was the position of the disciples. In the fearful mystery of the resurrected Jesus which brings us to our knees, Jesus said to them "Do not be afraid". Of what could they be afraid? Could they be afraid that in the presence of the Lord of Life they, we, will be called to so live our witness to the resurrection that others may find Jesus through us? Do we remember the rest of the Story? "Then Jesus said to them, 'Do not be afraid; go and tell my brothers (sisters) to go to Galilee; there they will see me.' "

Where does Easter begin? In the scripture it begins for the disciples in a shared witness. The first Easter begins in common mission, a communion of purpose, in communication, in the communion of communication.

There is a mystery here. It is a mystery, though, like the mysteries which are understood by children, who know love when they receive it. There is a mystery here but it is real nonetheless; it is real and revealed again when we share the gift, our hope of new life, received in Jesus. We are called to witness to this gift. But to reveal this there is no need for rhetorical flourish. Simple words will do.

Easter is a gift; a gift that gives the promise of new life, a gift that fills the simple words of forgiveness or the simple actions of mercy with the healing mystery of God. Easter is a gift of love from God who created life and called it good and refused to permit it to be wasted in the fires of anger, the firestorm of war, the smoldering ashes of despair and the burning coals of guilt or our secret addictions. God sent Jesus to lay his life down in the flames that we

April 11, 1993

have ignited. Christ extinguished the fire of our destruction in the light of love that shone from the cross. We have discovered, we can still discover this when we share the love of Christ. Then and there, in the moment where we begin to live the story we have heard, when we begin to share this story in the deepening life of faith shared in the church, we will discover that despite the fact that "it was on fire when we lay down on it", we can be released from the flames of self destruction to receive new life in the light of Easter and Christ's resurrection.

William Wesley Elkins
Bernardsville United Methodist Church
Bernardsville, New Jersey

APRIL 18, 1993

Second Sunday of Easter

Lessons:

Lessons:
Lutheran:	Acts 2:14a, 22-32	1 Peter 1:3-9	John 20:19-31
Roman Catholic:	Acts 2:42-47	1 Peter 1:3-9	John 20:19-31
Episcopal:	Acts 2:14a, 22-32	1 Peter 1:3-9	John 20:19-31
Pres/Meth/UCC:	Acts 2:14a, 22-32	1 Peter 1:3-9	John 20:19-31

Introductions to the Lessons

Lesson 1

Acts 2:14a, 22-32 (**Luth/Epis/Pres/Meth/UCC**). In the coming Easter season, we will hear readings from the Book of Acts rather than from the Old Testament. Today's 2nd Lesson is a portion of Peter's sermon on Pentecost. Peter preaches that Jesus' resurrection was a fulfillment of God's promise to David that a son of his would always be king. Furthermore he declares that he and the Apostles are witnesses to Jesus' resurrection.

Lesson 2

1 Peter 1:3-9 (**Luth/Epis/Pres/Meth/UCC**). For the rest of the Easter season we will hear a series of six passages from I Peter. In this first of the series Peter gives us reason to rejoice over the Resurrection. Because of it, we are given new life in Christ and a living hope of a future inheritance. Though we cannot see Jesus, we love and believe in him.

Gospel

John 20:19-31 (**Luth/Epis/Pres/Meth/UCC**). It is the night of Easter day. Jesus comes to the disciples who were all present except Thomas. It was a most important meeting, because Jesus gave them the Holy Spirit and the mandate to continue his work in the world. When the risen Christ returned a week later, Thomas was convinced that Jesus really rose from the dead. Faith, he learned, is believing without seeing.

Theme: We often do not experience forgiveness because we do not hope in Christ.

Thought for the day: "...Christian faith is faith in, Christian love is love through, and Christian hope is hope in God the Father, Son and Holy Spirit...If we tried to start with faith and love and hope, we would have still to go back to that free and higher other in which they have their basis." (K. Barth, Church Dogmatics, IV, 1, pp. 3-4).

April 18, 1993

Prayer of meditation: O Lord, give us more charity, more self-denial, more likeness to you. Teach us to sacrifice our comforts for others, and our likings for the sake of doing good. Make us kindly in thought, gentle in word, generous in deed. Teach us that it is better to give than to receive; better to minister than be ministered to. And to you, the God of love, be glory and praise for ever. Amen (Henry Alford in *The Communion of Saints: Prayers of the Famous*, ed. Horton Davies, Eerdmans, 1990)

Call to worship: Almighty and everlasting God, who in the Paschal mystery established the new covenant of reconciliation: Grant that all who have been reborn into the fellowship of Christ's Body may show forth in their lives what they profess by their faith; through Jesus Christ our Lord, who lives and reigns with you and the Holy Spirit, one God, for ever and ever. Amen. (*The Book of Common Prayer*, Charles Mortimer Guilford, custodian, 1977.)

Prayer of adoration: O Lord, most holy God, we praise you for your humility in Jesus Christ. O Lord, hidden in mystery, we thank you for revealing your mercy in the commonplace. O Lord, creator of life and all that is good, all that we have threatened to destroy, we thank you for revealing your hope of nature redeemed by grace. O Lord, most High God, we praise you for your intimate presence in each breath of our lives. May we continue through the Holy Spirit to be filled with prayer and praise. In the spirit of Christ. Amen.

Prayer of confession: Most merciful God, we confess that we have sinned against you in thought, word, and deed, by what we have done, and by what we have left undone. We have not loved you with our whole heart; we have not loved our neighbors as ourselves. We are truly sorry and we humbly repent. For the sake of your Son Jesus Christ, have mercy on us and forgive us; that we may delight in your will, and walk in your ways to the glory of your name. Amen. (*The Book of Common Prayer*, Charles Mortimer Guilford, custodian, 1977.)

Prayer of dedication of gifts and self: Christ, be with me, Christ before me, Christ behind me, Christ in me, Christ beneath me, Christ above me, Christ on my right, Christ on my left, Christ where I lie, Christ where I sit, Christ where I arise, Christ in the heart of everyone who thinks of me, Christ in every eye that sees me, Christ in every ear that hears me. Salvation is of the Lord. Salvation is of the Christ.

The Minister's Annual Manual

May your salvation, O Lord, be ever with us. (St. Patrick in *The Communion of Saints: Prayers of the Famous,* ed. Horton Davies, Eerdmans, 1990)

Sermon title: Something Hidden, Something Pro-found

Sermon thesis: The mystery of the resurrection is that it is so much more beyond us and so much more present to and within us that we misconstrue both the high holy majesty and deeply human humility of God. God is with us in Jesus Christ. In this hope we can be assured of completing our high calling through Jesus Christ.

Hymn for the day: *"We walk by faith"* "We may not touch his hands and side; we walk by faith, and not by sight." Henry Alford (1810-1871), who also gave us "Come, you thankful people, come," was a priest of the Church of England. In addition to his ministry at Leicestershire, London, and finally at Canterbury, he spent twenty years preparing a four-volume commentary on the Greek New Testament and was a member of the New Testament Revision Committee.

Announcements for next week:
   Sermon title: Know What You Need
   Sermon theme: We will experience forgiveness when we see Christ in and through broken lives and hearts.
   Sermon summary: The word of God is high and holy. We can understand its mysteries when we really know what we need. What we need is forgiveness. Yet we fear forgiveness more than sin. Despite this, Jesus forgives us, and we know and experience God's mercy because Jesus is the Lord of life.

Children's object talk:
We See What We Expect

Objects: One hidden Jesus Poster (The one in which Jesus is hidden in the unusual patterns and interchangeable patterns of foreground and background) One picture of a duck-rabbit.
Lesson: What we see is what we expect to see.

April 18, 1993

Outline: 1. Show children the picture of the duck rabbit. Question them on what they see.
2. Show children the "picture" of Christ. Question them on what they see.
3. Show the children that what they see depends upon what they expect to see.

I HAVE SOMETHING INTERESTING to show you. We found this in a child's coloring book. My son, (daughter, nephew, young friend etc.) wanted to know what color to use to color it. I said that what color we use depends upon what it is. What is it, I asked. He (she) did not know. I wasn't sure. Sometimes it looks like one thing and sometimes it looks like another. I said that I would show it to you and find out what you think. What do you think it is. (Some will say a duck, some will say a rabbit. If all say it is a duck or all say it is a rabbit, you can show that it can appear to be one or the other depending on whether we see the two diagonal lines as either rabbit ears or a duck's bill.) There is a problem here. Sometimes it is a duck and sometimes it is a rabbit. It all depends upon what we expect. What if all around the picture there were little ducks. Would it look like a duck? What colors would we use? Yes. If there were little rabbits around the picture then it would look like a rabbit, wouldn't it? What colors would we use? If we want ducks we see ducks. If we want rabbits we see rabbits. Now I want to show you something else (hidden "word" of Jesus.) For those of you who can read, what do we see here? Do we see anything at all? Is there a word here? What does that word look like? This is a word for Jesus. Why was Jesus hard to find? Was Jesus hidden? Not really. Jesus was always there. Jesus was hard to find because we did not expect to find Jesus in the picture. When we knew it was Jesus, was it easy to find? Yes. It was easy to find because we were expecting, hoping to find Jesus. This is what your mothers and fathers will be learning today: we find what we expect to find. In church we learn that we can find Jesus in places where we do not expect to find him. Sometimes we feel bad and we don't expect to find someone who loves us. In church we learn that no matter how we feel, we can find Jesus.

The sermon:
Something Hidden, Something Pro-found

Hymns:
   Beginning of worship: Christ Whose glory Fills the Skies
   Sermon hymn: Ask Ye What Great Thing I Know
   End of worship: Lift High the Cross

Scripture: John 20:19-31

Sermon Text: *If you forgive the sins of any, they are forgiven; if you retain the sins of any they are retained.* v. 23

THERE IS A CHINESE PAINTING that is sometimes found in art textbooks, sometimes in Chinese restaurants. It is a painting of seven trout in a crystal blue pond. Encountering this painting, our eyes may be drawn to the sense of peace portrayed there. Each blue-green trout appears to be suspended in or flowing within a moment that passes, only to renew itself. It seems that this artist, though most probably not a Christian, has caught in a few lines of color the perfection of Eden. But within this moment of ideal beauty there is something disturbing. Besides the six trout, who seem to be in the right place at the right time, there is a seventh trout that seems to be swimming upside down. This particular fish seems somewhat incongruous, almost twisted. This fish seems to be floating up towards the top of the painting. On first noticing this incongruity, we may not know what to make of it. Is this some form of Chinese religious symbolism? Is it a commentary upon an ancient ecological crisis to have a dead or dying fish floating near the surface of the pond?

In seeing all this we may be caught between mystery and uneasiness. But looking over the painting again we might discover something that we had not seen before. Well, we had seen it, but we had seen it

April 18, 1993

as something else. What we thought was a lily pad on the surface of the pond was really the ripples of a splash. The seventh fish was not dying, floating towards the surface of the pond. This trout is leaping into the air. The trouble with our original interpretation of the painting was that it was so calm in its each-fish-in-its-peaceful-right-place-at-the-right-time, that we could not imagine that this moment was actually an instant in which one trout, beyond all normal expectations, was dynamically transcending the limits of its natural life.

How was it possible that we could not see it? This painting is like those exercises in perspective in which we are presented with a collection of black and white blotches. We look and wait, knowing that something is hidden. Then in an instantaneous change of perspective, we see in the nonsense collection of foreground and background, a shepherd and his sheep, or Jesus, the resurrected Lord, who is now face to face with disciples.

It was the same way with the first disciples. In the mystery of Jesus' passion they did not know him as he really was and is and shall be. They feared the authorities, so they denied Jesus. These were the chosen, but in the war between hope and despair they had lost their faith. These were the beloved, who, from a distance looked toward the cross and only saw a dying man. But, unknown even to themselves, these broken men were to become apostles. They were the disciples, the chosen, the beloved, who, looking through the locked doors of their lives, saw and heard all that they had seen and heard in a new way. How was this possible? Jesus, the one they thought they knew so well, appeared to them and was known in a new way. Where they once heard cries of pain, they heard "Peace be with you." Where they heard, "It is finished," now they heard, "As the Father has sent me, so I send you." Where they knew fear and the despair of betrayal, they were given the Holy Spirit and were called to give to the world what they had received: "If you forgive the sins of any, they are forgiven." Jesus, the one they thought they knew so well, was not a dying man, nailed upon the cross to hang helpless in the shadow of death, denying them the horizon of their hope. Jesus was the resurrected Savior, who, in forgiveness, drew us from the darkness of our own death into the light of resurrection through the forgiveness of our sins. Jesus was the Christ, the re-creator of those who had lost their life. They had seen and heard all this before but they did not know as they were known.

If we now know that something can be seen but not really seen, heard but not understood, what about Thomas and the apparent judgment of Christ upon his doubt: "Have you believed because you have seen me? Blessed are those who have not seen and yet have come to believe."

Remember, the fish was not dying, it was leaping out of the pond. This is the way we must perceive this passage from John. Something other than what we first expect is happening here. "Peace be with you." "Forgive and sins are forgiven" This is not a ghost story where the dead walk and we are punished for our sins. Jesus is not the ghost of Christmas past who determines that we have betrayed our calling and we shall be marked for eternity to walk in the same and still smaller circle of guilt, until our lives are but a black singularity, a universe of unforgiven sin, alienating all light and life outside our guilt. No, this is a beginning, a beginning of something new. "As the Father has sent me, even so I send you." We are on a mission, a mission to the unforgiven, a mission for God. "If you forgive the sins of any, they are forgiven; if you retain the sins of any they are retained." So, we are called to forgive each other, and we should start with forgiving Thomas, for there is no difference between Thomas and ourselves. We will continue not to experience our own forgiveness really or fully. So, perhaps we should pray: "Forgive us our sins, as we forgive those who have sinned. In the forgiveness of sin offered, receive again, or for the first time, the perfect forgiveness that transcends and still transforms our lives.

William Wesley Elkins
Bernardsville United Methodist Church
Bernardsville, New Jersey

APRIL 25, 1993

Third Sunday of Easter

Lessons

Lutheran:	Acts 2:14a, 36-47	1 Peter 1:17-21	Luke 24:13-35
Roman Catholic:	Acts 2:14, 22-28	1 Peter 1:17-21	Luke 24:13-35
Episcopal:	Acts 2:14a, 36-47	1 Peter 1:17-23	Luke 24:13-35
Pres/Meth/UCC:	Acts 2:14a, 36-41	1 Peter 1:17-23	Luke 24:13-35

Introductions to the Lessons

Lesson 1

Acts 2:14a, 36-47 (**Luth/Epis**); *Acts 2:14a, 36-41* (**Pres/Meth/UCC**). Peter brings his Pentecost sermon to a close. His final thought is that the One they crucified, God made Lord and Messiah. This truth made the people feel so guilty that they asked, "What shall we do?" Peter instructed them to repent and be baptized and then they would receive the Holy Spirit and forgiveness. What a sermon! Three thousand responded!

Lesson 2

1 Peter 1:17-21 (**Luth**); *1 Peter 1:17-23* (**Epis/Pres/Meth/UCC**). At a great price we were set free from our sins. The price was the sacrifice of Christ, the Lamb of God. This was God's plan even before the creation of the world. Christ not only died for us but rose again in glory. Because of our faith and hope in him, we love each other and are born again as God's children through the Word of God.

Gospel

Luke 24:13-35 (**Luth/Epis/Pres/Meth/UCC**). It was Easter Sunday afternoon. Two friends of Jesus were walking from Jerusalem to Emmaus, a distance of seven miles. As they walked, they talked about the events of Good Friday and Easter morning. A third person joins them and explains from the Scriptures the meaning of what happened. Since it was getting dark, the men asked the stranger to have a meal with them. While at table, the stranger blessed, broke, and distributed bread. Then they realized that the stranger was the risen Christ. They rushed back to Jerusalem to tell the disciples the good news.

Theme: We will experience forgiveness when we see Christ in and through broken lives and hearts.

The Minister's Annual Manual

Thought for the day: "There is no present in which the justification of a person is not still (the) beginning of justification, and where, if it is recognized, it does not have to be continually recognized... The divine pardon does not burst into one's willingness but one's unwillingness. A person will always be a miracle and a puzzle to her/himself as she/he breaks out in this way." (Karl Barth, *The Church Dogmatics*, IV, 1, pp 575-76)

Prayer of meditation: O God, you have glorified our victorious Savior with a visible, triumphant resurrection from the dead and ascension into heaven, where he sits at your right hand; grant... that his triumphs and glories may ever shine in our eyes, to make us more clearly see through his sufferings, and more courageously endure our own; being assured by his example, that if we endeavor to live and die like him, for the advancement of your love in ourselves and others, you will raise our dead bodies again, and conforming them to his own glorious body, call us above the clouds and give us possession of your everlasting kingdom. (John Wesley 1703-1791 in *The Communion of Saints: Prayers of the Famous*, ed. Horton Davies, Eerdmans, 1990)

Call to worship: O God, whose blessed Son made himself known to the disciples in the breaking of bread: Open the eyes of our faith, that we may behold him in all his redeeming work; who lives and reigns with you, in the unity of the Holy Spirit, one God, now and for ever, Amen. *(The Book of Common Prayer,* Charles Mortrimer Guilbert, Custodian, 1977.)

Prayer of adoration: Almighty God, Father of all mercies, we your unworthy servants give you most humble and hearty thanks for all your goodness and loving-kindness to us, and to all. We bless you for our creation, preservation, and all the blessings of this life; but above all, for your inestimable love in the redemption of the world by our Lord Jesus Christ; for the means of grace, and for the hope of glory. And we beg you... that we may show forth your praise, not only with our lips, but in our lives: by giving up ourselves to your service and by walking before you in holiness and righteousness all our days; through Jesus Christ our Lord. Amen. (The General Thanksgiving of *The Book of Common Prayer*, 1662)

Prayer of confession: Merciful God, we confess that we have not loved you with our whole heart. We have failed to be an obedient church.

April 25, 1993

We have not done your will, we have broken your law, we have rebelled against your love, we have not loved our neighbors, and we have not heard the cry of the needy. Forgive us, we pray. Free us for joyful obedience, through Jesus Christ our Lord. Amen. *(The Book of Common Prayer,* Charles Mortimer Guilbert, Custodian, 1977.)

Prayer of dedication of gifts and self: O Lord, let me not henceforth desire health or life, except to spend them for you, with you, and in you. You alone know what is good for me; do therefore what seems best to you. Give to me, or take from me; conform my will to yours; and grant that, with humble and perfect submission, and in holy confidence, I may receive the orders of your eternal providence; and may equally adore all that comes to me from you; through Jesus Christ our Lord. Amen. (Blaise Pascal 1623-1662 in *The Communion of Saints: Prayers of the Famous,* ed. Horton Davies, Eerdmans, 1990)

Sermon title: Know What You Need

Sermon thesis: The word of God is high and holy. We can understand its mysteries when we really know what we need. What we need is forgiveness. Yet we fear forgiveness more than sin. Despite this, Jesus forgives us and we know and experience God's mercy because Jesus is the Lord of Life.

Hymn for the day: *"We sing the praise of him who died"* Thomas Kelly (1769-1855) was author of over 750 hymns, some of which rank among the finest hymns of the English language. After studying law for a time, he studied for the priesthood and was ordained in the Church of Ireland. He later left the Church of Ireland and became an independent preacher. A generous and humble man, he became a friend of the poor in Dublin and was especially helpful during the Irish famine in the 1840s. The hymn praises Christ who loved us and took our guilt away.

Announcements for next week:
Sermon title: We Know What You Said, But How Did You Mean It?
Sermon theme: The Word of God renews our lives in a new way each time we live it.
Sermon summary: The difference between just hearing the Word of God and understanding it is the difference discovered in living the meaning of God's mercy. We begin to live God's mercy when we open our hearts to the word of God, in a new way, each day. This mystery of "living-understanding" is made possible by Jesus Christ, who creates and recreates our lives in the light of his saving revelation.

Children's object talk:
We See Jesus in the Giving of the Bread

Objects: a penny, a nickel, a dime, a quarter
Lesson: We see Jesus in the persons giving the bread.
Outline: 1. Identify the coins and the persons on them.
2. Try to find Jesus on the coin.
3. Optional (start a weekly penny collection for the hungry and homeless)

HAVE YOU EVER SEEN these kinds of coins? Do you know what they are? (A penny, a nickel, a dime, a quarter). Does anyone know whose picture is on these coins? (Lincoln, Jefferson, Franklin Roosevelt, Washington). All these men were presidents. Each one is remembered for something he did. Lincoln helped free the slaves. Jefferson gave us religious freedom, Roosevelt helped stop poverty, and Washington helped free our nation. These were great men, so their pictures were put on these coins. I think that we can find a picture of someone greater than a president in these coins. I think that we can find Jesus. But where is Jesus? He is not in the pictures on the front; he is not in the pictures on the back. Where can we find Jesus in these coins? Well, what would happen if we took these coins, put them together with three more of each kind ($1.23) and bought a loaf of bread? What would happen if we took this loaf of bread and gave it to a hungry woman or man? Would we be able to find Jesus then? Yes, we would find Jesus, some of Jesus, in the man or woman who gave the bread to the hungry man. Jesus said to his first disciples, "Feed my sheep." Each time we feed the hungry we are becoming like Jesus. (Say, do you want to find Jesus in this church? Well, what if we collected change for the poor. What would you see if you went out into the church and collected change from the pockets or pocket books of all the people out there? I think that we just might find Jesus, not on the coin, but in the eyes of the people who give pennies, nickels, dimes, and quarters to feed the poor. Let's try to find Jesus each week in church. The children will help us to find the change for Jesus in our lives.)

April 25, 1993

The sermon:
Know What You Need

Hymns:
  Beginning of worship: Love Divine All Loves Excelling
  Sermon hymn: Fairest Lord Jesus
  End of worship: Sing With All the Saints in Glory

Scripture: Luke 24:13-35

Sermon Text: *"Was it not necessary that the Christ should suffer"*---v. 26... *"and---he was known to them in the breaking of the bread."* v. 35.

"....HE INTERPRETED to them in all the scriptures the things concerning himself." (Luke 24:27....Did not our hearts burn within us...while he opened to us the scriptures)
IS THIS HEART BURN or a heart strangely warmed? Are the words of Jesus a solution or a problem for us? Is it possible to understand Jesus, to have Jesus interpret for us the words of the scriptures, especially when Jesus does such strange things — draw near to us, walk with us, though his true identity is hidden? He shares a meal, opens the eyes of two apostles, and then vanishes from their sight. Is this a ghost? No, he walks. He has hands and feet. No ghost: He eats bread. But appearing and disappearing without prior and proper notice, this is unprecedented. Resurrected from the dead, isn't this an impossibility? Could someone like this possibly mean the same things that we mean with our ordinary words? Is it possible for his words to open our hearts to the scriptures?

It all depends upon who we are. We may say I love you and know that it is a risk. We promise faith and expect betrayal. We pray deliver us from evil and we hope that time will heal all wounds. But we suspect that avoiding harm and much of what little healing we receive is often a matter of luck. What then do we do with the words of someone who says "O foolish men (women)... slow of heart to believe all that the prophets have spoken! Was it not necessary that the Christ should suffer these things and enter into his glory?" He knows who we are. God protects children and fools but there just seems too much difference between us and the divine word. We fear suffering; we feel that it is unnecessary. Jesus accepts suffering because it is necessary. We glory in what we control and achieve for our lives. Jesus' glory is given for what is lost in the service of others. How could Jesus mean the same things that we mean when he says "I thirst." The Gnostics, perceptive though heretical, believed that since Jesus was the Son of God, he could not thirst, he could not suffer. They believed that when he "took bread, and broke it" sharing this bread with us, he was not sharing any human hunger. The Gnostics believed he was acting out a script in which, in the margin, the Director's notes read: "Appear hungry, appear sorrowful, appear dead, then vanish 'out of their sight.' "

When Jesus says "Father, forgive them; for they do not know what they do," is it possible that Jesus' forgiveness, because he is the Son of God, is so much beyond the forgive and forget of ordinary forgiveness that it cannot touch our ordinary lives? Are we capable of understanding this forgiveness and then witnessing to this forgiveness? We may love Jesus (Peter in Gospel of John), we may say the same words, preach "repentance and forgiveness of sins in his name." But how can we say these words and mean them in the same cross-suffering way? Can we understand the connection between "the redemption of Israel," the salvation of our lives, can we understand the connection between the suffering of Jesus and our own suffering? (Romans 8:17)

What is the problem here? We are seeking an understanding of our discipleship in the light of the crucifixion and the resurrection. This is often a problem for the church, not because we do not sin, but because we recognize that we need so much forgiveness. Often the church denies this. We refuse to recognize our need because we fear appearing vulnerable. Often this fear of vulnerability is the reason that many people don't associate with churches. It is not stylish to associate with people who need forgiveness. It is even more than a little insulting to discover that the sinners in the church claim the authority to forgive others. What is the problem here? The problem is that it appears that the words of the Son of God do not fit our lives very well. We sin and preach forgiveness. How can we do what we do and say what we say and not feel uncertain, more than a little uneasy? How can we preach forgiveness, understand forgiveness and then, so much more, live in the forgiveness of God?

Peter Bohler once said when John Wesley confessed that he could not preach because he did not have faith, "Preach faith until you have it, then preach faith." This is plain and direct. Often there is a plain and direct meaning in the scripture for anyone who has eyes to see

April 25, 1993

and ears to hear. What is it? "Repentance and forgiveness of sins is to be proclaimed in his name to all nations." We are called to offer forgiveness, not in our name, not upon our authority, not upon some inner assurance of our own salvation. We are called to witness to our common forgiveness solely upon the authority of Jesus Christ, who loved us even through death on a cross. Understanding Jesus and experiencing forgiveness all depends upon who we think we are. If we fear our sin so much that we will refuse to admit it, then Jesus must appear perfect because we believe that we, sinner or saint, should be invulnerable. But if we feel that we are not all that different than the people of Jerusalem, who prayed for redemption; if we read the news and fear for our world; if we read our own hearts and know that we threaten the lives of others, even the lives of those we love the most; if we recognize that we are children of God, injured, defensive, hoping against hope that we will be delivered from this body of death, from our politics of self defense, *then* we will recognize our own despair in the powers that we trust, *then* we will see Jesus. We will see Jesus become indignant when children are excluded and injured (Mark 7:14). We will see Jesus weep for men and women who have died, weep over souls and cities who refuse his loving mercy. We will see Jesus, truly human, truly divine, in the grieving, the broken, the hungry of body, heart and mind. We will then see Jesus and we understand the scriptures, for we will know that we need what he prayed for: "Father forgive them." In our need we will then find our forgiveness in the "breaking, blessing, and giving of the bread" of life through our crucified and resurrected Lord, Christ Jesus.

William Wesley Elkins
Bernardsville United Methodist Church
Bernardsville, New Jersey

MAY 2, 1993

Fourth Sunday of Easter

Lessons:

Lutheran:	Acts 6:1-9; 7:2a, 51-60	I Peter 2:19-25	John 10:1-10
Roman Catholic:	Acts 2:14a, 36-41	I Peter 2:20b-25	John 10:1-10
Episcopal:	Acts 6:1-9, 7:2a, 51-60	I Peter 2:19-25	John 10:1-10
Pres/Meth/UCC:	Acts 2:42-47	I Peter 2:19-25	John 10:1-10

Introductions to the Lessons

Lesson 1

(1) *Acts 6:1-9; 7:2a, 51-60* (**Luth/Epis**). The early church had a problem. Some members were being neglected. To solve this problem, the church decided to elect seven men to be in charge of administration to permit the Apostles to give full time to prayer and preaching. Stephen was one of the seven men and became the first martyr. Because his frank sermon enraged the people, he was stoned to death while Paul looked on.

(2) *Acts 2:42-47* (**Pres/Meth/UCC**). In response to Peter's Pentecost sermon, 3000 were baptized. This was the birth of the church. And it was an ideal one! They had very close fellowship and shared their possessions. Daily they worshiped in the temple and had their meals together in their homes. Every day the church membership increased.

Lesson 2

I Peter 2:19-25 (**Luth/Epis/Pres/Meth/UCC**). There are two kinds of suffering: deserved and innocent. According to Peter, God approves when we suffer for doing good. Jesus is our example in suffering. He absorbed the pain in himself rather than paying it back. Also, his suffering was redemptive. By his wounds we are healed.

Gospel

John 10:1-10 (**Luth/Epis/Pres/Meth/UCC**). Jesus tells a parable about a shepherd and sheep. A good shepherd enters the door to get to his sheep which, recognizing his voice, follow him. Jesus says he is the door of the sheep. If one goes through his door, the person will be saved, be fed, and will receive abundant life. To give abundance of life Jesus came to the world.

May 2, 1993

Theme: The Word of God renews our lives in a new way each time we live it.

Thought for the day: Now revelation is no more and no less than the life of God himself turned to us, the Word of God coming to us by the Holy Spirit. Therefore a biblical theology can never be more than a series of attempted approximations, a collection of individual exegeses. There can never be a question of any system... (Karl) Barth, *The Church Dogmatics*, 1, 2, p. 483).

Prayer of meditation: O God.... in the hearing of your word is the grace to receive it in true fear and humility ... Shine on us by your word so that we may not be blind at midday, nor willfully seek darkness. May we be roused daily by your words to present ourselves as a sacrifice to you, that you may peaceably rule and perpetually dwell in us, through Jesus Christ our Lord. (John Calvin in *The Communion of the Saints: Prayers of the Famous*, ed. Horton Davies, ed. Eerdmans, 1990).

Call to worship: O God, whose Son Jesus is the good shepherd of your people: Grant that when we hear his voice we may know him who calls us each by name, and follow where he leads; who, with you and the Holy Spirit, lives and reigns, one God, for ever and ever. Amen. (*The Book of Common Prayer*, Charles Mortimer Guilbert, Custodian, 1977.)

Prayer of adoration: O Lord God, in a world of words which mean little or nothing, your word creates life; "In the beginning was the Word." In a world of words which warp our hearts to "deceive" or "destroy," your Word "is light" and "the life" of all. In a world of words which can mean anything, covering all truth with darkness, we praise you for the Word which so "shines in the darkess" that the "darkness has not (will not and will never) overcome it." O Lord God, in a world of empty words we thank you for fulfilling and transforming our worldly words "in the way, the truth and the life" so that the words of our mouths and the meditation of our hearts may be acceptable to you, Our Lord and Redeemer. Amen.

Prayer of confession: Merciful God, we confess that we have not loved you with our whole heart. We have failed to be an obedient church. We have not done your will, we have broken your law, we have rebelled against your love, we have not loved our neighbors, and we have not heard the cry of the needy. Forgive us, we pray.

Free us for joyful obedience, through Jesus Christ our Lord. Amen. (*The Book of Common Prayer*, Charles Mortimer Guilbert, Custodian, 1977)

Prayer of dedication of gifts and self: O God, the Father of the forsaken, the help of the weak, the supplier of the needy ... teach us that love towards the human race is the bond of perfection, and the imitation of your blessed self; open our eyes and touch our hearts, that we may see and do ... the things which belong unto our peace. Strengthen us in the work we have undertaken; give us counsel and wisdom, perseverance, faith and zeal ... pour into us a spirit of humility; let nothing be done but in devout obedience to your will, thankfulness for your unspeakable mercies, and love to your ... Son Christ Jesus. Amen (Anthony Ashley Cooper in *The Communion of Saints: Prayers of the Famous*, ed. Horton Davies, Eerdmans 1990)

Sermon title: We know what you said, but how did you mean it?

Sermon thesis: The difference between just hearing the Word of God and understanding it is the difference discovered in living the meaning of God's mercy. We begin to live God's mercy when we open our hearts to the word of God, in a new way, each day. This mystery of "living-understanding" is made possible by Jesus Christ, who creates and recreates our lives in the light of his saving revelation.

Hymn for the day: *"Thy strong word"* This hymn of the Word of God, speaks of light and Christ's saving work on the cross. Martin Hans Franzmann (1907-1976) taught in Wisconsin for a number of years before taking a post at Concordia Lutheran Theological Seminary in St. Louis. In 1969 he was ordained at Westfield House in Cambridge England, where he taught until his death.

Announcements for next week:

Sermon title: In My Father's House

Sermon theme: Our true home is with Jesus before God in eternity.

Sermon summary: The home we long for is not to be found in this world. Let the griefs and disappointments of this life move you to put your trust in Jesus for beyond.

May 2, 1993

Children's object talk:
Who Do You Trust (to Cut the Pie)?

Objects: Two cardboard cut-outs from a pie tin: one divided equally, one divided unequally.
Lesson: We trust those who treat us as themselves.
Outline: 1. Tell the children the story.
2. Show children the two cut-outs.
3. Ask them how they would cut the pies if they could not choose first.

ONE DAY my mom baked a great pie. We had it for dinner and everybody loved it. Next day after school, my brother and I came home and we wanted a snack. So I got the pie out. There was one big piece left. (I was the big brother, he was the little brother.) So I began to cut it, a big piece for myself and a smaller piece for my little brother. He saw what I was beginning to do and thought it was unfair. We began to argue, we began to push, and we were almost beginning to fight when my mother stepped into the kitchen. (We pretended that nothing was going on). Do you know what she did then? She looked at the pie and asked who was going to cut the pie that way. She looked at me (I was pretending to be interested in the floor) and said "You cut the pie and then your brother will choose the first piece." How do you think I cut the pie? Do you think I cut the pie this way (unevenly) or this way (equal sizes)? What did I do? I took care to cut that piece of pie into two pieces that were as equal as I could make them. My brother looked and looked and then choose his piece. Why did I cut the pie in equal pieces? I knew that if one was bigger than the other, I would get the smallest. This became the rule in my house. The boy that cuts the pie, chooses last. After a while I learned that if my brother cut the pie I did not have to look. I knew they were equal. The same with him. We learned to trust each other. I knew that he would treat me the same. I knew that he would be fair. We learn to trust those people who treat us as themselves.

The sermon:

We Know What You Said, But How Did You Mean It?

Hymns:
Beginning of worship: Thine be the Glory
Sermon hymn: He Lives
End of worship: Spirit of the Living God

Scripture: John 10:1-10

Sermon Text: *"I am the door; if anyone enters by me, he will be saved..."* (v. 9)

"I LOVE YOU," she said. He heard, "Let's marry." She meant ... well, what they meant required some negotiation, the problem being that we often hear what is said without hearing what is meant. Putting this in biblical terms, we often hear the text without hearing the commentary. This is not uncommon. It even has a place in the comics. The comics, though, unlike real life have a solution. The little dotted balloons (as compared to the solid balloons) make it possible for one person to speak (in a solid balloon) while we can read what the other person is thinking (in the dotted balloon). Text and commentary at the same time. He says, "I promise." She hears, "I might." Often the commentary gives the heart of the matter, revealing the heart of the hearer. She says, "I hope." He hears (dotted balloon), "There's doubt."

But the comics, though they might be truer than life, are not real. The comics develop frame by frame. Time is stopped, held captive. We can read them over and over again if we do not get the point. And what is the point? Some recognition of our involvement in the silly or the absurd. But real time and real life do not proceed one scene at a time. In life we cannot move from frame to frame as we please until we find our sense of humor. In real life there are times in which the difference between understanding and not understanding is the difference between life and death; there is no second chance, and there is no humor in tragedy.

The Gospel, the Word of Jesus Christ, is real; it is true to life, it is the truth of life. In a moment we may hear, understand, and discover the difference between life and death. Why then do we read

May 2, 1993

and preach the same passages from year to year? We have all heard "Truly, truly, I say to you, I am the door of the sheep ... if anyone enters by me, he will be saved." Why then repeat this passage? Have we missed the point? Are we hoping for a better time, a time when have found our faith? It may seem a bit comic to repeat ourselves, as if we were looking for a key to a door that we had passed through or beyond the point of no return, to our salvation or judgment. So, why repeat it all over again? In faith the answer is this: when we hear or read the Word of God again we may discover that how we hear reveals a new way to live. Our lives are the commentary. Who we are, who we hope to be is revealed in the dotted, forever incomplete, broken halos that embody our limited understanding of the full and sufficient Word of God. In truth, when we hear the Word again we hope to hear it in a way in which "the way, the truth and the life" heal the broken fragments of our hearts. Let us take this to heart and try again to hear the word of God.

"Truly, truly, I say to you." This is one way that Jesus marks the times and places that he is speaking from the heart. Jesus is not being indirect or subtle. He is speaking the secrets of his heart. He is speaking from heart to heart. He is trying to enter our secret hearts. He is not, though, trying to trick us. "He who does not enter the sheepfold by the door" — which is the most direct and open way — "but climbs in by another way" — why would they attempt to enter indirectly without being observed? The answer is clear — "that man is a thief and a robber. But he who enters by the door is the shepherd of the sheep. To him the gatekeeper opens." We are the gatekeeper to our hearts. Jesus is attempting to give us a key to God's heart. We may accept it or refuse it. But why would we open our hearts? What do we need that we cannot supply from our own resources? The answer is in the beginning of the gospel, the beginning of life, the beginning of our lives. "In the beginning was the Word ... and the Word was God.... in him was life, and the life was the light of all people." (John 1.1 4) In the beginning we lived in and through the light of God. But we lost our way. How? The Gospel interprets our sin by the fact that "we love darkness rather than light, because (our) deeds are evil." But, this is not the final word, for despite our fragmented heart of darkness the gospel completes the interpretation of our situation by: "The light has come into the world ... he who does what is true comes to the light..." (John 3:19b, 21)

Why would we open our hearts to the light of God? Because Christ speaks directly to our hearts. But there may be others that try the direct approach. How do we distinguish between those that break and enter and those who con their ways into our hearts? The Scripture continues: "The sheep hear his voice, and he calls his own sheep by name and leads them out." What is the difference between a thief and a true shepherd? All of us, not just ministers, should ask this question, for we are, as Luther wrote, priests to each other. What then distinguishes those that "steal, kill and destroy" and the one who is the door, the way to safe pasture, the one that "came so that they may have life and have it abundantly"? The answer is clear. "The good shepherd lays down his (her) life for the sheep" (John 10:11). We all know this. This is the heart of the passage: Christ, the good shepherd, died so that we might pass through the valley of the shadow of death. But what does this mean, practically?

Last year (1991) in a movie title *The Doctor* we were able to see a surgeon who would rather "cut straight and care less" discover that he had cancer. This was only the first thing he discovered. The next was that a patient, even when he is a famous doctor, loses his name, loses his identity, and he is made to endure any indignity and delay that other doctors or the hospital determine he must suffer. He is a patient, passive, he cannot control his own life. He feels that he is becoming only another statistic: a number recording only that he lives or has died. He fears death, but more deeply he fears that no one cares what he suffers from and that no one cares what he hopes for. During his shock of receiving *A Taste of His Own Medicine* (the novel) (more expertise, less compassion) he discovered a young woman who is dying of a brain tumor. Recognizing that she has no hope of recovery, he lies to her about her condition. She senses the truth, though, and because she is committed to living her life day by day, speaking truth in love, she demands that if they speak at all then they must tell the truth. She also is determined that, despite her condition, she will continue to live each dying day in hope. Her tumor has given her freedom for only what is essential. But what is essential? What does the heart surgeon learn from this direct approach to life and death? He learns that the heart of it all is compassion. He learns that each person who suffers has a name. He learns, in his grief, that everyone has some deep hope that is threatened by illness. Finally he learns, above all, that "every doctor will

May 2, 1993

become a patient." In order to understand this simple wisdom, it was necessary for this doctor to fear for his life and then give up his career of "cutting straight and caring less." Someday we will all face death and then we will reach out, seek out, someone who knows our name, who speaks to the heart, who has suffered as we suffer, and who holds in his/her hands the light of compassion and hope that promises to guide us through our valley of the shadow of death. Speaking from the heart, let us hear, hear again, now and in a new way, that though we may suffer and learn compassion, the one "suffering servant," who has healed us body and soul, is Jesus Christ. For "surely, he has borne our griefs and carried our sorrows; yet we esteemed him stricken, smitten by God ... yet he bore the sin of many, and made intercession for (us)." (Isaiah 53:4-5, 12b) What is essential? What is a matter of life and death?

William Wesley Elkins
Bernardsville United Methodist Church
Bernardsville, New Jersey

MAY 9, 1993

Fifth Sunday of Easter

Lessons:

Lutheran:	Acts 17:1-15	I Peter 2:4-10	John 14:1-12
Roman Catholic:	Acts 6:1-7	I Peter 2:4-9	John 14:1-12
Episcopal:	Acts 17:1-15	I Peter 2:1-10	John 14:1-14
Pres/Meth/UCC:	Acts 7:55-60	I Peter 2:2-10	John 14:1-14

Introductions to the Lessons

Lesson 1

(1) *Acts 17:1-15* (**Luth/Epis**). Wherever Paul went there was either a revival or a riot. On his second missionary journey, he preached for three weeks in Thessalonica. A riot, led by jealous Jews, resulted, and Paul had to flee by night to Berea. There they received the Word with eagerness until the Jews from Thessalonica caused the same trouble in Berea. Again Paul had to flee.

(2) *Acts 7:55-60* (**Pres/Meth/UCC**). By the time Stephen finished his speech, the crowd was furious because he accused them of murdering Jesus, the Messiah. Stephen had a vision of Jesus standing at the right hand of God. The mob stoned him to death. Before dying Stephen knelt and prayed for their forgiveness.

Lesson 2

I Peter 2:4-10 (**Luth**); *I Peter 2:1-10* (**Epis**); *I Peter 2:2-10* (**Pres/Meth/UCC**). The church has been changed from being a nothing to being everything. As God chose Jesus, the church is also chosen. We are invited to come to Jesus, the living stone, and become living stones in the temple of God where we offer spiritual sacrifices. God has made something out of nothing. Now the people of the church are a chosen race, a royal priesthood, a holy nation, and God's own people. Behold what God has wrought!

Gospel

John 14:1-12 (**Luth**); *John 14:1-14* (**Epis/Pres/Meth/UCC**). Jesus has a one-on-one relationship with God the Father. Because of this oneness, he can go ahead and prepare a place in heaven for believers. Because of this oneness, we can see God in Jesus. Because of his oneness with the Father, prayers offered in Jesus' name will be answered.

Theme: Our true home is with Jesus before God in eternity.

May 9, 1993

Thought for the day: We all have a deep longing for home. But much of life as we experience it in America today only frustrates these longings. That our yearnings for home cannot be perfectly fulfilled in this life is meant to point us beyond to our true home in the next.

Prayer of meditation: Heavenly Father, cleanse my mind from all distraction and from all sin, that I may receive your word in the power of your Spirit. Grant to us today the grace of assurance, that we may know that we are numbered among those blessed ones who have washed their robes and made them white in the blood of the Lamb, who stand before your throne and serve you day and night in your holy temple, through Jesus Christ our Lord. Amen.

Call to worship: "Then Jacob awoke from his sleep and said, 'Surely the Lord is in this place; and I did not know it.... How awesome is this place! This is none other than the house of God, and this is the gate of heaven.' " (Gen 28:16, 17, RSV)

Prayer of adoration: Most blessed and most holy God, before the brightness of your presence the angels cover their eyes. In reverence show forth your glory, Father, Son, and Holy Spirit, eternal Trinity. Blessing and honor and glory and power be unto our God, for ever and ever. Amen.

Prayer of confession: Merciful God, we humble ourselves in your presence, as before you we must confess our sinfulness. We have broken your holy law. We have let false priorities come before your kingdom and righteousness. We have been anxious about many worldly things, while we have neglected the spiritual things which bring us true peace. We have not loved our neighbor as ourselves, nor done for others what we would have them do for us. Heavenly Father, you gave your own Son, Jesus Christ, to save your people from their sins. For his sake, forgive us, cleanse us, and renew a right spirit within us. We can plead for your forgiveness only through the grace of Jesus Christ, our Lord and Savior. Amen.

Prayer of dedication of gifts and self: Most bountiful Lord, all things come from you and of your own do we now give you. Accept us, O God, as your servants, and accept these offerings as our devotion to you. Give us grace always to serve you gladly, through Jesus Christ our Lord. Amen.

Sermon title: In My Father's House

The Minister's Annual Manual

Sermon thesis: The home we long for is not to be found in this world. Let the griefs and disappointments of this life move you to put your trust in Jesus for beyond.

Hymn for the day: *"I know that my Redeemer lives"*. This hymn of Jesus' resurrection reflects the Gospel especially in stanza 7 where we sing "He lives my mansion to prepare; He lives to bring me safely there." The author, Samuel Medley (1738-1799), lived in England where he apprenticed as an oilman and later joined the navy. A severe leg wound obliged him to return home. Impressed by a sermon by Isaac Watts he joined the Baptist church and later became a Baptist minister. For twenty-seven years he served as pastor of the Byron Street Baptist Church in Liverpool.

Announcements for next week:
Sermon title: What the Spirit Does
Sermon theme: The Spirit, living in our hearts, continues Jesus' ministry.
Sermon summary: Christ promised to carry on his ministry throughout all lands and times to come through a spiritual presence to be with us. What does the Spirit do?

Children's object talk:

Your Real Home

Objects: A photograph of my boyhood home
Lesson: Your Father in heaven loves you just for being you.
Outline: 1. When I was a boy my home made me feel cozy, because I was loved for just being me.
2. But I grew up, and my folks sold our home. No matter how much we want it, no home on earth lasts forever.
3. But Jesus has made us a home in heaven, where we are loved forever for simply being who we are.

THIS IS A PHOTO of the home where I grew up. I had good times there, playing with my brothers and with my friends in the neighborhood. Our parents loved us and took care of us, just because we were their children, even when we were naughty or when we did not do our best work in school.

I really liked my home. But I had to grow up and move away, just like all children do. My parents sold our old home, and we cannot go back there now. I have to work for a living now. No one pays me simply because of who I am, but only for what I do.

Sometimes I miss the home I grew up in, because my parents loved me just because I was their son, not because of what I did or didn't do. No home here on earth lasts forever. But I am glad that we have

May 9, 1993

a home to look forward to in heaven, which will last forever. Jesus has gone on ahead to get this home in his Father's house ready for us, where God will love us forever just because of who we are, brothers and sisters of his Son Jesus.

The sermon:

In My Father's House

Hymns:
Beginning of worship: Ye Watchers and Ye Holy Ones
Sermon hymn: O Jesus, I Have Promised
End of worship: The Church's One Foundation

Scripture: John 14:1-3 (RSV)

Sermon Text: *"Let not your hearts be troubled; believe in God, believe also in me. In my Father's house are many rooms; if it were not so, would I have told you that I go to prepare a place for you? And when I go and prepare a place for you, I will come again and will take you to myself, that where I am you may be also."*

FEW WORDS EVOKE such deep emotions as the word "home." "Home" gives us a sense of belonging, the feeling that we are loved simply for who we are. Home offers us rest and comfort after a day of hard work.

 We all have a deep longing for home. This longing has become particularly acute in America today, as we are losing our ties to family and to locale. A third of all children in our country are growing up in broken homes, and half of all marriages end in divorce. Every year one in five families moves to a new neighborhood, so fewer children than ever grow up in the same town their parents did. Much of life in America today only frustrates our deep longings for home.

 Yet, even the most warm, loving, and satisfying home someday must face death. No greater void can be left in the human heart than by the death of one's lifelong companion. That our longing for home cannot be perfectly fulfilled in this life is meant to point us beyond to our true home in the next.

Jesus came into this world in order to bring us to our true home with him in God. Most of Jesus' teachings sought to lift our focus above our concerns with this world and unto our true home he prepared for us in the next. His most comforting words about our eternal home Jesus spoke during his Last Supper with his disciples on the night in which he was betrayed. He promised them and us, "In my Father's house are many rooms." (v. 2)

Jesus knew the bitter disappointment and grief his disciples were to face on the following day. He sought to comfort them with the words, "Let not your hearts be troubled." (v. 1) It is comforting to know that our true home is not in this world, that the disappointments and grief we face are not life's final experiences. To know that our true home is beyond this world gives us strength not to let our hearts be troubled by this world.

We, too, in our lives must face disappointment, grief, and death. When we are young life seems long and bright with hope. But in a couple of decades we all realize how far short of our dreams we have fallen. No matter how much money we make we cannot put a price tag on our lives. That such disappointment seems built into the fabric of life is today much talked about as our "mid-life" crisis. Furthermore, the most loving, cherished relationships must someday end in grief, and we ourselves must face our own non-existence when "to dust thou shalt return." (Gen 3:19)

There in the Upper Room that night in which he was betrayed Jesus comforted his disciples with the promise that what they suffered had a meaningful role in God's plan. Jesus said, "I go and prepare a place for you." (v. 3) For three years the disciples had enjoyed Jesus' visible presence with them during his earthly ministry, hearing from his own lips the word of God and seeing his own hands care for them with the power of God. Now he was to be taken from their sight, and they would be left to face doubt and grief themselves.

We, too, must go through life without seeing the visible presence of Jesus with us. But his physical absence from us has a purpose. Jesus has gone on before us to prepare a place for us. Jesus left his disciples, and he leaves us today, to ready for us those many rooms in his Father's house.

The preparation for which Jesus had to leave his disciples was made in two stages; Calvary was the first, and Olivet the second, his crucifixion and his ascension. That Jesus had to make special

May 9, 1993

preparations is an implicit indictment of this life. Our true home in the next world is not a natural outcome of this world. Life now is out of harmony with God, and would result only in eternal separation from God. But to prepare for us the many rooms in his Father's house Jesus took upon himself everything that separates us from God, and bore it on Calvary's cross.

After Calvary came Olivet, from whose mount Jesus ascended from this world into heaven. There Jesus is today, continually offering before God his sacrifice on our behalf. Jesus is both the priest and the sacrifice, worshiping continually before his Father by presenting as sacrifice his own self. There he worships, still a man, body and soul, standing before God. His humanity is our entree as human beings into the very presence of God. There he prays for us daily, preparing our place before his Father's throne in glory.

There in the Upper Room that night in which he was betrayed Jesus promised his disciples that their deep longings for a true home would be fulfilled with him before God in glory. Our true home finally is where Jesus is, because he is humanity's only bridge to God. Jesus said to them, "Believe in God, believe also in me." (v. 1) No mere religious teacher ever dared to put belief in himself on an equal footing to belief in God. Jesus did, because he knew himself to be God's only-begotten Son. The Son of God became a man, so as to lift our humanity up into the life of God.

We are attached to Christ, and so brought before his Father, through our faith in him. Repeatedly Jesus commands us to believe in him. "Believe in God, believe also in me." (v. 1) This faith means trusting that what Christ sacrificed on Calvary is indeed enough to cleanse our guilt. Faith means asking Christ now in heaven to pray to his Father for us. Faith means wanting to find our true home with Christ before God. The purpose of this life is to grow year after year into increasingly deeper degrees of faith. We come to church week after week to foster our faith in Christ. We listen to his Word read and explained from the Bible. We sing his praises together with other believers. We eat his body and blood in the Lord's Supper, that through this sacrament we may feel our hearts lifted up spiritually into heaven where Christ is, seated at the right hand of God in glory.

Thus, we prepare ourselves now on earth by faith for the place which Christ has gone on before to prepare for us. Jesus promised, "In my Father's house are many rooms." (v. 2) This word "room" or "mansion" literally means "home," a permanent and secure dwelling. The true home after which every human heart longs is to be loved by God and be with Christ in God's presence. And there are "many" rooms, more than enough for all who want to come.

Bruce A. Hedman
Abington Congregational Church
Abington, Connecticut

MAY 16, 1993

Sixth Sunday of Easter

Lessons:

Lutheran:	Acts 17:22-31	I Peter 3:15-22	John 14:15-21
Roman Catholic:	Acts 8:5-8, 14-17	I Peter 3:15-18	John 14:15-21
Episcopal:	Acts 17:22-31	I Peter 3:8-18	John 15:1-8
Pres/Meth/UCC:	Acts 17:22-31	I Peter 3:13-22	John 14:15-21

Introductions to the Lessons

Lesson 1

Acts 17:22-31 (**Luth/Epis/Pres/Meth/UCC**). To escape bodily harm Paul left Berea in a hurry. He went to Athens where he waited for Timothy and Silas to join him. While waiting, he daily preached in the public square and attracted much attention. Out of curiosity the Town Council invited Paul to tell them about his new religion. He told them about a God who was unknown to them. When he spoke of Christ's resurrection, the meeting broke up into various factions.

Lesson 2

I Peter 3:15-22 (**Luth**); *I Peter 3:8-18* (**Epis**); *I Peter 3:13-22* (**Pres/Meth/UCC**). Like everybody, Christians are subject to suffering at the hands of a sinful world. But Christians are happy when they suffer for doing good. In this Jesus is our model. He suffered and died in behalf of sinners. As Noah and his family were saved from the flood, Christians are saved through the water of baptism, which is a spiritual cleansing. We are saved by the death, resurrection, and ascension of Christ, who is now in glory at the right hand of God.

Gospel

(1) *John 14:15-21* (**Luth/Pres/Meth/UCC**). This passage is a part of Jesus' discussion with his disciples in the Upper Room on the night he was betrayed. The cross comes tomorrow. Then the resurrection is followed by the ascension when he will leave the disciples. Thursday of this coming week is Ascension Day. To prepare them for his departure, he promises to send the Holy Spirit and assures them they will not be alone. If they love him, they will obey his commandments.

(2) *John 15:1-8* (**Epis**). Who is Jesus and what is our relationship to him? In this passage Jesus identifies himself as the vine and we are branches on the vine. As the branches must be a part of the vine to live and produce fruit, we must be in Christ.

The Minister's Annual Manual

Theme: The Spirit, living in our hearts, continues Jesus' ministry.

Thought for the day: Jesus' earthly ministry was confined to a radius of a hundred miles during a brief thirty-three years. Yet, what he did for one generation in one nation the Holy Spirit carries on "for ever," for all generations of Christians to follow.

Prayer of meditation: O Lord Jesus Christ, you are truth incarnate and the teacher of the faithful. Let your Spirit so overshadow us as we hear your Word read and preached, that the hearts of us all may be illumined by your revelation. May we so learn about you with sincere hearts, that we may be rooted and built up in you, who lives and reigns with the Father and the Holy Spirit, ever one God, world without end. Amen.

Call to worship: "Praise the Lord! Praise God in his sanctuary; praise him in his mighty firmament! Praise him for his mighty deeds; praise him according to his exceeding greatness! Let everything that breathes praise the Lord! Praise the Lord!" (Ps 150 RSV)

Prayer of adoration: Glory to you, Everlasting Father, as you sent your only Son into the world, so that we might live through him. Glory be to you, Lord Jesus Christ, as you brought eternal life to light through your gospel. Glory be to you, Holy Spirit, as you pour into our hearts the love of Christ. We bless you, Father, Son, and Holy Spirit, one God, eternal Trinity, for ever and ever. Amen.

Prayer of confession: We confess to you, merciful God, that we have sinned against heaven and in your sight, and we are not worthy to be called your children. We have forgotten you, and have broken your holy laws. We have been headstrong and disobedient. We have been selfish and unkind. For the sake of your Son our Savior we ask you to pardon our sins, to make clean our hearts within us, and to grant us your peace. Amen.

Prayer of dedication of gifts and self: Almighty God, our heavenly Father, you did not spare your own Son, but delivered him up for us all. In him you have given us freely all things. Receive now these offerings which we dedicate to you. By all our gifts enable us to yield ourselves to you, so that with body, soul, and spirit we may truly serve you, and in your service find our deepest joy, through Jesus Christ our Lord. Amen.

Sermon title: What the Spirit Does

May 16, 1993

Sermon thesis: Christ promised to carry on his ministry throughout all lands and times to come through a spiritual Presence to be with us. What does the Spirit do?

Hymn for the day: *"Alleluia! Sing to Jesus"* Written to fill a need for communion hymns in the Church of England, this hymn was first published in Dix's *Altar Songs*, 1867. William C. Dix (1837-1898), who also gave us "What child is this," was the manager of a marine insurance company. He made many fine contributions to hymnody, publishing four volumes. He also translated hymns from Greek and Abyssinian sources.

Announcements for this week: (Ascension Day)

Sermon title: You Are Witnesses
Sermon theme. With the apostles Christ has made us "witnesses of these things."
Sermon summary: Whereas we are not eyewitnesses to the events of Christ's death and resurrection, like the apostles, we nevertheless are witnesses *for* the meaning of these events, as we experience their power in our lives.

Announcements for next week:

Sermon title: Glorify Your Son
Sermon theme: We have confidence, not in ourselves, but in God's glory.
Sermon summary: Knowing our salvation is the result of love within the Persons of God gives us a confidence and joy that works righteousness can never know. Our salvation results from the Father and Son glorifying each other in the creation, in the cross, and in the consummation.

Children's object talk:

Jesus Inside Us

Objects: Pictures of Washington and Lincoln
Lesson: When Jesus lives inside us he helps us to want to do good for others.
Outline: 1. In school we learn about great people in history.
         2. But they are not alive to help us be good today.
         3. Jesus is alive. He gives us power on the inside to want to be like him.

I BET THAT YOU HAVE LEARNED in school how honest George Washington and Abraham Lincoln were. When George Washington was a little boy, he tried out his new hatchet on his father's cherry tree. When his father got angry, little George didn't lie or try to hide, but he told the truth, even at the risk of getting in trouble. As a young man Abraham Lincoln worked as a store clerk. One day he made a mistake, and short-changed a lady two cents. After work he walked twenty miles to her home to return her two cents.

You and I can hear stories like these about famous people, and we can respect their honesty. But George Washington and Abraham Lincoln are dead, and they cannot help you and me to be honest or kind or loving.

Unlike Washington and Lincoln, Jesus still is alive today. He sends his Spirit to live in our hearts. His presence with us inside our minds helps us to change, to want to be more honest, kinder, and more loving to those around us. He helps us want to be more like him.

The sermon:

What The Spirit Does

Hymns:
Beginning of worship: Joyful, Joyful, We Adore Thee
Sermon hymn: Spirit of God, Descend Upon My Heart
End of worship: Higher Ground

Scripture: John 14:15-17

Sermon Text: *"If you love me, you will keep my commandments. And I will pray the Father, and he will give you another Counselor to be with you for ever, even the Spirit of truth, whom the world cannot receive, because it neither sees him nor knows him; you know him, for he dwells with you, and will be in you."*

THERE IN THAT UPPER ROOM the night before he was to be crucified Jesus prepares his disciples for the grief they were to face the next day. For three years he has been their intimate companion. In him they have come to sense the very presence of God. Now as he is about to be taken from them, Jesus consoles his disciples with the promise of "another Counselor to be with [them] for ever," (v. 16) a Friend like himself, but who will never be taken away.

So with these words did Jesus that night begin to teach his disciples about the Holy Spirit who would extend his ministry throughout all lands and times to come. Jesus' earthly ministry was confined to a radius of a hundred miles during a brief thirty-three years. Yet, what he did for one generation in one nation the Holy Spirit would carry on, not only afterwards for the disciples themselves, but "for ever," for all generations of Christians to follow.

May 16, 1993

We today cannot know the intimacy of Jesus' bodily presence, as his disciples did, but we can know the intimacy of his spiritual presence through the ministry of the Holy Spirit within our hearts. And what specifically does the Holy Spirit do for us? Today we consider three benefits the Spirit brings which Jesus here promised to his disciples on that night in the Upper Room before he was crucified.

First, the Spirit convinces us of the truth in Christ. This "other Counselor," whose coming Jesus promised, he also called "the Spirit of truth." Throughout Scripture "truth" is never just a mental idea, but is the way to God. "Truth" is never just knowledge about God, but is knowing God. Thus, "truth" leads us to worship God, as Jesus said, "The true worshipers will worship the Father in spirit and truth."

Jesus was himself the very incarnation of the truth. His birth fused the life of God into human nature. His death broke down the barrier of sin separating us from a holy God. And his resurrection lifted human life up into the heart of God. Through his life, death, and resurrection Jesus Christ has opened up for us the way to God, and therefore is the ultimate truth of the universe. Of himself Jesus said, "I am the way, and the truth, and the life; no one comes to the Father, but by me." (Jn 14:6)

This "other Counselor" Jesus called the "Spirit of truth," because he communicates this truth to us. As a Spirit, he impacts our spirits, inwardly and invisibly. The Holy Spirit makes us rue the contrast between Christ's selfless, loving life and our own. The Spirit inspires the gratitude we feel over the sacrifice Jesus made for us on the cross. And through our faith in the cross the Holy Spirit releases the vitality of Christ's resurrected life into our hearts. The Spirit makes the words of Christ come alive to us and implants his grace in us. Of the Spirit Jesus said, "He will take what is mine and declare it to you."

Secondly, then, the Spirit comforts us with the peace of Christ. That night in the Upper Room, as Jesus was about to be taken from them, he consoled his disciples with the promise of "another Counselor." (v. 16) Jesus called the Holy Spirit a "counselor," literally "paraclete," meaning "one who is called alongside to help." This word could describe an attorney who gives legal counsel or an old friend who gives wise advice. Early English Bibles translated this as "Comforter," meaning "one who gives strength." I think of the "Paraclete" as a presence uplifting us in times of loneliness and stress.

The Minister's Annual Manual

Jesus called the Spirit "another" Counselor, implying that Jesus himself was the first. The Spirit continues to do for us what Jesus did for his disciples. Have you ever wished that you could have been with Jesus during his earthly ministry to see him calm the storm, to watch him heal the sick, and to hear him preach his Father's Word? But today through his Spirit Jesus yet calms the storms of our lives, heals our despair and loneliness, and quickens his words to our hearts. Through his Spirit Jesus is still to us today strength in weakness, wisdom in darkness, and victory in trouble.

This presence within the depths of our consciousness undergirds our lives with a sense of peace. Jesus gave the word "peace" an inner and personal meaning it did not have before. Such peace flows from sensing that our lives are anchored upon the foundation of the universe, no matter how we may be tossed about by the storms of life. Christians are often at a loss for words to describe to others this spiritual Presence who Jesus said "dwells with you, and will be in you." (v. 17) Truly, this is a peace "which passes all understanding," which keeps our hearts and minds in Christ Jesus. (Phil 4:7)

Thirdly, then, the Spirit connects us with the church of Christ. The Spirit, alive within our hearts, makes us love those in whom he also lives. Jesus said, "If you love me, you will keep my comandments." (v. 15) In John's gospel the commandments of Jesus always refer to loving fellow believers. "This is my commandment, that you love one another as I have loved you."

The Spirit always leads us into the church, into that community of love among those also indwelt by the Spirit. By its very nature love must be shared, and so hearts which know the love of Jesus yearn to share that love. Such is the character of love that Jesus could make this the acid test of his followers. "By this all people will know that you are my disciples, if you have love for one another." (Jn 13:35) There is no solitary Christianity. If the Spirit lives in our hearts, we are moved into community with other Christians. Augustine wrote, "He cannot have God for his father who refuses to have the church for his mother."

This mystical bond between Christians, inspired by the Spirit, we call the "communion of the saints." In the New Testament church Christians graphically lived out their love for one another. In Jerusalem they pooled all their possessions, so that all might have enough. When a famine struck Palestine all the churches throughout

May 16, 1993

the Mediterranean gathered their resources to relieve their hungry brethren. They called the church their "family" (1 Peter 2:17) and their "household of faith." (Gal 6:10) Their fellowship sets for us today the supreme example of that ideal community of love the Spirit of Jesus would make of us, as the Spirit dwells with us and will be in us for ever.

Bruce A. Hedman
Abington Congregational Church
Abington, Connecticut

MAY 20, 1993

Ascension Day

Lessons:

Lutheran:	Acts 1:1-11	Eph. 1:16-23	Luke 24:44-53
Roman Catholic:	Acts 1:1-11	Eph. 1:17-23	Matt. 28:16-20
Episcopal:	Acts 1:1-11	Eph. 1:15-23	Luke 24:49-53
Pres/Meth/UCC:	Acts 1:1-11	Eph. 1:15-23	Luke 24:44-53

Introductions to the Lessons

Lesson 1

Acts 1:1-11 (**Luth/Epis/Pres/Meth/UCC**). Luke opens his second book (Acts) with an account of Jesus' ascension to heaven. He reports that the risen Christ was on earth for 40 days during which he instructed the disciples to remain in Jerusalem and wait for the Holy Spirit who would give them power to witness to him. While they were conferring Jesus ascended in a cloud to his Father in heaven.

Lesson 2

Ephesians 1:16-23 (**Luth**); *Ephesians 1:15-23* (**Epis/Pres/Meth/UCC**). What is the significance of Jesus' ascension? In this pericope Paul explains that God raised Jesus from the dead, took him to heaven where he is seated in authority with his Father. In this position the ascended Christ has all power and authority, and all other powers are subject to him. It is this Christ who is the head of the Church.

Gospel

Luke 24:44-53 (**Luth**); *Luke 24:49-53* (**Epis**); *Luke 24:44-53* (**Pres/Meth/UCC**). Luke closes his gospel with the final scene of the risen Jesus with his disciples. He explained the Scriptures to them to show that his death and resurrection were necessary for the salvation of the world. Because of this, the disciples are to give the good news of forgiveness to all nations. In an act of blessing them, he departs to heaven.

Theme: With the apostles Christ has made us "witnesses of these things."

May 20, 1993

Thought for the day: "Witnesses" do not merely report facts but also persuade others as to the significance of these facts. Although we cannot share the apostles' physical experience of the resurrected and ascended Jesus, we are nevertheless able witnesses to the meaning of what they experienced.

Prayer of meditation: Gracious Father, since our salvation depends upon our having truly understood your holy Word, grant that my heart may be set free from worldly things, that I may receive your Word with diligence and faith. May we all gathered here this morning hear and apprehend your Word, that we may rightly understand and sincerely live according to your gracious will, through Jesus Christ our Lord. Amen.

Call to worship:
Lift up your heads, O gates!
   and be lifted up, O ancient doors!
   that the King of Glory may come in.
Who is this King of glory?
   The Lord of hosts,
   he is the King of glory. (Ps 24:9, 10 RSV)

Prayer of adoration: Almighty God, your blessed Son, our Savior, Jesus Christ, has ascended far above all heavens to the right hand of your throne in glory. There he prays for us continually and rules with you, so that he may fulfill our salvation. Mercifully give us faith to see that he even still abides with his Church on earth, just as he promised, even to the end of the world. Amen.

Prayer of confession: O Lord our God, you have searched us and known us, and are familiar with all our ways. You know our foolishness, and our sins are not hidden from you. But you are gracious, patient, and rich in mercy, forgiving iniquity, transgression, and sin. You have given your own Son to redeem us from our sin. By your mercy absolve us from all our guilt, cleanse us from hidden faults, restore to us the joy of your salvation, and uphold us with your Spirit, through Jesus Christ our Lord. Amen.

Prayer of dedication of gifts and self: O God, you do not need to be enriched by any gifts we may bring, but yet you do love the cheerful giver. Receive these our offerings which we now present before you, and with them receive ourselves, our souls and our bodies, a living sacrifice, through Jesus Christ our Lord. Amen.

The Minister's Annual Manual

Sermon title: You Are Witnesses

Sermon thesis: Whereas we are not eyewitnesses *to* the events of Christ's death and resurrection, like the apostles, we nevertheless are witnesses *for* the meaning of these events, as we experience its power in our lives.

Hymn for the day: *"Lift high the cross"* This hymn by George William Kitchin was revised by Michael Robert Newbolt and first published in the 1916 Supplement to *Hymns Ancient and Modern*. Both Kitchin (1827-1912) and Newbolt (1874-1956) were priests of the Church of England. Kitchin, who in 1990 was made chancellor of Durham University, published works in history, biography, and archaeology. Newbolt was from 1927 to 1946 canon of Chester Cathedral. This hymn of the victorious Christ bids us "Lift high the cross" to proclaim the love of Christ to all the world.

Children's object talk:

Tell People About Jesus

Objects: A photograph of Albert Schweitzer
Lesson: Jesus is counting on us to tell others that he is still present in our world and able to help them.
Outline: 1. When good things happen to us, we want to tell others.
2. Jesus is now ascended into heaven, but his invisible presence is still in our world.
3. He wants us to tell others that he is still present to help them.

I WANT TO TELL you a story about the man in this photograph. His name is Albert Schweitzer. He was a famous medical doctor who decided to spend his life helping poor people in Africa, because they didn't have any doctors. One day at his clinic he helped a blind man to see again. The man went away very, very happy. About a week later, the man came back to the clinic leading a long column of other blind men, each one holding the hand of the next in line ahead of him. The man whom Dr. Schweitzer had cured was so happy that he searched out other blind men, so that they, too, might experience again the joys of sight.

Jesus wants us to be like that. A long time ago Jesus went back up into heaven to be with his Father. But Jesus sends his Spirit to live inside of us to be with us when we are lonely, to comfort us when we are sad, and to teach us to be kinder people. His Spirit

May 20, 1993

will come into all who open their hearts. But the Spirit is invisible, so Jesus depends on us to tell others that the Spirit is here for us.

The sermon:

You Are Witnesses

Hymns:
  Beginning of worship: Crown Him with Many Crowns
  Sermon hymn: I Love to Tell the Story
  End of worship: You Servants of God, Your Master Proclaim

Scripture: Luke 24:45-48

Sermon Text: *Then [Jesus] opened their minds to understand the scriptures, and said to them, "Thus it is written, that the Christ should suffer and on the third day rise from the dead, and that repentance and forgiveness of sins should be preached in his name to all nations, beginning from Jerusalem. You are witnesses of these things."* v. 47

AFTER HE AROSE from the dead, Jesus appeared repeatedly to his disciples for forty days before he ascended into heaven. During those forty days he fulfilled the task he had undertaken three years before, that of teaching his disciples about his mission. For three years Jesus had clearly taught his disciples that he was to be delivered to the Gentiles, mocked, scourged, and killed, and that on the third day he was to rise. "But they understood none of these things." (Luke 18:34) Now Jesus could complete his teaching, because the disciples had seen with their own eyes the fulfillment of what he had taught. For this reason Jesus said to them, "You are witnesses of these things." (v. 48)

This word "witness" was a legal term for one who in a court of law told of what he or she had actually seen. The business of a witness is to tell the truth, the whole truth, and nothing but the truth. But a legal trial does not stop at mere fact-finding, but presses on for a verdict. These witnesses were not merely to report facts but were to persuade others as to the significance of these facts.

Christ's own charge to bear witness before the world of his sacrificial love has devolved from the apostles on to us. Yet, in what sense can we be called "witnesses of these things"? The apostles spoke of what they had heard, seen with their eyes, looked upon, and touched with their hands. (I John 1:1) We are separated from these events by time and space, living two thousand years later and over six thousand miles away. In what sense are we "witnesses of these things," like the apostles?

On a literal level the apostles were eyewitnesses to certain historical events, and this sense of the word "witness" we cannot share with the apostles. The apostles play a unique role in history, as only they can attest that these things actually did happen in real space and time. But their witness is vital, because Christianity is based not on ideas, but on real events. Christianity claims that God himself really entered our world and revealed himself to us in the life, death, and resurrection of Jesus. Facts, not ideas or myths, are at issue.

As witnesses, they were to convince people of what they had actually seen, that Jesus, who had truly died a gruesome death upon the cross, had been raised from the dead to newness of life. Repeatedly their argument took a two-pronged approach, that what the Scriptures had predicted they had seen come to pass. "Thus it was written, that the Christ should suffer and on the third day rise from the dead." (v. 46)

A common prophesy in the Old Testament was that the Messiah was to suffer. It was the cross that all Scripture pointed to. One of the most startling foreshadowings of the crucifixion is the Twenty-Second Psalm, which the New Testament writers quoted eleven times. Likewise, the apostles pointed to prophesies of the Messiah's triumph over death and his eternal life. On the day of Pentecost Peter quoted the Sixteenth Psalm as being fulfilled in Jesus. "For you will not abandon my soul to Hades, nor let your Holy One see corruption." (Acts 2:27)

The apostles were eyewitnesses of Christ's death and resurrection, so as to persuade people that these events really did occur. But on a deeper level the apostles were witnesses to the meaning of these events, so as to persuade people to believe in their eternal significance. Often a witness may be called upon not only to recount what was seen, but also to explain what it meant. Facts to be meaningful must evoke conviction and belief. For the apostles the facts of Christ's death and resurrection meant "that repentance and forgiveness of sins should be preached in his name to all nations." (v. 47)

Our repentance was made possible by Christ's death. "Repentance" literally means "do an 'about-face,' turn around, and start walking the other direction back towards God." But such is itself possible only by the help of God's grace, opening our eyes to see what we are and giving us the courage to change. And such grace can be given to us only through Christ's death. He reconciled us to God, and so we now may be given the grace to change. As Christ died, so can we now die to our old nature, and repent.

Our forgiveness was made possible by Christ's resurrection. "Forgiveness" literally means "to send far away." In forgiveness the sins are taken from the sinner and sent so far away that even God will not find them on Judgment Day. But such forgiveness is possible only through Christ's resurrection. By raising his Son from the dead, God showed that he accepted his Son's sacrifice on our behalf. He justified what his Son had done, and so accepted his Son's life as our righteousness.

The apostles were not just eyewitnesses to these historical events themselves, but were witnesses to their meaning and significance for human life. Therefore, this is the sense in which we also are "witnesses of these things" along with the apostles, if we experience the power of these events in our lives. The Old Testament predicted not only Christ's death and resurrection, but also the universal scope of the church, that "thus it was written" that the gospel should be preached "to all nations." (v. 47)

To bring the gospel to the ends of the earth required more witnesses than the original twelve. Already in the Book of the Acts the term "witness" was broadened to include those who attested to the profound meaning of these events. Paul never saw Jesus during his earthly life, yet he was said to be a witness *for* Jesus rather than *to* him. (Acts 22:15) This is the sense in which we also are "witness to these things," if we also have experienced his forgiveness and know the power of his resurrected presence in our lives.

Bearing witness before the world as to the reality of Christ's living presence above us and within us is the central activity of the church. Christians today carry on this apostolic commission in several ways. First, Christians should take care that solid, gospel preaching comes out of their own local pulpits, and should encourage good preaching. Second, Christians should generously support evangelical missionaries who carry the good news of the gospel to people throughout the world. Third, and most important, Christians are "witnesses to these things" by their own personal lives in that sphere of society in which they live, work, and play.

Bruce A. Hedman
Abington Congregational Church
Abington, Connecticut

MAY 23, 1993

Seventh Sunday of Easter

Lessons:

Lutheran:	Acts 1:(1-7)8-14	I Peter 4:12-17; 5:6-11	John 17:1-11
Roman Catholic:	Acts 1:12-14	I Peter 4:13-16	John 17:1-11a
Episcopal:	Acts 1:(1-7)8-14	I Peter 4.12-19	John 17:1-11
Pres/Meth/UCC:	Acts 1:6-14	I Peter 4:12-14; 5:6-11	John 17:1-11

Introductions to the Lessons

Lesson 1

Acts 1:8-14 (**Luth/Epis**); *Acts 1:6-14* (**Pres/Meth/UCC**). Today's Lesson serves as a bridge between the ascension and pentecost, which comes next Sunday. The risen Lord meets with his disciples for the last time on the Mount of Olives, a short distance from Jerusalem. After promising to send the Holy Spirit, he departs for heaven. The disciples return to Jerusalem. Along with Jesus' mother, brothers, and others, they meet regularly for prayer.

Lesson 2

I Peter 4:12-17; 5:6-11 (**Luth**); *I Peter 4:12-19* (**Epis**); *I Peter 4:12-14; 5:6-11* (**Pres/Meth/UCC**). Don't be surprised if as Christians you suffer for being a Christian. That is par for the course. Rather be glad that you share in the sufferings of Christ. In your suffering, be humble and God will exalt you. Let God carry your burdens. Resist temptations. Know that out of your suffering will come God's strength.

Gospel

John 17:1-11 (**Luth/Epis/Pres/Meth/UCC**). On this Sunday after the Ascension, the disciples are alone and challenged to continue the work of their Master. John 17 is known as the high priestly prayer offered by Jesus on the night before he was arrested. The prayer concludes the lengthy discourse Jesus had with the disciples in the Upper Room. He anticipates his departure and reports to his Father his accomplishments. Also, he prays for the followers he will leave behind that they may be preserved in God's name and made one with each other as he and the Father are one.

Theme: We have confidence, not in ourselves, but in God's glory.

Thought for the day: At some time all of us have thought that we come to God by being good people. But if this were true, we never could know any assurance or joy in God, because our behavior is so changeable. In contrast, the Christian gospel proclaims what God has already done for us.

Prayer of meditation: O Lord, give us humble, teachable, and obedient hearts, that we may receive what you have revealed and do what you command. As we do not live by bread alone, but by every word of God, grant that we may always hunger after this heavenly food, and find in it our daily provision on the way to eternal life, through Jesus Christ our Lord. Amen.

Call to worship: In the beginning was the Word, and the Word was with God, and the Word was God. He was in the beginning with God; all things were made through him, and without him was not anything made that was made. In him was life, and the life was the light of all. (John 1:1-4 RSV)

Prayer of adoration: O blessed Trinity, in you we know the Maker of all things visible and invisible, and the Savior of the world. By your Spirit so enable us now to worship you, that with all the company of heaven we may praise your glorious name, saying, "Holy, holy, holy is the Lord of hosts! The whole earth is full of his glory!" Amen.

Prayer of confession: Holy Father, we cannot justify ourselves before you, nor can we profess our innocence, We confess the evil of our ways, without concealment and without excuse. In the light of the sacrifice of your Son upon the cross, we see the hatefulness of our sins. But in that light we also see your great and wonderful mercy. Have mercy upon us, O God, according to your loving kindness. According to the multitude of your tender mercies blot out our transgressions, and grant us peace, through Jesus Christ our Lord. Amen.

Prayer of dedication of gifts and self: Almighty God, your loving hand has given us all that we possess. Grant us grace that we may honor you with our substance. As we remember the account which we must one day give, may we be faithful stewards of your bounty, through Jesus Christ our Lord. Amen.

Sermon title: Glorify Thy Son

May 23, 1993

Sermon thesis: Knowing our salvation is the result of love within the Persons of God gives us a confidence and joy that works righteousness can never know. Our salvation results from the Father and Son glorifying each other in the creation, in the cross, and in the consummation.

Hymn for the day: *"Thine is the glory"* Originally written in French, this hymn was the work of Edmond Budry (1854-1932), who for thirty-five years was a pastor of the Greek Church in Vevey, Switzerland. He translated a number of German, English, and Latin hymns to French. The hymn ascribes glory to the risen Savior.

Announcements for next week:
Sermon title: The Peace Christ Gives
Sermon theme: Jesus gives us a peace that we can experience nowhere else.
Sermon summary: Peace was a distinctive feature of Christ's ministry, unlike any peace people had ever experienced before. Through his Spirit Jesus brought this revolutionary peace into three relationships: peace with God, peace among people, and peace within ourselves.

Children's object talk:
Like Father, Like Son

Objects: Photographs of my father and myself
Lesson: We know what God is like, because we see his Son in Jesus.
Outline: 1. We cannot see God himself. So some people have thought that God was angry and mean.
2. But Jesus is God's Son. To know what God is like look at Jesus.
3. Jesus is kind, gentle, and patient with us.

NO ONE HAS EVER been able to see God. God is too big for anyone just to look at. God is a Spirit, and a spirit is simply invisible. Because they couldn't see God, some people thought that God didn't want to have anything to do with them. They thought that God was angry at them, or just simply mean. So some people live their lives as if God wasn't there.

But God wanted to show himself to us, and make us understand what he is like. To do that God sent his Son into our world, so that if we knew what the Son was like, we knew what God was like.

Here is a photograph of my father when he was about my age now. Do you see the resemblance? We have the same color hair and eyes. Our noses look similar, and we are both fat. We also talk alike, and have many of the same mannerisms.

"Like Father, like Son." God sent his Son Jesus, so that we would know what God is like through the character of Jesus. Jesus is kind, gentle, and forgiving. He isn't mad at us when we do wrong, but patiently waits for us to be sorry and do better. And he is always with us, so that we won't be alone.

The sermon:

Glorify Your Son

Hymns:
Beginning of worship: All Creatures of Our God and King

Sermon Hymn: Thine Is the Glory

End of worship: Revive Us Again!

Scripture: John 17:1-5

Sermon Text: *When Jesus had spoken these words, he lifted up his eyes to heaven and said, "Father, the hour has come; glorify your Son that the Son may glorify you, since you have given him power over all flesh, to give eternal life to all whom you have given him. And this is eternal life, that they know you the only true God, and Jesus Christ whom you have sent. I glorified you on earth, having accomplished the work which you gave me to do; and now, Father, glorify me in your own presence with the glory which I had with you before the world was made."* vs. 2-5

AT SOME TIME all of us have thought that we come to God by being good people. Instinctively we think of religion as something we do, such as leading moral and charitable lives, or showing pleasant personalities, or coming to church. But if our relationship with God depends upon what we do, we never can know any assurance or joy in God, because our behavior is so changeable. The guilt of our pasts and the uncertainty of our futures haunt our consciences.

In contrast, the Christian gospel proclaims, not what we must do to come to God, but what God has already done for us. Gratitude is a far better motivator than fear. The gospel proclaims the marvelous salvation God has already provided for us in Christ, so that out of gratitude we will love God in return and seek to serve him.

During his final night on earth, after his Last Supper with his disciples there in the Upper Room, Jesus "lifted up his eyes to heaven" (v. 1) and offered up his life to his Father, as on the next day he would be sacrificed upon the cross. Jesus prayed aloud, so that his disciples might hear how they were caught up in the glory the Father and the Son offered each other. To show his disciples that their salvation does not rest on flimsy human efforts, but on the unchangeable love between the Father and the Son, Jesus lays out for them the entire panorama of the history of salvation, as God showed forth his own glory from the creation, in the cross, and until the consummation.

First, in creation the Father glorified the Son by giving him the human race. To glorify God means to demonstrate his love. The Father glorified the Son in creation by so designing the human race that the Son might become human to redeem us in love. After his Last Supper with his disciples in the Upper Room, Jesus prayed aloud to his Father, "You have given [me] power over all flesh, to give eternal life to all whom you have given [me]." (v. 2)

Before the world was created, even before time began, God dwelt alone, and yet sufficient in himself. As God is love, and as love must be shared, we believe that within God are Persons, the Father, the Son, and the Holy Spirit, who share among themselves an eternal, divine love. This shared love is the bright glory of God's nature, extending back into eternity before the cosmos began. Jesus prayed aloud, "Father, glorify me in your own presence with the glory which I had with you before the world was made." (v. 5)

God created humankind in order to demonstrate his love. True love, God's love, is self-sacrificing, and will humble itself for the sake of the beloved. The Father so designed us that his Son might make himself small and become one of us, in order to lift us up to the throne of God. The Father glorified the Son by giving him this opportunity to exhibit his love, a love which stoops to conquer, a love whose power flows from his willingness to become weak for our sakes.

Second, upon the cross the Son glorified the Father by redeeming the human race. To glorify God means to demonstrate his love. On the cross Jesus showed us that the Father "so loved the world that he gave his only Son." (John 3:16) Without Christ we never would have known that we were reconciled with God. After his Last Supper with his disciples in the Upper Room, Jesus prayed aloud to his Father, saying, "I glorified you on earth, having accomplished the work you gave me to do." (v. 4)

The work the Father had given the Son was the cross. There the Son glorified the Father by bringing people to know him. We cannot come to know God simply in any way we choose, but only through the means God himself has chosen, through the cross of his own Son. Only Christ's cross shows us the sacrificial character of God's love, his willingness to give up himself for the sake of his beloved. Jesus prayed "that they may know you the only true God, and Jesus Christ whom you have sent." (v. 3)

To know God in this way is eternal life. Jesus does not bring us merely to know about God, but to know him personally. The Old Testament spoke of "knowing" someone as a euphemism for sexual intimacy. The knowledge of God Jesus brings is like the most intimate and personal relationship with our nearest and dearest in life, whose presence we enjoy and whom we are sorry to displease. Jesus prayed to his Father, "And this is eternal life, that they may know you."

Third, in the consummation at the end of history the Father will glorify the Son by resurrecting his church into their presence forever. After his Last Supper with his disciples in the Upper Room Jesus prayed aloud to his Father, saying, "Glorify your Son ... glorify me in your own presence." (v. 1, 5) This prayer the Father answered by raising Jesus from the dead. As the Son showed the world the Father's love by his crucifixion, so the Father glorified the Son in his resurrection.

Christ has been raised from the dead as the "first fruits" of those who belong to him. (I Cor. 15:23) All who in this life are united to Christ by faith will in the next be joined with him in his resurrection. What happened to him will happen to us. In the consummation of history at the end of this present age the Father will glorify his Son by demonstrating through us how great is his Son's love for us, that he endured the cross, despising its shame, for the joy that was set before him, to bring us before his Father's throne in glory. We will be raised up to exhibit the Son's self-sacrificing love

May 23, 1993

May 23, 1993

and so to glorify God, giving thanks for his amazing grace throughout eternity.

On the eve of his suffering Jesus prayed aloud to his Father, so as to lay before his disciples the great panorama of the history of salvation, from the creation to the cross until the consummation. He caught them up into his prayer to his Father, just as they were caught up in God's cosmic plan to exhibit his eternal love through them. This is the great vision of what God has done for us in creation and in the cross which Jesus would have so to grip our souls that we rejoice with a confidence based on him, not ourselves. As the recipients of his love and as channels of his glory, we, too, pray with Jesus to his Father, "Glorify your Son that the Son may glorify you." (v. 1)

Bruce A. Hedman
Abington Congregational Church
Abington, Connecticut

MAY 30, 1993

The Day of Pentecost

Lessons:

Lutheran:	Joel 2:28-29	Acts 2:1-21	John 20:19-23
Roman Catholic:	Acts 2:1-11	I Cor. 12:3b-7, 12-13	John 20:19-23
Episcopal:	Acts 2:1-11	I Cor. 12:4-13	John 20:19-23
Pres/Meth/UCC:	Acts 2:1-21	I Cor. 12:3b-13	John 20:19-23

Introductions to the Lessons

Lesson 1

Joel 2:28-29 (**Luth**). At a time of a devastating drought in Palestine, Joel calls upon the nation to repent. As a result of the people's repentance, the nation was blessed. God promises to pour out his Spirit on all people. The church believes that this promise was fulfilled on Pentecost.

(2) *Acts 2:1-11* (**Epis**); *Acts 2:1-21* (**Pres/Meth/UCC**). On Pentecost, 50 days after Easter, the disciples were gathered in Jerusalem as ordered by Jesus. Accompanied by a strong wind and fire, the Holy Spirit suddenly came upon them. As a result the disciples preached the Gospel in the native tongues of people present from various countries to the amazement of the people who heard them.

Lesson 2

(1) *Acts 2:1-21* (**Luth**). See above: Acts 2:1-11.

(2) *I Corinthians 12:4-13* (**Epis**); *I Cor. 12:3b-13* (**Pres/Meth/UCC**). As many church members today ask about the Holy Spirit, the people in the Corinthian church wrote to Paul for an explanation of the gifts of the Holy Spirit. The Spirit, Paul taught, gives a variety of nine gifts. There is only one Spirit who gives various gifts for a particular service. A different gift is given to each believer for the good of all.

Gospel

John 20:19-23 (**Luth/Epis/Pres/Meth/UCC**). According to John, the disciples received the Holy Spirit from the risen Lord who came to them on Easter Day. With the gift of the Holy Spirit came the authority to forgive or retain sins.

May 30, 1993

Theme: Jesus gives us a peace we can experience nowhere else.

Thought for the day: Through his Holy Spirit Christ gives us a deep sense of peace through his very presence in our hearts. This is a supernatural reality, when the Holy Spirit brings us into a living, dynamic union with our resurrected Lord.

Prayer of meditation: O Lord, as your holy Word is about to be opened before us, we ask you to open us to its sacred truths. Enable us to receive it as the true Word of God. O Holy Spirit, be our teacher, enlighten our minds, and prepare our hearts. Bring home some portion to our souls, through Jesus Christ our Lord. Amen.

Call to worship:
"Blessed be the name of the Lord from this
　　time forth and for evermore!
From the rising of the sun to its setting
　　the name of the Lord is to be praised!"

(Psalm 113:2, 3 RSV)

Prayer of adoration: Almighty God, send your Holy Spirit into our hearts, that we may be led according to your will and comforted in all trials and temptations. By your Holy Spirit keep us from all error, and teach us all truth. Breathe upon us fresh winds of your Spirit that we may be steadfast in faith, full of love and good works, and in the end obtain everlasting life, through Jesus Christ, your Son, our Lord. Amen.

Prayer of confession: We do not forget, O most holy God, that in your sight we are sinners. We have never perfectly loved you, nor tried completely to do your will. There is no commandment of your Word which we have not broken in thought, word, or deed. The drift of earthly concerns has come between our souls and you. We have walked in shadows, and have not believed the love which you have toward us. But merciful Father, in your infinite love you gave your own Son to take away our sin. Hear our confession, cleanse us from our guilt, and so renew us by your Holy Spirit, that from now on we may live more consciously for you, through Jesus Christ our Lord. Amen.

The Minister's Annual Manual

Prayer of dedication of gifts and self: Our Father, we count it a privilege to be allowed to share in the task of bringing others to know and love you. We are most glad to bring our offering, and we pray that your blessing will be upon it. May it be used wisely, so that human hearts may be set free from sin and your will may be done on earth as it is in heaven, through Jesus Christ our Lord. Amen.

Sermon title: The Peace Christ Gives

Sermon thesis: Peace was a distinctive feature of Christ's ministry, unlike any peace people had ever experienced before. Through his Spirit Jesus brought this revolutionary peace into three relationships: peace with God, peace among people, and peace within ourselves.

Hymn for the day: *"Peace, to soothe our bitter woes"* This hymn of Christ's peace was written by Nikolai Grundtvig (1783-1872), the greatest Danish hymnwriter of the 19th century. Grundtvig served as a Lutheran pastor and was also active in the educational and political life of Denmark.

Announcements for next week:
  Sermon title: Faith's Eternal Story
  Sermon theme: A story to tell!
  Sermon summary: The doctrine of the Trinity needs to be seen not as stale doctrine but as an encapsulation of the exciting story of God's saving activity.

Children's object talk:

Peace With God

Objects: A large drawing of a "peace symbol"
Lesson: Real peace between people flows from peace with God.
Outline: 1. People usually think of peace as just not fighting with others.
2. But real peace comes from knowing God. This is the peace that Jesus gives us.
3. Only this peace with God can bring peace between different people.

WHEN I WAS IN COLLEGE back in the sixties, many students wore this kind of symbol on their clothing or on necklaces. It meant that if everyone would just stop fighting, then there would be peace in the world. Many wanted to stop the Vietnam war. They didn't believe we needed armies or police, if everyone would love everybody else.

But most of those students have become grown-ups now, and have learned that the world just is not that simple. The Vietnam war is over, but we still need armies, because dictators keep cropping up. We need police more than ever, because people just cannot get along.

Real peace between people is not possible until they know peace with God. This is the new kind of peace Jesus brought into our world. When Jesus sends his Holy Spirit to live in our hearts, we experience a peace with God that makes us feel how much God loves us. Only this can bring peace between people. When we remember how much God loves them as well as us, we can find the strength to be kinder and more understanding.

The sermon:
The Peace Christ Gives

Hymns:
Beginning of worship: Rejoice, the Lord Is King
Sermon hymn: Dear Lord and Father of Mankind
End of worship: Jesus, Lover of My Soul

Scripture: John 20:19 RSV

Sermon Text: *On the evening of that day, the first day of the week, the doors being shut where the disciples were, for fear of the Jews, Jesus came and stood among them and said to them, "Peace be with you."*

IT WAS SUNDAY EVENING, and for the first time since Thursday night, when their Master had been arrested, the disciples again gathered together. They probably reassembled in the Upper Room where they had shared the Last Supper with their Lord. They gathered in secret, behind locked doors, fearing that the authorities sought to purge them along with their Master. Yet they had to assemble to share with one another the rumors that their crucified Lord had presented himself alive, to Mary, Joanna, Peter, and Cleopas. As they thus reassembled around the good news of Christ's resurrection, "Jesus came and stood among them and said to them, 'Peace be with you.'"

The Minister's Annual Manual

Here for the first time was the Christian church gathered around the good news of the gospel. Here was the resurrected Christ's first appearance to his assembled church. And here were his first words to his church, "Peace be with you." On such a momentous occasion these words were no longer an ordinary salutation, a wishful pleasantry. Whenever the church is gripped by the good news of the gospel, our resurrected and living Lord gives her a peace which passes all understanding, a peace which transforms human life.

Peace is a distinctive feature of Christ's ministry. The New Testament writers gave the word "peace" explicitly Christian connotations, using it to describe a sense of Christ's presence within us and above us. Today we will reflect on the peace Christ gives in three relationships; first, with God; second, with others; and third, within ourselves.

First, Christ gives us peace with God. On the cross Jesus took upon himself the punishment for the sins of the world, and thus made atonement for us. No longer does God look upon us in our state of sin and rebellion, but God looks upon us in Christ, and imputes to us Christ's righteousness.

Not only did Jesus bring us into objective reconciliation with God, but he also brought us into subjective, conscious fellowship with God. Not only did Jesus bring us into peace *with* God, he brought to us the peace *of* God. In his death on the cross Christ made atonement for our sins, and in his ascension into heaven he lifted sanctified human nature up into the very life of God. As we are united to Christ by faith, then through Jesus, who now is seated at the right hand of the Father, we share in the divine love between the Father and the Son in the very depths of the Godhead.

The second relationship to which Jesus brings his peace is between ourselves. Human history is a record of violence, war, cruelty, and injustice. Peace between humans is impossible, unless their hostile and selfish natures are changed from beyond themselves.

Henry Cabot Lodge, one of our most popular ambassadors to the United Nations, well understood this need, when he proposed that the doors of the U.N. be inscribed with this plea from a prayer of St. Francis of Assisi, "O God, make me an instrument of thy peace." Lodge's proposal, though, was rejected.

True peace can be found between people only as their old natures are changed, only as they are given a new heart through the work

May 30, 1993

of the Holy Spirit in their lives. As Jesus lifts us up into the presence of the Father, we are thereby drawn closer together. The early church experienced such a sense of love and peace between believers that they coined a new world to describe this unity they felt among Christians, "koinonia," which we translate "fellowship." This unity among Christians, this "one-ness" in Christ I believe is the meaning of the phrase "communion of saints" which we confess in the Apostles' Creed.

The third sphere into which Jesus brings a heretofore unimaginable peace is within ourselves. The Greek world had little concept of inner peace, peace within one's soul. Their closest approximation was the Stoic ideal of "calm," a state of mind so bleached of desire that neither pleasure nor sorrow would perturb it. But, for this stoic mind peace was only negative, only the absence of desire, a disconcern for pain or pleasure. But the peace Christ gives is positive, a presence inseparable from faith and joy.

The positive peace Christ gives us comes from his very presence in our hearts. This is a supernatural reality. Jesus promised his followers, "Those who love me will keep my word, and my Father will love them, and we will come and make our home with him." The objective peace with God which Christ earned for us on the cross leads to a subjective, conscious peace of God. The Holy Spirit applies Jesus' redemption personally to our hearts, and we enter into a living, dynamic union with the resurrected Christ.

Since such peace comes from Jesus, and him alone, nothing else can take it from us. Because the peace Jesus gives comes from his presence above and beyond this world, his peace in our hearts does not depend upon the outward circumstances in which we might find ourselves. The peace Christ gives the world neither understands, nor gives, nor can take away.

On the evening of that first Easter, as the disciples were assembled as the church for the first time around the good news of the gospel, Jesus continued their charge, saying, "Peace be with you. As the Father has sent me so I send you." The peace Christ gives never leads to mere quietism, a passive contemplation of the divine, but lays upon each believer the charge of the great commission, to spread the news of this great peace with God, peace with others, and peace within ourselves.

The Minister's Annual Manual

If you know the peace Christ gives, then, for the very love of God, there is laid upon you Christ's own commission to spread his peace and the knowledge of his presence throughout that sphere of society in which you live, work, and play, among family, co-workers, and friends. Christ's gracious invitation, "Come unto me, and I will give you rest," leads not to leisure, but to a positive peace by which we are impelled to the great commission, "Go therefore, and make disciples."

Bruce A. Hedman
Abington Congregational Church
Abington, Connecticut

JUNE 6, 1993

Trinity Sunday

Lessons:

Lutheran:	Gen. 1:1-2:3	2 Cor. 13:11-14	Matt. 28:16-20
Roman Catholic:	Ex. 34:4b-6, 8-9	2 Cor. 13:11-13	John 3:16-18
Episcopal:	Gen. 1:1-2:3	2 Cor. 13:(5-10) 11-14	Matt. 28:16-20
Pres/Meth/UCC:	Gen. 1:1-2:4a	2 Cor. 13:11-13	Matt. 28:16-20

Introductions to the Lessons

Lesson 1

Genesis 1:1-2:3 (**Luth/Epis**); *Gen. 1:1-2; 4a* (**Pres/Meth/UCC**). The work of God the Father was the creation of the universe out of nothing. He was pleased with all he created. The final creation was humanity. To man (male and female) he gave the task of controlling and caring for the rest of creation. By the seventh day all was finished and God rested.

Lesson 2

2 Corinthians 13:11-14 (**Luth/Epis**); *2 Cor. 13:11-13* (**Pres/Meth/UCC**). On this Trinity Sunday, Paul closes his second letter to the church in Corinth, Greece with a benediction that involves the blessing of the triune God upon this troubled church. He pronounces the blessing of the grace of God the Son, the love of God the Father, and the presence of God the Holy Spirit.

Gospel

Matthew 28:16-20 (**Luth/Epis/Pres/Meth/UCC**). Here are the last words Jesus spoke on earth. Jesus met with his disciples for the last time in Galilee. Before ascending to his Father, he gave them a mandate to make disciples of all peoples and to baptize them in the name of the Trinity: Father, Son, and Holy Spirit. As they go about their task, he assures them of his constant companionship.

Theme: A story to tell!

Thought for the day: The Christian faith is expressed in what seems to be a formal, difficult doctrine. But that doctrine, the Holy Trinity, is really a condensed version of the great drama of divine creation and redemption.

The Minister's Annual Manual

Prayer of meditation: Eternal and holy God, call us into a new consciousness of the mystery of your love. Make us more aware of how you love us as creator Lord, redeeming Son, and powerful Spirit. Let us not be satisfied with a shallow understanding or appreciation of your amazing ways but invite us to encounter the wonder of faith expressed in the Holy Trinity. Amen.

Call to worship: Come, let us bow before the Holy God of heaven and earth; let us praise God's name and sing to God's glory as one God in three persons, Holy Father, Holy Son, and Holy Spirit.

Prayer of adoration: Holy, Holy, Holy, Lord God we praise your name! You are holy in your creative power and love, fashioning a marvelous creation filled with beauty and endowed with life. O Holy God, your holiness is even more fully revealed in the gift of Jesus Christ. On the cross, we have seen the depths of your awesome purity and endless love. O God, Holy Spirit, in the movement of your Spirit among us you seek to make us holy, giving us gifts of grace and calling forth goodness from within. Holy, Holy, Holy, God, Father, Son and Spirit, we praise and adore you today and always. Amen.

Prayer of confession: Holy God, Creator of the heavens and earth, forgive our foolish ways with your creation. We waste and spoil the beauties of the earth you have given us. We misuse our own bodies and minds. Holy God, Redeemer of the world, forgive us for taking our redemption for granted. Remind us of the cost of our salvation, bought with your blood on the cross. Holy God, Spirit of power, forgive us for failing to trust in the power of your Spirit to work among us and in your world. Awaken us to your promptings in our lives and open us to your guiding will. Amen.

Prayer of dedication of gifts and self: Father, Son, and Holy Spirit, we bring before you today these gifts, humble offerings of our talents and time and treasure. They are signs of your creation, tokens of your saving grace in our lives, and responses to the movement of your Spirit within us. Accept them, we pray, and us with them, for we offer you ourselves as well. Amen.

Sermon title: Faith's Eternal Story

June 6, 1993

Sermon thesis: The doctrine of the Trinity needs to be seen not as stale doctrine but as an encapsulation of the exciting story of God's saving activity.

Hymn for the day: *"We all believe in one true God"* In its three stanzas this paraphrase of the creed speaks of each of the persons of the Trinity. Some hymnals contain a translation of the text by Luther; others use a later text by Tobias Clausnitzer. Luther based his hymn on the first two lines of a medieval hymn, expanding it to three stanzas, paraphrasing the three articles of the creed. The hymn very soon became a universally accepted substitute for the Latin Credo in the Lutheran liturgy. Clausnitzer (1619-1684) served as chaplain to the Swedish regiment at Leipzig and as such preached a sermon at St. Thomas' Church, Leipzig (later of J.S. Bach fame) on the accession of Queen Christina to the Swedish throne. Martin Luther (1483-1546) was born in Eisleben, Germany, and ordained a priest in 1507. While on the faculty at Wittenberg University he became aware of some of the corruptions in the church of his time. From there the story of the Reformation is well-known. A musician himself, Luther encouraged congregational hymn singing and wrote a number of fine hymns.

Announcements for next week:
Sermon title: Faith and Obedience
Sermon theme: The nature of faith.
Sermon summary: Faith and obedience are intimately and intrinsically linked. Our tendency is to psychologize or intellectualize faith, abandoning the action dimension of trust. There is no escaping Jesus' insistence that faith and obedience are two sides of the same coin. In discovering this, however, we also discover the deeper joy of true faith.

Children's object talk:
The Stories of God
Objects: A story book
Lesson: To show how the story of Jesus is the greatest of all stories.
Outline: 1. Read a story.
2. Tell about the stories of God.
3. Describe the greatest story of all.

BRING A STORY BOOK of a popular children's story. Begin reading a portion of the story. Read enough so that everyone is aware of this familiar tale. Then talk about how everyone loves a story. Tell the children how there are many wonderful stories of God, but there are three that are the best. These are the best because they are true and they never end! The story of how God created the whole world and everyone of us. The story of how God, saddened by our sin, sent Jesus to love us and save us from our sin. The story of how God sends God's Spirit so that we are never without God even though we can't see God. Those are the three great stories of God. Tell them this story has a name: The Trinity. Today we are here in worship to share that story. Thank them for coming to listen to the story and invite them to get to know the story well enough so they can tell it to others. It is the greatest story of all.

The sermon:
Faith's Eternal Story
Hymns:
Beginning of worship: Holy, Holy, Holy, Lord God Almighty.
Sermon hymn: Father most holy, merciful and tender
End of worship: I Love to Tell the Story

Scripture: Matthew 28:16-20

Sermon Text: *"Go therefore and make disciples of all nations, baptizing them in the name of the Father and of the Son and of the Holy Spirit, teaching them to observe all that I have commanded you, and lo, I am with you always, to the close of the age."*

MY FATHER WAS A GREAT STORY TELLER. He would come into my room to tuck me in bed and often would tell a story. I usually fell asleep before the story was finished but that didn't matter. It was still fun to hear the story. For some reason, all his stories began, "It was a dark and stormy night...."

What has happened to our ability to tell stories? Have we lost it? Some would say "yes." It may be that television, which absorbs us so, has robbed us of our ability to tell stories. We are good at watching them, but perhaps not so good at making them up or telling them.

I think the church has played its part in the loss of storytelling too. This place, which should be and can be so full of stories, is too often story-less. Rather than the great stories of faith, we in the church have too often fallen into the habit of turning everything into doctrine. In place of stories, we have formulas.

Take the doctrine of the Trinity as an example. We stand on most Sundays and confess our faith in "Father, Son, and Holy Ghost,"

June 6, 1993

or in "Creator, Redeemer, and Sustainer," or some similar formula of faith. We say we believe in one God in three persons or, more technically, "persona." Meanwhile, most of us, while knowing this doctrinal formula, are perplexed as to what it means.

The story is told of the great Cardinal Cushing of Boston who was once called to the side of a man who had collapsed on the floor in a department store. The Cardinal, then a parish priest, asked the man whom he thought was dying whether he believed in God the Father, God the Son, and God the Holy Spirit. The man opened one eye and said to those standing around, "Here I am dying, and he's asking me riddles."

This great doctrine of the Trinity is, however, not really a riddle. It isn't so perplexing as it sounds. That is especially true when we push past the doctrine to the great stories, true stories behind it. For the Trinity is really a short-hand title for the stories of faith. These are accounts, for the most part in the Bible, of who God is and what God does. It's interesting that while we won't find a pure and complete expression of the actual Trinitarian doctrine in the Bible, although there are references to it, we do find the faith-stories which inform the doctrine. This morning I invite you to recover some of those stories. Let's get behind the doctrine to the mystery, magic, and excitement of the story of God that informs the doctrine.

There is, for example, the story behind the first article of our Creed, "I believe in God, the Father almighty, creator of heaven and earth." That story is the powerful story of creation. All of Genesis is captured in this one brief phrase from the Apostles' Creed. Recite this part of the Creed, and suddenly before us is that marvelous story which says, "In the beginning when God created the heavens and the earth...." We can see the universe-making events spelled out one by one until we get to the seventh day when even the almighty must rest. We can smell the fresh garden in that Genesis 2 creation account. There before us are Adam and Eve, those representatives of all humanity.

What grandeur! What sweeping and magnificent events! What power and beauty we can behold and what an awesome God! The Trinity reminds us of these stories of the creation and the Creator. This is not dull doctrine. It is the very stuff of life!

The same stuff of life we have captured in the hundreds of stories of Jesus which begin with the gift of life, we are told, by the mysterious power of the Spirit to the Virgin Mary. Christmas, a manger, Joseph, angels, a star-filled night. Those are some of the dimensions of the Jesus story which began to pop into focus as we confess our faith not only in God the Father but in Jesus Christ, the second person of the Trinity. But the stories don't stop with Christmas. We move on to Jesus at age twelve in the temple, to his Baptism in the Jordan, to Christ's temptations, to his parables and teachings in Galilee, to the miracles of healing and compassion. Then, we walk with Jesus toward Jerusalem, entering triumphantly with him in a parade of palms, only to be led to a cross on a lonely hill. The story which begins at Christmas doesn't end with a cross, thank God. It includes also that wondrous account of an empty tomb and a Resurrection promise.

Can you begin to see how there is so much more to this Trinity "thing" than mere doctrine? Do you begin to catch something of the power and excitement of the faith-story which is behind it?

Speaking of excitement, that is the word for the Holy Spirit. There is the excitement of fire on Pentecost. There is the excitement of thousands who come to faith and the spread of the early church like a wild-fire across the Mediterranean world. There is the excitement of people of faith like Peter and Paul, Lydia and Lois. Wherever the Spirit is present, there is a living faith born and people with fire in their eyes, the fire of love and hope and joy.

Today we celebrate the Triune God. We share in confessing our faith in the Holy Trinity. You can see this is more than doctrinal formulations from ancient times. The Trinity captures in a few words much of the amazing story of God's mighty acts through the Bible in our lives today. The Trinity is a short way of telling the Good News of what God has done and continues to do to create, to save, and to guide.

The Church of Jesus Christ will never forget this doctrine called the Trinity. Even more, we will never forget the great and gracious God to whom it witnesses.

Gary Anderson
All Saints Lutheran Church
Minnetonka, Minnesota

JUNE 13, 1993

Lutheran: Second Sunday after Pentecost
Roman Catholic: Ninth Sunday of the Year
Episcopalian: Proper 4
Pres/Meth/UCC: Proper 4

Lessons:

Lutheran:	Deut. 11:18-21, 26-28	Rom. 3:21-25a	Matt. 7:(15-20) 21-29
Roman Catholic:	Deut. 11:18, 26-28	Rom. 3:21-25a, 28	Matt. 7:21-27
Episcopal:	Deut. 11:18-21	Rom. 3:21-25a, 28	Matt. 7:21-27
Pres/Meth/UCC:	Gen. 6:9-22	Rom. 1:16-17; 3:22b-28 (29-31)	Matt. 7:21-29

Introductions to the Lessons

Lesson 1

(1) *Deuteronomy 11:18-21, 26-28* (**Luth/Epis**). Because Moses in his righteous anger over the idolatry of the Israelites broke the two tablets of stone containing the Ten Commandments, God calls him back for another 40 days on Mt. Sinai to get another copy. As the Israelites are poised to enter the Promised Land, Moses urges his people to obey God's law. Not to obey brings a curse; to obey brings a blessing.

(2) *Genesis 6:9-22* (**Pres/Meth/UCC**). Today we begin a series of readings from the book of Genesis. We will learn about the great patriarchs beginning with Noah and continuing with Abraham, Isaac, Jacob, and Joseph. In this Lesson we learn of the only man God considered worthy of saving from a corrupt world, for he, without a fault, had a close relationship with God. In obedience to God, he built an ark in which humanity and the rest of creation were saved from the flood.

Lesson 2

Romans 3:21-25a (**Luth**); *Rom. 3:21-25a, 28* (**Epis**); *Rom. 1:16-17; 3:22b-28* (**Pres/Meth/UCC**). For the next 16 weeks we will be hearing from the book of Romans. It is St. Paul's most complete statement of the Gospel. In this Lesson Paul affirms the fact that all people are sinners. Christ came to put us right with God through his death and resurrection. We are made right with God by our faith in Christ's work on our behalf. Thus, we have no reason to boast in ourselves.

Gospel

Matthew 7:21-29 (**Luth/Pres/Meth/UCC**); *Matthew 7:21-27* (**Epis**). This passage constitutes the conclusion of the Sermon on the Mount. You have heard the teachings. What will you do about them? Jesus did not give the teachings primarily to entertain nor educate. He expects them to be put into practice. To obey them is like building your life on a rock; to disobey is to build on sand.

Theme: The nature of faith.

Thought for the day: How easy it is to say we believe, but how difficult it is to act on that faith. Everyone of us risks being a person who believes with our mind but fails to believe with our actions. Today we are invited to consider the linkages between belief and action. Jesus calls for both.

Prayer of meditation: God be in my head. God be in my heart. God be in my understanding. We pray that prayer today, dear God, as we seek to grow in faith. We also ask that you will be in our actions. So, to our prayer, O God, that you will be in my head, my heart, and my understanding, we add one more petition, "O God, be in my actions." Amen.

Call to worship: People of faith, we are called by the God we trust through faith to come to worship. Through faith we hear this call. Through faith we respond. Through faith we receive again the good news of forgiveness and life in Christ. Through faith we will leave to love and serve. O come, let us worship the Lord in faith, hope, and love.

Prayer of adoration: God of kindness and truth, we thank you that in Jesus Christ we have found our refuge and our righteousness. We thank you that you are always ready to lead us and guide us and deliver us by your strength. Help us to mirror that strength to others that they may see in our spirits a glimpse of your great love. Amen. (David C. Nelson)

Prayer of confession: Loving God, we confess that we have fallen short of your glory. We have yielded to the temptation to center our lives around those things which are hear today and gone tomorrow. We have grieved your heart by our busy building of castles of sand instead of grounding all that we have and are in the person of Jesus Christ. So our failings and fallings lead us to you who have promised ever and always to set us high upon the rock of redemp-

June 13, 1993
(Epis/Pres/Meth/UCC - Proper 4)

tion. Make us wise builders as your Holy Spirit leads us in our forgiveness. Amen. (David C. Nelson)

Prayer of dedication of gifts and self: O Lord our God, you have blessed us with gifts innumerable and we are so very grateful. We offer in return ourselves, our time and our possessions, signs of our thankfulness for your gracious love. Receive them for the sake of the one who offered everything for us, Jesus Christ our Lord. Amen. (Adapted from the *Lutheran Book of Worship*.)

Sermon title: Faith and Obedience

Sermon thesis: Faith and obedience are intimately and intrinsically linked. Our tendency is to psychologize or intellectualize faith, abandoning the action dimension of trust. There is no escaping Jesus' insistence that faith and obedience are two sides of the same coin. In discovering this, however, we also discover the deeper joy of true faith.

Hymn for the day: *"If God himself be for me"* This fine hymn of faith by Paul Gerhardt is founded on Romans 8 and has been described as worthy of a place alongside "A mighty fortress." Gerhardt (1607-1676) ranks with Martin Luther as a writer of German hymns. Ordained a Lutheran pastor, he served in churches in and near Berlin until 1666, when his refusal to sign a statement that he would not preach on doctrinal differences with the followers of Calvin resulted in his removal from the post. His last ten years were spent at Lübben on the Spree ministering to a rough and unsympathizing congregation.

Announcements for next week:
Sermon title: The Hospital of God
Sermon theme: The church as a healing place.
Sermon summary: The church is a place of acceptance not of perfection.

Children's object talk:
Believe in Jesus

Object: A small bicycle
Lesson: To try one's faith and put it to work.
Outline: 1. Here is a bicycle.
         2. Adam can't ride until he tries.
         3. Put your faith to work.

SHOW THE BICYCLE to the children and then tell a story about Adam who wanted to ride a bike. Tell how Adam went to the library and got books on bicycle riding. He watched other children ride bikes. He went to the bike store and looked at bikes. Finally, he asked his parents to give him a bike. Being kind and able to do so, they bought him a shiny new red bicycle. Everyone waited for Adam to ride the bike. But Adam just looked at it. He said, "I can ride a bike," to all his friends. He came in the house one day and told his mother, "I can ride a bike." But Adam never got on the bike. Can Adam really ride a bike?

Of course, Adam can't ride. We can't really ride a bike unless we try it. We have to do it. Maybe we'll fall a few times at first, but the only way to really say we can ride a bike is to try it.

Jesus tells us today that believing in him is something like my story about Adam. You can read books about Jesus. You can watch other people who believe in Jesus. You can go to church and even say you believe in Jesus. But Jesus says that unless we really follow him and do what he wants us to do, like loving other people, we don't truly believe any more than Adam really was a bike rider. Jesus says to us today that he wants us to try out our faith just like Adam needs to try out his bike. Let's hope Adam will really ride that bike, and let's pray that we will put our faith to work.

The sermon:

Faith and Obedience

Hymns:
   Beginning of worship: Faith of our Fathers, Living Still.
   Sermon hymn: My Faith Looks Up To Thee
   End of worship: My Hope Is Built on Nothing Less

Scripture: Matthew 7:21-29

Sermon Text: *"Not everyone who says to me, 'Lord, Lord,' shall enter the kingdom of heaven, but those who do the will of my Father who is in heaven."* v. 21

A RABBI AND A SOAPMAKER went for a walk one day. The soapmaker said, "What good is religion? Look at all the trouble and misery of the world! There is still such sin and sadness, even after years of teaching about goodness and truth and peace. If religion is good and true, why should this be?"

June 13, 1993
(Epis/Pres/Meth/UCC - Proper 4)

The rabbi said nothing. They continued walking until he happened to see a child playing in the street gutter. The rabbi said, "Look at that child. You say that soap makes people clean, but see the dirt on that youngster. Of what good is soap? With all the soap in the world, over all these years, the child is still filthy. I wonder how effective soap is after all!" "But Rabbi," the soapmaker protested, "soap cannot do any good unless it is used." "Exactly," said the rabbi. "Exactly."

In today's gospel, much more directly, Jesus makes the same point. Faith requires action. "Not everyone who says to me, 'Lord, Lord,' will enter the kingdom of heaven, but only the one who does the will of my Father in heaven." Faith has a "doing" component to it. As the epistle of James says, "Faith without works is dead." The soap has to be used!

This is very difficult for us to appreciate. It is especially difficult for Protestants who are accustomed to hearing countless sermons berating the vices of works-righteousness. Martin Luther, John Calvin and the other reformers of the 16th century protested mightily against a faith that was not really faith but self-achievement. They, and most Protestants since, rightly feared an attempt to please God by our efforts. The result, however, may be that we have forgotten that faith has an action component. Faith, of necessity, requires some doing.

Our fear or neglect of an acting faith is not only due to a long Protestant history of fear about works-righteousness; it also stems from our modern attitudes toward faith. In the 20th century, in particular, some things have happened which cause us to distort the true nature of faith.

One thing we have done is to psychologize faith. The 20th century is the great era of psychology. This is the century of Freud, Jung, and a whole host of influential psychologists; we have come to accept a psychological viewpoint as naturally as apple pie and ice cream. Unconsciously, (a good psychological word), we run many things through a psychological filter. Faith is one. As a result, faith has come to mean something largely interior to the human mind. It is perceived primarily as a kind of attitude or a feeling. Certainly faith is an attitude but it is far more than an attitude. And most definitely faith is a feeling—a feeling of trust or, as one great theologian called it, a feeling of "dependence." But faith is more than attitude or feeling, important as they are.

The 20th century is also a century in which learning and education have been exalted to new heights. We are much impressed with knowledge, as we should be. But this can result in a distortion of faith so that faith becomes only a matter of intellect. Consider how easily we substitute the word "belief" for faith. Faith clearly has an intellectual side. Faith seeks understanding and grows as our understanding grows. But faith is much more than intellectual knowledge of God. Faith is more than saying, "I believe."

Notice how both this psychologizing and intellectualizing lead to an interiorizing and personalizing of faith. Faith becomes something that happens largely within myself. Faith becomes private. Others cannot see or know it if it's only my feelings or only my knowledge of God.

The Bible understands faith in a much larger sense. Faith is something that is public, not just private. Faith is something to be experienced by others, especially through our deeds. Faith leads to action, in fact, includes action in its very essence.

C.S. Lewis, the agnostic Englishman who become a committed Christian and wrote so many wonderful books such as *The Screwtape Letters* and *The Chronicles of Narnia*, addressed himself to this connection between faith and action many times. In his fine little book, *A Grief Observed*, (Faber & Faber, London) the personal account of his grief over his wife's death, Lewis states:

"You never know how much you really believe anything until its truth or falsehood becomes a matter of life and death. It is easy to say you believe a rope to be strong as long as you are merely using it to cord a box. But suppose you had to hang by that rope over a precipice. Wouldn't you then first discover how much you really trusted it?"

It isn't difficult to catch Lewis' point. Faith requires use. If faith is, at its heart, trusting God, then trusting is what is to be done.

That includes trusting Christ when he calls us to obedience, to action. "You shall love the Lord your God with all your heart, mind and strength, and your neighbor as yourself," Jesus tells us. Faith calls forth the action of love for God, self, and, yes, for neighbor. No wonder Jesus has so much to say about acts of both kindness and justice toward others. No wonder every one of Paul's letters ends with strong instruction about how the Christian faith is to be put into practice. No wonder there is such an emphasis in our churches on responsible Christian stewardship. It is not only not

June 13, 1993
(Epis/Pres/Meth/UCC - Proper 4)

enough to say, "Lord, Lord, I believe," but it is impossible truly to say that without also acting on it.

And, in turn, that action strengthens and supports faith. There is a reciprocal relationship here. Faith leads, of necessity, to action, and the actions of faith in turn strengthen faith. As almost every pastor can say, "I've never met a tither who wasn't a strong believer."

Faith is a beautiful thing to behold in each of us. We are people of faith or we would not be here. That means we are also people of action, living out the trust and love that are at the center of faith in Jesus Christ. Pray that we might be strengthened in all the aspects of faith. Pray especially that we might be men and women, children and youth who both say "I believe" and do what faith requires.

Gary F. Anderson
All Saints Lutheran Church
Minnetonka, Minnesota

Pre-publication Advance Order Form

THE MINISTER'S ANNUAL MANUAL FOR PREACHING AND WORSHIP PLANNING 1993-1994

66 complete sermon and
worship planning helps
beginning August 1, 1993
through July 31, 1994

(Available by June 1, 1993)

$21.95

CLIP AND SEND NAME/ADDRESS WITH PAYMENT TO:

CHURCH MANAGEMENT, INC., P.O. Box 162527, Austin, TX 78716.
My check for $21.95, payable to CHURCH MANAGEMENT, INC., is enclosed for one copy of *The Minister's Annual Manual for Preaching and Worship Planning 1993-1994*.

Name _____

Address _____

City/State/Zip _____

JUNE 20, 1993

Lutheran: Third Sunday after Pentecost
Roman Catholic: Tenth Sunday of the Year
Episcopalian: Proper 5
Pres/Meth/UCC: Proper 5

Lessons:

Lutheran:	Hos. 5:15-6:6	Rom. 4:18-25	Matt. 9:9-13
Roman Catholic:	Hos. 6:3-6	Rom. 4:18-25	Matt. 9:9-13
Episcopal:	Hosea 5:15-6:6	Rom. 4:13-18	Matt. 9:9-13
Pres/Meth/UCC:	Gen. 12:1-9	Rom. 4:13-25	Matt. 9:9-13, 18-26

Introductions to the Lessons

Lesson 1

(1) *Hosea 5:15-6:6* (**Luth/Epis**). In desperation God tried everything good to regain the love and loyalty of his people, but failed. Now he decided to even abandon them in the hope that their suffering will bring them back. What does God want of his people? Not sacrifices but love.

(2) *Genesis 12:1-9* (**Pres/Meth/UCC**). A certain man named Terah had three sons, one of whom was Abraham. The family moved from Ur of the Chaldeans to Haran. After the death of his father, Abraham had a divine call to go to an unknown land. God called Abraham to follow him and promised to bless him in order that he in turn would be a blessing. Abraham obeyed and when he came to Canaan, he built an altar for worship.

Lesson 2

(1) *Romans 4:18-25* (**Luth**). In this chapter Paul is saying that it is by faith in Christ that we are made right with God. Abraham is an example of faith. When he and Sarah were childless and beyond the age of child-bearing, God promised them a son through whom he would have a multitude of descendants. Abraham did not doubt the promise. Because of this faith, Abraham was made right with God and received the promise.

(2) *Romans 4:13-18* (**Epis**); *Rom. 4:13-25* (**Pres/Meth/UCC**). In this chapter Paul explains that we are saved by grace through faith in God's promises apart from the keeping of God's Law. Abraham is an example of this. He received the promise of becoming a great nation not because he obeyed the Law but because he believed in God's promise.

The Minister's Annual Manual

Gospel

Matthew 9:9-13 (**Luth/Epis**); *Matt. 9:9-13, 18-26* (**Pres/Meth/UCC**). It is said that a person is known by the company that is kept. A good person is seen usually with good people. In today's gospel lesson, Jesus, the very best person, calls Matthew, a super-sinner and despised tax-collector, to be a disciple, and then Jesus had a meal with other outcasts. When Pharisees asked why Jesus associated with these malcontents, he explained that he came to call sinners to repentance.

Theme: The Church as a healing place.

Thought for the day: Everyone of us is welcome in the Church of Jesus Christ because it is not limited to those who have achieved success or perfection.

Prayer of meditation: Help us, O God, to understand ourselves in the light of your redeeming grace. Lead us away from false notions that we must be or even can be worthy of your love. Enable us to accept ourselves as we are and then to grow in the light of your grace. May we feel the warm welcome of your church as a place not for the perfect but for the sinful. Enable us, we pray, to share that same welcome with others that they too may discover your church as a place of grace-filled acceptance, even as Christ welcomed Matthew into his friendship. Amen.

Call to worship: God calls us to worship. "Follow me," he invited Matthew through the call of Jesus Christ. "Follow me," is the same word that comes to us today no matter who we are, what we have done, or from where we have come. Welcome to this service of worship whoever you are, in the name of the welcoming Christ. Amen.

Prayer of adoration: We stand in wonder at the depths of your love, O Christ. You welcomed even the tax collector, Matthew, as your disciple. You welcome and receive us despite our many failings and flaws. At such amazing grace we are filled with thanksgiving and awe. Praise be to you for an acceptance beyond all others. Praise be to you for a church that embodies your welcoming and saving ways. Praise be to God, Father, Son and Holy Spirit, the God of eternal grace. Amen.

Prayer of confession: We ask your forgiveness, O God of grace, for attempts at self-righteousness. We confess that we often mistakenly think we can be and need to be holy and pure. Too often, as a result, we sense only our failure and guilt. We may even stay

June 20, 1993
(Epis/Pres/Meth/UCC - Proper 5)

away from you, O God, and from prayer and worship. Enable us to sense again the freedom of your grace. Open our minds and hearts to the power of your acceptance in spite of our sinfulness, even as you freed Matthew for life, for love, and for witness through Jesus Christ. Amen.

Prayer of dedication of gifts and self: We bring before you, dear God, these offerings in thanksgiving for your healing grace. You give us these good things out of your boundless goodness. We return to you these signs of our love, not because we have to but because we want to. Receive them for the sake of Jesus Christ, our Lord. Amen.

Sermon title: The Hospital of God

Sermon thesis: The church is a place of acceptance not of perfection.

Hymn for the day: "O Christ, the healer, we have come". Frederick Pratt Green (b. 1903), a native of Liverpool, England, served for forty-five years as a minister of the Wesleyan Methodist Church. He began to write poetry at the age of forty, and did not begin writing hymns until he was over sixty years of age. This hymn speaks of Christ's healing of the world's disease of conflict as well as for individual healing.

Announcements for next week:

Sermon title: Follow the Leader
Sermon theme: The need for the leadership of Jesus Christ.
Sermon summary: To a people who, like sheep, are in need of a leader, Christ is there for us just as he was for the people of his time.

Children's object talk:

Church For Hearts

Objects: A big bandage or a whole box of bandages.
Lesson: The church can be a place to heal inner hurts.
Outline: 1. Show bandages and how they help heal hurts.
2. Inner hurts cannot be fixed by hospitals.
3. Use the church for other kinds of hurts.

SHOW THE BANDAGE to the children and ask them to describe it. Talk about how bandages are used when we have hurts. Point out there are other kinds of hurts for which we don't have bandages. Tell them about the inner kinds of hurts. Perhaps the children can even think of some, as when we feel sad or when we feel bad that we have done something wrong. There is the hurt of loneliness. Sometimes when we have hurt our bodies we have to go to the doctor or hospital and have the hurt healed with stitches or surgery and bandages. We are glad that our bodies can usually be fixed by doctors and hospitals. Tell them that the church is a kind of hospital too. Here you can't see the bandages because they are bandages of love. Here in the church Jesus Christ loves us, forgives us, and heals those inner hurts. Tell them how important it is to bring our inner hurts for healing. We shouldn't ever be afraid or ashamed. Just like the hospital is a good place to go when our bodies are sick, so the church is a good place to go when we have other kinds of hurts.

The sermon:

The Hospital of God

Hymns:
Beginning of worship: When Morning Gilds the Skies.
Sermon hymn: Jesus Sinners Will Receive
End of worship: Savior, Again to your Dear Name

Scripture: Matthew 9:9-13

Sermon Text: *"For I came not to call the righteous, but sinners."* v. 13

"PATIENTS STOP THINKING of themselves as bad people who need to be better and start realizing they are sick people who can get well."

That statement was made a few years ago by the Executive Director of the Betty Ford Center for the Treatment of Drug and Alcohol Abuse. It is an impressive statement about what is known to be a fine treatment center.

That statement could also serve as an excellent description for what the Church of Jesus Christ ought to be. For isn't that description the way Jesus dealt with people? Jesus didn't treat people as evil or bad who must somehow shape up their lives by their own efforts. Rather Christ regarded people as sick and in need of love, forgiveness and hope. With such medicines, they could get well.

Surely that is the way Jesus treated Matthew the tax collector. We may not know very much about tax collectors in first century Palestine, but we can easily imagine that they weren't the most popular people. Since they worked for the Roman government, they

June 20, 1993
(Epis/Pres/Meth/UCC - Proper 5)

were regarded by devout Jews as traitors, Quislings, among the most vile sort. What's more, most of them were known as thieves, engaging in a kind of white collar crime by skimming off some of the tax take for themselves.

As a result, tax collectors were grouped with the "sinners," those who were shut off from God by their lack of righteousness. Yet Jesus cares for just these kinds of people. Jesus sits down and shares dinner with tax collectors and sinners. He even calls one of them, Matthew, into his intimate circle as a disciple.

Clearly, Christ did not see Matthew or the other sinners who sat at the table with him as "bad people who must somehow get better," to use the words of the Betty Ford Center's Director, but rather as sick people who can, with God's love, get well.

That is also the calling of the Christian Church. The church, this church, is not a place for the holy and pure only, as if there are any such people, but it is above all a place for the sinful and weak. The church isn't a haven for those who have arrived at saintliness and righteousness, bad people who have somehow gotten better; but it is for those who know they are not perfect but depend on God's grace.

This means those of us in the church begin with a fresh realization of ourselves. We are here not because we are better than others or because we have somehow left all our "badness" behind, but because we know we are sinful people who desperately need love and forgiveness.

There is good reason that many congregations begin their worship with confession or include time for confession at some place in their service. Worship needs to include a recognition of who we are. We are people who have broken relationship with God, with our neighbors, and with ourselves. We are people who have sinned against God "in thought, word, and deed," as some of the ancient confessions express it.

Some today consider this too demeaning, too negative. It offends self-esteem, they claim. It isn't sufficiently positive. But it is the truth! The way to true self-esteem is through a truthful appraisal of ourselves and then the discovery of an acceptance far greater than mere self-affirmation. Jesus had it right when he said to the Pharisees who charged him with eating with the tax collectors and sinners, "Those who are well have no need of a physician, but those who are sick do."

Those of us in the church are among the sick. We know we need God's healing grace. That is the first and perhaps most important step in getting well. Those who deal with drug and alcohol abuse have discovered that truth. An essential first step is the recognition and admission of the disease. There can be no healing without it. So it is that in the church we come before God admitting our needs. "God help me" is our cry.

A prominent New York businessman came to see the famous Dr. Norman Vincent Peale, prominent pastor of a major church in that city years ago. The man laid out a tragic tale of confusion, frustration, and twisted values. When he finished describing his shameful life, he asked Pastor Peale, "What do you think I should do?" Dr. Peale said, "I have a solution for you. It is simple and you are a sophisticated and intelligent man. I doubt that you would want to hear it." The man said, "I think I would like to hear it." "No, I don't believe you would. It is too simple," Dr. Peale replied. Again, the man asked to hear it, even becoming angry. Finally Peale told him. "What I really think you need to do is to get down on your knees and tell God that you are a sinner and ask God to forgive you." I don't know if that man found his way into the church and into healing peace or not. But he belongs in the church. Because that is who the church is—not bad people who need to shape up, but sick people who, with forgiveness, get well.

This means not only a new way of seeing ourselves as individuals and as Christians, but it also means a new way of seeing the whole church. We need to see the church as a hospital, an image familiar to Martin Luther centuries ago. It is an image we may have lost. Too often for us the church is viewed as a place for the "goodie-goodie" types. Those not in the church often view it as a place for people who are better than they are. Notions of perfectionism keep many away from the church. How many people are there, I wonder, who stay away from worship because they feel they are not good enough?

It may be that entire groups, even whole congregations, labor under perfectionist misunderstandings.

We need to hear again the word, "I came not to call the righteous, but sinners." That includes a sinful, less than perfect, church.

This is not to excuse any of us from seeking to lead lives of moral integrity and responsibility. This is not to wink at immorality or wrong on the part of pastors or members. And this is not to say

June 20, 1993
(Epis/Pres/Meth/UCC - Proper 5)

congregations should be slovenly or lazy, failing to do their best to serve Christ and be God's people. But it is to say that if we have the image of the church as perfect institution made up of even nearly perfect people and pastors, we have it all wrong. We are, instead, a hospital where God's grace is the healing agent among the sick.

If that is true, then our mission is clear. The church exists to invite the tax collectors and sinners into its ranks! What a crazy job. What a ridiculous mission! It is, however, the one given to us who follow Christ. We exist for the Matthews of this world, the sinners whom we call into fellowship with us. The church isn't out looking only for the beautiful people. We aren't here for those who have achieved and arrived, although they are welcome too if there are truly such. This isn't a place only for the nice people. The church exists to reach out to the imperfect, the mixed-up, the mistaken, the guilty, the often lost people of this world. Our mission is to extend the same grace which has been given to us through the love and forgiveness of Jesus Christ.

A passage in Lorraine Hansberry's play, "A Raisin in the Sun," describes our mission well. The daughter in this play has "had it" with her brother and is about to give up trying to relate to him. Then her mother says to her: "There is always something left to love. And if you ain't learned that, you ain't learned nothing. Child, when do you think is the time to love somebody most; when they done good and made things easy for everybody? Well then, you ain't through learning, because that ain't the time at all. It's when he's at his lowest and can't believe in himself 'cause the world done whipped him so. When you start measuring somebody, measure him right, child, measure him right. Make sure you done taken into account those hills and valleys he come through before he got wherever he is."

That is the way Jesus Christ loves. Christ loves when people are at the lowest and worst, not just when they've done well. Such is our task in the church too. For this is the hospital of God, a place for sick people who, with Christ's love, can get well.

Gary F. Anderson
All Saints Lutheran Church
Minnetonka, Minnesota

JUNE 27, 1993

Lutheran: Fourth Sunday after Pentecost
Roman Catholic: Eleventh Sunday of the Year
Episcopalian: Proper 6 (June 13)
Pres/Meth/UCC: Second after Pentecost (June 13)

Lessons:

Lutheran:	Ex. 19:2-8a	Rom. 5:6-11	Matt. 9:35-10:8
Roman Catholic:	Ex. 19:2-6a	Rom. 5:6-11	Matt. 9:36-10:8
Episcopal:	Ex. 19:2-8a	Rom. 5:6-11	Matt. 9:35-10:8(9-15)
Pres/Meth/UCC:	Gen. 18:1-15 (21:1-7)	Rom. 5:1-18	Matt. 9:35-10:8 (9-23)

Introductions to the Lessons

Lesson 1

(1) *Exodus 19:2-8a* (**Luth/Epis**). The Israelites were released from Egypt and are now in the wilderness at the base of Mt. Sinai. Moses goes up the mountain to commune with God. Moses is told that if the people obey his commands, they will be his people and will serve him as priests. Moses reports this to his people who respond, "We will do everything the Lord has said."

(2) *Genesis 18:1-15 (21:1-7)* (**Pres/Meth/UCC**). On a very hot day while Abraham was sitting at the entrance to his tent, God came in the persons of three men. Abraham and Sarah urged the men to stay and have dinner with them. At the close of the meal one of the men promised that Sarah would have a son. Since Abraham was 100 years old and Sarah was in menopause, she laughed at the idea. In 9 months, however, Sarah had a boy named Isaac, meaning "Laughter."

Lesson 2

Romans 5:6-11 (**Luth/Epis/Pres/Meth/UCC**). Christ did not die because we were good and deserved it. We were sinful, estranged, and enemies of God. We were totally without merit or worthiness. While in this condition, Christ died for us because he loves us. By his death we made right with God and now we are his friends. We rejoice at what God has done for us in Christ.

Gospel

Matthew 9:35-10:8 (**Luth/Epis/Pres/Meth/UCC**). Jesus went to various towns in Galilee offering a threefold ministry to the people: preaching, teaching, and healing. He had compassion on the people because they were worried, helpless, and leaderless.

June 27, 1993
(Epis/Pres/Meth/UCC - June 13, 1993)

He compared the situation to a great harvest with few workers. To answer the need he chose twelve disciples and sent them out to expand his ministry.

Theme: The need for the leadership of Jesus Christ.

Thought for the day: We often sense our bewilderment and confusion. Life causes us to feel lost and confused, especially today. While we are in need of leadership, we often resist it, even from those we trust. Jesus Christ knows our situation and offers himself as one to lead us through life to hope. Can we trust and follow?

Prayer of meditation: Guide us, O God. Guide us in your paths of peace, of hope, of justice, of love. Guide us especially when we wander into ways of selfishness and destructiveness. Guide us when we are lost and confused. Guide us, O God, guide us in the way of Jesus Christ, our Shepherd and our Guide. Amen.

Call to worship: We gather as followers of Christ. We come today not only to worship Jesus Christ, but to seek Christ's guidance in our daily lives. Thanks be to God who sends us one we call the Good Shepherd. Come let us worship and follow as disciples of the one we call Savior. Amen.

Prayer of adoration: Praise and thanksgiving, Father, we offer for all things. Today we especially give you our praise and thanks for the gift of one who shows us the way through the sin, darkness, and confusion of our lives. Praise be for the leadership of Jesus Christ. Praise be for the gift of the one who said he was and is "the way, the truth, and the life." Amen.

Prayer of confession: We come in humble confession today, gracious Lord, of our frequent failure to trust and follow you. You have invited us to be your followers. You have called us into your discipleship and fellowship. You have shown us a way that is good and true. Your way is the way of love and hope. Yet we turn to ourselves. We even follow false leaders. We wander into error or wrong. Forgive our foolish ways. Lead us into deeper trust and obedience. Amen.

Prayer of dedication of gifts and self: We bring these gifts in grateful obedience as your servants, O Lord. You have shown us the way to live, a way that includes offering you our best and sharing with others. These gifts are tokens of our response as your disciples who seek to serve you, O Christ, and our neighbors. Amen.

Sermon title: Follow the Leader

Sermon thesis: To a people who like sheep are in need of a leader, Christ is there for us just as he was for the people of his time.

Hymn for the day: *"Lead on, O King eternal"* This hymn, which rejoices in the leadership of Christ, was written by Ernest Warburton Shurtleff (1862-1917). Born in Boston, Massachusetts. Shurtleff graduated from Andover Theological Seminary. This hymn was written for the Andover graduation ceremonies. Shurtleff served as a Congregational minister in Massachusetts and Minnesota, after which he went to Frankfurt-am-Main in Germany, where he established the American church. The next year he went to Paris, where he and his wife did relief work during World War I until the time of his death.

Announcements for next week:
Sermon title: Pennies and Sparrows
Sermon theme: Good news is God's love for each of us.
Sermon summary: Only when we understand that God loves and forgives us all can we see for ourselves the worth of everyone whose life surrounds ours—and the true value of our own lives, as well.

Children's object talk:
The Best Leader of All

Object: Several games.
Lesson: The importance of having good leaders.
Outline: 1. Play any game.
2. Can't decide which game to play.
3. Use Jesus as Leader of our lives.

TELL THE CHILDREN you would like them to play a game. Don't tell them what game. Just tell them they can play any game they like. Then wait a few minutes. Chances are they will all stand around wondering what to do. Ask them why they aren't playing. One of them will probably say, "We don't know what game to play." Sit down with the children if they have been standing and then share with them why it was hard to play a game—there was no leader. No one gave directions. Tell them that Jesus looked at the people of his time and saw that they had no leader. He said they were "like sheep without a shepherd." Talk with the children about the importance of having good leaders, loving and kind leaders who do the right thing. Point out that the best leader of all is Jesus. Invite the children to follow Jesus as leader for their lives.

June 27, 1993
(Epis/Pres/Meth/UCC - June 13, 1993)

The sermon:

Follow the Leader

Hymns:
Beginning of worship: When Morning Guilds the Skies
Sermon hymn: Spread, Oh, Spread, Almighty Word
End of worship: Savior, Again to Your Dear Name

Scripture: Matthew 9:35-10:8

Sermon Text: *"When he saw the crowds, he had compassion for them, because they were harassed and helpless, like sheep without a shepherd."* v. 36

"A NATION OF SHEEP." That was the title of a best-selling social commentary on the United States many years ago. It was a powerful title of a powerful book. It is a title which still applies. We are, for the most part, a nation of sheep; people who are without strong and effective leadership or who too often just wander around without direction.

This is not a political commentary. It is a commentary on the times in which we live and on our society. It is a commentary, an accurate one I believe, on our lives.

These are times when leadership is terribly difficult to begin with. Every leader is under constant public scrutiny. Their least flaw is examined and often magnified by the eye of television. While this makes it harder for crooks to be crooks, it also can cut the nerve of even the best leaders.

It is also a time of exaggerated individualism. We aren't much open to leadership. People want to be left alone and left to their own devices. Increasingly we are turning inward, to the private and personal dimensions of our lives. We become our own leaders and are less open to the leadership of others.

Then, too, we have been burned. We have been misled. While Vietnam and Watergate are a long way behind us, they are still not forgotten. On a smaller scale there are countless other leaders who have disappointed us, whether in government, business, or even the church.

Jesus looked at the people of his time and saw them as "sheep without a shepherd." You can almost hear the pain in Jesus' words as he sees the sad, lost state of his people.

To describe people as "sheep without a shepherd" was an image even more powerful in Christ's time than ours. Jesus and the people of that time were much more familiar with sheep and their wandering ways than we are.

A farmer once told a true story about a barn filled with sheep. There was one sheep who generally led the rest. One day the farmer noticed that the sheep did not come out of the barn. He went to see why. He noticed that the lead sheep was staring at a small beam of sunlight that was coming through the crack of the open barn door. The sheep thought the beam of light was some kind of obstacle like a chain or a rope preventing exit from the barn. But the old sheep finally figured it out. He got a little running start and jumped over the beam of light. The farmer stared in amazement and amusement as each of the sheep that followed also jumped over this imaginary barrier on their way out of the barn.

Jesus knew the need of sheep for a leader, a good leader, a trustworthy leader. Without such a leader, sheep are lost, vulnerable, and in great danger. We are told that Jesus had compassion on the people because he saw they were "harassed and helpless."

Those words describe us as well. Certainly many of us feel "harassed." Modern life has a way of harassing us. Modern life also often makes us feel helpless. We are victimized by the peer pressures around us. We are frightened by the growing violence in our society. We feel lost in the complexity and intimidated by the pace of our world. Often we sense we are turned into sheep, blindly following the trends and jumping over the beam of light that comes from our television sets. We need a good shepherd, a trustworthy leader.

Jesus offered himself to his people as such a leader and continues to offer himself to us today. "Follow me," Jesus called out to his disciples. That same invitation comes to us today. We cannot follow Christ in person but we can follow the way he charted for us. We can follow his Word.

We believe in Jesus. We sing the children's song, "Jesus loves me, this I know." We look up to Christ in worship and respect. But do we really follow him?

Dietrich Bonhoeffer asked that question in Germany during the 1930s. His famous book, *The Cost of Discipleship*, explores the question of obedience. He says too often we have an abstract Christology, a doctrinal system, or a general religious knowledge on the subject of grace or forgiveness. What is called for instead is an obedient

June 27, 1993
(Epis/Pres/Meth/UCC - June 13, 1993)

following. "The call to follow means ... adherence to the person of Jesus Christ and fellowship with him. The life of discipleship is not the hero-worship we would pay to a good master, but obedience to the Son of God." *(The Cost of Discipleship,* Macmillan Co., New York, 1963, p. 84)

Those are daring words to a people who were caught up in the hero-worship of an Adolph Hitler. It was also a strong challenge to people who had a vague sense of religion but did not have the kind of true obedience to Christ that Bonhoeffer saw as the essence of faith. As a result, they found themselves like sheep led to the slaughter by one they called "Der Fuehrer."

While our situation is far different, Bonhoeffer's words still apply. We too easily settle for hazy words about love and forgiveness and Jesus without hearing the call to obedience and following. We want the benefits of grace without the cost of commitment. As a result, we also miss out on the true leadership Christ can give for our lives. We, too, wind up being "sheep without a shepherd" or in the tow of false shepherds.

Today we discover again the Christ of great compassion who offers himself as a Good Shepherd to people so in need of leadership. But we also hear that if the leadership Christ can give us is to be effective in our lives, then we must follow Christ obediently. A tip of the hat to Jesus is not enough to receive the benefits of his leadership. An occasional remembrance of his name won't do. A desperate prayer when we are suddenly lost is better than no prayer at all, but constant communication is called for.

To a people who, like sheep, are in need of a leader, Christ is there for us just as he was for the people of his time. Will we follow or will we chose to wander, lost, confused, even misled? Let us pray that the answer is to give our trust and obedience to the one truly Good Shepherd.

Gary F. Anderson
All Saints Lutheran Church
Minnetonka, Minnesota

Dear Reader:

Are you a regular subscriber to THE CLERGY JOURNAL?

If not, please write for a sample copy.

We believe this magazine can be of help to you in your important work.

Our magazine is in its sixty-eighth year of helping America's church leaders to be more effective leaders.

We invite you to become one of the many pastors who find inspiration, advice and practical professional aid in our pages.

Why not send in the coupon below today?

The magazine about church administration, preaching, worship, finance, programming . . . practical, timely, popular . . . the clergy magazine that belongs in every congregation and on every pastor's desk.

SUBSCRIPTION ORDER:

CHURCH MANAGEMENT:

THE CLERGY JOURNAL

10 Issues annually

One year $27   Two years $51
(Foreign: add $6 per year)
(U.S. Banks only)

(Subscription rates include next May/June Planning Issue – $14.40 when purchases separately.)

Name _____

Street Address _____

City _____ State _____

Zip _____ Amount Enclosed: $ _____

(Sorry, we cannot bill)

☐ New
☐ Renewal
(Attach Label)

Church Management
P.O. Box 162527
Austin, TX 78716

Pre-publication Advance Order Form

THE MINISTER'S ANNUAL MANUAL FOR PREACHING AND WORSHIP PLANNING 1993-1994

66 complete sermon and
worship planning helps
beginning August 1, 1993
through July 31, 1994

(Available by June 1, 1993)

$21.95

JULY 4, 1993

Lutheran: Fifth Sunday after Pentecost
Roman Catholic: Twelfth Sunday of the Year
Episcopalian: Proper 7 (June 20)
Pres/Meth/UCC: Third after Pentecost (June 20)

Lessons:

Lutheran:	Jer. 20:7-13	Rom. 5:12-15	Matt. 10:24-33
Roman Catholic:	Jer. 20:10-13	Rom. 5:12-15	Matt. 10;26-33
Episcopal:	Jer. 20:7-13	Rom. 5:15b-19	Matt. 10:(16-23) 24-33
Pres/Meth/UCC:	Gen. 21:8-21	Rom. 6:1b-11	Matt. 10:24-39

Introductions to the Lessons

Lesson 1

(1) *Jeremiah 20:7-13* (**Luth/Epis**). Jeremiah is under divine orders to declare death and destruction to his people at the hands of the Babylonians because of their sins. As a result, Jeremiah is most unpopular among the people and his life is threatened. He wants to quit preaching, but he cannot because a divine call to preach is like fire in his bones. Nevertheless, Jeremiah is confident God will deliver him from his enemies.

(2) *Genesis 21:8-21* (**Pres/Meth/UCC**). After trying to be parents for many years

July 4, 1993
(Epis/Pres/Meth/UCC - June 20, 1993)

In baptism we died to self and sin with Christ, and now we live as Christ was raised from the dead. Physically we are born to life and eventually die. Spiritually we die first and then live forever.

Gospel

Matthew 10:24-33 (**Luth/Epis**); *Matt. 10:24-39* (**Pres/Meth/UCC**). Last Sunday we heard that Jesus sent out his disciples to preach and heal. What kind of treatment can they expect? In today's gospel lesson, Jesus tells them not to expect any more than what he receives. If they are persecuted, excluded, or maligned, it is no more than what their Master receives. However, disciples need to remember that God knows each one intimately and values each personally.

Theme: Good News is God's love for each of us.

Thought for the day: Today's lesson proclaims that God sees every sparrow that falls. God numbers the hairs on our heads. God has made each of us, values us, and loves us, no matter who we are. Our lives are in God's hands.

Prayer of meditation: Enter our hearts, O Holy Spirit; come in blessed mercy and set us free. Throw open, O Lord, the locked doors of our minds; cleanse the chambers of our thought for your dwelling; light there the fires of your own holy brightness in new understanding of truth. O Holy Spirit, very God, whose presence is liberty, grant us the perfect freedom to be your servants, today, tomorrow, evermore. Amen. (Eric Milner-White, in *The Oxford Book of Prayer*, alt.)

Call to worship:
Grace to you, and peace, from God our Creator, and from the
  Lord Jesus Christ.
Give to God the glory due to God's name.
Worship the Lord in the beauty of holiness.
Let us worship God in spirit and in truth.

Prayer of adoration: Grant to us, O Lord, to worship you in spirit and in truth; to submit all our nature to you, that our consciences may be quickened by your holiness, our minds nourished by your truth, our imaginations purified by your beauty. Help us to open our hearts to your love and to surrender our will to your purpose. So may we lift up our hearts to you in selfless adoration and love; through Jesus Christ our Lord. Amen. (George Appleton, in *The Oxford Book of Prayer*, alt.)

Prayer of confession: We confess to you, O God, that we have sinned against heaven and in your sight and are not worthy to be called your children. We have forgotten you; we have broken your holy laws; we have been wayward and disobedient; we have been selfish and unkind. For the sake of your dear Son, our Savior, we beseech you to pardon our sins; to cleanse our hearts within us; and to grant us your peace. Amen. *(The Book of Common Worship)*

Prayer of dedication of gifts and self: O God, of whose bounty we have all received: Accept this offering of your people: and so follow it with your blessing that it may promote peace and goodwill among all people, and advance the kingdom of our Lord and Savior Jesus Christ. Amen. *(The Book of Common Worship)*

Sermon title: Pennies and Sparrows

Sermon thesis: Only when we understand that God loves and forgives us all can we see for ourselves the worth of everyone whose life surrounds ours — and the true value of our own lives, as well.

Hymn for the day: *"O Lord of light"* This Latin hymn, which reviews the story of our forgiveness and salvation, dates from the early Middle Ages. It is found in a ninth-century manuscript at Bern, Switzerland, and in a tenth-century hymnal at Canterbury, England.

Announcements for next week:
 Sermon title: Some Basic Choices
 Sermon theme: Good news involves making basic choices.
 Sermon summary: Christians are called upon to make hard choices. In spite of conflict, strife, or persecution arising from those choices, Christians live within the realization that, regardless of any sacrifice we face, our sacrifice bears witness to Christ — whose victory was gained by his own sacrifice on the cross.

Children's object talk:

Whom Does God Love?

Object: 1. A magazine-picture collage of animals, birds, etc.
  2. A similar collage, showing all kinds of people.
  3. A small hand mirror.
Lesson: God loves everything God has created.
Outline: 1. Show "creature" collage, talk about different animals.
  2. Distinguish different people in the "people" collage.
  3. Pass around hand mirror; identify each child as loved by God.

July 4, 1993
(Epis/Pres/Meth/UCC - June 20, 1993)

WHOM DOES GOD LOVE? Can you tell me? Today I've brought some pictures with me that will give us some clues about that.

Look at these pictures. They show birds, and animals, and fish, and snakes. Can you find an elephant? A seagull? A whale? God made every one of these, and you know what? God loves every single one!

Here are some more pictures. What do they show? People! All different kinds of people. There are women, and men, girls and boys and little babies; there are old people and young people and people from all around the world. God made each one, and you know what? God loves every single one!

Now, I have a different kind of picture. Look at this little mirror. Whose picture do you see? Your own! God made each and every one of you, and God made me, too. If God loves all those animals and birds and other people, God must love you and me, too, in an extra-special way.

So, whom does God love? God loves everything and everyone God has made. And God loves you.

The sermon:

Pennies and Sparrows

Hymns:
Beginning of worship: All Things Bright and Beautiful
Sermon hymn: God Will Take Care of You
End of worship: Amazing Grace

Scripture: Matthew 10:24-33

Sermon Text: *"Are not two sparrows sold for a penny? Yet not one of them will fall to the ground apart from your Father ... So do not be afraid; you are of more value than many sparrows."* v. 29, 31

DURING THE SUMMER OF 1972, I worked as a counselor at a church-related camp, located along the Susquehanna River in northeastern Pennsylvania. In the first week of the season, Hurricane Agnes hit our area; for the rest of the summer, nothing went as we had planned and hoped in staff training. Many of our campers had lost their homes; the flooding river had ruined the whole lower end of the camp. Into this atmosphere, early in July, came 11-year-old Mary.

Mary was what we would now call a disadvantaged child. Her family was poor; she had been in marginal health since birth. The family had lost everything they owned in the flood. Mary had only two sets of clothing, unattractive and ill-fitting, which promptly made her the target of crude jokes, an object of laughter and derision among her fellow campers. We adults tried to end the cruelty, but the more angry we became with the kids for picking on Mary, the more persistent the taunts became.

Mary, as you might well imagine, was deeply hurt. She withdrew from most activities, preferring to walk alone in the woods, where no one told her she was "funny" or "different."

Our director that week knew Mary from other years at camp, and he became, quietly and unobtrusively, her friend. Each day, Mary and Bob spent time together. Not until the last night before the session ended did the rest of us find out what they had been doing.

Bob led us in worship, reading from Matthew, about sparrows being sold, two for a penny. Then, he asked Mary to step forward. She was clutching a brown paper grocery bag. Putting his arm around Mary's shoulder, Bob said, "My friend Mary has worked hard all week, and she has something for you." Mary began shyly to go around the circle, pressing a small object into each person's hands, until everyone in the room had a gift. The campers, who had teased Mary so cruelly, sat in embarrassed silence; some of the girls cried.

Mary's gift? She had made each of us a wooden cross, lashed with twine at the crosspiece and decorated with wild flowers.

Bob stilled the murmuring when he said, "Today, you have seen God's love. You may not think much of Mary, but God does. To God, Mary is a special person, with special gifts. In sharing herself with us, with these crosses, Mary has hinted at what it means to be loved by God."

I have that cross still, more than twenty years later.

"Are not two sparrows sold for a penny? Yet not one of them will fall to the ground apart from your Father ... So do not be afraid; you are of more value than many sparrows" (Matthew 10:29, 31, NRSV).

Matthew's comments today are directed to people living in his own time. Writing in the 70s, about forty years after the end of Jesus' earthly ministry, Matthew was especially concerned with Jewish converts to Christianity. For them, life was not easy. On one hand, the Jewish community viewed them as infidels, abandoning the legacy of faith. On the other, the Romans were beginning a pattern of suspicion and persecution of Christians that would last almost 300 years. Into this volatile situation, Matthew brings Good News: Have no fear. Romans can't kill your soul, for Christ has conquered death. You are valued; you are loved. Remain faithful.

Persecution was a fact of life in the ancient world. In recording these words, Matthew shows Jesus in direct opposition to this devaluation of human life. "Are not two sparrows sold for a penny? Yet not one of them will fall to the ground apart from your Father ... So do not be afraid; you are of more value than many sparrows."

We get the message, in many ways, in our highly sophisticated culture, that we should be concerned only with ourselves. Look out for Number One. Take every opportunity for self-gratification. Let your grandchildren worry about the environment or world starvation. Put the elderly, the homeless, the poor off into their own cubbyholes, and care for them in ways we don't have to see. We're fine; let someone else look after the unfortunates.

The Good News is not our colossal egotism. Jesus reminds us, again and again, that the people we think are undesirable, or lazy, or weak, are just as precious (if not more so, precisely because of our value judgments) in God's sight as we are. Only when we understand that God loves and forgives us all can we see for ourselves the worth of everyone whose life surrounds ours — and the true value of our own lives, as well.

In his book, *Damien the Leper*, John Farrow tells the true story of a young Belgian who hears, in a bishop's sermon, the call to priesthood and a challenge to minister to lepers on an island in the Hawaiian chain. In the last century, those who had contracted leprosy were quarantined, set apart, and because their condition was almost always fatal, the care extended to them was minimal.

For a number of years, Damien worked with these lepers. He dressed their wounds and dug their graves. He lobbied on their behalf for clinics and nurses. He built, often with his own hands, their churches and chapels, preached the Word, and administered the sacraments. He loved these people, proclaimed God's presence and love. By his own tender ministrations, he assured them that their horrible disease did not diminish them in either his eyes or God's.

On every occasion that he preached, Damien began his homily with the introduction, "My brothers and sisters in Christ." One day, he seemed to pause, just for a moment. Then, in words that were both a confession and a public acknowledgement of fact, he began with the words, "We lepers." Somehow, his illness gave a new dimension to his ministry. Even in his slow dying and his painful death, he continued to witness to God's presence and love.

Like Matthew long years before him, Damien was truly an evangel — a bringer of Good News. He carried Good News to some the world had cast aside; he was Good News, even as a leper.

"Are not two sparrows sold for a penny? Yet not one of them will fall to the ground apart from your Father ... So do not be afraid; you are of more value than many sparrows."

Nancy E. Topolewski
Kirkwood United Methodist Church
Sidney, New York

JULY 11, 1993

Lutheran: Sixth Sunday after Pentecost
Roman Catholic: Thirteenth Sunday of the Year
Episcopalian: Proper 8 (June 27)
Pres/Meth/UCC: Fourth after Pentecost (June 27)

Lessons:

Lutheran:	Jer. 28:5-9	Rom. 6:1b-11	Matt. 10:34-42
Roman Catholic:	2 Kings 4:8-11, 14-16a	Rom. 6:3-4, 8-11	Matt. 10:37-42
Episcopal:	Is. 2:10-17	Rom. 6:3-11	Matt. 10:34-42
Pres/Meth/UCC:	Gen. 22:1-14	Rom. 6:12-23	Matt. 10:40-42

Introductions to the Lessons

Lesson 1

(1) *Jeremiah 28:5-9* (**Luth**). Here are two prophets, Jeremiah and Hananiah, preaching opposite messages. Jeremiah says the nation, because of its sin, will remain in Babylonian captivity. Hananiah claims the exiles will return within two years. According to Jeremiah, the people will know who the true prophet is when his prophecy happens.

(2) *Isaiah 2:10-17* (**Epis**). Judah is saturated with wealth, leisure, and idolatry. Isaiah has a vision of God's judgment upon the nation. The day is coming when God will humiliate the proud, destroy the idols, and bring destitution to the nation. Then the Lord will be exalted.

(3) *Genesis 22:1-14* (**Pres/Meth/UCC**). What kind of a God would order you to kill the only son of your old age and burn his body as a sacrifice? That was the question Abraham asked when God told him to murder his miracle child, Isaac. Did Abraham love Isaac more than God? God put Abraham to the test and he passed it with flying colors!

Lesson 2

(1) *Romans 6:1b-11* (**Luth**); *Rom. 6:3-11* (**Epis**). If grace is the cure for sin, why not continue to sin in order to experience further grace? According to Paul, that is a foolish question. When we were baptized, we died to self and sin. If we are dead to sin, we cannot live in sin. As Jesus rose from death to eternal life, we also rise with him to newness of life. Now we live in Christ and share the life of Christ.

(2) *Romans 6:12-23* (**Pres/Meth/UCC**). Choose your slavery! All of us are slaves, either to sin or to righteousness, to Satan or to God. Before we accepted Christ, we were slaves to sin because we lived under the Law. Now that we are in Christ, we are slaves of God because we live under grace. To live as slaves of sin results in death, but to live as slaves of Christ we reap eternal life.

Gospel

Matthew 10:34-42 (**Luth/Epis**); *Matt. 10:40-42* (**Pres/Meth/UCC**). In this passage Jesus teaches us that discipleship has both a price and a reward. The price is to love Christ more than any other person including one's family, to carry one's cross, and to lose oneself wholly in Christ's cause. For those who pay this price there is a reward!

Theme: Good News involves making basic choices.

Thought for the day: " ... Although I knew that ... I was linked with the past that I had yielded up, inextricably and for ever, I found it not inappropriate that the years of frustration and grief and loss, of work and conflict and painful resurrection, should have led me through their dark and devious ways to this new beginning." (Vera Brittain, *Testament of Youth*)

Prayer of meditation: Father, behold your child: Creator, behold your creature: Master, behold your disciple: Savior, behold your redeemed one: Spirit, behold your cleansed one: Comforter, behold one whom you uphold: So I come to you, O infinite and unimaginable, to worship you. Amen. (Margaret Cropper, *The Oxford Book of Prayer* adapted)

Call to worship:
L. In the Name of the blessed and holy Trinity, one God, now and for ever.
P. Amen.
L. Let us bless the Lord.
P. God's holy name be praised.

Prayer of adoration: Almighty God, you have built your Church upon the foundation of the apostles and prophets, Jesus Christ himself being the chief cornerstone. Grant us so to be joined together in unity of spirit by their teaching, that we may be made a holy temple acceptable to you; through Jesus Christ our Lord, who lives and reigns with you and the Holy Spirit, one God, for ever and ever. Amen. (*The Book of Common Prayer*)

Prayer of confession: We confess to you, O God, that we have sinned against heaven and in your sight and are not worthy to be called

July 11, 1993
(Epis/Pres/Meth/UCC - June 27, 1993)

your children. We have forgotten you and have broken your holy laws. We have been wayward and disobedient. We have been selfish and unkind. For the sake of your dear Son, our Savior, we beseech you to pardon our sins; to make clean our hearts within us; and to grant us your peace. Amen. (*The Book of Common Worship*)

Prayer of dedication of gifts and self: O Lord our God, accept, of your infinite goodness, the offerings of your people, which, in obedience to your commandment and in honor of your name, we give and dedicate to you. Grant that these gifts, being devoted to your service, may be used for your glory; through Jesus Christ our Lord. Amen. (*The Book of Common Worship*)

Sermon title: Some Basic Choices

Sermon thesis: Christians are called upon to make hard choices. In spite of conflict, strife, or persecution arising from those choices, Christians live within the realization that, regardless of any sacrifice we face, our sacrifice bears witness to Christ — whose victory was gained by his own sacrifice on the cross.

Hymn for the day: *"We are the Lord's."* The hymn calls on us to "render no doubtful witness" and reminds us that whatever comes our way, "we are the Lord's." Karl Johann Philipp Spitta (1801-1859) was one of the leading hymnwriters of 19th-century Germany. He entered the ministry and, after working for a time as a chaplain at a prison, served as a parish pastor and later as superintendent of several districts. One of his sons, Johann August Philipp, wrote an important biography of J.S. Bach.

Announcements for next week:
Sermon title: "What is Real?," said the Rabbit
Sermon theme: Good news through innocent eyes.
Sermon summary: Four images are explored in such a way as to illustrate and reinforce the insight from today's Gospel lesson, that God's gracious will is that Good News can be seen by, and in, and through that which is childlike.

Children's object talk:
We Are A Family

Object: A camera (preferably instant developing) loaded with film.
Lesson: All belong to our Church Family.
Outline: 1. Ask who the children's families are, what they do together.
  2. Identify the church as being a family they are part of, too.
  3. Take a picture of the whole church family.

WHO IS YOUR FAMILY? Your mom, your dad, brothers and sisters, maybe aunts, uncles, cousins, grandparents—all of these people are part of your family. Would everybody here who is part of a family please stand?

What are some of the things you do with your families? Do you eat and maybe have picnics together? Do you play games? Do you go on trips? Do you read stories? Your families love you and take care of you, too. Would everybody here who likes to do these things together please stand?

We all are part of another family, a special family. It's called the church, we like to do things together, eat together, sing and read and play together. We love each other and take care of each other, too. What are some of the things you like to do with your church family? Will everybody who is a member of the church family please stand?

When our family is together, we like to take pictures to remember special times. Let's do that today with our church family. Then, we'll put the picture on the bulletin board, so we remember our time in church this Sunday. It will be our Church Family Picture. We surely are a big family!

The sermon:

Some Basic Choices

Hymns:
Beginning of worship: God, Whose Love is Reigning o'er Us
Sermon hymn: Must Jesus Bear the Cross Alone
End of worship: The Voice of God is Calling

Scripture: Matthew 10:34-42

Sermon Text: *"For I have come to set a man against his father, and a daughter against her mother, and a daughter-in-law against her mother-in-law ... whoever loves father or mother more than me is not worthy of me..."* v. 36, 37

A SHORT TIME BEFORE QUEEN VICTORIA'S DEATH, in 1896, Vera Brittain was born into the family of a middle-class factory owner. She was followed, in 1898, by a brother, Edward.

Their Victorian world was far different from our own. As Vera grew to adulthood, she began to confront both social conventions and parental attitudes which reflected that time and culture.

Most young ladies did not continue beyond, or even really complete, their high school education. Some went to "finishing schools," where they learned the female skills considered important by male society. Vera managed to coax her parents into letting her finish real high school; she graduated in 1912.

A year at home, stifled by provincial social amenities, convinced Vera that she wanted more than just respectable middle-class womanhood. But there was only enough money for one child to go to college; of course, that meant Edward. Vera was not deterred. After almost a year of pleading, she got her father to promise that if she could pass the entrance and scholarship exams for Oxford University — a major undertaking even for a man — she could go to college.

Her family assumed that Vera, as a woman, was intellectually inept, unable to function academically. She proved them wrong, not only passing the exams, but winning a prize in the process. Her astonished father could not but relent. In the spring of 1914, Vera entered St. Margaret's College, Oxford, the only school that officially accepted female students.

Suddenly, in August, 1914, the world went to war, and Vera's precious education, fought for so long and hard, was suspended. To do her part for the war effort, Vera became a Red Cross nurse. The ensuing years brought only hardship. Vera lived to see her brother, and all his friends — a whole generation of young men — slaughtered. Embittered and empty, Vera returned to a world irrevocably changed.

Somehow, though, by stubborn determination, Vera went back to Oxford. She became one of the first women ever to be granted an academic degree by the University. In spite of formidable obstacles placed in her way by social conventions, by war, and by her family's expectations, Vera got her education.

Vera Brittain made some important basic choices. She is remembered today as a pacifist, a tireless worker on behalf of humanitarian causes, and as an author, whose *Testament of Youth* stands beside Remarque's *All Quiet on the Western Front* as the only major book about the Great War written by a woman.

"For I have come to set a man against his father, and a daughter against her mother, and a daughter-in law against her mother-in-law ... Whoever loves father or mother more than me is not worthy of me; and whoever loves son or daughter more than me is not worthy of me; and whoever does not take up the cross and follow me is not worthy of me." (Matthew 10:35, 37-38, NRSV).

These comments of Jesus concerning the conflict which might be experienced within families, because of the choice to follow Jesus, are directed toward a new community of faith, emerging out of an older tradition, held in suspicion by governing authorities. The "sword" of which Jesus speaks may be both a symbol of strife and a symbol of persecution and martyrdom. Ironically, the "sword" is not in the hands of Jesus' followers, but rather, in the hands of their enemies — and Jesus himself brings the "sword!" Christians are called upon to make hard choices. In spite of conflict, strife, or persecution arising from such choices, Christians live within the realization that regardless of any sacrifice we face, our sacrifice bears witness to Christ — whose victory was gained by his own sacrifice on the cross.

In this passage, and others like it, Jesus is not speaking against families. Indeed, he calls upon his disciples to love their families, to honor fathers and mothers. What is absolutely clear, however, is that such honor and love must never stand in the way of obedience to God and the demands of God's kingdom. And really, this comes as no surprise; for as much as we love, are indebted to, and honor our families, only the most immature and self-deceiving of us would believe that our family is divine, or that its values are universal, or that what is good for me and mine is good for all. (The so-called "Pro-Family Movement" has made an idol of the family. Their insistence that all families must be, act, and believe in the same way is a travesty of both justice and the gospel.) Families are fine; they simply are not, and can never be, our sole or primary object of allegiance, or our only source of value and strength.

Joseph Donders, in his book, *Jesus the Stranger*, has some helpful insights about this aspect of Jesus' teaching. He asks, "Did you ever hear of the town in which Jesus had his own house? ... He did not settle; he did not even choose a partner. He never started his own home; he had friends — plenty of them; he had his lady-friends — plenty of them; but every time they wanted to keep him, to make him settle, or to lay a special claim upon him, he would say things like: Do not keep me, I have to go on, others are waiting, do not hold me, let me go.

"And he went, apparently forgetting about his mother, about his

July 11, 1993
(Epis/Pres/Meth/UCC - June 27, 1993)

family, about his parental home, about Nazareth, about Judea, about Galilee, about his country, and about his nation. His disciples did not understand this, although he asked some of them to do the same: to leave their father, to leave their mother, to leave their brothers and sisters, their wives, and consequently their homes.

"He did not forbid people to marry; he did not forbid us to start our own homes ... He told people to be faithful in their marriage, not to run away from each other. He hated people who did not take care of their children, but he added to all that a new dimension, that general brotherhood idea, that family of God idea, that world perspective."

"For I have come to set a man against his father, and a daughter against her mother, and a daughter-in-law against her mother-in-law ... Whoever loves father or mother more than me is not worthy of me; and whoever loves son or daughter more than me is not worthy of me; and whoever does not take up the cross and follow me is not worthy of me."

Nancy E. Topolewski
Kirkwood United Methodist Church
Sidney, New York

JULY 18, 1993

Lutheran: Seventh Sunday after Pentecost
Roman Catholic: Fourteenth Sunday of the Year
Episcopalian: Proper 9 (July 4)
Pres/Meth/UCC: Fifth after Pentecost (July 4)

Lessons:

Lutheran:	Zech. 9:9-12	Rom. 7:15-25a	Matt. 11:25-30
Roman Catholic:	Zech. 9:9-10	Rom. 8:9, 11-13	Matt. 11:25-30
Episcopal:	Zech. 9:9-12	Rom. 7:21-8:6	Matt. 11:25-30
Pres/Meth/UCC:	Gen. 24:34-38, 42-49, 58-67	Rom. 7:15-25a	Matt. 11:16-19, 25-30

Introductions to the Lessons

Lesson 1

(1) *Zechariah 9:9-12* (**Luth/Epis**). Zechariah writes during the difficult days of the post-exilic period. He expresses the people's longing for the coming of the Messiah who will bring peace and freedom for the captives. He calls upon the people to rejoice that the victorious Messiah will come.

(2) *Genesis 24:34-38, 42-49, 58-67* (**Pres/Meth/UCC**). Before Abraham died, he wanted to get a wife for his son Isaac. He sent his oldest servant back to his family in Haran. After prayer, the servant was led to Rebecca, the daughter of Bethuel, Abraham's brother, because she was generous in giving water to both him and his camels. Rebecca agreed to return with the servant and became the wife of Isaac who loved her.

Lesson 2

Romans 7:15-25a (**Luth/Pres/Meth/UCC**); *Rom. 7:21-8:6* (**Epis**). A Christian has a dual nature: a higher and a lower self, flesh vs. spirit. A Christian also has a duel nature. The two natures are in constant warfare. Paul describes the struggle in his life, a struggle we all share. The good we want to do, we do not; the evil we don't want to do, we do. Only Christ can deliver us from this inner conflict. To him we give thanks.

Gospel

Matthew 11:25-30 (**Luth/Epis**); *Matt. 11:16-19, 25-30* (**Pres/Meth/UCC**). Jesus has comforting words for his disciples. Previously his words demanded that he come first, that they bear a cross, and that judgment would fall on cities that rejected him. In

July 18, 1993
(Epis/Pres/Meth/UCC - July 4, 1993)

this passage he thanks his Father for revealing the truth to plain people. Because he is one with God, he invites all who are burdened to come to him for rest.

Theme: Good News through innocent eyes.

Thought for the day: Neither sophistication nor complexity is a prerequisite for receiving or sharing God's Good News in Jesus Christ. In fact, this gospel is often hidden from the wise and revealed to children.

Prayer of meditation: O God, you have taught us that in returning and rest we shall be saved, and that in quietness and confidence shall be our strength. Draw near to us now with your mighty power and steadfast love, that in your presence we may be still and know that you are God; through Jesus Christ our Lord. Amen. (*The Methodist Hymnal*, 1964, alt.)

Call to worship: Thus says the Lord: Do not let the wise boast in their wisdom, do not let the mighty boast in their might, do not let the wealthy boast in their wealth; but let those who boast boast in this, that they understand and know me, that I am the Lord; I act with steadfast love, justice, and righteousness in the earth, for in these things I delight, says the Lord. (Jeremiah 9:23-24, NRSV)

Prayer of adoration: Almighty God, the fountain of all wisdom, you know our necessities before we ask and our ignorance in asking: Have compassion on our weakness, and mercifully give us those things which for our unworthiness we dare not, and for our blindness we cannot ask; through the worthiness of your Son Jesus Christ our Lord, who lives and reigns with you and the Holy Spirit, one God, now and for ever. Amen. (*The Book of Common Prayer*)

Prayer of confession: Most merciful God, we confess that we have sinned against you in thought, word, and deed, by what we have done, and by what we have left undone. We have not loved you with our whole heart; we have not loved our neighbors as ourselves. We are truly sorry and we humbly repent. For the sake of your Son Jesus Christ, have mercy on us and forgive us; that we may delight in your will, and walk in your ways, to the glory of your name. Amen. (*The United Methodist Hymnal*, 1989)

Prayer of dedication of gifts and self: Gracious and bountiful Lord, the gifts we bring are expressions of who we are and how we love.

The Minister's Annual Manual

Use all that we are, and all that we bring, to the honor of your holy name. Amen.

Sermon title: "What Is Real?" said the Rabbit

Sermon thesis: Four images are explored in such a way as to illustrate and reinforce the insight from today's Gospel lesson, that God's gracious will is that Good News can be seen by, and in, and through that which is childlike.

Hymn for the day: *"How sweet the name of Jesus sounds."* John Newton (1725-1807) was seven years old when his mother died. Four years later he went to sea with his father. For many years he was involved in slave trade, which became more and more distasteful to him, until he finally gave it up in 1754. After meeting George Whitefield and the Wesleys he entered the ministry and became curate of Olney. Together with William Cowper, he prepared *Olney Hymns*, 1779, which contained this hymn. The hymn reflects on the graciousness of God.

Announcements for next week:
   Sermon title: Seeds, Seeds, Seeds
   Sermon theme: We are all sowers of seeds.
   Sermon summary: The biblical image of growing seeds provides an ongoing challenge to be about both the joy of receiving and the joy of sharing God's mercy and grace. Sometimes this grace comes to us in unexpected ways.

Children's object talk:

Drawing God's Love

Object: A box of Crayola crayons (preferably 64, with a built-in sharpener).
Lesson: You can share God's love.
Outline: 1. Distribute supplies.
   2. Give the assignment.
   3. Explore the possibilities.

GUESS WHAT I HAVE FOR YOU TODAY! Look, it's a brand-new, never-been-opened, unchewed box of 64 Crayola crayons. I bet almost everyone here has crayons at home. (Open the lid.) Tell me, what's your favorite color? Mine is Lemon Yellow.

I'm going to let you take this box of crayons, and these blank sheets of paper with you to the nursery. And I have an important job for you to do. I want you to draw me a picture of God's love. What do you think you might draw? A bird ... your house ...

July 18, 1993
(Epis/Pres/Meth/UCC - July 4, 1993)

your mother ... a big heart ... our church ... Jesus. Oh, boy, you've got a lot of great ideas.

After church, bring me your pictures, and we'll hang them on the bulletin board—your pictures of God's love.

The sermon:
"What Is Real?" said the Rabbit

Hymns:
Beginning of worship: How Can We Name a Love
Sermon hymn: Cuando El Pobre (When the Poor Ones)
End of worship: Forth in Thy Name

Scripture: Matthew 11:25-30

Sermon Text: *"I thank you, Father, Lord of heaven and earth, because you have hidden these things from the wise and the intelligent and have revealed them to infants; yes, Father, for such was your gracious will."* v. 25-26

EDWARD HICKS LIVED AND WORKED IN THE NINETEENTH CENTURY and is remembered today as a painter of children and animals. You can always tell a Hicks painting when you see one: The animals are many, wide-eyed and contented; a child plays among them; and what adults appear in the painting are there almost as an afterthought, standing somewhere in the rear.

Some incorrect conclusions could easily be drawn from these observations, assuming that the child-like quality of Hicks' work reflects an innocence that is psychologically naive, socially impossible, and historically deceiving. But such is not the case. Hicks titled many of his paintings after Isaiah's vision of the wolf and the lamb together, led by a child—a messianic child, who leads us all to "The Peaceable Kingdom." Hicks' vision is one shared by prophets and sages alike. His commitment, nurtured within his Quaker upbringing, is to the establishment of peace. His hero, one of the adults in the background of his paintings, is William Penn. Although the setting is Penn's Woods, Pennsylvania, his vision transcends time, personality, and place. It is the vision of an adult artist who trusts his own best child-like instincts and shares with us a dream of peace.

The tragedy "King Lear," by William Shakespeare, is one of his most complex and difficult plays to understand. It has been called both a tragedy of old age, and a plea for order. It can be viewed as one more variation on the Cinderella story, which is part of so many folklores and heritages. It ends on a most dismal note, as the powers of injustice and cruelty prevail.

But there is more to be said, for it is also the story of a man who, in his old age and with the advent of decreased mental powers, suffers the ingratitude of those children whom he has trusted, and is succored by the one child he had cast off. Having in his dotage been relieved of his position and might, Lear discovers in the father-child relationship between himself and Cordelia some meaning, some internal strength, some love which cannot be taken away. How well they know that when reason is abandoned, when natural ties and duties are violated, havoc and suffering are sure to follow. Yet, as an old man becomes a child, and a daughter returns to her father's side, there forms — or reforms — between them a bonding that endures.

At the end of the play, the forces of King Lear and his daughter are defeated in battle, and the two are led off to what they think will be their captivity, but which, in fact, will prove to be their death. In a moment of almost playful, demented wisdom, Lear speaks to Cordelia: "Come, let's away to prison; We two alone will sing like birds; th' cage, and take upon's the mystery of things as if we were God's spies."

Childlike, insightful, supportive, caring — what more could an old man and his daughter wish or want, even in the face of death?

There is a story about a small circus, which traveled from village to village, from town to town. The pattern was simple: The troupe would parade through the community, hand out announcements of their performances, and then depart for the edge of town, where they would set up their tent for the evening show.

One day, the tent caught fire an hour or so before the performance was to start. Everyone ran to help, and one individual was sent running into town, in order that others might come and assist in putting out the fire. The man cried out about the fire. He pleaded with people to bring their buckets, to come and help. But no one came, and the tent burned to the ground.

Why? Well, in all the excitement of the fire, nobody gave a thought to the fact that the man who had been sent for help was already in costume — he was dressed as a clown! His cries for help were (people thought) just one more way of drumming up a crowd.

July 18, 1993
(Epis/Pres/Meth/UCC - July 4, 1993)

Not until they saw the smoke in the sky did they recognize that there was a real man in the clown suit, whose message was urgent. You see, they heard the clown with their eyes, not with their ears.

So it is with us. We hear those who bear witness to the faith; we hear those who speak of Christ-likeness, child-likeness; we hear our children—with our eyes, and we do not hear what is being said.

Margery Williams is an adult who has heard children. She has made space for their ways and listened for the insights they hold and share. In her recreation of our common past, our time as children, she shares her own insights and commitment as well. Listen to this passage from *The Velveteen Rabbit*:

"The Skin Horse had lived longer in the nursery than any of the others. He was so old that his brown coat was bald in patches and showed the seams underneath, and most of the hairs in his tail had been pulled out to string bead necklaces. He was wise, for he had seen a long succession of mechanical toys arrive to boast and swagger, and by-and-by break their mainsprings and pass away, and he knew that they were only toys, and would never turn into anything else. For nursery magic is very strange and wonderful, and only those playthings that are old and wise and experienced like the Skin Horse understand all about it.

'What is Real?' asked the Rabbit, one day, when they were lying side by side near the nursery fender, before Nana come to tidy the room. 'Does it mean having things that buzz inside you and a stick-out handle?'

'Real isn't how you're made,' said the Skin Horse. 'It's a thing that happens to you. When a child loves you for a long, long time, not just to play with, but really loves you, then you became Real.'

'Does it hurt?' asked the Rabbit.

'Sometimes,' said the Skin Horse, for he was always truthful. 'When you are Real you don't mind being hurt.'

'Does it happen all at once, like being wound up,' he asked, 'or bit by bit?'

'It doesn't happen all at once,' said the Skin Horse. 'You become. It takes a long time. That's why it doesn't often happen to people who break easily, or have sharp edges, or who have to be carefully kept. Generally, by the time you are Real, most of your hair has been loved off, and your eyes drop out, and you get loose in the joints and very shabby. But these things don't matter at all, because once you are Real you can't be ugly, except to people who don't understand.' "

A painter's vision of Peace, a daughter's care for her father, the ability to hear with our ears, a child's story about love and maturity. In short, the Good News of God in Christ — the Gospel of our Lord.

"I thank you, Father, Lord of heaven and earth, because you have hidden these things from the wise and the intelligent and have revealed them to infants; yes, Father, for such was your gracious will."

John L. Topolewski
Superintendent, United Methodist Church
Sidney, New York

JULY 25, 1993

Lutheran: Eighth Sunday after Pentecost
Roman Catholic: Fifteenth Sunday of the Year
Episcopalian: Proper 10 (July 12)
Pres/Meth/UCC: Sixth after Pentecost (July 11)

Lessons:

Lutheran:	Is. 55:10-11	Rom. 8:18-25	Matt. 13:1-9 (18-23)
Roman Catholic:	Is. 55:10-11	Rom. 8:18-23	Matt. 13:1-23
Episcopal:	Is. 55:1-5, 10-13	Rom. 8:9-17	Matt. 13:1-9, 18-23
Pres/Meth/UCC:	Gen. 25:19-34	Rom. 8:1-11	Matt. 13:1-9, 18-23

Introductions to the Lessons

Lesson 1

(1) *Isaiah 55:10-11* (**Luth**); *Isa. 55:1-5, 10-13* (**Epis**). As the moisture from heaven causes agriculture to flourish, so also God's Word will accomplish its purpose. Our task is to proclaim the Word and God will produce the results. This is the church's task which she performs by proclaiming and administering the Word.

(2) *Genesis 25:19-34* (**Pres/Meth/UCC**). For 20 years Isaac and Rebecca had no children After prayer God gave her twins: Jacob and Esau. When the boys were grown, Esau was an outdoors man and Jacob, his mother's favorite, stayed at home. After hunting all day, Esau came home ravishingly hungry and asked Jacob to prepare him a meal. The price was Esau's giving to Jacob his birthright as the first-born son.

Lesson 2

(1) *Romans 8:18-25* (**Luth**). Paul teaches here that suffering is a part of the Christian life because they participate in Christ's suffering. The whole creation suffers and longs for the day when it will be free from decay. Likewise, we groan within until we attain the full liberty as children of God. This constitutes Christian hope.

(2) *Romans 8:9-17* (**Epis**). A Christian is born of the Spirit at baptism and lives thereafter according to the Spirit. Consequently, we are to live as the Spirit dictates. The Spirit in us witnesses to the fact that as children of God we can cry, "Abba Father." To live by the Spirit is to have life, for the Spirit is God who is life.

(3) *Romans 8:1-11* (**Pres/Meth/UCC**). Christians are free from God's condemnation because they live in and by the Spirit. If we lived by our human nature, the old Adam, or flesh, we would be condemned because we cannot perfectly keep the Law. Christ

473

fulfilled the Law for us by his sacrifical death. If Christ lives in us, we live by his Spirit who gives us life.

Gospel

Matthew 13:1-9 (**Luth**); *Matt. 13:1-9, 18-23* (**Epis/Pres/Meth/UCC**). Seated in a boat, Jesus preached to a crowd gathered on the beach of the Sea of Galilee. He tells them the parable of the sower whose seed fell on different kinds of soil and produced accordingly. Later the church, verses 18-23, gave an allegorical interpretation of the parable. The efficacy of the Word depends on the receptivity of the listener.

Theme: We are all sowers of seeds.

Thought for the day: Seeds, seeds, seeds everywhere: generously given, abundantly sown, gifts of love, gifts of life. The field awaits the sowing; the yield is still to come.

Prayer of meditation: Almighty and everlasting God, you are always more ready to hear than we to pray, and to give more than we either desire or deserve. Pour down upon us the abundance of your mercy, forgiving us those things whereof our conscience is afraid, and giving us those good things which we are not worthy to ask, but through the merits and mediation of Jesus Christ, your Son, our Lord. Amen. (*The Book of Common Worship*)

Call to worship:
O Lord, open our lips.
And our mouth shall show forth your praise.
Glory be to the Father, and to the Son, and to the Holy Spirit.
As it was in the beginning, is now, and ever shall be, world
　without end. Amen.

Prayer of adoration: New every morning is your love, great God of light, and all day long you are working for good in the world. Stir up in us desire to serve you, to live peacefully with our neighbors, and to devote each day to your Son, our Savior, Jesus Christ the Lord. Amen. (*The United Methodist Hymnal,* 1989)

Prayer of confession: Merciful God, we confess that we have not loved you with our heart. We have failed to be an obedient church. We have not done your will, we have broken your law, we have rebelled against your love, we have not loved our neighbors, and we have not heard the cry of the needy. Forgive us, we pray. Free us for joyful obedience, through Jesus Christ our Lord. Amen. (*The United Methodist Hymnal,* 1989)

July 25, 1993
(Epis/Pres/Meth/UCC - July 11, 1993)

Prayer of dedication of gifts and self: We give ourselves and our gifts with the constant petition: Your kingdom come, your will be done, on earth as in heaven; in Jesus' name. Amen.

Sermon title: Seeds, Seeds, Seeds

Sermon thesis: The biblical image of growing seeds provides an ongoing challenge to be about both the joy of receiving and the joy of sharing God's mercy and grace. Sometimes this grace comes to us in unexpected ways.

Hymn for the day: *"Almighty God, your Word is cast."* Based directly on the Matthew text, this hymn was written in 1815 by Thomas Cotterill (1775-1853). Born in Derbyshire, England, Cotterill attended Oxford University and served for nearly 40 years as curate of St. Ann's Chapel of Ease, Bewdley, in Worcestershire.

Children's object talk:

Planting Time

Objects: 1. A marigold plant
2. Marigold seeds
3. A prepared seedbed in the nursery
Lesson: We can work with God.
Outline: 1. Show the plant and the seeds it grew from.
2. Share the seeds for planting.
3. Emphasize that we can all do God's work.

LOOK AT THESE FLOWERS! Aren't they wonderful, all yellow and orange with green leaves. Does anyone here know what kind of flowers these are? That's right, they're marigolds. Now, look what I have in this dish. These are seeds, marigold seeds. It was from little seeds like these that these lovely flowers grew.

Do you have flowers and plants at home? Did you grow them from seeds? Well, I've spoken to your teacher, and when you go to the nursery today, she will help you plant these seeds, and in about two months, we'll have a new set of marigolds!

That makes us all farmers. Did you know God is a farmer, too? God plants seeds in our lives every day. God gives us love. And just like our flowers, it must be cared for.

Please take good care of your marigolds, and good care of God's love.

The sermon:

Seeds, Seeds, Seeds

Hymns:
Beginning of worship: O God in Heaven
Sermon hymn: We Plow the Fields and Scatter
End of worship: Lord, Whose Love through Humble Service

Scripture: Matthew 13:1-9

Sermon Text: *"Listen! A sower went out to sow."* v. 3

THE SOWER IS SOWING HIS SEED EVERYWHERE, generously, abundantly, hands-full of seed: That seed is the life of Jesus, and it falls all over us, over us all, a gift from heaven; just as all we have and all we are is a gift of God. We are invited to receive that seed and let it grow into fruit.

Now, as we are reminded in the parable, and in the writings of the White Father Joseph Donders, there are many things that can go wrong with such a gift, a gift of seed, a gift of Jesus, a gift of life. It can fall on the concrete, on the smoothness and the tightness of the people who do not want to live or to get old, who do not want to mature and to get wrinkles, who do not want to live at all. It can fall on our walkways, where there are too many footsteps, too much business, too much work, too much running to be able to survive and to enjoy and to thank. It can fall among the thorns and be too over-stimulated, over-excited, to be able to live.

In spite of these dangers, yet the sower continues to sow: Seeds, seeds, seeds; the gift of Jesus, the gifts of life.

But he is not the sower alone; we, too, bear responsibility for, and witness to, God's kingdom. The gifts of life are our gifts to give, as well; our seeds are everywhere, too. That life and that seed are not only gifts that should develop in me, because of myself, but also because of others. My life is not only a gift to me; it is God's gift to you, as well, just as your life is not only a gift to you, but also to me. The sower's seeds are everywhere: Generous seeds, abundant seeds, hands-full of seeds.

For over 500 years, Western art was dominated by two themes: Church and state, faith and the crown, the king and the King of Kings. A number of years ago now, if you're a closet Anglophile like me, you will remember watching what was billed as the "wedding

July 25, 1993
(Epis/Pres/Meth/UCC - July 11, 1993)

of the century." The Prince of Wales, heir to England's throne, had, in the words of the ancient liturgy, taken to himself a bride. And what a glorious "taking" it was, filled with all the pageantry and theater the English, and the institution of the crown, could bring to bear, coupled with the ceremony, the vestments, and the music of the church. Art and life were one, as the sovereigns-to-be walked the aisle of St. Paul's Cathedral and processed through London's sand-strewn streets. In a common re-living of our childhood past, the Fairy Princess and Prince Charming were united in marriage and began to live what we then thought to be happily ever after.

What do you think about when you go to a wedding? At first, we probably think about our apprehensions: She's so young! Does she really know what she's letting herself in for? Is he ready, really ready? Then we tend to forget about our anxieties as we become involved in the ceremony itself and as we hear again those ancient and wise words. Perhaps – perhaps we even remember our own wedding, and find ourselves in some unconscious, yet meaningful way, re-living those sacred vows.

In a sense, the wedding of Charles Philip Arthur George (Did I get them in the right order?) and Diana Frances was not theirs alone; in a very real way, it was also your wedding and mine. How appropriate that the Archbishop of Canterbury should remind us all that in the marriage rite of the Eastern Orthodox, every bride and groom have a crown placed on their heads, and all become princes and princesses. In ways that we will never begin to measure, the institution of marriage was strengthened; ties of love were drawn closer; our lives were ennobled by that wedding. The seeds were everywhere, as numerous as the grains of sand spread upon the roads: Seeds of love and life, seeds sown by the sower, and sown by the church, sown for you and me.

At the very time when I was so involved in watching the royal wedding, the news broadcast was continually being interrupted by a local story of tragic dimensions. It came as a reminder that much can go wrong with the gift of life. Two small children were reported missing; two days later, our worst fears and suspicions proved true, as their bodies were discovered. Later that week, a neighbor, a young man, was arrested and charged with the crime. Did he do it? That question would be settled through the judicial process. If he did it, why? That question remains unanswered.

We can blame this tragedy on any number of factors: A broken home, the state of the economy, kids today, lack of parental control—we do not find it difficult to come up with easy answers. What we do find difficult to accept is the fact that no one single, simple answer, or any combination of answers, for that matter, will *ever* answer, "Why?" The seeds were sown; they must have been sown; but they did not take. The seeds did not take. And our sense of tragedy comes from the fact that we do not know why.

Many of us have had the experience of receiving a note or a call or a visit from someone out of our past who reminds us of some word, some event shared in common, and, quite often, a word, an event that we have forgotten. "I'll never forget when you said..." "I'll always remember when..." "You don't know how much it meant to me when..." You see, we scatter seeds even when we're not the least bit aware of it. Seeds, seeds, everywhere, all the time; generously given, abundantly sown, gifts of love, gifts of life. If all of us could understand and live that reality, the field of this, our world, could yield a crop—a hundred, a thousand-fold.

"A sower went out to sow. And as he sowed..." Jesus is the sower, and his seeds fall all over us, over us all, a gift of heaven. You are the sower, and so am I, and our seeds are abundant. Please, let them be seeds of love, seeds of life.

John L. Topolewski
Superintendent, United Methodist Church
Sidney, New York

Pre-publication Advance Order Form

THE MINISTER'S ANNUAL MANUAL FOR PREACHING AND WORSHIP PLANNING 1993-1994

66 complete sermon and worship planning helps beginning August 1, 1993 through July 31, 1994

(Available by June 1, 1993)

$21.95
(plus 10% for postage/handling)

CLIP AND SEND NAME/ADDRESS WITH PAYMENT TO:

CHURCH MANAGEMENT, INC., P.O. Box 162527, Austin, TX 78716.
My check for $24.15, payable to CHURCH MANAGEMENT, INC., is enclosed for one copy of *The Minister's Annual Manual for Preaching and Worship Planning 1993-1994.*

Name _____   _____

Address _____

City/State/Zip _____

Preach Like Jesus

by John R. Brokhoff*

In the middle of the week, a pastor asked another, "What are you going to preach about this Sunday?" She replied, "Jesus." It was a good answer which St. Paul would approve. "We preach Jesus Christ our Lord." (II Cor. 4:5) But, how do we preach Christ? Do we preach like Jesus preached? If we want to be like Jesus, to be forgiving, as Jesus was, to be compassionate, to be kind and good like Jesus was, to live like Jesus, can we preach like Jesus?

Every preacher needs a role model, someone to look up to. After hearing a great sermon, one says, "I want to preach like that!" Of course, this can be carried to an extreme. Slavish imitation can be disastrous. Years ago Oscar Blackwelder was probably the most popular Lutheran preacher in America. A young man just out of seminary so admired Blackwelder that he imitated him in gestures, tone of voice, and language. He became known as "the little Blackwelder." No, one must be one's own person. Preaching is truth through one's unique personality shared by no other person. Yet, one needs a role model as a goal or an ideal. One does not want to be a carbon-copy of another preacher, but the techniques and methods of a greater one can give direction to one's own efforts.

If you want and need a role model as a preacher, you need to choose the very best. Who is the greatest preacher of all time? Is there a greater than Chrysostom, Augustine, Luther, Calvin, or John Knox? Can one surpass a preacher like Jonathan Edwards, Phillips Brooks, Harry Emerson Fosdick, and Billy Graham? Indeed, there

---

*John R. Brokhoff is Professor Emeritus of Homiletics, Candler School of Theology, Emory University. He lives in Clearwater, Florida.

Appendix

is one greater than the greatest. We commonly refer to him as Messiah, teacher, or miracle worker. But, Jesus was a preacher, the best that ever spoke. He had both power and popularity. He began his ministry with the act of preaching. (Mark 1:4) People "marveled at the eloquent words that he spoke." (Luke 4:22) "Large crowds followed him from Galilee." (Matthew 4:25) Because of Jesus' popularity with the masses, the religious authorities *secretly* plotted his death. (Luke 22:2) They had to use an undercover agent, Judas Iscariot, to arrest him at a time when the public was unaware of the plot. They negotiated with Judas "to hand Jesus over to them without the people knowing about it." (Luke 22:6) His preaching made police foget that they came to arrest him. When they returned, they were asked why they did not arrest him. They explained, "No man ever spoke like this man.' (John 7:45-46) The people heard Jesus gladly. They crowded to hear him. When he preached in one home, it was so full that a paralyzed man had to be lowered through the roof to get to Jesus. When he preached on the beach, the crowd so

---

"If we are going to preach like Jesus, we must preach with authority."

---

pressed to get to hear him that he had to speak from a boat. Five thousand men, not counting women and children, followed him to the wide open spaces where food was not available. This resulted in the miracle of feeding the multitude with two fish and five loaves of bread, a boy's lunch!

I Must Preach

If we are going to preach like Jesus, how did he preach? Let us look, first, at his motivation for preaching. Undoubtedly, Jesus felt a divine necessity to preach: "I *must* preach the good news of the Kingdom of God . . . because that is *what God sent me to do*." (Luke 4:43) Jesus felt he had a destiny. It was to proclaim the good news of the Kingdom. It was not a matter of choice but of necessity.

What he had to say was what his Father gave him to say. He did not speak out of his own authority, wisdom, or experience. He explained, "What I teach is not my own teaching, but it comes from

God who sent me." (John 7:16) Again, "I say only what the Father has instructed me to say." (John 8:28)

For us to preach like Jesus is to have a similar motivation. You should preach because you *want* to not because you *have* to. For this reason a preacher lives and serves. A preacher therefore needs to preach to fulfill life's meaning and purpose. A missionary in Burma was engaged in street preaching. A hostile crowd shouted him down and interrupted him. Just when he was about to give up, a Buddhist monk came by and shouted to the crowd, "Listen to this man. Don't you know he needs to tell you about his God?" A true preacher feels like Elihu, who said to Job, "I can hardly wait to speak. I can't hold back the words. If I don't get a chance to speak, I will burst like a wineskin full of new wine. I can't stand it; I have to speak." (Job 32:18-20)

A preacher has to speak because he/she is not speaking for him/herself. A pulpiteer is a spokesperson for God. With the prophets, a preacher says, "Thus saith the Lord." He/she is God's mouthpiece.

"For us to preach like Jesus is to have a similar motivation. We should preach because we want to not because we have to."

A sermon is an acoustical event. The church is God's mouth house. This constitutes a preacher's highest honor and privilege as God's herald and ambassador, and at the same time it is a preacher's heaviest responsibility. Listen to the sermon — is it really God speaking? This makes preaching more than an occupation or a profession. It is a calling. God calls us to speak for him. And there is no inner peace until we do it. Unlike an occupation or profession, we are not paid to preach. The church meets our expenses to enable us to give full time to God's service as a preacher and pastor.

Say Something!

A preacher is supposed to be one who has a message from God to the people. It is not a matter of having to say something Sunday morning but having something to say. Some years ago preachers had a message without relevance to life. Now, many have relevance without a message.

Appendix

Jesus is our model in having something to say. The Scriptures were constantly referred to. In his very first sermon at Nazareth, Jesus used a text from Isaiah 61. (Luke 4:16-21) It was a liturgical and lectionary sermon coming from the assigned lesson for that day. He also used the Scriptures as a resource by quoting them from time to time. After his baptism, he was tempted for 40 days. He turned down each temptation by quoting the Scriptures. (Matthew 4:1-10) When a rich young ruler wanted to know how to get eternal life, Jesus listed some of the Ten Commandments. When a Biblical scholar challenged Jesus to give the greatest law, Jesus gave the two greatest commands: love God and neighbor. (Matthew 22:34-44) Even when near death on the cross, Jesus cried in agony words from a psalm, "My God, why. . .?" (Psalm 21:1)

To have something to say to a congregation each Sunday, a preacher must get the message from the Bible. It is necessary for a sermon to have a text, as necessary as it is to have thread to weave a garment. It is not enough to use a passage as background music to the sermon, not as a jumping off place for one's own ideas. The preacher must let the text speak for itself by providing the theme and main points of the sermon. Then God is speaking in the words of the preacher. Until the Word is proclaimed, the Bible is a dead-letter book. When preached, the Bible comes alive. It is like a musical score. On paper there is no music, no melody. When a musician plays the notes on the score, you get wonderful music — a Brandenburg concerto or a Hallelujah Chorus. People do not care what a preacher thinks or feels. They do not come to church for that purpose. They want to know what God has to say about life and its meaning. When they hear God's voice in the preacher's voice, they go home feeling that it was worth the time and trouble of going to church. And they will be back next Sunday to hear more. To preach like Jesus one must preach a message from the Bible.

How to Say It

Say it with authority. Jesus' preaching was characterized by authority. In the Sermon on the Mount, Jesus put his interpretation on Mosaic statements by saying, "But I say to you." (Matthew 5:21-22) At Capernaum the people were amazed at his teaching, "because he spoke with authority." (Luke 4:32) He could speak with authority because he was God's Son. Moreover, he could be certain about his preaching because it was his Father's message and not his. Being the truth, he spoke the truth with power, conviction, and certainty.

If we are going to preach like Jesus, we must preach with authority. This does not mean that we are authoritarian in terms of lording it over people or as one who knows it all. The preacher's authority is in the Word which is proclaimed. It gives the preacher courage to say what otherwise he/she would be afraid to say. A preacher can say, "If you don't like what is said, don't blame me. Blame God who said it in the Scriptures." Unless you repent, you will perish. I did not say that; God did. (Luke 13:3) The tithe is the Lord's, not yours. I didn't say that; God did. (Malachi 3:10) If you do not tithe, you steal from God. I did not say that; God did!

The preacher's authority can be seen and heard in and through his/her convictions. Powerful preaching results when the preacher believes so deeply in the truth proclaimed that he/she would be willing to die for it. In 1991 President Bush received popular approval

---

"Powerful preaching results when the preacher believes so deeply in the truth proclaimed that he or she would be willing to die for it."

---

of his State of the Union address. *Time* magazine observed, "No speaker is more compelling than one who believes what he is saying." Convictions result from a preacher's faith and are expressed with enthusiasm and zeal. Jesus had convictions of who he was and what his purpose in life was. If we are going to peach like Jesus, we must have deep convictions about spiritual truths taught in the Bible and expressed in the ecumenical creeds of the church.

Say it with boldness. Jesus did. He was frank, direct, and fearless in his preaching and teaching. One time some Pharisees urged Jesus to flee from Jerusalem, because King Herod wanted to kill him. Jesus replied, "Go and tell that fox . . ." (Luke 13:32) He refused to run away and used the unflattering term "fox" for his king! When it came to describing the religious leaders of his day, he was so bold that he called them what they were: "hypocrites," "white-washed sepulchres" (Matthew 23), "liars" (John 8:55) and "children of your father, the Devil." (John 8:44)

In the Book of Acts, the distinguishing mark of apostolic preaching

Appendix

was boldness. The members of the city council of Jerusalem were amazed to see how bold Peter and John were. The apostles frankly declared, "We cannot stop speaking of what we ourselves have seen and heard." (Acts 4:20) Paul asked his people to pray that he might be bold in his preaching. (Ephesians 6:19).

To preach like Jesus we will tell it like it is without pulling any punches. We will expose evil regardless of where it is and who does it. The Word of God consists of Law and Gospel. The Law needs to be preached, for it convicts and brings us to a realization of our sin. Why are some of us preachers so timid, so noncommital? Why do we try to carry water on both shoulders hoping to please everybody? Are we afraid of losing favor or of offending a member? Do we fear that some may walk out during the sermon? Is our job in jeopardy? Will it mean a decline in salary? Indeed, boldness in preaching may demand a price. It cost John the Baptist his head. It threw Jeremiah into a pit. It chased Amos back home. It cost Jesus death on a cross. John Chrysostom and John Calvin were driven from their pulpits. We are in a war with Satan, and, as in every war, there are casualties. Therefore, Paul advised us to put on the whole armor of God and then speak up and speak out the truth. Let the pieces fall where they will!

Ways of Saying It

Jesus never enrolled in a seminary. He had no course in Homiletics on how to prepare a sermon. In his day there was no course on practice preaching to perfect the delivery of a sermon. But Jesus had a message and a love for people. Instinctively he knew how to get the message across and into the minds and hearts of his listeners.

For one thing, Jesus used many illustrations in his messages. He used similes such as "as a hen gathers her brood." (Matthew 23:37) At times he used metaphors: "You are the salt of the earth." (Matthew 5:13) Thirty-five percent of his teaching consisted of parables, examples, cases, life situations, and stories. Without a parable he did not teach them. (Mark 4:34) In his presentations Jesus used concrete references, the things with which common people were familiar: bread, water, sheep, birds, grass, wheat, flowers, etc. He avoided the general and abstract, the theoretical and academic. Jesus talked about specific items: two sparrows for a penny (Matthew 10:29), and the hairs of your head. (Matthew 10:30) By these illustra-

The Minister's Annual Manual

tions, he made deep, eternal truths simple and plain for everyone, even a child.

To preach like Jesus means to use plenty of homiletical materials to make plain the Scriptures. Illustrations prevent platitudes, generalities, and boredom. They help to make the message interesting and real. An illustration can make plain the point you are trying to make. At the same time an illustration gives the congregation a break from serious, concentrated thought, especially when humor is used. Because of this need for illustrative materials, a preacher is on the lookout for this material every waking hour of the day and night. A sermon without illustrations is like a building without windows and with no interior lighting.

Another method Jesus used in preaching was the dialogical method. Jesus spoke to people and involved people in his preaching. By doing this he succeeded in getting their interest, in making them think, and in helping them to find answers for themselves. How did he do this? Consider—

1. Questions—In the gospels Jesus asked 153 questions, such as—
"Which man of you?" (Luke 15:4)
"What father among you?" (Luke 11:11)
"What do you think?" (Matthew 21:28)
"Who do you say that I am?" (Matthew 16:15)
"How do you read?" (Luke 10:26)
2. Life situations.
Jesus used life situations as opportunities for learning. It was the case method, such as—
Pilate's massacre of Galileans (Luke 13:1-5)
Man with a withered hand (Mark 3:1-6)
A man born blind (John 9:1-3)
3. Inductive method.
Usually Jesus did not begin with a general truth. He used the inductive method by starting with the specific and going to the general. In the case of the Samaritan woman at the well in John 4, Jesus began with a request for water and went to a theological question on worship to a moral question of adultery to the revelation that he was the Messiah.
4. A fourth method Jesus used was the application of the message to daily life. He did not speak for the sake of speaking. There was to be a practical outcome. Consider some cases:
• A woman caught in adultery: "Go, and sin no more." (John 8:11)

Appendix

- The story of the Good Samaritan: "Go and do likewise." (Luke 10:37)
- The conclusion to the Sermon on the Mount: obedience. (Matthew 7:24-27)

When a sermon is finished, do we ask, "So what? What difference does it make? What am I to do about it?" When John the Baptizer finished a sermon, the people responded, "What are we to do then?" (Luke 3:10) Likewise, at the end of Peter's Pentecost sermon, the people asked, "What shall we do, brothers?" (Acts 2:37) To make a sermon applicable and practical, a preacher needs to ask him/herself, "What difference does this truth make — what difference to your life, to your work, to your family, to your church? Your sermon was about love. But, tell me how can I love the unlovely? You preach about faith? Well and good, but how do I get faith? If a sermon is going to do anybody any good, it must get down to where people are and give specific know-how to live a Christian life in a naughty world.

To preach like Jesus is as difficult as it is to live like Jesus every day in every way. It is a perfect goal which takes a lifetime to approximate. Little by little, year by year with God's help we aspire to reach the goals. As we long to be like Jesus, we preachers long to preach like Jesus. We have not yet attained the goal but we press on "until we all attain . . . to the measure of the stature of the fullness of Christ" as preachers par excellence! (Ephesians 4:13) ■

Preaching from the Common Lectionary

Resources for Preaching

by David H. Schmidt*

One-volume commentaries to be used throughout the three year cycle include:
James L. Mays, general editor, *Harper's Bible Dictionary,* (Harper & Row, 1988). Published in cooperation with the Society of Biblical Literature, this one-volume commentary provides good brief information which reflects the current state of scholarship. There are good overview articles as well as comments on each book (including the Apocrypha). A second current one-volume work is Raymond E. Brown et al. *The New Jerome Biblical Commentary,* Revised edition (Paulist Press, 1989). While Roman Catholic in origin, it is a valuable tool for all. About two-thirds of revised edition is new material.

Books for study of the Psalter for all three years:
Overview and Theology
H.J. Kraus, *Theology of the Psalms* (Augsburg, 1986) is a good discussion by a scholar who has also published a major commentary (below). A briefer but insightful work is C. Westermann, *The Living Psalms* (Eerdmans, 1988). It would serve as a fine introductory study.

---

*David H. Schmidt is Campus Minister at the Wesley Foundation, United Methodist Church, Northern Illinois University in Dekalb, Illinois.

Appendix

Commentaries

H.J. Kraus, *Psalms 1-59* and *Psalms 60-150* (Augsburg, 1987, 1989) is one of the most detailed works of this century. For those who want a less formidable study, A.A. Anderson, *The Book of Psalms*, The New Century Bible Commentary (Eerdmans, 1972) is a solid, yet inexpensive two volume set that will serve the pastor well. Don't overlook C. Stuhlmueller in the Harper's commentary above.

ORDINARY TIME, Aug. 2 to Nov. 22, 1992

For the study of the Gospel lessons:

Overviews

F.W. Danker, *Luke*, Proclamation Commentary, 2nd rev. ed (Fortress, 1987) will provide a good discussion on Luke which is gospel for the year C. C. Talbert, *Reading Luke* (Crossroad, 1982) offers a literary and theological review with stimulating ideas.

Commentaries

A most detailed and helpful set is Joseph Fitzmyer, *The Gospel According to Luke*, Anchor Bible 28, 28A (Doubleday, 1981, 1985). Add to this the new expository work by Fred Craddock, *Luke*, Interpretation Commentaries (John Knox, 1990) for good preaching help. Eduard Schweizer, *The Good News According to Luke* (John Knox, 1987) provides a nice combination of exegetical and pastoral insight. I. Howard Marshall, *The Gospel of Luke*, New International Greek Commentary (Eerdmans, 1978) offers a solid evangelical study of the Greek text.

Studies

Walter E. Pilgrim, *Good News to the Poor* (Augsburg, 1981) offers a provocative sermon starter on issues of wealth and poverty. Likewise J. Massyngbaerde Ford, *My Enemy is My Guest* (Orbis, 1984) stimulates one on the issues of non-violence in Luke. Both books invite one to look at the gospel from a new perspective.

Books for the study of Epistle lessons during this time (Colossians five times, Hebrews four times, I & II Timothy seven times, II Thessalonians three times):

For Colossians/Philemon one could start with Peter T. O'Brien, *Colossians, Philemon*, Word Biblical Commentary (Word, 1982) for good current evangelical scholarship. Eduard Lohse, *Colossians and*

Philemon, Hermeneia (Fortress, 1971) provides a detailed commentary on the Greek text.
F. F. Bruce, *The Epistle to the Hebrews*, rev. ed., The New International Commentary on the New Testament (Eerdmans, 1990) is a solid place to begin for Hebrews. Harold W. Attridge, *Hebrews*, Hermeneia (Fortress, 1989) is a fine study on the Greek text, but the book is designed so others can use it without too much trouble. Ernst Kaesemann, *The Wandering People of God* (Augsburg, 1984) is a well recognized treatise which might be read along with one of the above commentaries.
For the pastorals, J.N.D. Kelly, *A Commentary on the Pastoral Epistles*, Harper's New Testament Commentaries (Harper, 1963) is a good traditional approach, while M. Dibelius and Hans Conzelmann, *The Pastoral Epistles*, Hermeneia (Fortress, 1972) provides a detailed study from the deutero-Pauline perspective. The new expository work by Thomas C. Oden, *First and Second Timothy and Titus*, Interprepation Commentaries (John Knox, 1989) may be of assistance. His decision to group passages topically is annoying to some.
Leon Morris, *The First and Second Epistles to the Thessalonians*, New International Commentary on the New Testament, rev. ed. (Eerdmans, 1991) provides a sound evangelical start for II Thessalonians, while Ernest Best, *A Commentary on the First and Second Epistles to the Thessalonians*, Harper's New Testament Commentaries (Hendrickson, 1972) continues to offer solid scholarly assistance.

Books for the study of some of Old Testament texts:
For Jeremiah, Ronald Clements, *Jeremiah*, Interpretation Commentaries (John Knox, 1989) offers a good expository study. John Bright, *Jeremiah*, Anchor Bible 21 (Doubleday, 1965) has a fresh translation and helpful insight. R. Carroll, *Jeremiah: A Commentary*, Old Testament Library (Westminster, 1986) is one of several solid newer works for those wanting more exegetical material.

The Nativity Cycle and Sundays after Epiphany, A
Books for the study of the Matthean Gospel lessons:
Overviews
Two books that provide the reader with an overview of the gospel used in cycle A are: Jack Kingsbury, *Matthew, Proclamation Commentary*, 2nd ed. (Fortress, 1986) which gives a good overview by

Appendix

a leading scholar on Matthew, and D. Senior, *What Are They Saying About Matthew?* (Paulist Press, 1983) which summarizes the current state of discussion on Matthew.

Commentaries

Eduard Schweizer, *The Good News According to Matthew* (John Knox, 1975) is where I start. He keeps the pastor in mind. A good complement, also focused on the pastor, is David Hill, *The Gospel of Matthew*, The New Century Bible Commentary (Eerdmans, 1981). For detailed study, W.D. Davies and Dale C. Allison, *A Critical and Exegetical Commentary on the Gospel According to Saint Matthew*, International Critical Commentary, vol. 1 (Clark, 1988) gives summaries of many positions plus analysis by key scholars on Matthew for Chap. 1-7. Second volume now available covers chap. 8-18 with third to follow, making this expensive! An alternative for the same chapters is Ulrich Luz, *Matthew 1-7, A Commentary* (Augsburg, 1989). Again the cost is high when the set is completed.

Studies

D. Bonhoeffer, *Cost of Discipleship* (Macmillan, 1948) gives excellent reflections on the Sermon on the Mount and Matthew 10. Robert A. Guelich, *The Sermon on the Mount* (Word, 1982) is a helpful study as well.

Books for the study of the Old Testament texts (mostly Isaiah):

R. Clements, *Isaiah 1-39*, New Century Bible Commentary (Eerdmans, 1980) and R.N. Whybray, *Isaiah 40-66*, New Century Bible Commentary (Eerdmans, 1975) provide good inexpensive commentaries. A more detailed set would be O. Kaiser, *Isaiah 1-12*, Old Testament Library, 2nd ed. (Westminster, 1983) and *Isaiah 13-39*, Old Testament Library (Westminster, 1974) plus C. Westermann, *Isaiah 40-66*, Old Testament Library (Westminster, 1969). Wolfgang Roth, *Isaiah*, Knox Preaching Guides (John Knox, 1988) gives a good concise overview.

Books for the study of some of the Epistle lessons:

For Romans, Paul J. Achtemeier, *Romans*, Interpretation Commentaries (John Knox, 1985) provides excellent expository materials for pastors and church teachers. One might couple it with one of the following exegetical books. C.K. Barrett, *Romans*, Harper's New Testament Commentaries (Harper & Row, 1958) continues to be a good concise resource. C.E.B. Cranfield, *A Critical and Exegetical Commentary on the Epistle to the Romans*, 2 vol., International Critical Commentary (Clark, 1975, 1979) is a strong new ICC contribution on the Greek text. E. Kaesemann, *Commentary on Romans* (Eerdmans, 1980) has many insights, but it will be helpful to be familiar with current discussion about Romans.

For Ephesians, Markus Barth, *Ephesians*, Anchor Bible 34, 34A (Doubleday, 1974) is a detailed study which will provide the pastor with plenty of material. A smaller work that can be a suitable starter is C.L. Mitton, *Ephesians*, The New Century Bible Commentary (Eerdmans, 1976).

For I Corinthians, C.K. Barrett, *I Corinthians*, Harper's New Testament Commentaries (Harper & Row, 1968) continues to be a solid help. Gordon D. Fee, *The First Epistle to the Corinthians* New International Commentary on the New Testament (Eerdmans, 1987) is a good detailed new evangelical study. H. Conzelmann, *I Corinthians*, Hermeneia (Fortress, 1977) is a scholarly work based on the Greek text. C. Talbert, *Reading Corinthians* (Crossroads, 1987) provides a fine literary and theological supplement to any of the above.

The Paschal Cycle 1993

For the study of the Gospel lessons (in addition to the above on Matthew):

Overviews

D. Moody Smith, *John*, Proclamation Commentary, 2nd ed. (Fortress, 1986) will provide a good overview for John. A more detailed discussion may be found in Robert Kysar, *The Fourth Evangelist and His Gospel: An Examination of Contemporary Scholarship* (Augsburg, 1975).

Commentaries

Raymond E. Brown, *The Gospel According to John*, Anchor Bible 29, 29A (Doubleday, 1966, 1970) is an excellent work for exegetical study. Couple this with the expository effort of Gerald Sloyan, *John*, Interpretation Commentaries (John Knox, 1988) for a solid set of resources. For those who desire more on the Greek, C.K. Barrett, *The Gospel According to St. John*, 2nd rev. ed. (Westminster, 1978) continues to be popular.

Books for the study of Acts:

W.H. Willimon, *Acts*, Interpretation Commentaries (John Knox, 1988) gives a sound expository start for the pastor. E. Haenchen,

Appendix

The Acts of the Apostles: A Commentary (Westminster, 1971) is the top scholars' commentary at present. C.S.C. Williams, *The Acts of the Apostles*, Harper's New Testament Commentaries (Hendrickson, 1957) or F.F. Bruce, *The Book of the Acts*, The New International Commentary on the New Testament, rev. ed. (Eerdmans, 1988) provide solid alternatives that may be easier to use.

Books for the study of epistle lessons (See above for Romans):
For I Peter, a well-balanced treatment can be found in J.N.D. Kelly, *I and II Peter*, Harper's New Testament Commentaries (Hendrickson, 1969). The newer evangelical commentary by J.R. Michaels, *I Peter*, Word Biblical Commentary (Word, 1988) can be a solid help. An old exhaustive work on the Greek with word studies is E.G. Selwyn, *The First Epistle of St. Peter* (Macmillan, 1964).

ORDINARY TIME, June 13 - July 25, 1993

For the Gospel lessons from Matthew, see above.

For study of some of the Old Testament lessons:
Genesis is well served by the expository work of Walter Brueggemann, *Genesis*, Interpretation Commentaries (John Knox, 1982). Add to this C. Westermann, *Genesis, Text and Interpretation* (Eerdmans, 1988) for a brief commentary for pastors and laity drawn from his massive three volume work.

For Exodus, N.M. Sarna, *Exploring Exodus: The Heritage of Biblical Israel* (Schocken Books, 1986) provides some interesting insights for clergy and laity. B. Childs, *The Book of Exodus, A Critical and Theological Commentary*, The Old Testament Library (Westminster, 1974) offers a unique exegetical study which includes reflection on the text's usage throughout history. Terence E. Fretheim, *Exodus*, Interpretation Commentaries (John Knox, 1991) is a new expository work.

For study of the Epistle (Romans, seven times) see above.

LECTIONARY LESSONS

(Series C to November 22, 1992; Series A beginning November 29, 1992)

August 2, 1992 — Eighth Sunday after Pentecost
(Roman Catholic — 15th Sunday of the Year)
(July 12: Episcopal — Proper 10; Pres/Meth/UCC — 5th after Pentecost)

Lutheran:	Deut. 30:9-14	Col. I:1-14	Luke 10:25-37
Roman Catholic:	Deut. 30:10-14	Col. 1:15-20	Luke 10:25-37
Episcopal:	Deut. 30:9-14	Col. 1:1-14	Luke 10:25-37
Pres/Meth/UCC:	2 Kings 2:1, 6-14	Col. 1:1-14	Luke 10:25-37

August 9, 1992 — Ninth Sunday after Pentecost
(Roman Catholic — 16th Sunday of the Year)
(July 19: Episcopal — Proper 11; Pres/Meth/UCC — 6th after Pentecost)

Lutheran:	Gen. 18:1-10a (10b-14)	Col. 1:21-28	Luke 10:38-42
Roman Catholic:	Gen. 18:1-10a	Col. 1:24-28	Luke 10:38-42
Episcopal:	Gen. 18:1-10a (10b-14)	Col. 1:21-29	Luke 10:38-42
Pres/Meth/UCC:	2 Kings 4:8-17	Col. 1:21-29	Luke 10:38-42

August 16, 1992 — Tenth Sunday after Pentecost
(Roman Catholic — 17th Sunday of the Year)
(July 26: Episcopal — Proper 12; Pres/Meth/UCC — 7th after Pentecost)

Lutheran:	Gen. 18:20-32	Col. 2:6-15	Luke 11:1-13
Roman Catholic:	Gen. 18:20-32	Col. 2:12-14	Luke 11:1-13
Episcopal:	Gen. 18:20-32	Col. 2:6-15	Luke 11:1-13
Pres/Meth/UCC:	2 Kings 5:1-15ab	Col. 2:6-15	Luke 11:1-13

August 23, 1992 — Eleventh Sunday after Pentecost
(Roman Catholic — 18th Sunday of the Year)
(August 2: Episcopal — Proper 13; Pres/Meth/UCC — 8th after Pentecost)

Lutheran:	Eccl. 1:2, 2:18-26	Col. 3:1-11	Luke 12:13-21
Roman Catholic:	Eccl. 1:2, 2:21-23	Col. 3:1-5, 9-11	Luke 12:13-21
Episcopal:	Eccl. 1:12-14, 2:(1-7, 11)18-23	Col. 3:(5-11) 12-17	Luke 12:13-21
Pres/Meth/UCC:	2 Kings 13:14-20a	Col. 3:1-11	Luke 12:13-21

Appendix

August 30, 1992 – Twelfth Sunday after Pentecost
(Roman Catholic – 19th Sunday of the Year)
(August 9: Episcopal – Proper 14; Pres/Meth/UCC – 9th after Pentecost)

Lutheran:	Gen. 15:1-6	Heb. 11:1-3, 8-16	Luke 12:32-40
Roman Catholic:	Wisd. 18:6-9	Heb. 11:1-2, 8-19	Luke 12:32-48
Episcopal:	Gen. 15:1-6	Heb. 11:1-3, (4-7) 8-16	Luke 12:32-40
Pres/Meth/UCC:	Jer. 18:1-11	Heb. 11:1-3, 8-19	Luke 12:32-40

September 6, 1992 – Thirteenth Sunday after Pentecost
(Roman Catholic – 20th Sunday of the Year)
(August 16: Episcopal – Proper 15; Pres/Meth/UCC – 10th after Pentecost)

Lutheran:	Jer. 23:23-29	Heb. 12:1-13	Luke 12.49 53
Roman Catholic:	Jer. 38:4-6, 8-10	Heb. 12:1-4	Luke 12:49-53
Episcopal	Jer. 23:23-29	Heb. 12:1-7, (8-10) 11-14	Luke 12:49-56
Pres/Meth/UCC:	Jer. 20:7-13	Heb. 12:1-2, 12-17	Luke 12:49-56

September 13, 1992 – Fourteenth Sunday after Pentecost
(Roman Catholic – 21st Sunday of the Year)
(August 23: Episcopal – Proper 16; Pres/Meth/UCC – 11th after Pentecost)

Lutheran:	Is. 66:18-23	Heb. 12:18-24	Luke 13:22-30
Roman Catholic:	Is. 66:18-21	Heb. 12:5-7, 11-13	Luke 13:22-30
Episcopal:	Is. 28:14-22	Heb. 12:18-19, 22-29	Luke 13:22-30
Pres/Meth/UCC:	Jer. 28:1-9	Heb. 12:18-29	Luke 13:22-30

September 20, 1992 – Fifteenth Sunday after Pentecost
(Roman Catholic – 22th Sunday of the Year)
(August 30: Episcopal – Proper 17; Pres/Meth/UCC – 12th after Pentecost)

Lutheran:	Prov. 25:6-7	Heb. 13:1-18	Luke 14:1, 7-14
Roman Catholic:	Sir. 3:19-21, 30-31	Heb. 12:18-19, 22-24a	Luke 14:1, 7-14
Episcopal:	Ecc. 10:(7-11), 12-18	Heb. 13:1-8	Luke 14:1, 7-14
Pres/Meth/UCC:	Ezek. 18:1-9, 25-29	Heb. 13:1-8	Luke 14:1, 7-14

September 27, 1992 – Sixteenth Sunday after Pentecost
(Roman Catholic – 23rd Sunday of the Year)
(September 6: Episcopal – Proper 18; Pres/Meth/UCC – 13th after Pentecost)

Lutheran:	Prov. 9:8-12	Phil. 1, (2-9), 10-21	Luke 14:25-33
Roman Catholic:	Wis. 9:13-18	Phil. 9b-10, 12-17	Luke 14:25-33
Episcopal:	Deut. 30:15-20	Phil. 1-20	Luke 14:25-33
Pres/Meth/UCC:	Ezek. 33:1-11	Phil. 1-20	Luke 14:25-33

The Minister's Annual Manual

October 4, 1992 – Seventeenth Sunday after Pentecost
World Wide Communion Sunday
(Roman Catholic – 24th Sunday of the Year)
(September 13: Episcopal – Proper 19; Pres/Meth/UCC – 14th after Pentecost)

Lutheran:	Ex. 32:7-14	1 Tim. 1:12-17	Luke 15:1-10
Roman Catholic:	Ex. 32:7-11, 13-14	1 Tim. 1:12-17	Luke 15:1-32
Episcopal:	Ex. 32:1, 7-14	1 Tim. 1:12-17	Luke 15:1-10
Pres/Meth/UCC:	Hos. 4:1-3; 5:15-6:6	1 Tim. 1:12-17	Luke 15:1-10

October 11, 1992 – Eighteenth Sunday after Pentecost
(Roman Catholic – 25th Sunday of the Year)
(September 20: Episcopal – Proper 20; Pres/Meth/UCC – 15th after Pentecost)

Lutheran:	Amos 8:4-7	1 Tim. 2:1-8	Luke 16:1-13
Roman Catholic:	Amos 8:4-7	1 Tim. 2:1-8	Luke 16:1-13
Episcopal:	Amos 8:4-7 (8-12)	1 Tim. 2:1-8	Luke 16:1-13
Pres/Meth/UCC:	Hos. 11:1-11	1 Tim. 2:1-7	Luke 16:1-13

October 18, 1992 – Nineteenth Sunday after Pentecost
(Roman Catholic – 26th Sunday of the Year)
(September 27: Episcopal – Proper 21; Pres/Meth/UCC – 16th after Pentecost)

Lutheran:	Amos 6:1-7	1 Tim. 6:6-16	Luke 16:19-31
Roman Catholic:	Amos 6:1a, 4-7	1 Tim. 6:11-16	Luke 16:19-31
Episcopal:	Amos 6:1-7	1 Tim. 6:11-19	Luke 16:19-31
Pres/Meth/UCC:	Joel 2:23-30	1 Tim. 6:6-19	Luke 16:19-31

October 25, 1992 – Twentieth Sunday after Pentecost
(Roman Catholic – 27th Sunday of the Year)
(October 4: Episcopal – Proper 22; Pres/Meth/UCC – 17th after Pentecost)

Lutheran:	Hab. 1:1-3; 2:1-4	2 Tim. 1:3-14	Luke 17:1-10
Roman Catholic:	Hab. 1:2-3; 2:2-4	2 Tim. 1:6-8, 13-14	Luke 17:5-10
Episcopal:	Hab. 1:1-6 (7-11), 12-13; 2:1-4	2 Tim. 1:(1-5) 6-14	Luke 17:5-10
Pres/Meth/UCC:	Amos 5:6-7, 10-15	2 Tim. 1:1-14	Luke 17:5-10

October 25, 1992 – Reformation Sunday

Protestant: Jeremiah 31:31-34   Romans 3:19-29   John 8:31-36

November 1, 1992 – Twenty-first Sunday after Pentecost
(Roman Catholic – 28th Sunday of the Year)
(October 11: Episcopal – Proper 23; Pres/Meth/UCC – 18th after Pentecost)

Lutheran:	Ruth 1:1-19a	2 Tim. 2:8-13	Luke 17:11-19
Roman Catholic:	2 Kings 5:14-17	2 Tim. 2:8-13	Luke 17:11-19
Episcopal:	Ruth 1:(1-7) 8-19a	2 Tim. 2:(3-7) 8-15	Luke 17:11-19
Pres/Meth/UCC:	Mic. 1:2; 2:1-10	2 Tim. 2:8-15	Luke 17:11-19

Appendix

November 1, 1992 — All Saints' Day

Lutheran:	Is. 26:1-4, 8-9, 12-13, 19-21	Rev. 21:9-11, 22-27 (22:1-5)	Matt. 5:1-12
Roman Catholic:	Dan. 7:1-3, 15-18	Eph. 1:11-23	Luke 6:20-36
Episcopal:	Ecc. 2:(1-6) 7-11	Eph. 1:(11-14) 15-23	Luke 6:20-26 (27-36)
Pres/Meth/UCC:	Dan. 7:1-3, 15-18	Eph. 1:11-23	Luke 6:20-36

November 8, 1992 — Twenty-second Sunday after Pentecost
(Roman Catholic — 29th Sunday of the Year)
(October 18: Episcopal — Proper 24; Pres/Meth/UCC — 19th after Pentecost)

Lutheran:	Gen. 32; 22-30	2 Tim 3:14-4:5	Luke 18:1-8a
Roman Catholic:	Ex. 17:8-13	2 Tim. 3:14-4:2	Luke 18:1-8
Episcopal:	Gen. 32:3-8, 22-30	2 Tim. 3:14 4:5	Luke 18:1-8a
Pres/Meth/UCC:	Hab. 1:1-3; 2:1-4	2 Tim. 3:14-4:5	Luke 18:1-8

November 15, 1992 — Twenty-third Sunday after Pentecost
(Roman Catholic — 30th Sunday of the Year)
(October 25: Episcopal — Proper 25; Pres/Meth/UCC — 20th after Pentecost)

Lutheran:	Deut. 10:12-22	2 Tim. 4:6-8, 16-18	Luke 18:9-14
Roman Catholic:	Sir. 35:12c-14, 16-18b	2 Tim. 4:6-8, 16-18	Luke 18:9-14
Episcopal:	Jer. 14: (1-6) 7-10, 19-22	2 Tim. 4:6-8, 16-18	Luke 18:9-14
Pres/Meth/UCC:	Zeph. 3:1-9	2 Tim. 4:6-8, 16-18	Luke 18:9-14

Twenty-fourth Sunday after Pentecost
(Roman Catholic — 31st Sunday of the Year)
(November 1: Episcopal — Proper 26; Pres/Meth/UCC — 21st after Pentecost)

Lutheran:	Ex. 34:5-9	2 Thess. 1:1-5, 11-12	Luke 19:1-10
Roman Catholic:	Wis. 11:22-12:2	2 Thess. 1:11-2:2	Luke 19:1-10
Episcopal:	Is. 1:10-20	2 Thess. 1:1-5 (6-10) 11-12	Luke 19:1-10
Pres/Meth/UCC:	Hab. 2:1-9	2 Thess. 1:5-12, 11-12	Luke 19:1-10

Twenty-fifth Sunday after Pentecost
(Roman Catholic — 32nd Sunday of the Year)
(November 8: Episcopal — Proper 27; Pres/Meth/UCC — 22nd after Pentecost)

Lutheran:	1 Chron. 29:10-13	2 Thess. 2:13-3:5	Luke 20:27-38
Roman Catholic:	2 Macc. 7:1-2, 9-14	2 Thess. 2:16-3:5	Luke 20:27-38
Episcopal:	Job 19:23-27a	2 Thess. 2:13-3:5	Luke 20:27 (28-33) 34-38
Pres/Meth/UCC:	Zech. 7:1-10	2 Thess. 2:13-3:5	Luke 20:27-38

Twenty-sixth Sunday after Pentecost
(Roman Catholic—33rd Sunday of the Year)
(November 15: Episcopal—Proper 28; Pres/Meth/UCC—23rd after Pentecost)

Lutheran:	Mal. 4:1-2a	2 Thess. 3:6-13	Luke 21:5-19
Roman Catholic:	Mal. 4:1-2a	2 Thess. 3:7-12	Luke 21:5-19
Episcopal:	Mal. 3:13-4:2a, 5-6	2 Thess. 3:6-13	Luke 21:5-19
Pres/Meth/UCC:	Mal. 4:1-6	2 Thess. 3:6-13	Luke 21:5-19

Twenty-seventh Sunday after Pentecost
(Roman Catholic—34th Sunday of the Year, Christ the King, November 22)
(November 22: Episcopal—Proper 29; Pres/Meth/UCC—Christ the King)

Lutheran:	Is. 52:1-6	1 Cor. 15:54-58	Luke 19:11-27
Roman Catholic:	2 Sam. 5:1-3	Col. 1:12-20	Luke 23:35-43
Episcopal:	Jer. 23:1-6	Col. 1:11-20	Luke 23:35-43
Pres/Meth/UCC:	2 Sam. 5:1-5	Col. 1:11-20	John 12:9-19

November 22, 1992—Last Sunday after Pentecost
(Christ the King)

Lutheran:	Jer. 23:2-6	Col. 1:13-20	Luke 23:35-43
Roman Catholic:	2 Sam. 5:1-3	Col. 1:12-20	Luke 23:35-43
Episcopal:	Jer. 23:1-6	Col. 1:11-20	Luke 23:35-43
Pres/Meth/UCC:	2 Sam. 5:1-5	Col. 1:11-20	John 12:9-19

November 26, 1992—Thanksgiving Day (U.S.)

Lutheran:	Deut. 8:1-10	Phil. 4:6-20	Luke 17:11-19
Pres/Meth/UCC:	Joel 2:21-27	I Tim. 2:1-7	Matt. 6:25-33
Episcopal:	Deut. 8:1-3, 6-10 (17-20)	Jas. 1:17-18, 21-27	Matt. 6:25-33
Pres/Meth/UCC:	Deut. 26:1-11	Phil. 4:4-9	John 6:25-35

(End of Series C in the Lectionary series)
(Beginning of Series A in the Lectionary Series.)

November 29, 1992—First Sunday in Advent

Lutheran:	Is. 2:1-5	Rom. 13:11-14	Matt. 24:37-44
Roman Catholic:	Is. 2:1-5	Rom. 13:11-14	Matt. 24:37-44
Episcopal:	Is. 2:1-5	Rom. 13:8-14	Matt. 24:37-44
Pres/Meth/UCC:	Is. 2:1-5	Rom. 13:11-14	Matt. 24:36-44

Appendix

December 6, 1992 — Second Sunday in Advent

Lutheran:	Is. 11:1-10	Rom. 15:4-13	Matt. 3:1-12
Roman Catholic:	Is. 11:1-10	Rom. 15:4-9	Matt. 3:1-12
Episcopal:	Is. 11:1-10	Rom. 15:4-13	Matt. 3:1-12
Pres/Meth/UCC:	Is. 11:1-10	Rom. 15:4-13	Matt. 3:1-12

December 13, 1992 — Third Sunday in Advent

Lutheran:	Is. 35:1-10	James 5:7-10	Matt. 11:2-11
Roman Catholic:	Is. 35:1-6a, 10	James 5:7-10	Matt. 11:2-11
Episcopal:	Is. 35:1-10	James 5:7-10	Matt. 11:2-11
Pres/Meth/UCC:	Is. 35:1-10	James 5:7-10	Matt. 11:2-11

December 20, 1992 — Fourth Sunday in Advent

Lutheran:	Is. 7:10-14 (15-17)	Rom. 1:1-7	Matt. 1:18-25
Roman Catholic:	Is. 7:10-14	Rom. 1:1-7	Matt. 1:18-25
Episcopal:	Is. 7:10-17	Rom. 1:1-7	Matt. 1:18-25
Pres/Meth/UCC:	Is. 7:10-16	Rom. 1:1-7	Matt. 1:18-25

December 24, 1992 — Christmas Eve

Lutheran:	Is. 9:2-7	Titus 2:11-14	Luke 2:1-20
Roman Catholic:	Is. 9:2-7	Titus 2:11-14	Luke 2:1-24
Episcopal:	Is. 9:2-4, 6-7	Titus 2:11-14	Luke 2:1-14 (15-20)
Pres/Meth/UCC:	Is. 9:2-7	Titus 2:11-14	Luke 2:1-14 (15-20)

December 25, 1992 — Christmas Day

Lutheran:	Is. 52:7-10	Heb. 1:1-9	John 1:1-14
Roman Catholic:	Is 62:11-12	Titus 3:4-7	Luke 2:15-20
Episcopal:	Is. 62:6-7, 10-12	Titus 3:4-7	Luke 2:(1-14) 15-20
Pres/Meth/UCC:	Is. 62:6-12	Titus 3:4-7	Luke 2:(1-7) 8-20

December 27, 1992 — First Sunday after Christmas

Lutheran:	Is. 63:7-9	Gal. 4:4-7	Matt. 2:13-15, 19-23
Roman Catholic:	Sir. 3:2-6, 12-14	Col. 3:12-21	Matt. 2:13-15, 19-23
Episcopal:	Is. 61:10-62:3	Gal. 3:23-25; 4:4-7	John 1:1-18
Pres/Meth/UCC:	Is. 63:7-9	Heb. 2:10-18	Matt. 2:13-23

January 3, 1993 — Second Sunday after Christmas

Lutheran:	Is. 61:10-62:3	Eph. 1:3-6, 15-18	John 1:1-18
Roman Catholic:	Jer. 31:7-14	Eph. 1:3-6, 15-18	John 1:1-18
Episcopal:	Jer. 31:7-14	Eph. 1:3-6, 15-19a	Matt. 2:13-15, 19-23
Pres/Meth/UCC:	Jer. 31:7-14	Eph. 1:3-14	John 1:(1-9) 10-18

The Minister's Annual Manual

January 6, 1993 — The Epiphany

Lutheran:	Is. 60:1-6	Eph. 3:2-12	Matt. 2:1-12
Roman Catholic:	Is. 60:1-6	Eph. 3:2-3, 5-6	Matt. 2:1-12
Episcopal:	Is. 60:1-6, 9	Eph. 3:1-12	Matt. 2:1-12
Pres/Meth/UCC:	Is. 60:1-6	Eph. 3:1-12	Matt. 2:1-12

January 10, 1993 — First Sunday after Epiphany, The Baptism of Our Lord

Lutheran:	Is. 42:1-7	Acts 10:34-38	Matt. 3:13-17
Roman Catholic:	Is. 42:1-4, 6-7	Acts 10:34-38	Matt. 3:13-17
Episcopal:	Is. 42:1-9	Acts 10:34-38	Matt. 3:13-17
Pres/Meth/UCC:	Is. 42:1-9	Acts 10:34-43	Matt. 3:13-17

January 17, 1993 — Second Sunday after Epiphany

Lutheran:	Is. 49:1-6	I Cor. 1:1-9	John 1:29-41
Roman Catholic:	Is. 49:3, 5-6	I Cor. 1:1-3	John 1:29-34
Episcopal:	Is. 49:1-7	I Cor. 1:1-9	John 1:29-41
Pres/Meth/UCC:	Is. 49:1-7	I Cor. 1:1-9	John 1:29-34

January 24, 1993 — Third Sunday after Epiphany

Lutheran:	Is. 9:1b-4	1 Cor. 1:10-17	Matt. 4:12-23
Roman Catholic:	Is. 9:1-4	1 Cor. 1:10-13, 17	Matt. 4:12-23
Episcopal:	Amos 3:1-8	1 Cor. 1:10-17	Matt. 4:12-23
Pres/Meth/UCC:	Is. 9:1-4	1 Cor. 1:10-18	Matt. 4:12-23

January 31, 1993 — Fourth Sunday after Epiphany

Lutheran:	Mic. 6:1-8	1 Cor. 1:26-31	Matt. 5:1-12
Roman Catholic:	Zeph. 2:3; 3:12-13	1 Cor. 1:26-31	Matt. 5:1-12a
Episcopal:	Mic. 6:1-8	1 Cor. 1:(18-25) 26-31	Matt. 5:1-12
Pres/Meth/UCC:	Mic. 6:1-8	1 Cor. 1:18-31	Matt. 5:1-12

February 7, 1993 — Fifth Sunday after Epiphany

Lutheran:	Is. 58:5-9a	1 Cor. 2:1-5	Matt. 5:13-20
Roman Catholic:	Is. 58:7-10	1 Cor. 2:1-5	Matt. 5:13-16
Episcopal:	Hab. 3:1-6, 17-19	1 Cor. 2:1-11	Matt. 5:13-20
Pres/Meth/UCC:	Is. 58:1-9a (9b-12)	1 Cor. 2:1-12 (13-16)	Matt. 5:13-20

Appendix

February 14, 1993 — Sixth Sunday after Epiphany

Lutheran:	Deut. 30:15-20	1 Cor. 2:6-13	Matt. 5:20-37
Roman Catholic:	Sir. 15:15-20	1 Cor. 2:6-10	Matt. 5:17-37
Episcopal:	Ecc. 15:11-20	1 Cor. 3:1-9	Matt. 5:21-24, 27-30, 33-37
Pres/Meth/UCC:	Deut. 30:15-20	1 Cor. 3:1-9	Matt. 5:21-37

Seventh Sunday after Epiphany

Lutheran:	Lev. 19:1-2, 17-18	1 Cor. 3:10-11, 16-23	Matt. 5:38-48
Roman Catholic:	Lev. 19:1-2, 17-18	1 Cor. 3:16-23	Matt. 5:38-48
Episcopal:	Lev. 19:1-2, 9-18	1 Cor. 3:10-11, 16-23	Matt. 5:38-48
Pres/Meth/UCC:	Lev. 19:1-2, 9-18	1 Cor. 3:10-11, 16-23	Matt. 5:38-48

February 21, 1993 — Transfiguration

Lutheran:	Ex. 24:12, 15-18	2 Pet. 1:16-19 (20-21)	Matt. 17:1-9
Roman Catholic:	Is. 49:14-15	1 Cor. 4:1-5	Matt. 6:24-34
Episcopal:	Ex. 24:12 (13-14) 15-18	Phil. 3:7-14	Matt. 17:1-9
Pres/Meth/UCC:	Ex. 24:12-18	2 Peter 1:16-21	Matt. 17:1-9

February 24, 1993 — Ash Wednesday

Lutheran:	Joel 2:12-19	2 Cor. 5:20b-6:2	Matt. 6:1-6, 16-21
Roman Catholic:	Joel 2:12-18	2 Cor. 5:20b-6:2	Matt. 6:1-6, 16-18
Episcopal:	Joel 2:1-2, 12-17	2 Cor. 5:20b-6:10	Matt. 6:1-6, 16-21
Pres/Meth/UCC:	Joel 2:1 2, 12-17	2 Cor. 5:20b-6:10	Matt. 6:1-6, 16-21

February 28, 1993 — First Sunday in Lent

Lutheran:	Gen. 2:7-9, 15-17; 3:1-7	Rom. 5:12 (13-16) 17-19	Matt. 4:1-11
Roman Catholic:	Gen. 2:7-9; 3:1-7	Rom. 5:12-19,	Matt. 4:1-11
Episcopal:	Gen. 2:4b-9, 15-17, 25-3:7	Rom. 5:12-19, (20-21)	Matt. 4:1-11
Pres/Meth/UCC:	Gen. 2:15-17; 3:1-7	Rom. 5:12-19	Matt. 4:1-11

March 7, 1993 — Second Sunday in Lent

Lutheran:	Gen. 12:1-8	Rom. 4:1-5, 13-17	John 4:5-26 (27-30) (39-42)
Roman Catholic:	Gen. 12:1-4a	2 Tim. 1:8b-10	Matt. 17:1-9
Episcopal:	Gen. 12:1-8	Rom. 4:1-5 (6-12) 13-17	John 3:1-17
Pres/Meth/UCC:	Gen. 12:1-4a	Rom. 4:1-5, 13-17	John 3:1-17

The Minister's Annual Manual

March 14, 1993 – Third Sunday in Lent

Lutheran:	Is. 42:14-21	Eph. 5:8-14	John 9:1-41
Roman Catholic:	Ex. 17:3-7	Rom. 5:1-2, 5-8	John 4:5-42
Episcopal:	Ex. 17:1-7	Rom. 5:1-11	John 4:5-26 (27-38) 39-42
Pres/Meth/UCC:	Ex. 17:1-7	Rom. 5:1-11	John 4:5-42

March 21, 1993 – Fourth Sunday in Lent

Lutheran:	Hos. 5:15-6:2	Rom. 8:1-10	Matt. 20:17-28
Roman Catholic:	1 Sam. 16:1b, 6-7, 10-13a	Eph. 5:8-14	John 9:1-41
Episcopal:	1 Sam. 16:1-13	Eph. 5:(1-7) 8-14	John 9:1-13 (14-27) 28-38
Pres/Meth/UCC:	1 Sam. 16:1-13	Eph. 5:8-14	John 9:1-41

March 28, 1993 – Fifth Sunday in Lent

Lutheran:	Ez. 37:1-3 (4-10) 11-14	Rom. 8:11-19	John 11:1-53
Roman Catholic:	Ez. 37:12-14	Rom. 8:8-11	John 11:1-45
Episcopal:	Ez. 37:1-3 (4-10) 11-14	Rom. 6:16-23	John 11:(1-17) 18-44
Pres/Meth/UCC:	Ez. 37:1-14	Rom. 8:6-11	John 11:1-45

April 4, 1993 – Passion/Palm Sunday

Lutheran:	Is. 50:4-9a	Phil. 2:5-11	Matt. 27:11-54
Roman Catholic:	Is. 50:4-7	Phil. 2:6-11	Matt. 26:14-27:66
Episcopal:	Is. 45:21-25	Phil. 2:5-11	Matt. (26:36-75) 27:1-54 (55-66)
Pres/Meth/UCC:	Is. 50:4-9a	Phil. 2:5-11	Matt. 27:11-54

April 8, 1993 – Maundy Thursday

Lutheran:	Ex. 12:1-14	1 Cor. 11:17-32	John 13:1-17, 34
Roman Catholic:	Ex. 12:1-8, 11-14	I Cor. 11:23-26	John 13:1-15
Episcopal:	Ex. 12:1-14a	I Cor. 11:23-26 (27-32)	John 13:1-15
Pres/Meth/UCC:	Ex. 12:1-4 (5-10) 11-14	1 Cor. 11:23-26	John 13:1-17, 31b-35

April 9, 1993 – Good Friday

Lutheran:	Is. 52:13-53:12	Heb. 4:14-16, 5:7-9	John 19:17-30
Roman Catholic:	Is. 52:13-53:12	Heb. 4:14-16, 5:7-9	John 18:1-19:42
Episcopal:	Is. 52:13-53:12	Heb. 10:1-25	John (18:1-40) 19:1-37
Pres/Meth/UCC:	Is. 52:13-53:12	Heb. 4:14-16, 5:7-9	John 18:1-19:42

Appendix

April 11, 1993 – Easter Day. The Resurrection of our Lord.

Lutheran:	Acts 10:34-43	Cor. 3:1-4	Matt. 28:1-10
Roman Catholic:	Acts 10:34a, 37-43	Col. 3:1-4	John 20:1-9
Episcopal:	Acts 10:34-43	Col. 3:1-4	John 20:1-10 (11-18)
Pres/Meth/UCC:	Acts 10:34-43	Col. 3:1-4	Matt. 28:1-10

April 18, 1993 – Second Sunday of Easter

Lutheran:	Acts 2:14a, 22-32	1 Peter 1:3-9	John 20:19-31
Roman Catholic:	Acts 2:42-47	1 Peter 1:3-9	John 20:19-31
Episcopal:	Acts 2:14a, 22-32	1 Peter 1:3-9	John 20:19-31
Pres/Meth/UCC:	Acts 2:14a, 22-32	1 Peter 1:3-9	John 20:19-31

April 25, 1993 – Third Sunday of Easter

Lutheran:	Acts 2:14a, 36-47	1 Peter 1:17-21	Luke 24:13-35
Roman Catholic:	Acts 2:14, 22-28	1 Peter 1:17-21	Luke 24:13-35
Episcopal:	Acts 2:14a, 36-47	1 Peter 1:17-23	Luke 24:13-35
Pres/Meth/UCC:	Acts 2:14a, 36-41	1 Peter 1:17-23	Luke 24:13-35

May 2, 1993 – Fourth Sunday of Easter

Lutheran:	Acts 6:1-9; 7:2a, 51-60	1 Peter 2:19-25	John 10:1-10
Roman Catholic:	Acts 2:14a, 36-41	1 Peter 2:20b-25	John 10:1-10
Episcopal:	Acts 6:1-9, 7:2a, 51-60	1 Peter 2:19-25	John 10:1-10
Pres/Meth/UCC:	Acts 2:42-47	1 Peter 2:19-25	John 10:1-10

May 9, 1993 – Fifth Sunday of Easter

Lutheran:	Acts 17:1 15	1 Peter 2:4-10	John 14:1-12
Roman Catholic:	Acts 6:1-7	1 Peter 2:4-9	John 14:1-12
Episcopal:	Acts 17:1-15	1 Peter 2:1-10	John 14:1-14
Pres/Meth/UCC:	Acts 7:55-60	1 Peter 2:2-10	John 14:1-14

May 16, 1993 – Sixth Sunday of Easter

Lutheran:	Acts 17:22-31	1 Peter 3:15-22	John 14:15-21
Roman Catholic:	Acts 8:5-8, 14-17	1 Peter 3:15-18	John 14:15-21
Episcopal:	Acts 17:22-31	1 Peter 3:8-18	John 15:1-8
Pres/Meth/UCC:	Acts 17:22-31	1 Peter 3:13-22	John 14:15-21

May 20, 1993 – Ascension Day

Lutheran:	Acts 1:1-11	Eph. 1:16-23	Luke 24:44-53
Roman Catholic:	Acts 1:1-11	Eph. 1:17-23	Luke 28:16-20
Episcopal:	Acts 1:1-11	Eph. 1:15-23	Luke 24:49-53
Pres/Meth/UCC:	Acts 1:1-11	Eph. 1:15-23	Luke 24:44-53

The Minister's Annual Manual

May 23, 1993 – Seventh Sunday of Easter

Lutheran:	Acts 1:(1-7) 8-14	1 Peter 4:12-17; 5:6-11	John 17:1-11
Roman Catholic:	Acts 1:12-14	1 Peter 4:13-16	John 17:1-11a
Episcopal:	Acts 1:(1-7) 8-14	1 Peter 4:12-19	John 17:1-11
Pres/Meth/UCC:	Acts 1:6-14	1 Peter 4:12-14; 5:6-11	John 17:1-11

May 30, 1993 – The Day of Pentecost

Lutheran:	Joel 2:28-29	Acts 2:1-21	John 20:19-23
Roman Catholic:	Acts 2:1-11	I Cor. 12:3b-7, 12-13	John 20:19-23
Episcopal:	Acts 2:1-11	I Cor. 12:4-13	John 20:19-23
Pres/Meth/UCC:	Acts 2:1-21	1 Cor. 12:3b-13	John 20:19-23

June 6, 1993 – Trinity Sunday

Lutheran:	Gen. 1:1-2:3	2 Cor. 13:11-14	Matt. 28:16-20
Roman Catholic:	Ex. 34:4b-6, 8-9	2 Cor. 13:11-13	John 3:16-18
Episcopal:	Gen. 1:1-2:3	2 Cor. 13:(5-10) 11-14	Matt. 28:16-20
Pres/Meth/UCC:	Gen. 1:1-2:4a	2 Cor. 13:11-13	Matt. 28;16-20

June 13, 1993 – Second Sunday after Pentecost
(Roman Catholic – 9th Sunday of the Year; Episcopal – Proper 4)

Lutheran:	Deut. 11:18-21, 26-28	Rom. 3:21-25a	Matt. 7:(15-20) 21-29
Roman Catholic:	Deut. 11:18, 26-28	Rom. 3:21-25a, 28	Matt. 7:21-27
Episcopal:	Deut. 11:18-21, 26-28	Rom. 3:21-25a, 28	Matt. 7:21-27
Pres/Meth/UCC:	Gen. 6:9-22	Rom. 1:16-17; 3:21-28 (29-31)	Matt. 7:21-29

June 20, 1993 – Third Sunday after Pentecost
(Roman Catholic – 10th Sunday of the Year; Episcopal – Proper 5)

Lutheran:	Hos. 5:15-6:6	Rom. 4:18-25	Matt. 9:9-13
Roman Catholic:	Hos. 6:3-6	Rom. 4:18-25	Matt. 9:9-13
Episcopal:	Hosea 5:15-6:6	Rom. 4:13-18	Matt. 9:9-13
Pres/Meth/UCC:	Gen. 12:1-9	Rom. 4:13-25	Matt. 9-13, 18-26

Appendix

June 27, 1993 – Fourth Sunday after Pentecost
(Roman Catholic – 11th Sunday of the Year)
(June 13: Episcopal – Proper 6; Pres/Meth/UCC – 2nd after Pentecost)

Lutheran:	Ex. 19:2-8a	Rom. 5:6-11	Matt. 9:35-10:8
Roman Catholic:	Ex. 19:2-6a	Rom. 5:6-11	Matt. 9:36-10:8
Episcopal:	Ex. 19:2-8a	Rom. 5:6-11	Matt. 9:35-10:8 (9-15)
Pres/Meth/UCC:	Gen. 18:1-15 (21:1-7)	Rom. 5:1-8	Matt. 9:35-10:8 (9-23)

July 4, 1993 – Fifth Sunday after Pentecost
(Roman Catholic – 12th Sunday of the Year)
(June 20: Episcopal – Proper 7; Pres/Meth/UCC – 3rd after Pentecost)

Lutheran:	Jer. 20:7-13	Rom. 5:12-15	Matt. 10:24-33
Roman Catholic:	Jer. 20:10-13	Rom. 5:12-15	Matt. 10:26-33
Episcopal:	Jer. 20:7-13	Rom. 5:15b-19	Matt. 10:(16-23) 24-33
Pres/Meth/UCC:	Gen. 21:8-21	Rom. 6:1b-11	Matt. 10:24-39

July 11, 1993 – Sixth Sunday after Pentecost
(Roman Catholic – 13th Sunday of the Year)
(June 27: Episcopal – Proper 8; Pres/Meth/UCC – 4th after Pentecost)

Lutheran:	Jer. 28:5-9	Rom. 6:1b-11	Matt. 10:34-42
Roman Catholic:	2 Kings 4:8-11, 14-16a	Rom. 6:3-4, 8-11	Matt. 10:37-42
Episcopal:	Is. 2:10-17	Rom. 6:3-11	Matt. 10:34-42
Pres/Meth/UCC:	Gen. 22:1-14	Rom. 6:12-23	Matt. 10:40-42

July 18, 1993 – Seventh Sunday after Pentecost
(Roman Catholic – 14th Sunday of the Year)
(July 4: Episcopal – Proper 9; Pres/Meth/UCC – 5th after Pentecost)

Lutheran:	Zech. 9:9-12	Rom. 7:15-25a	Matt. 11:25-30
Roman Catholic:	Zech. 9:9-10	Rom. 8:9, 11-13	Matt. 11:25-30
Episcopal:	Zech. 9:9-12	Rom. 7:21-8:6	Matt. 11:25-30
Pres/Meth/UCC:	Gen. 24:34-38, 42-49, 58-67	Rom. 7:15-25a	Matt. 11:16-19, 25-30

July 25, 1993 – Eighth Sunday after Pentecost
(Roman Catholic – 15th Sunday of the Year)
(July 11: Episcopal – Proper 10; Pres/Meth/UCC – 6th after Pentecost)

Lutheran:	Is. 55:10-11	Rom. 8:18-25	Matt. 13:1-9 (18-23)
Roman Catholic:	Is. 55:10-11	Rom. 8:18-23	Matt. 13:1-23
Episcopal:	Is. 55:1-5, 10-13	Rom. 8:9-17	Matt. 13:1-9, 18-23
Pres/Meth/UCC:	Gen. 25:19-34	Rom. 8:1-11	Matt. 13:1-9, 18-23

NAMES AND ADDRESSES OF AUTHORS

Andrea La Sonde Anastos
The First Church of Deerfield
PO Box 276
Deerfield, MA 01342
October 25 (2), November 1 (2), 1992

Richard Andersen
St. Timothy's Lutheran Church
5100 Camden Avenue
San Jose, CA 95124
November 29, December 6, 13, 20, 1992

Gary F. Anderson
All Saints Lutheran Church
15915 Excelsior Blvd.
Minnetonka, MN 55345
June 6, 13, 20, 27, 1993

David deFreese
Immanuel Lutheran Church
104 Galvin Road North
Bellevue, NE 68005
January 6, 10, 17, 24, 1993

William Wesley Elkins
Bernardsville United Methodist Church
22 Church Street
Bernardsville, NJ 07924
April 11, 18, 25, May 2, 1993

Beth Marie Halvorsen
Shepherd of the Hills Lutheran Church
3525 Bee Cave Road
Austin, TX 78746
February 24, 28, March 7, 14, 1993

Bruce A. Hedman
Abington Congregational Church
Routes 44 and 97
Abington, CT 06230
May 9, 16, 20, 23, 30, 1993

Miles Walter Jackson
United Methodist Church
352 Legg Road
Bow, WA 98232
Proper 28, Proper 29, November 22, 26, 1992

Marie C. Jerge
Assistant to the Bishop
Upstate New York Synod, ELCA
49 Linwood Ave.
Buffalo, NY 14209
December 24, 25, 27, 1992, January 3, 1993

Stephen M. Larson
Evangelical Lutheran Church of Geneva
20 rue Verdaine
1204 Geneva, Switzerland
March 21, 28, April 4, 8, 9, 1993

Ronald H. Love
Summit United Methodist Church
1510 Townhall Road, West
Erie, PA 16509
November 8, 15, 1992, Proper 26, Proper 27

David N. Mosser
First United Methodist Church
410 E. University
Georgetown, TX 78626
January 31, February 7, 14, 21, 1993

Appendix

David Z. Ring III
Paradise Hills United Methodist Church
4700 Paradise Blvd., N.W.
Albuquerque, NM 87114
September 27, October 4, 11, 18, 1992

John L. Topolewski
Superintendent, Wyoming Annual Conference
United Methodist Church
1 Circle Drive
Sidney, NY 13838
July 18, 25, 1993

Nancy F. Topolewski
Kirkwood United Methodist Church
1 Circle Drive
Sidney, NY 13838
July 4, 11, 1993

E. Dean Windhorn
Christ Church, the Lutheran Church
600 North Ford Road
Zionsville, IN 46077
August 2, 9, 16, 23, 1992

Theodore A. Youngquist
Redemption Lutheran Church
4481 North Glenway
Wauwatosa, WI 53225
August 30, September 6, 13, 20, 1992

FOUR YEAR CHURCH YEAR CALENDAR

	Series C 1991	Series A 1992	Series B 1993	Series C 1994
Advent begins	Dec. 1	Nov. 29	Nov. 28	Nov. 27
Christmas	Dec. 25	Dec. 25	Dec. 25	Dec. 25
	1992	1993	1994	1995
Epiphany	Jan. 6	Jan. 6	Jan. 6	Jan. 6
Ash Wednesday	March 4	Feb. 24	Feb. 16	March 1
Passion Sunday	April 12	April 4	March 27	April 9
Maundy Thursday	April 16	April 8	March 31	April 13
Good Friday	April 17	April 9	April 1	April 14
Easter Day	April 19	April 11	April 3	April 16
Ascension Day	May 28	May 20	May 12	May 25
Pentecost	June 7	May 30	May 22	June 4
Trinity Sunday	June 14	June 6	May 29	June 11
Reformation	Oct. 31	Oct. 31	Oct. 31	Oct. 31
All Saints	Nov. 1	Nov. 1	Nov. 1	Nov. 1

The Minister's Annual Manual

1992

JANUARY	FEBRUARY	MARCH	APRIL
S M T W T F S	S M T W T F S	S M T W T F S	S M T W T F S
1 2 3 4	1	1 2 3 4 5 6 7	1 2 3 4
5 6 7 8 9 10 11	2 3 4 5 6 7 8	8 9 10 11 12 13 14	5 6 7 8 9 10 11
12 13 14 15 16 17 18	9 10 11 12 13 14 15	15 16 17 18 19 20 21	12 13 14 15 16 17 18
19 20 21 22 23 24 25	16 17 18 19 20 21 22	22 23 24 25 26 27 28	19 20 21 22 23 24 25
26 27 28 29 30 31	23 24 25 26 27 28 29	29 30 31	26 27 28 29 30

MAY	JUNE	JULY	AUGUST
S M T W T F S	S M T W T F S	S M T W T F S	S M T W T F S
1 2	1 2 3 4 5 6	1 2 3 4	1
3 4 5 6 7 8 9	7 8 9 10 11 12 13	5 6 7 8 9 10 11	2 3 4 5 6 7 8
10 11 12 13 14 15 16	14 15 16 17 18 19 20	12 13 14 15 16 17 18	9 10 11 12 13 14 15
17 18 19 20 21 22 23	21 22 23 24 25 26 27	19 20 21 22 23 24 25	16 17 18 19 20 21 22
24 25 26 27 28 29 30	28 29 30	26 27 28 29 30 31	23 24 25 26 27 28 29
31			30 31

SEPTEMBER	OCTOBER	NOVEMBER	DECEMBER
S M T W T F S	S M T W T F S	S M T W T F S	S M T W T F S
1 2 3 4 5	1 2 3	1 2 3 4 5 6 7	1 2 3 4 5
6 7 8 9 10 11 12	4 5 6 7 8 9 10	8 9 10 11 12 13 14	6 7 8 9 10 11 12
13 14 15 16 17 18 19	11 12 13 14 15 16 17	15 16 17 18 19 20 21	13 14 15 16 17 18 19
20 21 22 23 24 25 26	18 19 20 21 22 23 24	22 23 24 25 26 27 28	20 21 22 23 24 25 26
27 28 29 30	25 26 27 28 29 30 31	29 30	27 28 29 30 31

1993

JANUARY	FEBRUARY	MARCH	APRIL
S M T W T F S	S M T W T F S	S M T W T F S	S M T W T F S
1 2	1 2 3 4 5 6	1 2 3 4 5 6	1 2 3
3 4 5 6 7 8 9	7 8 9 10 11 12 13	7 8 9 10 11 12 13	4 5 6 7 8 9 10
10 11 12 13 14 15 16	14 15 16 17 18 19 20	14 15 16 17 18 19 20	11 12 13 14 15 16 17
17 18 19 20 21 22 23	21 22 23 24 25 26 27	21 22 23 24 25 26 27	18 19 20 21 22 23 24
24 25 26 27 28 29 30	28	28 29 30 31	25 26 27 28 29 30
31			

MAY	JUNE	JULY	AUGUST
S M T W T F S	S M T W T F S	S M T W T F S	S M T W T F S
1	1 2 3 4 5	1 2 3	1 2 3 4 5 6 7
2 3 4 5 6 7 8	6 7 8 9 10 11 12	4 5 6 7 8 9 10	8 9 10 11 12 13 14
9 10 11 12 13 14 15	13 14 15 16 17 18 19	11 12 13 14 15 16 17	15 16 17 18 19 20 21
16 17 18 19 20 21 22	20 21 22 23 24 25 26	18 19 20 21 22 23 24	22 23 24 25 26 27 28
23 24 25 26 27 28 29	27 28 29 30	25 26 27 28 29 30 31	29 30 31
30 31			

SEPTEMBER	OCTOBER	NOVEMBER	DECEMBER
S M T W T F S	S M T W T F S	S M T W T F S	S M T W T F S
1 2 3 4	1 2	1 2 3 4 5 6	1 2 3 4
5 6 7 8 9 10 11	3 4 5 6 7 8 9	7 8 9 10 11 12 13	5 6 7 8 9 10 11
12 13 14 15 16 17 18	10 11 12 13 14 15 16	14 15 16 17 18 19 20	12 13 14 15 16 17 18
19 20 21 22 23 24 25	17 18 19 20 21 22 23	21 22 23 24 25 26 27	19 20 21 22 23 24 25
26 27 28 29 30	24 25 26 27 28 29 30	28 29 30	26 27 28 29 30 31
	31		

ADDITIONAL WORSHIP PLANNING RESOURCES

Litanies and readings for dedication services are frequently needed by those planning special worship services. For more than thirty years, *The Clergy Journal* has annually published a variety of dedications, litanies and rededication services. All of these have been used in real situations and are now available in book form.

The following litanies, dedications, and readings are available in these three books compiled by the editors of *The Clergy Journal*. The books are available from Church Management, Inc., PO Box 162527, Austin, TX 78716 at $9.95 each. Or any two are available for $18.50, all three for $26.90. Please send payment with order.

Dedication Services for Every Occasion
Ground breaking and site dedication
Service for laying a cornerstone
Dedication of a new church building
Dedication of new educational wing
Dedication of stained glass windows
Dedication of new office and study
Dedication of a new church kitchen
Dedication service for a memorial library
Dedication of the church sign
Litany for burning the church mortgage
Litany for the anniversary of building the sanctuary
Rededication of a church building
Litany for closing a sanctuary
Dedication of chancel memorials
Dedication of altar memorial vases
Dedication of a chalice
Dedication of communion ware
Dedication of cross and candlesticks
Litany for dedication of candelabra
Dedication of baptismal font or baptistry
Litany for dedication of new offering plates
Litany for the dedication of candlelighters
Dedication of a pulpit Bible
Organ dedication and celebration
Dedication of a piano
Dedication of a church bell
Dedication of a carillon
Dedication service for handbells
Dedication of hymnals
Dedication of choir robes
Dedication of chair lift or elevator
Dedication of Christian and national flags
Litany for a manse site dedication
Dedication of a parsonage
Dedication of a home

The Minister's Annual Manual

Dedications and Readings for Church Events

Ground Breaking
Commemoration of the Sanctuary
Rededication of a Church Building
Church Building Roof
Ramp (for benefit of the handicapped)
Cross (for Children's Church)
Parking Lot
Placing of a Cornerstone
New Sanctuary
Church Bell
Tree of Life
Rose Garden
Parish Hall Stage
Razing of a Church Building
Church Offices
Church Van
New Pews
Cross and Candlestick Holders
New Paraments
Organ
Pulpit Chairs
Pew Bibles
Clock
Literature Rack
Tables, Cushions, Choir Robes
Hearing Assist System
Sound System
Library
Communications Center
Installation of Director of Christian Education
Farewell of a Family
Dedication for an Historical Roster of the Church's Pastors
Setting Apart of Church School Teachers
Commissioning of a Director of Music
Installation of Church Officers and Board
Installation of a Scholarship Trust Fund
Renewal of Marriage Vows
Celebration of a Church Anniversary
Recognition of a Church School Class
Blessing for a Home
Dedication of an Ethnic Social Club Building
Post Recognition of Baptism in Hospital
Dedication of a Community Building
Rededication of the Parsonage

More Dedications and Readings for Church Events

Acolyte Robes and Stoles
Adoption of Child
Altar
Altar Candelabra
Ashes at Sea
Attendance Pads and Covers
Audio Visual Equipment (TV, VCR, etc.)
Baptismal Bowl
Bible Stand
Building Addition
Building Committee
Chalice
Chapel
Chimes/Carillons
Choir Robes
Church Sign
Cornerstone Laying
Cross Lifting
Debt Retirement
Doors
Funeral Home
Funeral Pall
Ground Breaking
Headstone
Hospital
Hymn Books
Kneeling Bench
Lectern, Amplified
Merging Congregations
Office Equipment
Organ and Chimes
Parking Lot
Pastors, Former
Pledges
Public School Educators
Senior Home Groundbreaking
Stained Glass Windows
Steeple and Bell
Swimming Pool
Tree Planting
Visitation Teams
Welcome Card Pew Racks

INDEX OF SERMON TEXTS

Genesis 2:7-9, 15-17; 3:1-7,
  Lent I 310
Genesis 12:1-8, Lent II 317
Joel 2:12-19, Ash Wednesday 304
John 1:1-14, Christmas Day 233
John 1:1-18, Christmas II 246
John 1:29-41, Epiphany II 267
John 8:31-36, Reformation 109
John 9:1-41, Lent III 324
John 10:1-10, Easter IV 384
John 11:1-53, Lent V 337
John 13:1-17, 34,
  Maundy Thursday 350
John 14:1-12, Easter V 391
John 14:15-21, Easter VI 398
John 17:1-11, Easter VII 412
John 19:17-30, Good Friday 356
John 20:19-23, Pentecost 419
John 20:19-31, Easter II 370
Luke 2:1-20, Christmas Eve 227
Luke 10:25-37, Proper 10,
  Pentecost 8 18
Luke 10:38-42, Proper 11,
  Pentecost 9 24
Luke 11:1-13, Proper 12,
  Pentecost 10 33
Luke 12:13-21, Proper 13,
  Pentecost 11 41
Luke 12:32-40, Proper 14,
  Pentecost 12 49
Luke 12:49-53, Proper 15,
  Pentecost 13 56
Luke 13:22-30, Proper 16,
  Pentecost 14 63
Luke 14:1, 7-14, Proper 17,
  Pentecost 15 70
Luke 14:25-33, Proper 18,
  Pentecost 16 77
Luke 15:1-10, Proper 19,
  Pentecost 17 85
Luke 16:1-13, Proper 20,
  Pentecost 18 93

Luke 16:19-31, Proper 21,
  Pentecost 19 100
Luke 17:1-10, Proper 22,
  Pentecost 20 117
Luke 17:11-19, Proper 23, Pentecost
  21, Thanksgiving Day 187
Luke 18:1-8, Proper 24,
  Pentecost 22 139
Luke 18:9-14, Proper 25,
  Pentecost 23 146
Luke 19:1-10, Proper 26,
  Pentecost 24 152
Luke 20:27-38, Proper 27,
  Pentecost 25 159
Luke 21:5-19, Proper 28,
  Pentecost 26 165
Luke 19:11-27, Proper 29,
  Pentecost 27 173
Luke 23:13-35, Easter III 377
Luke 23:35-43, Christ the King ... 180
Luke 24:44-53, Ascension Day ... 405
Matt. 1:18-25, Advent IV 218
Matt. 2:1-12, Epiphany 252
Matt. 2:13-15, 19-23,
  Christmas I 239
Matt. 3:1-12, Advent II 202
Matt. 3:13-17, Epiphany I 259
Matt. 4:12-23, Epiphany III 274
Matt. 5:1-12, All Saints,
  Epiphany IV 125, 278
Matt. 5:13-20, Epiphany V 286
Matt. 5:20-37, Epiphany VI 292
Matt. 7:21-29, Proper 4,
  Pentecost 2 432
Matt. 9:9-13, Proper 5
  Pentecost 3 440
Matt. 9:35-10:8, Proper 6,
  Pentecost 4 447
Matt. 10:24-33, Proper 7,
  Pentecost 5 455
Matt. 10:34-42, Proper 8,
  Pentecost 6 463

The Minister's Annual Manual

Matt. 11:25-30, Proper 9,
  Pentecost 7 469
Matt. 11:2-11, Advent II 209
Matt. 13:1-9, Proper 10,
  Pentecost 8 476
Matt. 17:1-9, Transfiguration 299

Matt. 20:17-28, Lent IV 332
Matt. 24:37-44, Advent I 194
Matt. 27:11-54, Passion Sunday .. 345
Matt. 28:1-10, Easter Day 363
Matt. 28:16-20, Trinity 426